SOUTHERN COMMUNITIES

SOUTHERN COMMUNITIES

Identity, Conflict, and Memory in the American South

EDITED BY Steven E. Nash
AND Bruce E. Stewart

The University of Georgia Press
Athens

© 2019 by the University of Georgia Press
Athens, Georgia 30602
www.ugapress.org
All rights reserved
Designed by Kaelin Chappell Broaddus
Set in 11/13.5 Garamond Premier Pro
by Kaelin Chappell Broaddus

Most University of Georgia Press titles are
available from popular e-book vendors.

Printed digitally

Library of Congress Cataloging-in-Publication Data
Names: Nash, Steven E., editor. | Stewart, Bruce E.,
editor. | Inscoe, John C., 1951– honouree.
Title: Southern communities : identity, conflict, and memory in the
American South / edited by Steven E. Nash and Bruce E. Stewart.
Description: Athens [Georgia] : The University of Georgia
Press, [2019] | Includes bibliographical references.
Identifiers: LCCN 2018054029| ISBN 9780820355115
(hardcover : alk. paper) | ISBN 9780820355122 (pbk.
: alk. paper) | ISBN 9780820355139 (ebook)
Subjects: LCSH: Community life—Southern States—History—
19th century. | Southern States—Social life and customs—19th
century. | Southern States—History—19th century.
Classification: LCC F209 .S729 2019 | DDC 975/.03—dc23
LC record available at https://lccn.loc.gov/2018054029

For John C. Inscoe

CONTENTS

Introduction: Southern Communities during the Long Nineteenth Century
STEVEN E. NASH AND BRUCE E. STEWART 1

PART 1: CREATING COMMUNITIES

Gullah and Ebo: Reconsidering Early Lowcountry African American Communities
RAS MICHAEL BROWN 21

The Ties That Bind: Slaveholding Kinship Networks in the Toe Valley
KEVIN W. YOUNG 39

Divided Loyalties: The Fain Family in an East Tennessee Civil War
KATHARINE S. DAHLSTRAND 59

An Emotional Rebellion: Wrecking the Old South's Emotional Community
KYLE N. OSBORN 77

PART 2: CONFLICTING COMMUNITIES

A Slaveholding Unionist in the Secession Crisis: Reverend Dr. George Junkin and Lexington, Virginia, in Peace and Civil War
BARTON A. MYERS 93

"In Search of All That Was Near and Dear to Me": Desertion as a Window into Community Divisions in Caldwell County during the Civil War
JUDKIN BROWNING 113

Fighting the "Laurel War": The Civil War inside the Henry Household
STEVEN E. NASH 132

Reinterpreting John Noland: Community Coercion
Theory and the Black Confederate Debate
MATTHEW C. HULBERT 148

"Full of Danger to the Community":
Driving the Mormons from Brasstown in Late
Nineteenth-Century North Carolina
MARY ELLA ENGEL 161

Community and the Commons: Richmond Pearson and
the Buncombe County Stock Law Revolt of 1885–87
LUKE MANGET 174

PART 3: RE-CREATING COMMUNITIES

Too South of the South: A Louisiana Family
Searches for Community in Cuba
ROBERT C. POISTER 195

"Yankees Invade the South Again": Race, Reconciliation,
and the 1913 National Grand Army of the Republic
Encampment at Chattanooga, Tennessee
SAMUEL B. MCGUIRE 211

The Lucy Cobb Institute: Mildred Lewis Rutherford and Her
Mission to Preserve an Idealized Southern Community
KATHERINE E. ROHRER 230

Rocks in a Whirlwind: Protest and Alienation
in Southern Autobiography
GEORGE W. JUSTICE 246

Afterword: The Inscoe Connection
STEPHEN BERRY 265

Contributors 271

Index 275

SOUTHERN
COMMUNITIES

INTRODUCTION

Southern Communities during the Long Nineteenth Century

STEVEN E. NASH AND
BRUCE E. STEWART

CADES COVE, THE SUBJECT OF DURWOOD DUNN'S CLASSIC study, was a vibrant Appalachian community throughout the nineteenth century. There, kinship ties and shared experiences created a sense of community among residents, who—contrary to popular belief—were neither backward nor isolated from the outside world. The realities of this tight-knit community would eventually be obscured by the federal government's creation of the Great Smoky Mountains National Park during the 1930s. Cades Cove was located within the park's boundaries, and locals were forced to sell their properties via eminent domain and abandon their homes. The National Park Service demolished all modern buildings but preserved log cabins and other "primitive" structures in an attempt to portray Cades Cove as a pioneer settlement.[1]

Today, visitors to the Cades Cove exhibit can experience the splendor of nature and a sense of simplicity and may find themselves yearning for the past. They can touch the log cabins and barns, sit in the wooden pews at the Cades Cove Primitive Baptist Church, and walk through the area's cemeteries, the final resting places of those men and women who made the community. Cades Cove is trapped in time, cut off from the world as if a great bubble encircled it.

The millions of tourists who visit Cades Cove each year could be interpreted as an "imagined community"—an imagined community whose members could be, say, naturalists who feel a certain peace or communion with nature there, Appalachians who want to understand their heritage, or Americans who envision themselves as heirs of a nation girded by rugged individualism, all of whom continue to add to the cove's story. Whatever lures them to the peaks, valleys, and farmsteads in Cades Cove, these visitors can be seen as bonding through a given identity.

In the strictest sense, a community requires people. While we could argue over whether modern visitors constitute a sort of community of their own, such temporary residents are not the people who built those cabins, barns, and churches at Cades Cove. They are not the people who lived in that neighborhood. Family names still adorn the buildings and farms, but the residents who breathed life into Cades Cove are gone. So, clearly, whatever we imagine or however we feel when we visit this place says more about us than the households that once gave Cades Cove meaning.

The key terms we have used here—"community," "neighborhood," "place," and "household"—were used knowingly and interchangeably. Did you notice? Perhaps you did. But what do they mean? Are they the same thing? Southerners often tout their claims to community, referencing their family ties, religion, heritage, and place. Indeed, it is the strong bonds of community that supposedly continue to make the South—dare we say—exceptional. "Southerners have a unique sense of time and place, of belonging, of community," historian David Mathews observed. "Southerners have roots. They have an identity. A Southerner—whatever his station, whatever his color—has a 'home.'"[2] Still, the definition of community remains elusive, especially from a historical perspective. Is it a neighborhood, a place, a household, or maybe something else entirely?

Cades Cove is part of the South, which in many ways is itself an imagined community, marked by Confederate monuments, road names, and other daily reminders of an idealized past. Historians have attempted to move us beyond nostalgia, using community as a mode of analysis to answer those elusive questions posed to Mississippian Quentin Compson in William Faulkner's novel *Absalom, Absalom!*: "Tell [us] about the South. What's it like there. What do they do there. Why do they live there. Why do they live at all."[3] Many of these studies have focused on the nineteenth-century South, a region where—according to many contemporary Americans—people lived in communities unmarred by conflict, competition, and change. Historians have not only challenged the romanticized image of nineteenth-century southern communities but have also revealed that community—or whatever term you wish to use—is more than just a physical space. It is the product of interpersonal relationships and associations, common experiences and feelings, and a shared past that connects people together. It may be connected to a specific place or region, but it does not have to be. Community is much more than a feeling. It is the ties that bind, imagined and real, for better and for worse; it is the web of personal relationships that links disparate people together and gives meaning to their interactions.

MODERN HISTORIANS' DEFINITION OF COMMUNITY ORIGINATED with the rise of the new social history in the 1960s. Influenced by the civil rights, feminist, and other protest movements, scholars shifted away from "traditional" narratives based on national figures and started focusing on the histories of ordinary people. Writing "bottom up" history encouraged many academics to embrace community-based studies.[4] Leading the way were colonial New England historians, who employed community as a unit of analysis to chart change over time, drawing on local records such as inventories, tax lists, and wills. In many ways, it was a logical place to start. Americans long identified Puritan towns and town meetings as building blocks of a larger national identity. While fundamental to historians' later use of the concept, colonial New England scholars' understanding of community remained rather limited. For them, community was simply a nucleated settlement of people who shared a common culture.[5]

If New England communities defined the idea of strong community in early America, it stood to reason that the bonds of community must have remained weak in rural regions like the South. Even into the nineteenth century, most southerners—living in disparate and racially diverse farmsteads and plantations—supposedly lacked access to the "communal public institutions" that made community possible.[6] Following the lead of sociologists and anthropologists, however, historians since the 1970s have developed "more flexible definitions" of community and, in the process, have discovered that southerners indeed created a multitude of communities during the long nineteenth century.[7] Many of these scholars first turned their attention to the region's largely overlooked African American population.

Riding a revisionist wave through the civil rights era, historians in the 1970s emphasized the existence of an autonomous "slave community." Scholars, notably John W. Blassingame and George A. Rawick, argued that enslaved people created a cultural space—the slave quarters—in which the interplay between African and Euro-American cultures placed slaves beyond their masters' reach. In many ways, this version of community mirrored colonial New England historians' emphasis on culture. The slave community served as the foundation for what scholars in subsequent years described as a separate African American nationalism. Depicting slaves' cultural practices as consciously and fundamentally African, researchers showed how culture bound African American slaves together and created cohesiveness typical of a community, despite concerted efforts by whites to control it.[8]

Even as this concept gained traction, several historians challenged the notion of an autonomous slave community. In *Roll, Jordan, Roll: The World the Slaves Made*, Eugene D. Genovese illustrated how enslaved people exercised agency within a slave system that placed tremendous power in the hands of paternalistic masters. Advocates for the slave community emphasized the enslaved people's autonomy and cultural independence from their master. Genovese and other critics embraced African American slaves' historical agency in a way that incorporated what they saw as slave owners' hegemonic power. For Genovese, the source of this seeming contradiction was paternalism, which he believed "created a tendency for the slaves to identify with a particular community through identification with its master" while weakening "their identification with each other as a class." Still, Genovese recognized that community necessitated that everyone, whether master or slave, "find some measure of self-respect and self-interest." Genovese argued that paternalism inextricably linked the enslaved and the enslaver in a single community based upon reciprocal—though highly unequal—relationships between white slave owners and their slaves.[9]

In the 1980s, community-focused studies of the nineteenth-century South further evolved as historians increasingly sought to understand how southerners, regardless of race, sex, or class, created and sustained community within a given locale. This task was made easier due to the work of several scholars, most notably Thomas Bender, who urged historians to change the way they defined community. According to Bender, community was not a place but a "network of social relations" and experiences that bound people together for better or worse. "This network," he explained, "is the essence of community, and it may or may not be coterminous with a specific, contiguous territory."[10] Community, then, was not confined solely to compact settlements such as the colonial New England town. It could occur anywhere, even in the most rural environs of the nineteenth-century South.

Armed with this new definition, historians uncovered the "web of relationships" that defined southerners' lives and communities during the long nineteenth century. Many scholars used the county as their unit of analysis. Though these historians acknowledged that it was an artificial political subdivision, the county contained institutions that united people residing in "dispersed and randomly scattered farms."[11] In particular, the county seat functioned as the center of communal life, providing residents with the opportunity to buy and sell goods, communicate with one another, and—for white men—participate in politics. Moreover, as Gail O'Brien argued, "social institutions such as newspapers and voluntary institutions such as agricultural societies usually served an entire county."[12] Seen in this way, the county was the arena in which most southerners intermingled and formed the "social networks" crucial to building community.[13]

One objection to this "county as community" model was that it failed to take into account the fact that counties often contained multiple communities that frequently crossed county lines. Skeptics also maintained that the model's reliance on public records obscured women and other minority groups' roles in community formation. To rectify this omission, in the 1990s, a number of historians introduced a new unit of analysis for studying community: the household. More than just places of residence, households served as "the constituent units of society, organizing the majority of the population ... in relations of legal and customary dependency to the propertied male head."[14] However, these households did not function independently from the outside world. Kinship, religious, and economic ties connected individual households, even those situated in more remote parts of the South, to their neighbors. It was within these networks of households that southerners—especially women and African Americans—interacted most often with each other and created a sense of community.[15]

Within the county as community model, historians have teased out local subsections, such as neighborhoods, within rural communities. Often, several neighborhoods organized themselves around a church, a country store, a courthouse, a school, or some other node that connected people to each other and a particular locale. The importance of locality to the neighborhood brought spatial and material elements to the study of southern communities, allowing a sense of place—a central aspect of southern identity—to develop among residents. Christopher C. Morris depicted neighborhoods as a cluster of households bound by kinship and economic ties. Specifically, he defined neighborhoods as rural spaces of twenty to thirty square miles (often adjoining plantations and farms) containing two to three dozen households "linked by friendship, family, or proximity." Morris posited that the highly rigid patriarchal order of these neighborhoods—organized around elite families owning significant real and slave property—gave these neighborhoods, which were no more or less harmonious than other types of communities, a distinctly southern character.[16]

The spatial and local element of the neighborhood also reshaped historians' understanding of the slave community. In *Joining Places: Slave Neighborhoods in the Old South*, Anthony E. Kaye applied the spatial neighborhood approach to southern slavery. Kinship, labor, religion, and other intimate relationships and cultural practices were as central to the slave community as to the white-centered neighborhood. Influenced by the field of human geography, Kaye tied these relationships to a specific place that was both material and socially constructed. Enslaved people's daily interactions gave meaning to their neighborhoods, but the landscape also circumscribed what was possible in a given place. Kaye did not view the slave community as an idealized cultural space independent of the master's authority. Instead, slave neighborhoods were surrounded by and part of the slave owner's neighborhood. Further, Kaye's emphasis on neighborhoods as the locus of the intimate relationships of daily life conformed to Bender's relationship-based view of community. So, as Kaye moved beyond the slave community, he also reaffirmed the importance of community as a historical construct.[17]

Kaye's use of social construction was site specific, but it hinted at larger ways of imagining community. Place is a vital component of southerners' sense of community, which often calls to mind smaller rural settings. A person's understanding of place grew out of their sex, race, and position within society. An enslaved man or woman might have occupied and lived on the same plantation or cluster of farms in a rural area as slave owners, but they understood the landscape differently. The crop fields represented hard work and exploitation to slaves but profit and wealth to masters. Slave quarters represented personal relationships and communal bonds to a slave, while a master could only view those spaces as an outsider. A grove of trees might have been beautiful or relaxing to a white observer, but a black person might have recognized it as a place of torture and pain. Whites might have seen a swamp as an unhealthy place to be avoided, whereas African Americans might have hailed it as a place of refuge or escape.

But there is also a broader sense of being *southern*, which is equally cultural and historical. The secession of eleven southern states and the formation of the Confederate States of America forced whites across the region to reimagine themselves during the 1860s and beyond. While they shared language, political traditions, religious views, and other bonds with the now-foreign free states, white southerners increasingly approached those cultural connections differently. This new nationalism helped define a collective regional community in the South during the late nineteenth and early twentieth centuries. Dozens of scholars have argued ably about the creation, absence, limits, endurance, and collapse of Confederate nationalism. However, what matters to us in terms of the South as a community is the fact that the region actively strove to define itself as unique. Failure to secure independence left the South with terrible physical and metaphysical burdens that forced whites to rebuild and redefine themselves in the shadow of defeat.[18]

As Benedict Anderson noted in *Imagined Communities*, nationalism was sometimes tied to the process of remembering and forgetting. Our opening example of Cades Cove is an excellent illustration of this process. The Great Smoky Mountains National Park created a version of the cove that stripped away the residents' modernity in favor of a primitive version of the past. Visitors to the park are invited to imagine themselves as part of a larger American nation built on pioneers' taming of pristine wilderness. On a regional level, Cades Cove fits within a southern cultural identity built on memory. More broadly, white southerners, burdened with the linked histories of slavery and military defeat on their own soil, worked hard and creatively to establish a harmonious imagined community well into the twentieth century. The so-called Lost Cause represented these southerners' attempts to create a version of the Civil War that found dignity in defeat while simultaneously memorializing the antebellum South as a lost idyllic community. Slavery was retroactively divorced from secession and a heightened emphasis was placed on American republican ideals. Such imagining left no room for class divisions among a supposedly united white population, and "happy slave" monuments and stories at the turn of the twentieth century purported that enslaved people were content in bondage. In short, the Lost Cause mythology provided the white South with a sort of alt-nationalism that cast Confederate generals as gods, white southern women as angels of mercy, southern soldiers as mythic warriors, and enslaved people as loyal servants. To the determined veterans of the conflict, their children, and later generations desperate to believe that their ancestors had not sacrificed hundreds of thousands of young lives to preserve human property, the Lost Cause imposed a harmony on the antebellum South that never existed while exalting those who fought as the true heirs of the founding fathers.[19]

Community is an evolving and complex concept that historians have applied to localities, counties, and the South as a whole. It allows historians to ground larger issues in the day-to-day lives of all segments of society. These social networks can unite or divide people, they might mirror or transcend political boundaries, or they may exist solely in the cultures of likeminded people. Historians' use of the concept has changed significantly since the 1960s, but the core value of community as a historical tool has not been contested. As

Eudora Welty argued in the 1970s, "One place comprehended can make us understand other places better. Sense of place gives equilibrium; extended, it is sense of direction too."[20]

THESE ESSAYS, WRITTEN AND COMPILED IN HONOR OF HISTORIAN John C. Inscoe, explore the nature of southern communities during the long nineteenth century. Building on previous scholarship, they view community not simply as a place but also as an idea that is always being redefined. The essays reaffirm that there was never a singular southern community. Southerners, they reveal, constructed an array of communities across the region and beyond. Nor do the contributors romanticize these communities. Far from being "places" of cooperation and harmony, southern communities were rife with competition and discord during the long nineteenth century. Indeed, conflict constituted a vital part of southern communal development. Taken together, the essays remind us how community-focused studies can bring us closer to answering the questions posed to Quentin Compson in *Absalom, Absalom!*

Historians in recent decades have debunked the notion that most nineteenth-century southerners lacked a sense of community. Throughout the antebellum and postbellum periods, whites and blacks created multiple real and imagined communities. Within their neighborhoods, households, counties, and minds, they interacted with one another, forging the "web of relationships" that made—and continue to make—community possible. The essays in part 1, "Creating Communities," document the construction of four of these distinct southern communities before and during the Civil War: the enslaved, the slaveholding, the Confederate, and the emotional.

Leading off the section is Ras Michael Brown's essay on the origins of Gullah and Ebo as social identities within Lowcountry African American communities. By the nineteenth century, both nation names had become the dominant ethnonyms tying the region's culturally diverse slave population together. Brown traces the beginnings of the use of Gullah and Ebo back to the 1730s and 1740s, when the vast majority of captive Africans who arrived in the Lowcountry were from Angola (West-Central Africa) and Igbo (the Bight of Biafra). According to Brown, these slaves—in a conscious attempt to create a pluralist identity and culture—fashioned themselves as either Gullah (a contracted form of the word Angola) or Ebo (a label referring to those who had resided in communities defined culturally and socially as Igbo). Despite the massive influx of slaves from outside Angola and Igbo to the Lowcountry at the turn of the nineteenth century, the use of Gullah and Ebo as social and cultural markers endured, largely because most native-born slaves, who now constituted more than three-fourths of the region's African-descended population, originated from the first generation of Gullah and Ebo women forced to live on the coast of South Carolina and Georgia.

Kevin W. Young recounts the rise of the Toe Valley's slaveholding community in the section's second essay. Situated within western North Carolina and encompassing around seven hundred square miles, the Toe Valley was home to some eighty-three hundred people on the cusp of the Civil War. The region's numerous waterways—most notably the North Toe, South Toe, and Cane rivers—served as "connecting arteries" that enabled valley inhabitants to communicate and trade with one another and forge a sense of community. But, beginning in the 1830s, wealth within the Toe Valley became increasingly concentrated in the hands of a slaveholding class. Growing economic inequality restricted membership within the community, Young explains, as slaveholders capitalized on kinship ties to acquire slaves and consolidate power. By 1860, an exclusive community of long-term slaveholding families owned 99 percent of Toe Valley slaves. "In a cruel irony," Young concludes, "slavery threatened family bonds among the enslaved but bolstered kinship ties among slave owners."

As Katharine S. Dahlstrand affirms in her essay, one's understanding of history plays a crucial role in the construction of identity and community. Dahlstrand juxtaposes the lives of Hiram Fain and John Anderson, second cousins who lived within miles of each other in Hawkins County, Tennessee. While both men idolized George Washington, their different interpretations of the founding father led one (Fain) to endorse the Confederacy and the other (Anderson) to support the Union. Fain saw Washington as a symbol of defiance, a man who defended citizens' rights against a tyrannical government. It was the image of Washington the revolutionary, Dahlstrand argues, that Fain used to defend secession and his allegiance to the Confederate community. On the other hand, Anderson invoked the memory of President Washington, the commander in chief who suppressed the Whiskey Rebellion in order to preserve the republic. For Anderson, the Union *was* Washington's legacy and duty demanded that he defend it.

In the section's final essay, Kyle Osborn chronicles a largely overlooked revolution transpiring below the Mason-Dixon Line in the months before and after secession. Antebellum elite women belonged to an "emotional community" that obligated them to suppress their emotions, so as to not corrupt the moral sanctuary of the home. But, as Osborn explains, a new, less restrictive "emotional community" emerged in the South during the secession crisis. The

Confederate cause inspired wealthy young women, in particular, to unleash public expressions of indignation and disgust toward their northern neighbors. These emotional outbursts quickly met with the approval of men eager to unite white southerners across party, state, class, and gender lines. Anger and hatred—as long as they remained directed at Yankees and African Americans—had now become accepted female emotions. Unfortunately, these women—freed from the shackles of the antebellum South's "emotional community"—would pass their disdain for their "enemies" on to the next generation. "It was the [white] children of secession who ... violently overthrew Reconstruction, launched Jim Crow, and condoned the heinous lynching wave that haunted the southern landscape," Osborn writes. "They mythologized the Old South of their parents and the justness of the Lost Cause, maintaining (if sometimes sub rosa) the anti-Yankee enmity of the secessionist movement."

For many Americans, the term "community" evokes the feelings of conviviality and nostalgia one often associates with Norman Rockwell's art. Relationships that bind community members are assumed to be intimate and amicable. Reciprocity and a shared sense of purpose supposedly encourage members to subordinate their self-interest to the common good. Community is "the commonwealth and common interests ... of people living in a place and wishing to continue to do so," novelist and poet Wendell Berry believes. "[It] is a locally understood interdependence of local people, local culture, local economy, and local nature."[21] However, there is a darker side of community, one marked by exclusion, racism, competition, and violence, that challenges communal bonds and promotes disharmony. As the six essays in part 2, "Conflicting Communities," demonstrate, discord frequently defined nineteenth-century southern communities wrought by civil war, emancipation, and modernization.

Barton A. Myers's essay on George Junkin, a slaveholding Unionist who served as president of Washington College in Lexington, Virginia, in the 1850s, looks at what can happen when an individual's personal beliefs do not align with their community. Though born in Pennsylvania, Junkin's anti-abolitionist writings quickly endeared him to proslavery ideologues across the South. The toast of Lexington, he became friends with prominent community members, including Thomas "Stonewall" Jackson, who married Junkin's daughter in 1853. Junkin's charmed life in Lexington ended abruptly during the secession crisis. Despite his support of slavery, Junkin had always valued the Union and the U.S. Constitution above all else, which alienated him from Lexington's prosecession community and forced him to flee his adoptive hometown in 1861.

The next two essays examine other ways the Civil War strained the bonds of community. In his essay, Judkin Browning argues that community cohesion and support for the Confederate cause in Caldwell County, North Carolina, eroded as food shortages and guerrilla violence became a facet of daily life. Poorer residents from rural districts, whose sons deserted from the Confederate army at higher rates than men from neighborhoods adjoining the county's commercial center of Lenoir, began to focus more on survival than sustaining the war effort following the Battle of Gettysburg in July 1863. Meanwhile, as Steven E. Nash reveals in his essay, the Civil War wreaked havoc on William and Cornelia Henry's household, which served as the focal point of the Sulphur Springs community in Buncombe County, North Carolina. A wealthy slaveholding family, the Henrys lost control over both enslaved and free white laborers under the strains of war and emancipation, which altered forever the relationships that had defined their household and community. Debt and family infighting further upended the Henrys' world, causing William to ultimately become a tenant on the land he once owned.

Batting fourth in the section's lineup is Matthew C. Hulbert's reinterpretation of John Noland, a Missouri slave who has become the darling of many Confederate heritage groups in recent decades. These groups insist that Noland regularly rode with William Quantrill's band of Confederate guerrillas as they raised hell along the Missouri-Kansas border during the Civil War. Confederate heritage groups use Noland as clear and undeniable proof that African Americans voluntarily fought for the Confederacy and that the preservation of slavery was not a cause of disunion. Hulbert debunks these claims in his essay, arguing that Noland's involvement with Quantrill's band was limited and not motivated by pro-Confederate sentiment. Because he lacked the mobility or opportunity to escape bondage and lived in a white community that frequently used violence to maintain the racial status quo, self-preservation dictated Noland's decision to cooperate with Quantrill's men and later attend the group's reunions.

The section's final two essays highlight the persistence of community cohesion in the face of external threats and economic change during the late nineteenth century. Mary Ella Engel chronicles the unfortunate experiences of Joseph Parry, a Mormon missionary who visited Brasstown, North Carolina, to recruit converts in 1879. The town's Baptist and Methodist preachers—casting themselves as community protectors—quickly united locals against the unwelcomed guest, resulting in a series of violent events that forced Parry to leave the state altogether. Less than a decade later, rural farmers in Buncombe County rallied against a more serious threat to their communities: the closing of the open range. As Luke Manget demonstrates in his essay, Buncombe residents who had long relied on the commons to earn a living vehemently opposed New South boosters' attempts to pass a countywide fence law during the 1880s and even managed—via the political system—to prevent the operation of the law in several districts. By the early twentieth century, modernizers had successfully passed legislation that made all of Buncombe County subject to the stock law, a blow from which the open range and commons culture would never recover.

Postbellum southerners struggled to adapt to the myriad changes wrought by Confederate defeat. For African Americans, emancipation provided an opportunity to reconstitute old or build new communities. Kinship networks, shared experiences, and local institutions united African American communities despite continued racial injustice.[22] Meanwhile, white southerners sought to reconstruct communities in ways that preserved the Old South's racial and gender status quo. They also hoped to forge a reunited (white) American community, a task made easier by many of their northern counterparts' embrace and promotion of the Lost Cause.[23] Perhaps it is unsurprising, as the essays in part 3, "Re-Creating Communities," highlight, that white southerners often turned to memory and nostalgia to escape the turbulence of the New South. An ideology of white supremacy established the contours of an imagined South that served as both a refuge from and a critique of the United States well into the twentieth century.

Hoping to eschew the hardships of war and "Yankee" rule, thousands of white southern families emigrated to the Caribbean and other foreign lands during the 1860s. Robert C. Poister's chapter chronicles the experiences of one such family: the McHattons. In 1862, James and Eliza McHatton fled their sugar plantation near Baton Rouge, Louisiana, eventually settling in Cuba three years later, where they hoped to re-create the culture and community they had left behind. James, a wealthy slaveholding planter, viewed the island as an ideal location to reconnect with business associates and maintain the Old South's slave-based plantation economy, and Eliza saw Cuba as a new "home" in which to resume her life as a southern plantation mistress. Debt, violence, and cultural isolation, however, ultimately undermined the McHattons' belief that Cuba could become an extension of the antebellum southern community. Only their son, Henry, who lived most of his childhood on the island and was raised on stories of a lost South, would consider Cuba to be an appropriate substitute for his parents' homeland.

Shifting back to the Continental United States, Samuel B. McGuire's essay explores southern and northern whites' symbolic attempt to re-create a unified postwar American community. In September 1913, the Grand Army of the Republic (GAR) held its national encampment in Chattanooga, Tennessee, the only time a national meeting would be held in the former Confederacy. Praised by southerners and northerners alike as an opportunity to further promote reconciliation, the encampment included a parade in which some white GAR members, on a whim, invited several former Confederates to participate. This veneer of solidarity, McGuire discovers, quickly succumbed to sectional and racial tensions. When a GAR officer, for instance, presented a resolution to support congressional legislation granting federal aid to ex-Confederates, most GAR members, believing that their former adversaries had committed treason, rejected the proposal. White Union veterans also remained ambivalent on race, refusing to condemn Jim Crow laws that discriminated against the GAR's black members. "Though white and black GAR members marched side by side during the encampment parade and former Rebels and Federals claimed lingering war wounds had fully healed," McGuire concludes, "it was unclear to perhaps many concerned how far the nation had yet to travel for both of those idyllic gestures to be fully realized."

In the section's third essay, Katherine E. Rohrer takes a grassroots look at how many white southerners sought to re-create a romanticized version of the Old South community well into the twentieth century. The Lucy Cobb Institute, a girls' school founded in Athens, Georgia, in 1859, played a key role in this effort. Under the leadership of Mildred Rutherford—who served as the matriarch of the school between 1880 and 1928—Lucy Cobb became a "factory" that trained young white women to become antebellum southern belles. "The institute functioned as a microcosm of the Old South, an enduring legacy of a region in which racial and sexual subordination was de rigueur," Rohrer explains. "[It] offered Rutherford opportunities to embrace and promote [such] conservative values." Rutherford's devotion to preserving the Old South community, however, caused her to reject new pedagogies and societal norms that encouraged southern women to be more independent and to find employment outside the home. Unable to attract enough students and funding to stay afloat, Lucy Cobb closed in 1931, the victim of Rutherford's rigid devotion to a romanticized past.

By the end of the nineteenth century, southern whites—with the assistance of many of their northern counterparts—had created the so-called Jim Crow South, a regional community committed to maintaining white supremacy that would persist throughout most of the twentieth century. In the section's final essay, George W. Justice explores how three southern writers—Lillian Smith, Richard Wright, and William Alexander Percy—failed to find a sense of belonging within this broader cultural community. A white liberal and advocate for racial equality, Smith rejected the Jim Crow South, while Wright, an African American raised in Mississippi, ultimately developed an identity apart from a community determined to oppress him. Percy also grew disenchanted, but for a different reason. The son of a prominent white planter, he believed that the Jim Crow South had begun to abandon its past and no longer held a place for aristocrats—like him—who championed the traditions of the Old South.

Much has changed in our understanding of community. As historians, we must embrace revision of both concepts and interpretation. Sometimes, however, we come perilously close to discarding the baby with the bathwater. The survey of works in this introduction—though far from definitive—makes clear that we have learned a lot about the South during the long nineteenth century through community-focused studies. Like many of the highlighted works, these essays strive to show the continued strength of community as a historical approach. As Christopher Morris argued, we must recognize the interplay and connections of these different uses. Community was, perhaps always, the larger meanings and relationships that bound people across place and time. Households, neighborhoods, and other terms are layers of analysis that ultimately seek to elucidate similar concepts. Scholars recognizing gaps related to gender, race, and other elements of southern life criticized and revised community's historical meaning. Yet, here we are decades later, and Thomas Bender's call to historians seems as loud as ever. Perhaps the number of voices has grown, a clear sign that the differences of interpretation and definition have borne fruit. But let us not lose sight of what community has taught us: "By knowing one small place well we can understand better the larger society which it is a part."[24]

NOTES

1. Durwood Dunn, *Cades Cove: The Life and Death of a Southern Appalachian Community, 1818–1937* (Knoxville: University of Tennessee Press, 1988).

2. Quoted in Stephen A. Smith, *Myth, Media, and the Southern Mind* (Fayetteville: University of Arkansas Press, 1986), 116.

3. William Faulkner, *Absalom, Absalom!* (New York: Modern Library, 1993), 142.

4. For more on the new social history, see Francis G. Couvares, Martha Saxton, Gerald N. Grob, and George Athan Billias, eds., *Interpretations of American History: Patterns and Perspectives*, vol. 1: *Through Reconstruction* (New York: Free Press, 2000), 16–20.

5. For a sample of this scholarship, see Summer C. Powell, *Puritan Village: The Formation of a New England Town* (Middletown, CT: Wesleyan University Press, 1963), Page Smith, *As a City Upon a Hill: The Town in American History* (New York: Knopf, 1966), Richard L.

Bushman, *From Puritan to Yankee: Character and the Social Order in Connecticut, 1690–1765* (Cambridge, MA: Harvard University Press, 1967), John Demos: *A Little Commonwealth: Family Life in Colonial Plymouth* (New York: Oxford University Press, 1970), Kenneth A. Lockridge, *A New England Town, the First Hundred Years: Dedham, Massachusetts, 1636–1736* (New York: Norton, 1970), and Michael Zuckerman, *Peaceable Kingdoms: New England Towns in the Eighteenth Century* (New York: Knopf, 1970).

6. John Mack Faragher, "Open-Country Community: Sugar Creek, Illinois, 1820–1850," in *The Countryside in the Age of Capitalist Transformation: Essays in the Social History of Rural America*, ed. Steven Hahn and Jonathan Prude (Chapel Hill: University of North Carolina Press, 1985), 235.

7. Orville Vernon Burton and Robert C. McMath Jr., eds, *Class, Conflict, and Consensus: Antebellum Southern Community Studies* (Westport, CT: Greenwood, 1982), xi.

8. John W. Blassingame, *The Slave Community: Plantation Life in the Antebellum South*, rev. ed. (New York: Oxford University Press, 1972); George P. Rawick, *From Sundown to Sunup: The Making of the Black Community* ser. 1, vol. 1, *The American Slave: A Composite Autobiography* (Westport, CT: Greenwood, 1972). A fuller analysis of the persistence of African cultural practices and their significance in the formation of a distinctive black nationalism within the United States can be found in Sterling Stuckey, *Slave Culture: Nationalism Theory and the Foundations of Black America* (New York: Oxford University Press, 1987). For close analysis of a single slave community that similarly emphasizes the role a shared creole culture played in creating slave unity, see Charles Joyner, *Down by the Riverside: A South Carolina Slave Community* (Urbana: University of Illinois Press, 1984).

9. Eugene D. Genovese, *Roll, Jordan, Roll: The World the Slaves Made* (New York: Vintage Books, 1976), 6. Additional critics emerged in subsequent decades as historians used gender, class, and other analytic tools to strengthen and diversify our understanding of African American life in the nineteenth-century South. For example, see Paul D. Escott, *Slavery Remembered: A Record of Twentieth-Century Slave Narratives* (Chapel Hill: University of North Carolina Press, 1979), William L. Van Deburg, *The Slave Drivers: Black Agricultural Labor Supervisors in the Antebellum South* (Westport, CT: Greenwood, 1979), Peter Kolchin, "Reevaluating the Antebellum Slave Community: A Comparative Perspective," *Journal of American History* 70, no. 3 (1983): 579–601, Deborah Gray White, *Ar'n't I a Woman? Female Slaves in the Plantation South* (New York: Norton, 1985), and Brenda E. Stevenson, *Life in Black and White: Family and Community in the Slave South* (New York: Oxford University Press, 1996).

10. Thomas Bender, *Community and Social Change in America* (Baltimore, MD: Johns Hopkins University Press, 1978), 7, 122. Like Bender, Darrett Rutman also urged historians to view community as a "network of relationships" instead of a place. See Darrett B. Rutman with Anita H. Rutman, *A Place in Time: Middlesex County, Virginia 1650–1750* (New York: Norton, 1984), and *Small Worlds, Large Questions: Explorations in Early American Social History, 1600–1850* (Charlottesville: University Press of Virginia, 1994), chap. 3. It is important to note that Bender questions the classic definition of social change espoused by German sociologist Ferdinand Tönnies, who describes the process by which community (*Gemeinschaft*) transitioned to urban society (*Gesellschaft*). Many sociologists and others view this change as inevitable or total due to its connection to the growth of capitalism and urbaniza-

tion. Bender observes that social change plays out differently in unique places. In short, the shift from the more personal social networks and face-to-face interactions of community to the impersonal urban and capitalistic society is not a zero-sum game. Community and society might overlap, and, significantly, one may never completely replace the other. See Bender, *Community and Social Change in America*, especially chap. 2.

11. Faragher, "Open-Country Community," 235.

12. Gail W. O'Brien, "The Systematic Study of Power in the Nineteenth-Century South," in *Class, Conflict, and Consensus*, 268.

13. Most of these county-based studies published in the 1980s focus on how southern communities changed between the antebellum and postbellum periods. Some of these works stress continuity between the Old and New South, while others maintain that much had changed in these communities economically, politically, and socially. Since the 1990s, historians of the Civil War, in particular, have used the county as community model to examine the impact of the war on communities. For examples of 1980s scholarship that uses the county as a unit of analysis, see Crandall A. Shifflett, *Patronage and Poverty in the Tobacco South: Louisa County, Virginia, 1860–1900* (Knoxville: University of Tennessee Press, 1982), Randolph B. Campbell, *A Southern Community in Crisis: Harrison County, Texas, 1850–1880* (Austin: Texas State Historical Association, 1983), Michael Wayne, *The Reshaping of Plantation Society: The Natchez District, 1860–1880* (Baton Rouge: Louisiana State University Press, 1983), Richard R. Beeman, *The Evolution of the Southern Backcountry: A Case Study of Lunenburg County, Virginia, 1746–1832* (Philadelphia: University of Pennsylvania Press, 1984), J. William Harris, *Plain Folk and Gentry in a Slave Society: White Liberty and Black Slavery in Augusta's Hinterlands* (Middletown, CT: Wesleyan University Press, 1985), and Orville Vernon Burton, *In My Father's House Are Many Mansions: Family and Community Edgefield, South Carolina* (Chapel Hill: University of North Carolina, 1985).

14. Stephanie McCurry, *Masters of Small Worlds: Yeoman Households, Gender Relations, and the Political Culture of the Antebellum South Carolina Low County* (New York: Oxford University Press, 1995), 6.

15. Historians remain divided over whether southern women, especially wealthy plantation mistresses, forged distinct female communities during the nineteenth century. Some argue that elitism and racism prevented white women from identifying with other members of their sex. Others maintain that women, sharing similar experiences under the roofs of male-dominated households, managed to form a common culture and sense of community. For scholarship on southern households during the nineteenth century, see McCurry, *Masters of Small Worlds*, Elizabeth Fox-Genovese, *Within the Plantation Household: Black and White Women of the Old South* (Chapel Hill: University of North Carolina Press, 1988), Joan E. Cashin, *Our Common Affairs: Texts from Women in the Old South* (Baltimore, MD: Johns Hopkins University Press, 1996), Laura F. Edwards, *Gendered Strife and Community: The Political Culture of Reconstruction* (Urbana: University of Illinois Press, 1997), and Nancy C. Bercaw, *Gendered Freedoms: Race, Rights, and the Politics of Household in the Delta, 1861–1875* (Gainesville: University Press of Florida, 2003).

16. Burton, *In My Father's House Are Many Mansions*, 32, 60, 75, 81–82; Christopher C. Morris, *Becoming Southern: The Evolution of a Way of Life* (New York: Oxford University Press, 1995), 84–85, 87–92, 95, 133–34.

17. Anthony E. Kaye, *Joining Places: Slave Neighborhoods in the Old South* (Chapel Hill: University of North Carolina Press, 2007), 4–6, 9–12; Anthony E. Kaye, "'In the Neighborhood': Towards a Human Geography of US Slave Society," *Southern Spaces: A Journal about Real and Imagined Space and Places of the US South and Their Global Connections*, September 8, 2008, https://southernspaces.org/2008/neighborhood-towards-human-geography-us-slave-society.

18. Benedict Anderson, *Imagined Communities: Reflections on the Origin and Spread of Nationalism*, rev. ed. (London: Verso, 2016); James M. McPherson, "Antebellum Southern Exceptionalism: A New Look at an Old Question," *Civil War History* 29, no. 3 (1983): 230–44. On Confederate nationalism, see John McCardell, *The Idea of a Southern Nation: Southern Nationalists and Southern Nationalism, 1830–1860* (New York: Norton, 1979), Emory M. Thomas, *The Confederate Nation: 1861–1865* (New York: Harper and Row, 1979), Richard E. Beringer, Herman Hattaway, Archer Jones, and William N. Still Jr., *Why the South Lost the Civil War* (Athens: University of Georgia Press, 1986), Drew Gilpin Faust, *The Creation of Confederate Nationalism: Ideology and Identity in the Civil War South* (Baton Rouge: Louisiana State University Press, 1988), Gary W. Gallagher, *The Confederate War: How Popular Will, Nationalism, and Military Strategy Could Not Stave Off Defeat* (Cambridge, MA: Harvard University Press, 1997), Jason Phillips, *Diehard Rebels: The Confederate Culture of Invincibility* (Athens: University of Georgia Press, 2007), and Michael T. Bernath, *Confederate Minds: The Struggle for Intellectual Independence in the Civil War South* (Chapel Hill: University of North Carolina Press, 2010). On southern identity, see James C. Cobb, *Away Down South: A History of Southern Identity* (New York: Oxford University Press, 2005).

19. Anderson, *Imagined Communities*, chap. 11; Dunn, *Cades Cove*. On the Lost Cause, see Thomas L. Connelly, *The Marble Man: Robert E. Lee and His Image in American Society* (1977), Charles Reagan Wilson, *Baptized in Blood: The Religion of the Lost Cause* (Athens: University of Georgia Press, 1980), Gaines M. Foster, *Ghosts of the Confederacy: Defeat, the Lost Cause, and the Emergence of the New South, 1865–1913* (New York: Oxford University Press, 1987), William Garrett Piston, *Lee's Tarnished Lieutenant: James Longstreet and His Place in Southern History* (Athens: University of Georgia Press, 1988), William C. Davis, *The Cause Lost: Myths and Realities of the Confederacy* (Lawrence: University Press of Kansas, 1996), Gary W. Gallagher and Alan T. Nolan, eds., *The Myth of the Lost Cause and Civil War History* (Bloomington: Indian University Press, 2000), Karen L. Cox, *Dixie's Daughters: The United Daughters of the Confederacy and the Preservation of Confederate Culture* (Gainesville: University Press of Florida, 2003), Paul A. Shackel, *Memory in Black and White: Race, Commemoration, and the Post-Bellum Landscape* (Lanham, MD: AltaMira, 2003), especially chap. 3; David W. Blight, *Race and Reunion: The Civil War in American Memory* (Cambridge, MA: Harvard University Press, 2001), Caroline E. Janney, *Burying the Dead but Not the Past: Ladies' Memorial Associations and the Lost Cause* (Chapel Hill: University of North Carolina Press, 2008), and Caroline E. Janney, *Remembering the Civil War: Reunion and the Limits of Reconciliation* (Chapel Hill: University of North Carolina Press, 2013).

20. Eudora Welty, *The Eye of the Story: Selected Essays and Reviews* (New York: Random House, 1978), 128–29.

21. Quoted in Orville Vernon Burton, "Reaping What We Sow: Community and Rural History," *Agricultural History* 76, no. 4 (2002), 641.

22. For an excellent discussion on the reconstitution of old and the construction of new African American communities following the Civil War, see Steven Hahn, *A Nation under Our Feet: Black Political Struggles in the Rural South from Slavery to the Great Migration* (Cambridge, MA: Harvard University Press, 2003). Hahn draws on the work of political scientist Victor V. Magagna, who argues that being able to ascertain who has control of and access to community institutions represents the key to understanding power and political action in rural societies. See Victor V. Magagna, *Communities of Grain: Rural Rebellion in Comparative Perspective* (Ithaca, NY: Cornell University Press, 1991), ix–x, 12–21.

23. For more on reconciliation, see Blight, *Race and Reunion*, Janney, *Remembering the Civil War*, K. Stephen Prince, *Stories of the South: Race and Reconstruction of Southern Identity, Stories of the South* (Chapel Hill: University of North Carolina Press, 2016), Edward J. Blum, *Reforging the White Republic: Race, Religion, and American Nationalism, 1865–1898* (Baton Rouge: Louisiana State University Press, 2005), and Nina Silber, *The Romance of Reunion: Northerners and the South, 1865–1900* (Chapel Hill: University of North Carolina Press, 1993).

24. Don H. Doyle, *Faulkner's County: The Historical Roots of Yoknapatawpha* (Chapel Hill: University of North Carolina Press, 2001), 4.

PART I

CREATING COMMUNITIES

Gullah and Ebo

*Reconsidering Early Lowcountry
African American Communities*

RAS MICHAEL BROWN

WHEN WE REVISIT THE COMMUNITIES OF ENSLAVED AFRICAN-descended people, we enter a landscape scarred by violence but also consecrated with landmarks of hope. Large tracts of the unknown between these visible points leave us unsure of how to reach out to those we find in this place, as we catch glimpses of what looks familiar at the same time we confront much that we have never experienced. How do we portray relationships among people whose connections to each other could never be assumed to be stable or voluntary? How do we make sense of supposedly basic forms of affinity such as kinship in a world where bonds of blood failed to prevent separation of mother from child? What kind of community had any chance of existing in this realm?

We may imagine that the kind of community that could survive in such an environment had to be unified and strong in the ways implied by the muscular term "the slave community." Indeed, the inspiring, even miraculous, perseverance of African-descended people and their cultures through generation after generation within enslavement testifies to a resilience and creativity that exceeds our more prosaic notions of a community passively formed by the coincidental occupancy of the same time and space. Yet we may also worry that commemoration of social and cultural tenacity could veer uncritically toward a romanticized vision of the lives of enslaved people.[1]

Our survey of the contested terrain of community in early African America reveals that every tie required endeavors well beyond our usual expectations for what we may consider necessary for even the most mundane relationships. We can venture into the "neighborhoods" organized across the boundaries of plantations, farms, and households within which enslaved people created dense local social webs.[2] Efforts by enslaved women and men to establish marriages and families outside of the immediate spaces of their captivity provide testimony to the inclination to create bonds that needed exceptional care and entailed the interaction of communities, not solely individuals. The overall proportion of "abroad marriages" in the antebellum South may not have exceeded one-third, but in certain circumstances the proportion exceeded one-half and almost reached three-fourths.[3] Further, the commitment to visiting separated family and friends with or without the sanction of enslavers provided additional nourishment for communities outside of the normal confines of everyday work routines and social interactions.[4] These direct and personal methods of fostering the attachments of community attest to the meanings of close relationships among enslaved people across distances, some small and others vast. The difficulty in keeping them intact made them all the more remarkable.

My engagement with community in this essay moves beyond these intimate relationships and neighborhoods to the outer edges of the usual conceptions of community. This space is delineated by the connection of close personal bonds to those ideas and practices that allowed diverse, transient individuals to find "their people" in crowds of strangers and draw cultural nourishment from unfamiliar environments. The brutality of captivity and enslavement required African-descended people to fashion these outer edges into channels that carried countless waves of newcomers from social death to community as they passed from one place to another and, too often, to another and another. In the end, we find in this supposedly peripheral space of our conventional understandings of community the elements of the processes that sparked the creation of exceptionally complex Lowcountry African American communities in the first instance/place.

One of the earliest expressions of this complexity appears in the pluralist origins and uses of the terms Gullah and Ebo as social and cultural markers both within and outside Lowcountry African American communities in the eighteenth century. In identifying a pluralist formation of African-descended communities, I rebuff the notion that the heterogeneity of captive Africans meant that communities quickly emerged in tandem with the development of "new" creolized cultures that did not depend on specific African identities or cultures to define them. Further, I move on from the idea that captive Africans from certain key regions arrived in numbers large and homogeneous enough to re-create their identities and cultures for several generations before an African American identity and culture came to predominate. Instead of regarding cultural difference as the determinative factor that either inhibited community formation or ensured the insular integrity of distinct ethnicities, I recognize that captives taken to the Lowcountry came from societies in West and Central Africa that typically embraced cultural differences and developed ways to connect people across those differences. I do not imagine that identity and culture moved along a continuum with African at one end and African American at the other and that, at some point sooner or later, African-descended communities crossed a threshold that marked their transformation from African to African American. No, African-descended people in the Lowcountry did not seem to conform to this conception of a cultural continuum. Instead, they ultimately remodeled Gullah and Ebo into transethnic identities and attached ideas of cultural pluralism to those labels. In doing so, they collaboratively created interdependent identities that incorporated both diverse African-born and increasingly Lowcountry-born people within their communities without sacrificing cultural differences.

The nurturing of plural identities and cultures remains an underappreciated element in the formation of early African American communities.[5] The suffering induced by enslavement and its enabling institutions made such efforts essential, as diverse people constantly passed in and out of African-descended communities through birth, death, flight, and forced relocation. A newcomer to life or a place entered as an individual but had to be turned into "people," a part of a community, to belong and to have personhood. Groups that shared much or little in terms of language or religion or any other aspect of culture had to inhabit the same spaces, at the very least, and to flourish, in the best of circumstances. The methods needed to achieve all of this had already been developed in West and Central Africa well before the arrival of the first European vessels along African coasts, before the first barracoons, before the Middle Passage.[6] Deeply rooted within African and then African-Atlantic cultures, these strategies were transplanted by captive Africans and their descendants everywhere throughout the diaspora.

Gullah and Ebo as social identities within Lowcountry African American communities developed over multiple generations in ways unlike other African-derived identities and ethnonyms that once had currency in the Lowcountry. Whereas the many other "nation names" (names ostensibly derived from African ethnonyms) and other indicators of ethnic or cultural distinction persisted into the nineteenth century, they seemed to have purposes less pliable and enduring than Gullah and Ebo.[7] One of the more striking examples of the distinction afforded to Gullah and Ebo as ethnonyms appears in accounts of Denmark Vesey's planned uprising in 1822.[8] The details of the plot and subsequent trials do not pertain to the current inquiry other than to show that the units formed and recruited for the event included two with nation names, the Gullah band and the Ebo company. Many from a wide array of backgrounds participated in the planning, including a "French band" consisting of people relocated from Saint-Domingue and men from Senegambia, identified as Gambians, at least one of whom played a leading role. In the end, however, only two units, the Gullah band and the Ebo company, had nation names, and the leaders of these two companies, Gullah Jack Pritchard and Monday Gell, formed the core leadership along with Vesey. The composition of the force with its Gullah and Ebo factions amid numerous anonymous units suggests that the naming and pairing of the Gullah and Ebo divisions was intentional and not just a product of the circumstantial demographic backgrounds of the participants in the planning. Had the ethnicities of participants been determinative, the liberation force would have included a Gambia company, for example. It did not, as those known to have come from Senegambia participated in other units, including at least one in the Ebo company. Gullah and Ebo together in this revealing moment conveyed some special meaning. Maybe the combination projected a message about an alliance of spiritual power in conjure (Gullah), obeah (Ebo), and Christianity that was needed to overthrow oppression.[9] Maybe the pairing signaled to potential recruits and all who would have witnessed the uprising that the intended revolution emanated from a whole African-descended community united across affiliations of nation, language, religion, and status. Above all, it appears to have been a clear expression of the value of plural identities and cultures within an evolving African American community.

The need to contemplate the special meanings attached to Gullah and Ebo arises from the fact that these identities remained in use after emancipation and gained prominence within the collective memory and identity of Lowcountry African American communities. Most significantly, Gullah has emerged as the preeminent identity for those who wish to assert connections to the unique heritage of African-descended communities in coastal South Carolina and Georgia.[10] Though Ebo did not retain its function as a social identity the way Gullah did, it continues to resonate throughout the Lowcountry in "Ibo landing" stories that recount how a group of enslaved Africans chose to drown together in their rejection of enslavement and their hopes of returning home.[11] Both terms in their modern forms, then, continue to be spoken, shared, and cherished as names of power that serve to define Lowcountry African American communities. Given the special meanings of Gullah and Ebo over time, we must attempt to explain how this history of their pairing in the shaping of early Lowcountry African American communities began.

OUR SEARCH BEGINS WITH THE OBSERVATIONS OF JAMES BARCLAY, who related about his time among the sixty people enslaved on Cypress plantation in the 1770s that "there are some provinces from whence they are brought, whereof people have a violent antipathy to one another, and they are brought over here, the same antipathy subsists." As an example, he claimed that "those of the Gulli or Gully, and Iba are the chief. The one will say to the other, 'You be Gulli Niga, what be use of you, you be good for nothing.' The other will reply 'You be Iba Niga; Iba Niga great' askal [rascal]."[12] Barclay clearly mistook verbal sparring for ethnic antipathy, as the significant distance and lack of direct contact between West-Central Africans (Gulli, or Gullah) and those from the Bight of Biafra (Iba, or Ebo in historical usage and Igbo in modern form) presented no opportunities for them to develop animosities while still in Africa.[13] This error in understanding identity and culture among enslaved people should not obscure the significance of the reference to Gulli and Iba people, however. Of all the possible ethnic labels current then in the Lowcountry, Barclay repeated the two most deeply imprinted in Lowcountry African American culture. The pattern through which Gullah and Ebo became paired as transethnic identifiers appeared to be already established by the time that Barclay encountered African-descended people in South Carolina, even though such a pairing would not have been predicted given the prevalent trends in the coerced relocation of captive Africans beginning in the middle of the eighteenth century.

At least 61,483 captive Africans disembarked in South Carolina between 1750 and 1774. Among these people, no less than 45,691 came from places other than West-Central Africa and the Bight of Biafra. Almost three-fourths of captive newcomers during this period left Africa from the broad regions called Senegambia, Sierra Leone, the Windward Coast, the Gold Coast, the Bight of Benin, and Southeast Africa, in addition to unspecified regions of Africa. At least 9,879 (16.1 percent) and 5,913 (9.6 percent) of the captives started their transatlantic crossings in West-Central Africa and the Bight of Biafra, respectively. The preponderance of those from Senegambia (15,337, or 24.9 percent), Sierra Leone (8,798, or 14.3 percent), and the Windward Coast (7,141, or 11.6 percent), many of whom came from Mande societies, suggests that Mandingo and Bambara would figure prominently in the lexicon of Lowcountry ethnicity.[14] Notices from wardens of the workhouse in Charleston bear this out, as over half of the African "fugitives" linked to Upper Guinea (the designation for the combination of Senegambia, Sierra Leone, and the Windward Coast) nation names in notices had an association with Mandingo or Bambara. Additionally, nearly one-third of those with Upper Guinea ethnonyms were members of a variant of Kishee, a cultural group that spoke a non-Mande language, though their culture closely corresponded with Mande-speaking neighbors.[15] People taken from Senegambia made up the first cohorts of Africans carried directly from Africa to the Lowcountry, preceding the massive influx of captives from Upper Guinea regions in the decades following 1750. Although the regional origins of a sizable proportion of captive Africans remains unknown during the period stretching from 1701 to 1749 (11,839 of 33,121, or 35.7 percent), as many as 4,592 (21.6 percent of 21,282) came from Senegambia and Sierra Leone combined among those with a known regional provenience.[16] Those from Senegambia numbered prominently in the trade during the 1720s, so it is not surprising that probate inventories from the 1730s record the presence of six men from this region, including Bambro, Bambra, Bambrea, Bambra Jack, Mundingo Jack, and Mundingo Tom.[17] Further, probate inventories from 1740 through 1751 reveal people from Upper Guinea identified as Mondingo/Mundingo and Bambora/Bambra/Bambro through nation names prefixed to their personal names in proportions similar to that seen in the workhouse notices.[18]

With their significant presence in early African-descended communities, people from Upper Guinea societies exerted considerable cultural influence over several generations.[19] Certainly, the African-born population in the Lowcountry during Barclay's time, the 1770s, would have included a disproportionately high number of people carried from Senegambia, Sierra Leone, and the Windward Coast. They may have had more or less success in re-creating communities based on linguistic or cultural coherence, possibly identified through the sharing of nation names in some cases. Yet any outward expression of affinity did not appear to resonate in the same way as the pairing of Gullah and Ebo even though for more than two decades, large numbers of people from Upper Guinea had made up enslaved communities. This does not mean that Mandingo or Kishee or other African-based ethnicities in the Lowcountry were insignificant or lacked influence. Still, Barclay must have heard the pairing of Gullah and Ebo frequently for him to indicate that "they are the chief" among the identities expressed by enslaved people.[20] In light of the provenience of many captives, it appears that Gullah and Ebo did a different kind of work in the complex dynamics of community formation and elaboration, and evidence of this peeks through in the passing comment from James Barclay in the 1770s.

In order to sort out this special status for Gullah and Ebo, we need to return once again to the first half of the eighteenth century, particularly the 1730s and 1740s, as it was then that Gullah and Ebo first began to be paired in probate inventories and advertisements for enslaved people who absconded. Prior to the 1720s, no sources exist that indicate any nation names for captives. The silence of the archive regarding this early period, as well as subsequent eras, must be understood in the context of a remark from Gideon Johnston, first commissary of the Anglican mission in South Carolina: "I had something to say of the Negroes here, but cannot now."[21] This was all that he could trouble himself to write about African-descended people in July 1710, despite the fact that by the time that Johnston was composing this letter, African-descended people constituted over half of the population in the colony, and proselytization among enslaved people remained a high priority for the Anglican mission.[22] Still, Johnston felt no need to offer more than these twelve words as justification for his omission, and whatever he had to "say of the Negroes here" never made it into the record later.

Given the nature of intercolonial trade before the 1720s, people who would have been identified later as Gullah and Ebo almost certainly lived in the Lowcountry before the 1720s. Though in the direct transatlantic trade from Africa, vessels only moved between Sierra Leone or Senegambia and South Carolina, the continuing, though diminishing, significance of intercolonial commerce ensured the presence of captive Africans from other regions.[23] Probate inventories attest to this fact, as we find a small, but illustrative, range of nation names in the 1720s. The eight Africans named Gambo, Gamboa, Carantee Maria, Cormuntee Will, Popow Phillis, Golla, Gola Maria, and Angola Phillis appear to identify men and women from Senegambia (Gambo and Gambo), the Gold Coast (Carantee Maria and Cormuntee Will), the Bight of Benin (Popow Phillis), and West-Central Africa (Golla, Gola Maria, and Angola Phillis).[24] Evidence of the genesis of Gullah as a social label known to enslaved people and enslavers alike emerges from these three names noted in the 1720s, though there would be no mentions of people called Ebo until the following decade.

The 1730s appear to have determined the preeminence of Gullah and Ebo, as people carried from West-Central Africa and the Bight of Biafra dominated numerically among newly arrived captive Africans. Voyage data for the transatlantic trade indicate that all of the West-Central Africans taken to the Lowcountry arrived in 1730 and afterward, though we already know this to be an incomplete picture of the presence of West-Central Africans. Between 1730 and 1749, nearly two-thirds of the captive Africans with known regional origins (11,615 of 18,375, or 63.2 percent) came from West-Central Africa and over one-fifth (3,983, or 21.7 percent) entered the Middle Passage through ports in the Bight of Biafra region.[25] Taken together, more than eight out of every ten African newcomers could have been called Gullah or Ebo during these two decades that fundamentally redefined life on Lowcountry plantations.[26]

The 1730s produced the first mentions of the Ebo identity in the nation names of Ebo Jack, Ebo Joo, and Ebo Peter in inventories of estates.[27] Another first included the use of Congo or Congoe as a one-word nation name seen in the examples of four men with no other personal names. They joined Angola Jack as West-Central Africans in these sources.[28] The continued use of Senegambia nation names seen in variations of Bambara and Mandingo likely reflected the aging of those brought to the Lowcountry in the 1720s, as well as the steady, through relatively small by the standards of the 1730s, removal of captive Africans from Senegambia to South Carolina. The new presence of Ebo and Congo captives derived from the extension of direct importation from the Bight of Biafra and West-Central Africa that may have started in the 1720s and certainly accelerated in the subsequent decade. By the 1740s, when direct importation from all regions of Africa ceased almost entirely as a result of European wars and the Stono Rebellion, the number of nation names in estate inventories reflects the importation figures of the 1730s. Of the seventy nation names present in inventories created in the 1740s, twenty-four (34.3 percent) are variants of Angola (Gola, Golah, Gulla, and Gullah) and eighteen (25.7 percent) are variants of Ebo and Eboe, while only eight (11.4 percent) are forms of Gambia (Gambia, Gamboa, Gamba, and Gambo), five (7.1 percent) are variations of Bambara (Bambora, Bambra, and Bambro), and three (4.3 percent) are forms of Mandingo labels (Mondingo and Mundingo).[29]

The two predominant nation names, Angola/Gola and Ebo/Eboe, reflected two different, though parallel, paths to social identity in the coming generations. For those called Ebo, the label likely referred to people who hailed from communities defined culturally and socially as Igbo. No less than three-fourths of the people carried from Bight of Biafra ports shared an Igbo background.[30] The nation name Ebo could therefore have served as an ethnonym in the most conventional sense in both an African setting as well as in the Lowcountry. The use of Ebo may have been complicated by the poor reputation that people from the Bight of Biafra had with enslavers throughout the British Atlantic. This judgment, best summarized by an academic luminary inclined to disparaging African-descended people, held that "as to the Eboes... described as having a sickly yellow tinge in their complection, jaundiced eyes, and prognathous faces like baboons, the women were said to be diligent but the men lazy, despondent and prone to suicide."[31] Henry Laurens, a Carolina trader and enslaver, communicated an early version of this message in 1756, when he advised an associate that "slaves from the River Gambia are prederr'd to all others with us save the Gold Coast, but there must not be a Callabar among them."[32] Callabar in this phrase reflected the favored term among traders and enslavers in the eighteenth century for people from the Bight of Biafra. By way of contrast, captive people from the Bight of Biafra region chose to call themselves Ebo, not only in the Lowcountry but in the larger Igbo diaspora as well.[33] This distinction matters as we see special meanings attached to the Ebo identity in later generations.

A similar distinction appears to have been made by African-descended people with the names Angola and Gola. The temptation to see the prevalence of Angola/Gola as solely or primarily the artifacts of the minds of traders and enslavers may be strong for those who forget about the imbalance in the authorship of historical sources and the fact that the cultural worlds of enslaved people remained hidden for many reasons. Those who perpetuated the captivity of African-descended people certainly had their perspectives on the identities held by and imposed upon enslaved communities. We have plenty of evidence of those views, as manifested in their commentary about people called Callabar or Ebo. Ideas among African-descended people on the meanings of Angola and Gola (which became Gullah) during these formative stages of the label in the Lowcountry are hard to suss out, however. Still, we can gain some insight from two standout features of the use of Angola/Gola labels. The term Angola was used to identify all West-Central Africans in the Lowcountry, but not in any other part of the British Atlantic or the diaspora. If the term derived essentially from the functional terminology of transatlantic trade in captive Africans, why would the word that all British merchants used to identify the region of West-Central Africa (i.e., Angola) stick as the generic name for certain Africans in the Lowcountry alone and nowhere else? Further, we see that the name Angola coexisted with Gola, among many others, until Gullah emerged as the predominant form for the nation name. This contraction was used only in the Lowcountry and not in the extensive documentation for the transatlantic trade. The closest we get to a reference in the records is in a published notice that the ship *Liberty* put into Charleston harbor in 1806 with over four hundred captives carried from "Congo and 'Gulah.'"³⁴ The scare-quoting of "Gulah" in the advertisement indicates an awareness of the particular usage of the term in the Lowcountry and the adoption of the contraction among traders and enslavers there. How did this contraction originate in the Lowcountry? It came from African-descended people and their efforts to create plural communities.

It is important to remember that Angola and Gola in the eighteenth century represented a public discourse about social identity to which both enslaved people and those who enslaved them contributed, and so there can be no simplistic either-or account of the origins and use of these names. The most direct evidence of this discourse appears in two items published in 1795 in Savannah, Georgia. Tom, London, and Caesar together left their enslaver, and the first two men ended up in the custody of the workhouse warden in Savannah. They indicated to the warden that they came "from GOLA country and belong to Dr. Hague." Given that the warden had no prior knowledge about their backgrounds, this information had to come from Tom and London themselves. The next week's issue of the same newspaper that published the warden's notice included an advertisement from a subscriber that stated a Tom and London "from ANGOLA country" had run away. Both notices refer to the same men and reveal variations of an identity associated with them. According to the pen of an enslaver, Tom and London came from "ANGOLA country." According to Tom and London themselves, they came from "GOLA country."³⁵

In addition to this contemporary documentary link, we have cultural evidence. An interesting observation from the twentieth-century testimony of an African-descended man in coastal Georgia asserted that enslaved people "what come from Africa or overseas was call 'Golla,'" and "they talk was call 'Golla' talk." This "Golla talk" included words such as "musungo" (tobacco), "mulafo" (whiskey), "sisure" (chicken), "gombay" (cow), and "gulluh" (hog), all of which came from the Kongo language in particular and in some cases other closely related languages in West-Central Africa.³⁶ A deeper, cultural phenomenon affords us a more historical perspective on linguistic evidence, specifically a phonological principle in certain African languages and the creole language that emerged in the Lowcountry. When speakers of Kikongo and related languages encountered words that had the n- or m- prefix or began with a nasal vowel, they tended to drop it, producing the contracted form.³⁷ As used in the British Atlantic world and the Lowcountry, the term Angola in its Anglicized form began with an open vowel that sounded different from the nasalized "an-" Portuguese speakers used to replicate the kiMbundu word "ngola," a political title in the Ndongo kingdom and a widely used word meaning "power" or "force," from which the name of the Portuguese colony in West-Central Africa was derived.[38] To mirror the same sound heard at the beginning of the kiMbundu term, the Portuguese wrote "an-," as they did with every other local Bantu word that had either the n- or m- prefix. Speakers of the Kongo and Mbundu languages used many words that began with these prefixes, and they often dropped them with words that stood alone or did not follow a vowel sound in a preceding word.[39] Captive West-Central Africans certainly recognized Angola as a term from their vocabularies, regardless of how traders and enslavers used it, and did with Angola what they did with other Bantu terms that had the n- or m- prefix. They turned Angola into Gola.

This common phonological practice in the Kongo, Mbundu, and the Lowcountry creole (Gullah) languages reveals a key, though generic, approach to enunciating a large corpus of terms. A purely phonological explanation, however, misses what may be the most important reason why African-descended people said Angola as Gola and then Gullah. They contracted Angola to Gola to mark it as their own nation name conversant with but distinct from the label affixed by enslavers. Like their Ebo counterparts, African-descended people known by the name Gola and its variants intended to name themselves. The peculiar irony we see over time is that enslavers eventually adopted the name Gola/Gullah people established for themselves. The use of these names by whites is most notable in the nineteenth-century references to the 1739 Stono Rebellion as the Gullah War and in the use of Gullah to identify Jack Pritchard and his militia.[40]

The first step the African-descended people who named the Gola nation took was different from that taken by Ebo people in the Lowcountry. Instead of using a term that replicated a specific ethnonym, they chose a term that communicated an encompassing identity. A shift in the nation names in estate inventories reveals how this process unfolded. Whereas the inventories from the 1730s include a high proportion of people identified by the term Congo, the following decade presents only one such example and one additional nation name, Loango, which was an attempt at greater specificity for West-Central Africans than the broader Angola or Gola/Gullah was capable of. All kinds of personal identifications, including markers of ethnicity, likely circulated within enslaved communities, though outside of earshot of enslavers.[41] Yet in the strange space where the language of the transatlantic trade, captivity, and social identity met in documented nation names known to the enslaved and enslavers alike, forms of Angola took precedence as indicators of collective identity, rather than Congo, as typically seen in other parts of the diaspora.[42]

In later years, some would attempt to clarify distinctions, as in a runaway advertisement in 1768 that claimed that Toby, Agnes, and Roxana "are said to be of the Congo country (not Angola's frequently called Congo's)."[43] Enslavers appeared content to use Angola in public discourse well before then, as all of the references to West-Central Africans in newspaper advertisements during the 1730s and 1740s used this term.[44]

Newspaper advertisements were intended to be public and so they reveal how nation names were used broadly. Estate inventories, by contrast, were private; they documented the significance of nation names for the people within individual plantation communities. By all measures, Congo should have appeared frequently to identify relationships within plantation communities, as a large share of the West-Central Africans carried to the Lowcountry in the 1730s came from specifically Kongo communities.[45] Instead, variations of Angola predominated within plantation communities to the extent of rendering narrower nation names, such as Congo and Loango, as exceptional. With the emphasis on Angola and especially Gola, we witness the genesis of a pan-Bantu Gola/Gullah community as a means to incorporate diverse, displaced West-Central Africans into a mutually supportive group within a larger plural community.

One estate inventoried in 1746 may reveal the heart of this complex community formation. In it, three West-Central Africans (two named Gola Grippa and one Gola Clarinda), three women from the Bight of Biafra (Eboe Pathina, Eboe Venus, and Eboe Lucy), and three others (Echaw Peter, Echaw Jack, and Itchaw Susy) are named.[46] Two significant features emerge in this notable cluster of people with nation names. First, we see three identities (Gola, Eboe, and Echaw/Itchaw) mentioned in one community. Second, six women figured among the eight people with nation names, including two Gola women and three Eboe women. This is significant because women made up just under one-fourth of the people inventoried with nation names during the 1740s. Eight Angola/Gola women and seven Ebo/Eboe women together made up all but two of the total number of women with nation names in a larger group of enslaved people that had a much wider range of nation names among the men as well. The relatively small number of women serves only to amplify the absolute prevalence of Angola/Gola and Ebo/Eboe women among those identified by nation names and requires us to consider what this meant for enslaved communities going forward. Before 1740, those born in the Lowcountry only made up one-third of the African-descended population, but within the next two generations after 1740, those born in the Lowcountry came to make up three-fourths of this population.[47] These Gullah and Ebo women were the mothers of the first generation in this new era and the matriarchs of the communities that continued to grow in subsequent years. The Lowcountry-born people who formed a numerical majority by the start of the American War of Independence, then, were the children of the Gullah and Ebo nations.

When James Barclay considered it "diverting to hear" people "in their quarrels, reproaching one another with their respective countries," he assumed, as have scholars, that he was hearing the voices of Africans born across the Atlantic in "Gulli" and "Iba" countries and relocated to Cypress plantation on the Ashley River.[48] We must consider, however, that while he did indeed hear Gullah and Ebo people sparring with each other, some may have been born in Africa, and others may have been born into Lowcountry communities then raised in the Gullah and Ebo nations created by their parents. Further, others may have been born in Africa but not necessarily into communities in West-Central Africa or the Bight of Biafra regions. Contrary to the dominant scholarly narratives that have shaped our understandings of culture and identity in recent decades, communities of enslaved people required neither one kind of homogeneity as Africans nor another kind as "creolized" African Americans to participate in collective cultural processes.[49] Indeed, not only did they have no need for homogeneity, but they also appeared to want to cultivate a polycultural community in those realms of culture and identity they directed.

In all possible permutations of their composition in the 1770s, Gullah and Ebo people embodied diverse, distinct identities coexisting and interacting within one community. The lasting legacy of this early stage in forming plural identities and cultures in Lowcountry African American communities comes into view time and time again in subsequent generations. It was apparent when Gullah Jack Pritchard went into the countryside near Charleston to recruit men for Vesey's liberation force and thousands reportedly responded to the call of the Gullah and Ebo nations.[50] It endures in the sites people mark as sacred to their heritage, as with Igbo Landing. It lives on from the name Gola that African-descended people first gave themselves in the eighteenth century to the name Gullah now embraced by their descendants as they proclaim their dedication to the continuation of communities born long ago.

NOTES

1. The enduring scholarly discussion of "the slave community" was initiated by John W. Blassingame in *The Slave Community: Plantation Life in the Antebellum South* (New York: Oxford University Press, 1972). For brief historiographical context, see Brenda E. Stevenson, "The Question of the Slave Female Community and Culture in the American

South: Methodological and Ideological Approaches," *Journal of African American History* 92, no. 1 (2007): 80, and Dylan C. Penningroth, *The Claims of Kinfolk: American Property and Community in the Nineteenth-Century South* (Chapel Hill: University of North Carolina Press, 2003), 8. We should not move forward without noting Orlando Patterson's notion of natal alienation as fundamental to the condition of slave status. Natal alienation served to negate the possibility of membership in "any formally recognized community," though "informal social relations" existed for enslaved people (*Slavery and Social Death: A Comparative Study* [Cambridge, MA: Harvard University Press, 1982], 5–6). The understandings of community that most inform this essay come from Charles Joyner, *Down by the Riverside: A South Carolina Slave Community* (Urbana: University of Illinois Press, 1984), Margaret Washington Creel, *"A Peculiar People": Slave Religion and Community-Culture among the Gullahs* (New York: New York University Press, 1988), 1–2, and Michael A. Gomez, *Exchanging Our Country Marks: The Transformation of African Identities in the Colonial and Antebellum South* (Chapel Hill: University of North Carolina Press, 1998), 6.

2. Philip D. Morgan, *Slave Counterpoint: Black Culture in the Eighteenth-Century Chesapeake and Lowcountry* (Chapel Hill: University of North Carolina Press, 1998), 519–24; Stephanie M. H. Camp, *Closer to Freedom: Enslaved Women and Everyday Resistance in the Plantation South* (Chapel Hill: University of North Carolina Press, 2004); Anthony E. Kaye, *Joining Places: Slave Neighborhoods in the Old South* (Chapel Hill: University of North Carolina Press, 2007); Sergio A. Lussana, *My Brother Slaves: Friendship, Masculinity, and Resistance in the Antebellum South* (Lexington: University Press of Kentucky, 2016).

3. Paul D. Escott, *Slavery Remembered: A Record of Twentieth-Century Slave Narratives* (Chapel Hill: University of North Carolina Press, 1979), 50–52; Emily West, *Chains of Love: Slave Couples in Antebellum South Carolina* (Urbana: University of Illinois Press, 2004), 43–54; Diane Mutti Burke, *On Slavery's Border: Missouri's Small Slaveholding Households, 1815–1865* (Athens: University of Georgia Press, 2010), 200–201, 311; Brenda E. Stevenson, *Life in Black and White: Family and Community in the Slave South* (New York: Oxford University Press, 1996), 208–12, 229–31; Kaye, *Joining Places*, 74.

4. Wilma King, *Stolen Childhood: Slave Youth in Nineteenth-Century America* (Bloomington: Indiana University Press, 1995), 3–4, 17–19; Kaye, *Joining Places*, 38–39; Morgan, *Slave Cotunterpoint*, 524–30.

5. "Plural identities and cultures" are not equivalent to identities and cultures produced by creolization. The latter requires the total synthesis of identities and cultures into one construct, but the former does not. For a fuller account of this distinction, see Gomez, *Exchanging Our Country Marks*, 8–13.

6. Boubacar Barry, *Senegambia and the Atlantic Slave Trade*, trans. Ayi Kwei Armah (New York: Cambridge University Press, 1998); Toby Green, *The Rise of the Trans-Atlantic Slave Trade in Western Africa, 1300–1589* (New York: Cambridge University Press, 2012), chaps. 1 and 2. This fact that different groups in West and Central Africa had already developed strategies to make inhabiting in the same spaces possible should caution scholars against misinterpreting all forms of cultural interchange involving African-descended people in postcontact Africa and the diaspora as fundamentally dependent on creolization or the emergence of the Atlantic world, as enticing as both concepts may be.

7. The value of nation names and personal names in understanding cultural processes is discussed in John C. Inscoe, "Carolina Slave Names: An Index to Acculturation," *Journal of Southern History* 49, no. 4 (1983): 527–54, Cheryll Ann Cody, "There Was No 'Absalom' on the Ball Plantations: Slave-Naming Practices in the South Carolina Low Country," *American Historical Review* 92, no. 3 (1987): 563–96, Jerome S. Handler and JoAnn Jacoby, "Slave Names and Naming in Barbados, 1650–1830," *William and Mary Quarterly*, 3rd ser., 53, no. 4 (1996): 685–728, John K. Thornton, "Central African Names and African-American Naming Patterns," *William and Mary Quarterly*, 3rd ser., 50, no. 4 (1993): 727–42, and Gwendolyn Midlo Hall, *Slavery and African Ethnicities in the Americas: Restoring the Links* (Chapel Hill: University of North Carolina Press, 2005), 52–54.

8. Gomez, *Exchanging Our Country Marks*, 1–3; Walter Rucker, *The River Flows On: Black Resistance, Culture, and Identity Formation in Early America* (Baton Rouge: Louisiana State University Press, 2006), 152–79.

9. For the broad religious context, see Rucker, *The River Flows On*, 163–69. For the link between obeah and Igbo, see Douglas B. Chambers, "'My Own Nation': Igbo Exiles in the Diaspora," *Slavery and Abolition* 18, no. 1 (1997): 72–97. An interesting pairing of Gullah and Ebo as potent spiritual practices appears in the proto-ethnographic story "The Lazy Crow: A Story of the Cornfield," in William Gilmore Simms, *The Wigwam and the Cabin*, 2nd ser. (London: Wiley and Putnam, 1845), 99–126.

10. For diverse expressions of this identity and heritage in recent times, see of Marquetta L. Goodwine and the Clarity Press Gullah Project, eds., *The Legacy of Ibo Landing: Gullah Roots of African-American Culture* (Atlanta: Clarity Press, 1998).

11. Gomez, *Exchanging Our Country Marks*, 118–20; Ras Michael Brown, *African-Atlantic Cultures and the South Carolina Lowcountry* (New York: Cambridge University Press, 2012), 139–42; Douglas B. Chambers, "The Igbo Diaspora in the Era of the Slave Trade," in *Igbo in the Atlantic World: African Origins and Diasporic Destinations*, ed. Toyin Falola and Raphael Chijokwe Njoku (Bloomington: Indiana University Press, 2016), 161–62.

12. James Barclay, *The Voyages and Travels of James Barclay, Containing Many Surprising Adventures, and Interesting Narratives* (Dublin: printed for the author, 1777), 26.

13. The perpetuation of this misinterpretation appears in Morgan, *Slave Counterpoint*, 457–58.

14. List of voyages, 1750–74, *Voyages: The Trans-Atlantic Slave Trade Database*, www.slavevoyages.org/voyages/edoSG6nI.

15. Sean M. Kelley, *The Voyage of the Slave Ship* Hare: *A Journey into Captivity from Sierra Leone to South Carolina* (Chapel Hill: University of North Carolina Press, 2016), 168–71, 214; Gomez, *Exchanging Our Country Marks*, 89, 102–3.

16. List of voyages, 1701–49, *Voyages: The Trans-Atlantic Slave Trade Database*, www.slavevoyages.org/voyages/y5Hy4rAX.

17. All inventories are contained in the miscellaneous records of South Carolina, Secretary of State, Recorded Instruments, South Carolina Department of Archives and History, and are identified here by name, date of inventory, and volume number the inventory is recorded in. See Henry Nicholas, April 12, 1730, vol. H, 1729–31, Elias Horry, October 3, 1737, vol. II, 1736–39, William Sanders, May 22, 1736, vol. CC, 1732–36, Wilson Sanders, July 26, 1736, vol. CC, 1732–36, Levi Guichard, June 23, 1731, vol. H, 1729–31.

18. See vol. KK, 1739–43, vol. LL, 1744–46, vol. MM, 1741–48, and vol. B, 1748–51.

19. Creel, *"A Peculiar People,"* 285–95; Matt Schaffer, "Bound to Africa: The Mandinka Legacy in the New World," *History in Africa* 32 (2005): 321–69; Edda Fields-Black, *Deep Roots: Rice Farmers in Africa and the African Diaspora* (Bloomington: Indiana University Press, 2008), 161–86.

20. Barclay, *The Voyages and Travels of James Barclay*, 26.

21. Gideon Johnston, *Carolina Chronicle: The Papers of Commissary Gideon Johnston, 1707–1716*, ed. Frank J. Klingberg (Berkeley: University of California Press, 1946), 61.

22. Johnston's letter extended over sixty-eight hundred words, which prompted him to apologize at the end of his correspondence "for the length of this," so the failure to elaborate on the enslaved stands out that much more (*Carolina Chronicle*, 61). The classic treatment of this period remains Peter Wood, *Black Majority: Negroes in South Carolina* (New York: Knopf, 1974), 95–130. For the Anglican missions, see Creel, *"A Peculiar People"*, 67–74, and Travis Glasson, *Mastering Christianity: Missionary Anglicanism and Slavery in the Atlantic World* (New York: Oxford University Press, 2012).

23. Brown, *African-Atlantic Cultures and the South Carolina Lowcountry*, 71–74.

24. Thomas Stewart, March 28, 1723, vols. B and C, 1722–26; Gesper Baskerfild, August 24, 1725, vol. D, 1724–25; Phillip Gendroon, May 8, 1724, vols. B and C, 1722–26; Elias Hancock, vol. H, 1729–31; John Cawood, January 4, 1725, vol. E, 1726–27; Francis Courage, August 13, 1725, vol. D, 1724–25.

25. List of voyages, 1730–49, *Voyages: The Trans-Atlantic Slave Trade Database*, http://www.slavevoyages.org/voyages/LbEHPMwb.

26. Wood, *Black Majority*, 131–66.

27. George Smith, December 3 and 4, 1730, vol. H, 1729–31; William Downing, September 30, 1732, vol. I, 1731–33; George Smith, February 21, 1734, vol. CC, 1732–36; Thomas Rose, December 12, 1733, vol. CC, 1732–36; William Moore, September 21, 1736, vol. II, 1736–39.

28. Samuell West, July 12, 1731, vol. H, 1729–31; Jonathan Jamer, April 2, 1731, vol. I, 1731–33; Joseph Mackey, August 9, 1736, vol. II, 1736–39; Gilson Clapps, January 24, 1738, vol. II, 1736–39; William Downing, September 30, 1732, vol. I, 1731–33.

29. Ralph Izard, January 25, 1743–44, vol. KK, 1739–43; Royal Spry, May 16, 1747, vol. MM, 1741–48; William Guy, January 29, 1750, vol. B, 1748–51; Noah Serre, February 11, 1746, vol. LL, 1744–46; William Wateis, July 30, 1743, vol. KK, 1739–43; Hugh Hext, March 25, 1745, vol. LL, 1744–46; Bengamin Donning, October 20, 1741, vol. MM, 1741–48; Alexander Hext, June 26, 1742, vol. MM, 1741–48; Barnebe Reily, April 7, 1747, vol. MM, 1741–48; Benjamin Godin, June 20 and 21, 1749, May 24, 1749, vol. B, 1748–51; Daniel Britton, January 19, 1749, vol. B, 1748–51; William Elliot, March 25, 1751, vol. B, 1748–51; Andrew Broughton, July 30, 1743, Vol. KK, 1739–43.

30. Chambers, "The Igbo Diaspora in the Era of the Slave Trade," 156, 158.

31. Ulrich Bonnell Phillips, *American Negro Slavery: A Survey of the Supply, Employment, and Control of Negro Labor as Determined by the Plantation Régime* (New York: Appleton, 1918), 43. For a broader survey of stereotypes associated with captive Africans from the Bight of Biafra, see Gomez, *Exchanging Our Country Marks*, 115–17.

32. *The Papers of Henry Laurens*, 16 vols., ed. George Rogers Jr. (Columbia: University of South Carolina Press, 1968), 2:186.

33. Gwendolyn Midlo Hall, "The Clustering of Igbo in the Americas: Where, When, How, and Why?" in *Igbo in the Atlantic World*, 140–42.

34. Elizabeth Donnan, ed., *Documents Illustrative of the History of the Slave Trade to America*, 4 vols. (Washington, DC: Carnegie Institute of Washington, 1930–35), 4:513.

35. *Georgia Gazette* (Savannah), August 13, 1795, August 20, 1795.

36. Georgia Writers' Project, Savannah Unit, *Drums and Shadows: Survival Studies among the Georgia Coastal Negroes* (1940; repr., Athens: University of Georgia Press, 1986), 66.

37. For phonological variations of Gullah, see Lorenzo Dow Turner, *Africanisms in the Gullah Dialect* (Chicago: University of Chicago Press, 1949), 194.

38. Joseph C. Miller, *Kings and Kinsmen: Early Mbundu States in Angola* (Oxford, UK: Clarendon, 1976), 58–86.

39. John K. Thornton, *The Kongolese Saint Anthony: Dona Beatriz Kimpa Vita and the Antonian Movement, 1684–1706* (Cambridge: Cambridge University Press, 1998), 9.

40. Lionel H. Kennedy and Thomas Parker, *An Official Report of the Trials of Sundry Negroes, Charged with an Attempt to Raise an Insurrection in the State of South Carolina* (Charleston, SC: James B. Schenck, 1822), "Extracts," 2.

41. A twentieth-century testament to this appears in the massive compilation of "basket names" once used in Lowcountry communities documented in Turner's classic *Africanisms in the Gullah Dialect*, 43–190.

42. Hall, *Slavery and African Ethnicities in the Americas*, 35.

43. *Georgia Gazette* (Savannah), November 9, 1768. For the other examples of the use of Congo in runaway advertisements, see *South Carolina Gazette and Country Journal* (Charleston), October 28, 1766, *South Carolina Gazette and General Advertiser* (Charleston), October 7–14, 1774.

44. Daniel C. Littlefield, *Rice and Slaves: Ethnicity and the Slave Trade in Colonial South Carolina* (Baton Rogue: Louisiana State University Press, 1981), 115–33, 118–22 (table 3); Daniel C. Littlefield, "'Abundance of Negroes of that Nation': The Significance of African Ethnicity in Colonial South Carolina," in *The Meaning of South Carolina History: Essays in Honor of George C. Rogers, Jr.*, ed. David R. Chesnutt and Clyde N. Wilson (Columbia: University of South Carolina Press, 1991), 19–38.

45. John K. Thornton, "African Dimensions of the Stono Rebellion," *American Historical Review* 96, no. 4 (1991): 1101–13.

46. Noah Serre, February 11, 1746, vol. LL, 1744–46.

47. Morgan claims that the proportion of the Lowcountry-born people within the enslaved population grew from 34 percent in 1740 to 77 percent in 1790 (*Slave Counterpoint*, 61).

48. Barclay, *The Voyages and Travels of James Barclay*, 26.

49. The most notable works that posit foundational ideas for these opposing interpretations include Sterling Stuckey, *Slave Culture: Nationalism Theory and the Foundations of Black America* (New York: Oxford University Press, 1987) and Sidney W. Mintz and Richard

Price, *The Birth of African-American Culture: An Anthropological Perspective* (Boston: Beacon Press, 1992).

50. James Hamilton, *Negro Plot: An Account of the Late Intended Insurrection among a Portion of the Blacks of the City of Charleston, South Carolina* (Boston: Joseph W. Ingraham, 1822), 38.

The Ties That Bind

Slaveholding Kinship Networks in the Toe Valley

KEVIN W. YOUNG

SHORTLY BEFORE HIS DEATH IN 1843, THOMAS LEE RAY OF THE Toe Valley in western North Carolina composed his will. With twenty-two slaves, Ray was the largest slaveholder in the Toe Valley. "I give and bequeath to my sons," he wrote, "all my Negroes to be equally divided among them share and share alike." For the next two decades Ray's heirs profited from this slaveholding legacy. In 1860, his descendants owned a total of forty-five persons, over half of whom had been born in the years following Thomas Lee Ray's death.[1]

In a cruel irony, slavery threatened family bonds among the enslaved but bolstered kinship ties among slave owners. Widows and children inherited slaves, while men who married into slaveholding families obtained slaves as well as wives. Relatives sold slaves to one another at favorable prices, and at estate auctions, belonging to the family of the deceased slaveholder gave potential buyers a significant advantage over other bidders. There were extensive kinship ties among slaveholders throughout western North Carolina, including the Toe Valley. Encompassing about seven hundred square miles along the Tennessee border, the Toe Valley was a widely dispersed rural community, with local waterways serving as connecting arteries and corridors for communication. Within this community, slaveholders constituted an elite socioeconomic class, bound together by shared economic interests and close family ties.[2]

Euro-Americans began settling the Toe Valley after the American Revolution, and by the eve of the Civil War, about eighty-three hundred people lived in the region. From 1790 to 1860, slaves consistently made up around 4 percent of the local population, and slave labor played a vital role in the economy. In 1850, the Toe Valley's ten largest corn farmers were all slave owners, as were the twelve men with at least $1,500 in livestock. Fifty-four slaveholders, owning a total of 288 slaves, resided in the Toe Valley in 1850. Identifying precisely where these slaveholders lived underscores the close correlation between slaveholding and physical terrain; throughout the region, slaveholders were concentrated along waterways. Virtually all the owners in 1850 had slaveholding roots dating back two decades or more. Examining the identity of new owners in 1860 demonstrates the importance of kinship ties in acquiring slaves. By the antebellum era, Toe Valley slaveholders had become a firmly established class, and entry into this class was limited almost exclusively to those who were born or married into long-time slaveholding families.[3]

RATHER THAN A LARGE FLAT BASIN, THE TOE VALLEY IS A WATERshed containing three main rivers—the North Toe, South Toe, and Cane rivers. From its headwaters at the Toe Valley's northeastern end, the North Toe runs westward, twisting and turning across the northern half of the watershed. The highest mountain chain in the eastern United States—the Black Mountains—extends for a dozen miles south to north, dividing the southern half of the region into two separate river valleys. Beginning on opposite slopes of the Black Mountains, the South Toe and Cane rivers run northward and consecutively join the North Toe. These three rivers and their tributaries are not commercially navigable, but their banks provide the flattest and most arable land in this mountainous region.[4]

In 1850, only four men held slaves on the northeastern end of the Toe Valley. In a large meadow a mile downstream from the juncture of Roaring Creek and the North Toe was a farm called the Crab Orchard. Managed by a local overseer, the farm belonged to Isaac T. Avery, the scion of a wealthy and politically prominent Burke County family. Upon his father's death in 1821, Avery had inherited the family plantation near Morganton and at least seventy-five slaves, as well as the Crab Orchard and several thousand acres at the head of Roaring Creek that he used for raising hundreds of cattle. By 1850, Avery owned over 130 slaves, fourteen of whom lived year-round at the Crab Orchard, and every August additional slaves were temporarily sent there from Burke County to cut and gather hay.[5]

Unlike Avery, the other three slave owners in the upper Toe Valley were local residents. At the confluence of Powdermill Creek and the North Toe, Loderick Oakes operated a gunpowder mill and held a single slave, a man in his

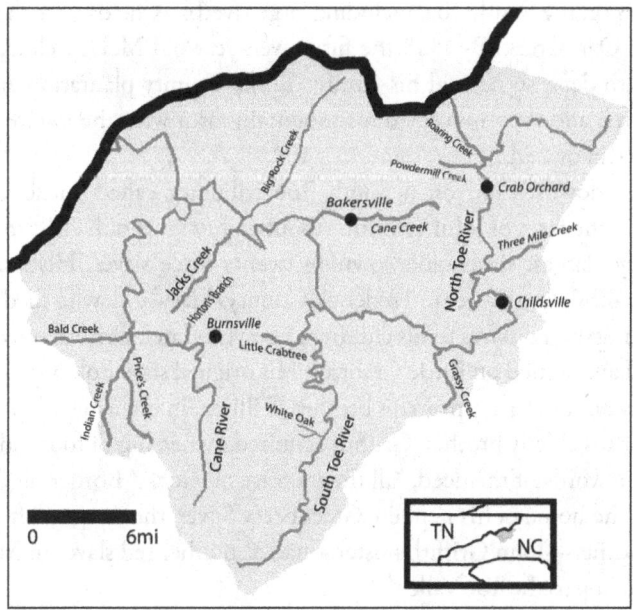

MAP 1. The Toe Valley of Western North Carolina

twenties. Two decades earlier Oakes had owned five persons, including two boys—one of whom was likely the same individual listed in his possession in 1850. Further down the North Toe, on a tributary called Three Mile Creek, lived seventy-nine-year-old Jacob Carpenter, the owner of two female slaves. Prior to 1840, census records had never listed Carpenter as a slaveholder; he probably inherited these two women—one middle aged, the other in her twenties—from his father, a large Ashe County slaveholder who died in 1835. One of Carpenter's neighbors was Albertus Childs, a Massachusetts native who had recently arrived in North Carolina. In the 1840s, Childs's brother Lysander had moved to Lincoln County, North Carolina, where he married a mill owner's daughter and acquired over twenty slaves. Lysander Childs then persuaded his parents and brothers to join him in the South, and he probably facilitated his siblings' acquisition of slaves. In the summer of 1850, Albertus Childs settled a farm near Three Mile; the slave schedule that year listed him as owning a man and two children.[6]

From its headwaters on the eastern slopes of the Black Mountains, the South Toe River flowed northward and intersected the North Toe. The only slaveholder along the upper South Toe was James McDowell, a member of a prominent Burke County slaveholding family. In 1839, McDowell purchased

1,740 acres on the South Toe, including large riverbank fields near the mouth of White Oak Creek. By 1848 the fifty-seven-year-old McDowell had fallen heavily into debt, so he sold his family's Burke County plantation and most of his slaves, and then moved to his mountain farm with the twelve persons whom he still owned.[7]

Further downstream, on a South Toe tributary called Little Crabtree Creek, was the farm of John Griffith. About eighty years old, Griffith was the Toe Valley's largest slaveholder, owning twenty-three slaves. His father had been a wealthy slave owner in Frederick County, Maryland, who died in 1801, bequeathing several slaves to his children. Five years later, Griffith moved from Maryland and settled on Little Crabtree. His original slave holdings were augmented by an 1825 legacy from his brother William. In exchange for promising to care for his elderly brother, Griffith acquired ownership of four individuals and, in the words of the deed, "all the increase on stock." Bordering Griffith's farm was the home of his nephew Greenberry Silver, the owner of five slaves. Silver's mother—John Griffith's sister—had also inherited slaves in Maryland before moving to the Toe Valley.[8]

The remaining slaveholders in the lower South Toe area were four brothers—Thomas, George, Wesley, and John Young—who lived along tributary streams and held a total of fifteen slaves. Around 1815 their grandfather in Burke County purchased a girl named Airey, whose owners had recently moved to western North Carolina from Virginia. Over the next two decades, Airey gave birth to numerous children. Two of her children were owned by the Youngs' father, Strawbridge Young, who settled on the lower South Toe and died there in 1834. Over time, the Young family developed extensive kinship ties to other local slave owners. Strawbridge Young's wife Martha Wilson was possibly the sister of Cane River slaveholder Edward "Ned" Wilson, and Young's widowed sister-in-law married John Griffith. Such ties helped Young's children acquire additional slaves. In March 1834, John Griffith traded a woman named Charlotte "and her issues" to George Young in exchange for ten acres of land, a mill, two stills, and other merchandise.[9]

A few miles downstream from the convergence of the North Toe and South Toe rivers was Cane Creek. Seven slaveholders lived along the creek, which flowed through the tiny village of Bakersville. The son of a large Burke County slaveholder, Bakersville merchant Isaac Pearson Jr. owned six slaves. A short distance up Cane Creek lived Reuben Young, the largest pig farmer in the Toe Valley. In addition to his two hundred pigs, Young kept a large herd of sheep and grew corn. With eight slaves, he was the largest slaveholder in the Bakersville area. Though he may have been distantly related to the slave-owning Youngs on the lower South Toe, Reuben Young's parents were nonslaveholders of modest means. However, he had married the daughter of Simeon Burleson, whose slaveholdings dated back to at least 1820. Simeon Burleson and his brother Aaron had both owned slaves, and the other slaveholders living along Cane Creek included Simeon Burleson's widow and Aaron Burleson's son.[10]

Most Toe Valley slaveholders resided on prized farmland along rivers and streams, but slave owners in the village of Burnsville were an exception. Located on a small hill flanked by higher mountains, Burnsville had been established in 1833 as a county seat for newly created Yancey County. A simple settlement with wooden buildings and dirt streets, the village had a few commercial establishments and a courthouse. In 1850, slaveholders accounted for six of the eighteen households in Burnsville—a far higher percentage than in the surrounding countryside. In addition, three other slave owners lived on the outskirts of the village. These nine men held a total of sixty-one slaves—slightly over 20 percent of the Toe Valley's entire slave population.[11]

Some Burnsville slave owners had moved there comparatively recently, lured by business opportunities in the new county seat. Thirty-year-old Joshua Williams had arrived from Sevier County, Tennessee, in the 1840s and opened a linseed oil mill and tannery; by 1850 he owned three slaves. The son of a Buncombe County slaveholder, Milton Penland had various business enterprises in Burnsville, including a general store, tannery, and gristmill. Married to the niece of North Carolina governor David Swain, Penland held seven slaves. The Toe Valley's wealthiest resident was thirty-eight-year-old Samuel Fleming, an attorney and representative in the state legislature, who had moved to Burnsville in the 1830s. The 1850 census listed Fleming as owning $42,000 in real estate, an enormous sum for the time and place. As Fleming once remarked to a business associate, he "had commenced life . . . in poverty" but "married a fortune." In 1835 he had instantly ascended to the slaveholding elite by marrying Hannah Greenlee, an heiress whose grandfather had accumulated immense wealth in land, cattle, and slaves. By 1850 Fleming held seven slaves in the Toe Valley, but he owned at least another two dozen people in McDowell County, his wife's birthplace.[12]

Like Fleming, Burnsville store owner John McElroy had acquired slaves from the Greenlee family. In 1840, elderly Toe Valley resident James Greenlee wished "to make ample provisions for his wife," who was some twenty years younger than him. He therefore set up a trust account, and for the sum of $1 transferred ownership of his eight slaves to McElroy, specifying that they should be held "in trust for & to the sole & separate use & benefit of my said wife Mary." In 1850, both Greenlee and his wife were still alive, but no longer listed as slaveholders, while McElroy now owned sixteen slaves, including eight children.[13]

Burnsville slaveholders Joseph Shepherd and John Wesley Garland had both married daughters of Zephaniah Horton Sr., a local slave owner who died in 1844. However, Shepherd and Garland came from very different backgrounds. Shepherd was descended from a long-time slaveholding family. His grandfather had held slaves as early as the 1780s; his father, Thomas Shepherd, arrived in the Toe Valley in the 1790s and by 1820 owned thirteen slaves. Thomas Shepherd later relocated to Macon County, where his slaveholdings steadily increased, but his son Joseph remained in the Toe Valley. Upon his father's death in 1842, Joseph Shepherd inherited at least ten slaves, and the subsequent census showed him owning thirteen people—including four children. Unlike Shepherd, John Wesley Garland had been born into a nonslaveholding family in eastern Tennessee. He moved to Burnsville, where he established a linseed oil mill and earned a reputation as a shrewd businessman. "Good but tricky, needs close watching," an anonymous credit agent wrote of Garland. His business acumen and the ties he established through marriage helped him acquire slaves. In 1844 he purchased a female slave from his wife's family, and by 1850 he owned eight people.[14]

The remaining three slave owners living in or near Burnsville in 1850 were sons or sons-in-law of local slaveholders and had obtained slaves through these family connections. Alabama native Isaac Broyles had married the daughter of Joseph Shepherd, who provided the couple with three slaves. Court clerk William Lewis was married to Cecilia Wilson, the daughter of Cane River slaveholder Edward "Ned" Wilson. In 1850, Lewis owned a teenage girl whom his father-in-law had given to Cecilia. Twenty-one-year-old James M. Ray—the youngest slaveholder in the Toe Valley—lived on the outskirts of Burnsville. His father, Hiram, who died in 1839, had bequeathed nine slaves to his wife and children. Throughout the 1840s, two of these slaves—a woman and a boy—were held in guardianship for James M. Ray by his older brother, and in 1848 the enslaved woman gave birth to a child. By 1850, Ray was married, headed his own household, and owned three slaves.[15]

In the lower Toe Valley, the Cane River began on the rugged western slopes of the Black Mountains. The mountains along the river's headwaters were unsuitable for farming, but further downstream the river looped westward for several miles. This long arc in the waterway was flanked by expansive river bottoms and fed by several tributaries, including Indian Creek, Price's Creek, and

Bald Creek. The flat fields along this stretch of the river provided fertile farmland. In 1850 nineteen slave owners—holding over 40 percent of the Toe Valley's slave population—lived along the Cane River or on one of its tributaries.[16]

Immediately west of Burnsville, on a stream known as Horton Branch, lived Zephaniah Horton Jr., the owner of eight slaves. Horton had acquired these slaves from his late father, and he had extensive family ties to other local slaveholders; at least three of his brothers-in-law owned slaves. To the north of Horton Branch was Jacks Creek, where Baptist minister Samuel Byrd lived. In February 1832, Byrd had purchased three female slaves—apparently a mother and her two young daughters—from an estate sale. In 1850 Byrd still held these three slaves, while his son Cornelius was now the owner of two children.[17]

In 1850, two extended families dominated the ranks of Toe Valley slaveholders. The Rays and Wilsons had been among the earliest Euro-American settlers along the Cane River, and by 1850 at least sixteen slaveholders in the Toe Valley—nearly 30 percent of local slave owners—were either descendants of or had married into these two families. Family patriarchs Thomas Lee Ray and Edward "Ned" Wilson had arrived in the 1790s. Ray came from Virginia, while Wilson had lived in South Carolina for several years before heading to the North Carolina mountains. Apparently neither Ray nor Wilson owned slaves when they first arrived in the Toe Valley, but during the 1810s and 1820s several members of the two families became slaveholders. The families developed close kinship ties, for Thomas Lee Ray's son Henry married Ned Wilson's youngest daughter.[18]

Thomas Lee Ray owned hundreds of acres where Price's Creek and Bald Creek flowed into the Cane River. There he built a gristmill and developed a thriving business, transporting produce to Charleston, South Carolina, and returning with various goods. In 1810, neither he nor his father held slaves; a decade later, Ray owned eight persons, including young women who would give birth to numerous children. By the time of his death in 1843, Ray had become the largest slave owner in the Toe Valley. In 1850 his sons James, Jesse, William, and Henry—as well as his grandson Nathan Boone—were all slaveholders, owning a total of thirty-two people. James, William, and Henry Ray were three of the largest corn farmers in the Toe Valley, using slave labor to grow thousands of bushels of corn annually along the banks of the Cane River.[19]

Born in South Carolina around 1769, Ned Wilson would accumulate several hundred acres of land on the Cane River and Jack's Creek. A farmer and blacksmith, Wilson owned at least one slave in the early 1800s. His slave holdings dramatically increased in the 1820s, and by 1830 he held eight persons, including five women and girls. Family ties helped Wilson acquire additional slaves; in 1847 he purchased a woman and two children from a relative in Union County, Georgia. Three years later, Wilson owned a total of eleven people. In addition to Wilson's son-in-law Henry Ray, seven other slaveholders in the Cane River area were members of Wilson's family. His sons William and James resided near Price's Creek, as did James's son-in-law Andrew Roberts. Nearby lived Calvin Edney, who had married Wilson's daughter. To the west of the Cane River, on a tributary known as Bald Creek, lived Wilson's nephew William Wilson Sr.; the two other slaveholders residing on Bald Creek were William Wilson Sr.'s son Samuel and son-in-law David Proffitt. These seven slaveholders held a total of twenty-two slaves.[20]

By 1850, Ned Wilson's son James was an even larger slaveholder than his father, having used various family connections to acquire a total of thirteen slaves. In 1830 he bought "a certain negro man, by the name of Will," from his brother-in-law William Lewis. James Wilson's father-in-law was Blake Piercy, who had moved from Georgia to the Cane River area around 1800. Upon his arrival, Piercy became the largest slaveholder in the western Toe Valley, but on April 14, 1829, heavily in debt, he sold most of his human chattel. James Wilson bought five of these slaves for $1,000, while Piercy's son Ephraim purchased seven of them. In 1850, Ephraim Piercy lived at the southwestern edge of the Toe Valley, on a six-hundred-acre farm along Indian Creek, and held twelve slaves. One of Piercy's neighbors was Dorothy Shepherd. Like Mary Burleson on Cane Creek—the only other woman in the Toe Valley listed as a slave owner in 1850—Shepherd was a slaveholder's widow and the owner of one female slave. In 1842, her husband—the nephew of prominent slaveholder Joseph Shepherd—had paid his mother $400 for a young slave girl; eight years later, Dorothy Shepherd owned a seventeen-year-old female slave.[21]

By 1850, slaveholding among the Ray, Wilson, Piercy, and Shepherd families extended over multiple generations. In contrast, Cane River slaveholders Thomas Gardner and Henry Rowland had not yet transferred slaves to their children. The owners of neighboring farms, Gardner and Rowland had lived in the area since the early nineteenth century. In 1808, Rowland purchased 155 acres; five years later, the twenty-one-year-old Gardner, a native of Virginia, bought 100 acres in "the Caney River settlement." Over the next two decades, the two men each accumulated over five hundred acres that they used to grow corn and raise livestock. By 1830, both Gardner and Rowland had acquired slaves; in 1850, Rowland would be listed as owning seven people. Gardner's slaveholdings were more extensive. In 1830 he owned a boy under age ten and a male teenager. Two years later, he bought "a certain negro girl by the name of

Polly, aged about sixteen years, with a child named Affection about one year old" from two Virginia slave traders. By 1850 Thomas Gardner had become the second-largest slaveholder in the Toe Valley, owning twenty-one persons.[22]

Of the nineteen slaveholders in the western Toe Valley, eighteen were the children of slave-owning parents, had married into long-time slaveholding families, and/or had personally owned slaves since at least the early 1830s. The sole exception was thirty-six-year-old Logan Henry Dellinger. He had grown up in a Lincoln County community of German settlers, many of whom owned slaves. Dellinger's parents, however, were not slaveholders. In 1829, they moved to the Toe Valley, settling near Three Mile Creek. Their son subsequently relocated twenty miles down the valley and began operating a gristmill, which brought him into frequent contact with local slaveholding farmers. Dellinger's business prospered and he acquired thirty-four hundred acres of land and over forty cattle. By 1850 he had become a slaveholder, owning a woman and two girls. Like Thomas Lee Ray before him, Dellinger apparently used the profits from a gristmill to invest in slave labor, and he developed extensive business and family ties to other slaveholders. In the 1850s he bought several hundred acres along the Cane River from Thomas Gardner and William Ray, and three of Dellinger's children would marry into the Ray family.[23]

Of the Toe Valley's fifty-four slaveholders in 1850, only nineteen (35 percent) had been listed as local slave owners a decade earlier; however, nearly all the region's owners belonged to slaveholding kinship networks that had facilitated their acquisition of slaves. All seven slave owners in the South Toe area were the children of slaveholders. Of the nine slave owners in or near Burnsville, at least seven had slaveholding fathers or fathers-in-law, while an eighth had acquired slaves for the nominal sum of $1. In the western Toe Valley, eighteen of the nineteen slaveholders either had slave-owning parents or fathers-in-law or had personally held slaves for many years. Two of the four owners in the North Toe area were the sons of slaveholders; a third—whose ancestry cannot be discerned—had owned slaves for at least two decades, while the fourth was a wealthy native of a free state whose parents had been legally precluded from holding slaves.

In addition to inheriting slaves directly, members of slaveholding families had other advantages in acquiring slaves. If the buyer and seller of a slave were closely related, then the purchaser frequently paid a substantially reduced price. In December 1841, John Wesley Garland purchased a seven-year-old boy named Jacob from Samuel Fleming. Three years later, Garland bought "a negrow [sic] woman named Leah, about 26 years of age," from his brother-in-law Zephaniah Horton Jr. The price of a woman of child-bearing age should have been equal to, if not more than, the price of a young boy; however, whereas Garland paid $400 for Jacob, he bought Leah from his brother-in-law for $100. Other Toe Valley slave transactions demonstrate the same pattern. In September 1841, James Carter purchased a "Negro Girl named Mareah" from a nonrelative for $400; four months later, William A. Wilson paid his kinsman William Wilson Jr. $100 for "a Negro girl Named Canthea" (Cynthia).[24]

Estate auctions seem to have been the most common form of slave transactions in the Toe Valley. If bidders at an estate sale were members of the deceased's family, then they often purchased slaves at a reduced price, for other potential buyers deferred to the bids made by surviving family members. In 1843, a North Carolina resident counseled his sister about buying slaves at a family estate sale. "Bid for them yourself," he advised, "and you will be likely to get them at moderate prices." This general principle held true in the Toe Valley. When Simeon Burleson died in 1840, his two slaves Joseph and Mary were put up for sale. Estate administrators received $915 for Joseph but sold fourteen-year-old Mary for $100. Though Joseph, a twenty-one-year-old man, was perhaps more valuable than the teenage girl, the price differential was far greater than one would expect. An unidentified buyer had purchased Joseph, while Burleson's widow had paid a reduced price for Mary. In 1852, Jackson Gardner died. Gardner had only recently become a slaveholder, owning a thirty-year-old woman named Phyllis and her two children Mary and Elijah. He probably acquired these individuals from his father, Cane River slaveholder Thomas Gardner, and when his estate was sold at auction, Thomas Gardner purchased his son's three slaves for $589. In comparison, the previous year, tight-fisted Burnsville businessman John W. Garland had paid $950 for a thirty-six-year-old woman and her eleven-year-old daughter, and in 1853 Garland bought a seven-year-old girl and five-year-old boy for $650.[25]

Comparing the Toe Valley's 1850 slaveholders with the owners in 1860 makes clear the importance of kinship ties in acquiring slaves. In 1860, there were sixty-one slaveholders in the Toe Valley, holding 362 slaves. Thirty-two of these owners had not appeared on the previous local slave schedule, and the percentage of Toe Valley slaveholders owning only one slave had dramatically increased (see table 1). Of the twenty-three owners of a single slave in 1860, seventeen had not been listed on the previous slave schedule. Examining who the new slaveholders in 1860 were—and how they had acquired their human chattel—sheds light on the dispersal of slaves through extended families and reveals how inaccessible slave ownership had become to those who lacked such kinship ties.[26]

TABLE 1. Number of Slaves Owned by Toe Valley Residents, 1850 and 1860

Number of Slaves Owned	1850 Slaveholders (Percentage of Total Owners)	1860 Slaveholders (Percentage of Total Owners)
20 or more	2 (3.7%)	4 (6.6%)
10–19	9 (16.7%)	10 (16.4%)
5–9	10 (18.5%)	7 (11.5%)
2–4	18 (33%)	17 (27.9%)
1	15 (27.8%)	23 (37.7%)

Only two new owners in 1860 held ten or more slaves, and both were sons of large slaveholders. With twenty-six slaves, John Orlando Griffith was the second-largest slaveholder in the Toe Valley. The only child of John Griffith, who died in 1853, he had inherited his father's property. Twenty-three-year-old George Greenlee had recently moved to the Toe Valley. His father, Samuel Greenlee, had been a prominent Burke County slaveholder who died in 1848. An estate administrator had hired out these slaves, reaping large profits for Greenlee's heirs; in one year's time, young George had gained $185.75. In addition to slaves, the younger Greenlee inherited a 640-acre farm on Grassy Creek, a tributary of the North Toe, and by 1860 he had moved there. With twenty-three slaves, Greenlee instantly became one of the Toe Valley's largest slaveholders.[27]

Four of the other new owners held at least five slaves. Robert Penland had not personally owned slaves in 1850, but he was the brother of Burnsville slaveholder Milton Penland. Throughout the 1850s, aided by an inheritance from their slaveholding Buncombe County father, the Penland brothers accumulated thousands of acres of land and several slaves. In 1853, Milton Penland paid $1,400 for James M. Ray's four slaves, and at the 1858 estate sale of George Roberson—a local resident who had held a few slaves for many years—he bought two enslaved men for $1,616. By 1860, Milton Penland was the largest slaveholder in the Toe Valley, owning thirty-one people. Occasionally the Penland brothers jointly purchased slaves; in 1852, they bought an enslaved boy named Manson from Cane Creek slaveholders Wilson and William Burleson. Like his brother, Robert Penland was involved in numerous business enterprises, including running a general store, and by 1860 he owned nine slaves.[28]

The new owners in 1860 were scattered throughout the Toe Valley. In 1850, Massachusetts native Albertus Childs had settled on the North Toe and become a slaveholder. Soon thereafter, his parents and his brother Eben joined him, establishing the small community of Childsville. Despite their Massachusetts background, the Childs family showed no aversion to slavery, and by 1860 Eben Childs owned six people. At the other end of the Toe Valley, on Indian Creek, lived Jackson Shepherd, son of the widow Dorothy Shepherd. In 1850 Dorothy Shepherd had owned one female slave. By 1860, her son held the enslaved woman in guardianship for his own children; however, his mother continued to use the woman's labor, hiring her for the nominal sum of twenty-five cents annually. During the 1850s the woman had given birth to four daughters, making Jackson Shepherd the owner of five slaves.[29]

Six of the new slave owners were sons and sons-in-law of Thomas Gardner, who died in 1857. In his will, Gardner dispersed twenty-nine slaves among his wife and children. Through direct inheritance, his sons John and William Gardner, and his sons-in-law Thomas Baker, William Banks, Reuben Sawyer, and Jasper Roland, all became slaveholders. In other cases, slaveholding parents were still living but had transferred ownership of some slaves to their children. Greenberry and Moses Young were sons of Cane Creek slaveholder Reuben Young. Though Reuben Young was still alive and still owned slaves in 1860, his sons had almost certainly obtained their slaves from him. Among Reuben Young's holdings in 1850 were two boys, ages twelve and seven. By 1860, these two individuals were no longer in his possession, but his sons now owned two men, ages twenty-two and eighteen.[30]

One of the new Toe Valley slaveholders in 1860 was Robert Vance. A member of a prominent Buncombe County slaveholding family, Vance did not reside locally, but he owned an enslaved woman and her three daughters who were being held by his father-in-law, Burnsville resident John McElroy. In May 1858, McElroy had experienced serious financial problems, so Vance paid him $3,000 for five slaves, including the woman and her two daughters (the third daughter was born the following year). That same month, McElroy and Vance arranged a deal involving Vance's brother, future North Carolina governor Zebulon Vance. Together with a business partner, Robert Vance served as security for $1,350 that McElroy borrowed from an Asheville bank. In return, for the nominal sum of $1, McElroy sold Zebulon Vance a "negro girl named Eliza," who was "about eighteen years old" and had "a yellow complexion." The deed specified that if Robert Vance was ever pressed for repayment of the bank loan, then Zebulon would "provide to sell at public auction after thirty days advertisement the said girl Eliza & any children she may then have to the highest bidder for cash and the proceeds he shall apply to the discharge of said Bank note." In 1860, McElroy no longer owned any slaves, but thanks to his son-in-law he continued to enjoy the benefits of slave labor.[31]

Among the new owners in 1860 were three widows—Margaret Carpenter, Cecilia Lewis, and Cordelia Adams. Carpenter was the widow of Three Mile Creek slaveholder Jacob Carpenter, and at the 1858 auction of her husband's estate, she purchased a middle-aged female slave for the discounted price of $102.50. After Cecilia Lewis's husband died in 1853, she assumed outright ownership of Jane, a young slave whom her father Ned Wilson had given to the couple. Cordelia Adams was the daughter of Joseph Shepherd, who died in early 1860. In his will, Shepherd bequeathed "my boys Manson & Julius" to his widowed daughter Cordelia. Whereas Julius was indeed a young boy, Manson was in his forties and had likely belonged to the Shepherd family since birth.[32]

Five of the Toe Valley's new slaveholders were Amos, Hiram, J. B., William, and Jesse Ray. Descendants of the prominent Cane River slave-owning family, each of the men owned one slave. The slaveholding ranks of the Ray family had also grown through marriage. Dr. Benjamin Whittington had not owned slaves in 1850, but ten years later he held three individuals. Marriage—not his professional status—accounted for Whittington's ability to enter the slaveholding class; his wife was a daughter of large slaveholder Henry Ray. Though new owner James C. Proffitt was the son of a slaveholder, this family connection did not explain how Proffitt acquired a slave; in 1850 his father had owned a single male slave, while ten years later Proffitt held a twelve-year-old girl. Like Whittington, Proffitt had become a slave owner by marrying a daughter of Henry Ray, who had given the enslaved girl to the couple.[33]

The new slave owners in 1860 ranged greatly in age. Only eighteen years old, Presley Blankenship was the Toe Valley's youngest slaveholder, owning a teenage girl. His father had been a nonslaveholding farmer of modest means; an advantageous marriage was the cause of Blankenship's change in status. In February 1860, he married into the Ray family, taking sixteen-year-old Martha Louisa Ray for his wife. Ray's father, Jesse, had died five years before, bequeathing to his daughter "two beds & furniture and also one Negro girl named Jane," who had been annually hired out throughout the late 1850s for over $30 a year. Among the Toe Valley's oldest new slaveholders was fifty-eight-year-old farmer Alfred Hampton. Hampton's wife, Rebecca, was the daughter of Nathan Deyton, who upon his death in 1849 left an estate that included a "Black woman named Phebe." The following year Rebecca Hampton's brother William Deyton owned two slaves, including an elderly woman. After William Deyton died in the early 1850s, the subsequent census showed his brother-in-law Alfred Hampton owning an elderly woman who had almost certainly been in the Deyton family for decades.[34]

In all, twenty-nine of the thirty-two new owners in 1860 had demonstrably close kinship ties to previous slaveholders; these twenty-nine owners had a parent, sibling, father-in-law, or son-in-law who had owned slaves. Of the 362 slaves in the Toe Valley, 359 of them—over 99 percent—were held by members of long-term slaveholding families. Only three new owners—each owning a single slave—had no discernable relation to 1850 slave owners, and two of these individuals—J. C. Kilpatrick and Hulda Webb—had moved to the Toe Valley in the 1850s and came from unknown family backgrounds.[35]

Of the Toe Valley's sixty-one slaveholders in 1860, only one owner—fifty-three-year-old Jackson Stewart—had been a nonslaveholding local resident ten years earlier and had no close family ties to other slaveholders. In the words of one contemporary observer, Stewart was "of low and humble parentage." His sister Frankie Stewart Silver had been hanged in 1833 for killing her husband and then dismembering and burning his body—the most notorious murder in Toe Valley history. Stewart's personal history suggests financial malfeasance probably played a role in his anomalous rise to the slaveholding class. Throughout the 1850s, a credit agent filed multiple reports warning that Stewart was "a most noted scoundrel" and "not to be trusted at all." Nevertheless, he was appointed sheriff of Yancey County; his duties included overseeing public auctions of property—including slaves—that had been seized from individuals who either owed taxes or had defaulted on bank loans. In August 1854, Stewart was charged with illegally rigging these auctions by having an accomplice submit winning bids and then transferring ownership of the property to himself. Though convicted on these charges, Stewart continued serving as sheriff. Three years later, he was indicted for misappropriating tax money, which resulted in Yancey County owing the state more than $1,000. He eventually resigned after reaching an agreement with state officials: the new sheriff would be responsible for settling the delinquent tax bill, and Stewart would not be held liable for it. Following his resignation, his legal problems continued. In 1859, he was jailed in South Carolina for passing counterfeit money; he then forfeited bail by failing to appear for trial.[36]

There is no record how Jackson Stewart obtained the middle-aged female slave whom he owned in 1860, but his history of rigging public auctions and passing counterfeit money is certainly suggestive. The sole Toe Valley resident to enter the slaveholding class without the benefit of family ties, Stewart is the exception who proves the rule: by the 1850s, becoming a slaveholder in the Toe Valley nearly always depended on kinship ties established by birth or marriage.

AS WITH ANY COMMUNITY STUDY, A HISTORY OF TOE VALLEY slaveholders inevitably raises the question of typicality. In other regions of the South, did kinship ties play such a decisive role in providing entry into the slaveholding class? To answer this question conclusively, one would have to research the family background and marital history of all slaveholders in another region, determining how and when each of these individuals acquired slaves. Historian Stephen West has shown that over 75 percent of slaveholders in the Upper Piedmont of South Carolina in 1860 had either owned slaves or had lived with slaveholding parents in 1850. Yet even this large percentage underestimates the late antebellum stratification between slaveholding and nonslaveholding classes, for it does not include owners who married into slaveholding families or inherited slaves after having been out of their parents' household for more than ten years.[37]

Throughout the early 1800s, Toe Valley residents with no previous history of slaveholding occasionally acquired slaves. By the 1830s, however, the economic divide between nonslaveholders and slaveholders had grown so large that unless individuals were born or married into slaveholding families or owned some means of production such as a grist mill, then they had little possibility of ever accumulating enough money to purchase a slave. On his 1854 journey through the southern Appalachians, Frederick Law Olmsted visited the Toe Valley. A local resident informed Olmsted that wage-earning manual laborers could find work only a few months each year and could hope to earn at most around $75 annually. In comparison, at an auction in 1858, Burnsville merchant Milton Penland bought one hundred acres of land for $124, while a male slave named Joe was sold for $935. An able-bodied male slave thus cost over seven times more than one hundred acres of land—and the purchase price of such a slave represented a manual laborer's entire earned income for over a dozen years.[38]

When compared with slavery in the Deep South, slavery in the Toe Valley may seem a grain of sand. But this grain of sand helps illustrate far larger patterns. Investigating how individual slaveholders in the late antebellum period had acquired their human chattel reveals a stark economic divide between slaveholders and nonslaveholders. From examining the kinship ties among Toe Valley slaveholders, one learns that slave transactions in the American South did not always follow the dictates of formal economics; the family relationship between buyer and seller often played an important role in determining the prices paid in such transactions. Finally, and perhaps most importantly, the history of Toe Valley slaveholding highlights the process by which wealth within a community is consolidated in an elite socioeconomic class; this class becomes an endogamous group, fostering their shared interests by cultivating kinship ties among each other—while ignoring the humanity of the people from whom they profit.[39]

NOTES

I wish to thank Paul Kardulis of Burnsville, North Carolina, for his help in identifying places of residence of Toe Valley slaveholders.

1. Yancey County Clerk of Court, will book 1, 72–74; U.S. Census, 1840, 1860, free inhabitant and slave schedules, Yancey County; Lloyd Bailey, ed., *Toe River Valley Heritage*, 21 vols. (Marceline, MO: Walsworth, 1994), 1:382 (hereafter *TRVH*).

2. Jason Basil Deyton, "The Toe River Valley to 1865," *North Carolina Historical Review* 24, no. 4 (1947), 424; John C. Inscoe, *Mountain Masters: Slavery and the Sectional Crisis in Western North Carolina* (Knoxville: University of Tennessee Press, 1989), 116–17. As Inscoe notes, "The extent of kinship ties among western Carolina slaveholding families" was remarkable; these families "tied themselves to each other through marriage," thus ensuring a multigenerational "continuity of wealth and power" (117). For the role of waterways in forming extended rural communities within the Appalachians, see Altina L. Waller, *Feud: Hatfields, McCoys, and Social Change in Appalachia, 1860–1900* (Chapel Hill: University of North Carolina Press, 1988), 25. For the concept of community, see Thomas Bender, *Community and Social Change in America* (Baltimore, MD: Johns Hopkins University Press, 1991), 6–7, 17. In the Toe Valley, internal waterways connected local residents, while surrounding mountain ranges served as barriers to neighboring regions, and so all inhabitants occupied a shared community geographically. As defined by Bender, however, community entails more than a shared geography; in Bender's words, a community consists of "a limited number of people in a somewhat restricted social space or network held together by shared understandings and a sense of obligation" (7). Based on this definition, I argue that Toe Valley slaveholders formed their own tightly knit community, for they were a socioeconomically elite class that played a dominant role in local politics. In 1834, the first two Toe Valley residents to serve in the state legislature were sent to Raleigh from newly formed Yancey County; both men were slaveholders, as were all the region's representatives in state government for the next sixteen years. Though fewer than 6 percent of local households owned slaves, the first five county commissioners were slaveholders, as were most of their successors. On a local level, county officials acted in accordance with slaveholders' interests, including by establishing and maintaining regular slave patrols (Yancey County Court of Pleas and Quarter Sessions, minute docket, January and June terms, 1834; John H. Wheeler, *The Legislative Manuel and Political Register of the State of North Carolina* [Raleigh, NC: Josiah Turner, 1874], 371; Yancey County Court of Pleas and Quarter Sessions, minute docket, April session, 1838).

3. U.S. Census, 1790–1860, free inhabitant and slave schedules, Burke, Buncombe, and Yancey counties; U.S. Census, 1850, agricultural schedule, Yancey County; Edward W. Phifer, "Slavery in Microcosm: Burke County, North Carolina," *Journal of Southern History* 28, no. 2 (1962): 140–41. The 1850 Yancey County census listed 71 slaveholders and 346 slaves. However, the following seventeen slaveholders lived outside the Toe Valley in what would become

Madison County (1851): Jesse Anderson, Nathan Anderson, Levi Bailey, Elizabeth Carter, William Keith, James Metcalf, Joseph Pitman, John Ponder, John Radford, William Ramsey, James Ray (a relative of Toe Valley slaveholder James Ray), Thomas W. Ray, Joseph Rice, John Roberts, Isam Woodard, John Woodard, Joshua Young.

4. John Hairr, *North Carolina Rivers* (Charleston, SC: History Press, 2007), 91. The Toe Valley has been part of various counties. Burke County (established 1777) included the entire region. In 1791, the southeastern Toe Valley became part of newly formed Buncombe County. Carved from Burke and Buncombe, Yancey County (1833) included the Toe Valley and adjacent areas that were later incorporated into Watauga (1849) and Madison (1851). From 1851 to 1861 Yancey's boundaries were contiguous with the Toe Valley. Following the formation of Mitchell (1861) and Avery (1911), the Toe Valley now includes three counties—Yancey, Mitchell, and part of Avery (David Leroy Corbitt, *The Formation of the North Carolina Counties, 1663–1943* [Raleigh: State Department of Archives and History, 1950], 239–43).

5. Edward W. Phifer, "Saga of a Burke County Family," pt. 1, *North Carolina Historical Review* 39, no. 1 (1962), 1–17, Edward W. Phifer, "Saga of a Burke County Family," pt. 2, *North Carolina Historical Review* 39, no. 2 (1962), 140–47, Edward W. Phifer, "Saga of a Burke County Family," pt. 3, *North Carolina Historical Review* 39, no. 3 (1962), 305–39; John Preston Arthur, *A History of Watauga County* (Richmond, VA: Everett Waddey, 1915), 53–54; U.S. Census, 1820, population schedule, Burke County; U.S. Census, 1850, slave schedules, Burke and Yancey counties; "Roll Book of Slaves of the Avery Family from 1766 to 1865," North Carolina State Archives, Raleigh, NC.

6. Horton Cooper, *History of Avery County, North Carolina* (Asheville, NC: Biltmore Press, 1964), 32 (Cooper states that Oakes eventually earned enough money to purchase this single slave, but census records show otherwise—see U.S. Census, 1830, 1840 population schedules, Burke County); Maggie Palmer Lauterer, *Sweet Rivers* (Asheville, NC: Folk Heritage Books, 1997), 31–35; Marty Grant, "Mathias Carpenter (1750/55) and Elizabeth Miller of Surry, Wilkes and Ashe C o, NC," www.martygrant.com/gen/carpenter/carpenter-mathias.htm#children; Claudia Hill McGough, *Childsville* (privately published, 2003); U.S. Census, 1850, slave schedule, Lincoln County; Jeannette Holland Austin, *North Carolina–South Carolina Bible Records* (Westminster, MD: Heritage Books, 2008), 260; U.S. Census, 1810–30, population schedules, Ashe County; U.S. Census, 1840, population schedule, Yancey County.

7. Paul Kardulis, "Col. James Moffitt McDowell (1791–1854) and Margaret Caroline Erwin (1801–1831)," *Mountain Echoes* 2, no. 2 (1996): 19–22; U.S. Census, 1840, population schedule, Burke County.

8. R. R. Griffith, *Genealogy of the Griffith Family* (Baltimore, MD: William K. Boyle and Son, 1892); Frederick County, MD, inventory and accounts, 1797–1802, liber GM no. 3, 549–50; *TRVH*, 1:406; Yancey County Register of Deeds, record book 1, 8–9.

9. Burke County Court of Equity, March term 1833, reprinted in Perry Deane Young, *Our Young Family* (Johnson City, TN: Overmountain Press, 2003), 505; abstract of George Young papers, photocopy in the author's possession. A fifth slaveholding brother, Joshua Young, lived just outside the Toe Valley.

10. Frederick Law Olmsted, *A Journey in the Back Country* (New York: Mason Brothers, 1860), 267; "A Winter in the South," *Harper's New Monthly Magazine*, November 1857, 731; U.S. Census, 1820, 1840, 1850, population schedules, 1850 slave schedule, Burke County; Phifer, "Slavery in Microcosm," 160; Young, *Our Young Family*, 412, 414; U.S. Census, 1850, agricultural schedule; Yancey County Clerk of Court, will book 1, 106; Marie W. Holland, *Cane Creek Cousins* (Statesville, NC: Atavus, 2001).

11. Corbitt, *The Formation of the North Carolina Counties, 1663–1943*, 239–43; A. R. Newsome, ed., "The A. S. Merrimon Journal, 1853–1854," *North Carolina Historical Review* 8, no. 3 (1931), 329; U.S. Census, 1850, agricultural schedule, Yancey County.

12. U.S. Census, 1840, population schedule, Sevier County, TN; U.S. Census, 1850, agricultural schedule, Yancey County; U.S. Census, 1830, 1840, population schedules, Buncombe County; *TRVH*, 1:361; Ralph Stebbins Greenlee and Robert Lemuel Greenlee, *Genealogy of the Greenlee Families* (Chicago: privately published, 1908), 251; William L. Byrd III and John H. Smith, eds., *North Carolina Slaves and Free Persons of Color: McDowell County* (Bowie, MD: Heritage Books, 2003), 238; W. Conard Gass, "'The Misfortune of a High Minded and Honorable Gentleman': W. W. Avery and the Southern Code of Honor," *North Carolina Historical Review* 56, no. 3 (1979): 278–97; Phifer, "Saga of a Burke County Family," pt. 3, 307–11; Yancey County Court of Pleas and Quarter Sessions, minute docket, June session, 1835; U.S. Census, 1850, slave schedule, McDowell County.

13. *TRVH*, 2:305–6; Yancey County Register of Deeds, record book 1, 304; U.S. Census, 1850, free inhabitant schedule, Yancey County.

14. North Carolina State Census, 1787, Wilkes County; *TRVH*, 1:404; U.S. Census, 1800–1820, population schedules, Buncombe and Macon counties, will book 1, 24–27; Paul Kardulis, "John Wesley Garland," *Mountain Echoes* 1, no. 3 (1995), 17–20; U.S. Census, 1850, agricultural schedule, Yancey County; David C. Hsiung, ed. *A Mountaineer in Motion: The Memoir of Abraham Jobe* (Knoxville: University of Tennessee Press, 2009), 50; North Carolina, 25:592, R. G. Dun and Company Collection, Baker Library, Harvard Business School; John Wesley Garland Papers, private collection of Paul Kardulis, Burnsville, NC.

15. *TRVH*, 1:404; Yancey County Clerk of Court, will book 1, 417–18; Buncombe County Register of Deeds, record book 16, 435; Yancey County, settlements of estates, wills, inventories, and accounts, 1855–69, vol. 1A, 15–18 (microfilm no. C.107.50011); Yancey County Clerk of Court, will book 1, 51–52, 147–53. James M. Ray was the nephew of Thomas Lee Ray.

16. *TRVH*, 4:45.

17. U.S. Census, 1840, population schedule, Yancey County; Young, *Our Young Family*, 28; *TRVH*, 1: 177–78; Yancey County Register of Deeds, record book 1, 335.

18. *TRVH*, 1:382–85; U.S. Census, 1800–20, population schedules, Buncombe County; U.S. Census, 1840, population schedule, Yancey County; Yancey County Clerk of Court, will book 1, 72.

19. U.S. Census, 1820, population schedule, Buncombe County; U.S. Census, 1840, population schedule, Yancey County; Yancey County Clerk of Court, will book 1:72; *TRVH*, 1:384–85.

20. Yancey County Register of Deeds, record book 3, 27; *TRVH*, 1:404, 95; U.S. Census,

1800–20, population schedules, Buncombe County; Buncombe County Register of Deeds, record book 17, 196, record book 16, 423.

21. *TRVH*, 1:404, 95; U.S. Census, 1800–20, population schedules, Buncombe County; Buncombe County Register of Deeds, record book 13, 381–82, record book 17, 196, record book 16, 423.

22. Yancey County Register of Deeds, record book 3, 257; Buncombe County Register of Deeds, record book 12, 451, record book 13, 82, 497, record book 15, 182, 179, 250, record book 16, 182; *Images of Yancey* (Burnsville, NC: Yancey History Association, 1993), 162; *TRVH*, 1:212.

23. François Michaux, *Michaux's Travels to the West of the Alleghany Mountains* (Bedford, MA: Applewood Books, n.d.), 292; Yancey County Register of Deeds, record book 5, 81, record book 3, 391; *TRVH*, 1:193.

24. John Wesley Garland Papers; Yancey County Register of Deeds, record book 3, 2, record book 2, 150; *TRVH*, 1:222.

25. Walter G. Jones to Mary C. Jones, November 20, 1843, Harper-Beall Family Papers, Correspondence Series, 1826–1959, W. L. Eury Collection, Appalachian State University, Boone, NC; Yancey County Clerk of Court, will book 1, 106, 277–78; U.S. Census, 1850, 1860, slave schedules, Yancey County; Yancey County Register of Deeds, record book 3, 278; John Wesley Garland Papers. As Steven Hahn has noted, public auctions in the nineteenth-century South "had a decidedly nonmarket character," for "family members retrieved ... property at much reduced prices" (*The Roots of Southern Populism* [New York: Oxford University Press, 1983], 81).

26. U.S. Census, slave schedule, 1860, Yancey County. Among the thirty-two new slaveholders in 1860 was Jesse Ray—the nephew of the Jesse Ray listed in 1850. The thirty-two new slaveholders do not include the following two cases. Bacchus Young is listed on the 1860 schedule but only as an employer of slaves rented from a McDowell County owner—his first-cousin and brother-in-law Zephaniah Young. The Nathan Ray listed in 1860 was the illegitimate son of William Ray; in 1850 he had been listed with his mother's surname as Nathan Boon.

27. Griffith, *Genealogy of the Griffith Family*; *TRVH*, 1:254–55; Phifer, "Slavery in Microcosm," 157–58.

28. *TRVH*, 9:179; North Carolina, 25:590, 592, R. G. Dun and Company Collection, Baker Library, Harvard Business School; U.S. Census, slave schedule, 1860, Yancey County; Buncombe County estate records, 1815–1924, Pearson (folder 2), microfilm no. G.013.1674238; Buncombe County Register of Deeds, record book 25, 456; Yancey County Clerk of Court, will book 1, 298; Yancey County Register of Deeds, record book 4, 163; Henry E. Colton, *Mountain Scenery* (Raleigh, NC: W. L. Pomeroy, 1859), 98.

29. McGough, *Childsville*; Yancey County Clerk of Court, will book 1, 323, 326, 329.

30. Yancey County, settlements of estates, wills, inventories and accounts, 1855–69, vol. 1A, microfilm no. C.107.50011; Young, *Our Young Family*, 414.

31. *TRVH*, 2:305–6; Gordon B. McKinney, *Zeb Vance: North Carolina's Civil War Governor and Gilded Age Political Leader* (Chapel Hill: University of North Carolina Press, 2004), 11; Yancey County Register of Deeds, record book 3, 297, 298.

32. Yancey County Clerk of Court, will book 1, 332, 302, 15–18.

33. Yancey County Clerk of Court, will book 1, 72; Whittington family bible, Old Buncombe County Genealogical Society, Asheville, NC; *TRVH*, 1:377.

34. Yancey County Clerk of Court, will book 1, 260, 182; 1850 U.S. Census, slave schedule, Yancey County.

35. U.S. Census, 1850, 1860, free inhabitant and slave schedules, Yancey County.

36. Perry Deane Young, *The Untold Story of Frankie Silver* (Asheboro, NC: Down Home Press, 1998), 148, 163; North Carolina 25:592, R. G. Dun and Company Collection, Baker Library, Harvard Business School; *Cases at Law Argued and Determined in the Supreme Court of North Carolina*, vol. 49, pt. 4 (Raleigh, NC: Seaton Gales, 1858), 483; John Wesley Garland Papers; *Images of Yancey*, 162.

37. Stephen West, *From Yeoman to Redneck in the South Carolina Upcountry, 1850–1915* (Charlottesville: University of Virginia Press, 2008), 23–45.

38. Olmsted, *A Journey in the Back Country*, 260; *TRVH*, 1:101.

39. The role of kinship ties in Toe Valley slave transactions could be interpreted as an example of substantivist economics, and the importance of such kinship ties recalls historian Richard White's description of trade in the Great Lakes region: "The relation of the buyer and the seller was not incidental to the transaction; it was critical" (*The Middle Ground* [New York: Cambridge University Press, 1991], 98).

Divided Loyalties

The Fain Family in an East Tennessee Civil War

KATHARINE S. DAHLSTRAND

During his own lifetime, George Washington's successes transformed him into apocryphal legend. In the decades after his death, Washington's example of selfless service to a young nation inspired Americans to do better and be better citizens. He personified a noble cause as a revolutionary. He encapsulated strength as the founding father of a perpetual union. The truth of George Washington's opinions, his humanity, and his physical and ideological legacies became less instructive. George Washington became whatever was needed of him. George Washington the revolutionary excused actions that could be considered treason. On the other hand, George Washington the first president of a democracy and a perpetual union inspired a citizenry to pick up arms and fight against rebellion. Both of these ideas contributed to his birthday becoming a holiday in the infant nation. Fabled stories about the "Cincinnatus of the West," appeared in newspapers and magazines throughout the continent and beyond.

To subsequent generations of Americans, George Washington's *actual* thoughts about slavery and the parameters for rebellion did not matter, but the justifications Washington's worshippers used to defend their loyalties to the Union or the Confederacy do matter. They demonstrate the power of rhetoric. The generational buildup of carefully crafted historical accounts can compel men and women in the same family to pledge loyalty to opposite sides of the same war.

When sectional divisions developed in the mid-nineteenth century in east Tennessee, both the idea of the Revolution as ushering in a perpetual union and the idea of treason being justifiable in the face of certain acts had pull. Its landscape and elevation were unsuited to large plantations, ensuring that the debate over slavery and secession stood on an already uncertain ground. As communities split over these issues throughout the mountain South, identity played a key role in determining loyalties. The early American period allowed east Tennesseans to defend or attack secession based on historical perspective. Whichever narrative each man and woman internalized informed their worldview.

The Fain family, descended from Nicholas the "emigrant," had options. Nicholas Fain, born in Ireland in 1730, immigrated to Chester County, Pennsylvania, with his wife, Elizabeth Taylor, in the early 1750s, and eventually settled in what is now Washington County, Tennessee, prior to the American Revolution. The Fains possessed a "remarkable military record," Nicholas holding the "unusual record" of having fought with the Patriots at Kings Mountain with five of his sons and his only son-in-law. Fain and all seven of his sons would ultimately serve during the Revolution.[1]

John Fain, son of Nicholas, a seasoned combat veteran who had participated in the Battle of Point Pleasant as a part of the Virginia militia in October 1774, arrived at Kings Mountain in October 1780 to join his comrades and family in the fight for independence. A year later, he married Nancy McMahon. Between 1782 and 1788, the Fains had four children. Then, when military forces ignored a Cherokee land treaty that had been in place since 1780, the Native Americans aggressively defended their land. White settlers lived in fear and requested military aid. On August 8, 1788, John Fain set out with a team of scouts to gather intelligence and, along the way, entered an apple orchard, "where carelessly they began to gather the fruit." Indians were lying in wait. Fain and his men were surrounded, driven into the nearby Tennessee River, and sixteen of the twenty-one men were killed, including John Fain.[2] The youngest of his children never knew his father because John Fain died the year he was born.

A later generation of Fains confronted a different type of revolution. The descendants of John Fain's eldest and youngest sons lived through the American Civil War. Heirs of a Revolutionary War soldier, these men faced difficult decisions about which side deserved their loyalties. Examining how Hiram Fain's and John Fain Anderson's choice of which side to support was defined by their understanding of Revolutionary history offers a lens on how identity and historical perspective informed allegiances to either the Union or the Confederacy. The Fain family famously fought for both the Federal Union and the Confederate States. On both sides, the Revolution and subsequent formation of a perpetual union were venerated and used to defend their respective loyalties.³

The communities with which Hiram Fain and John Fain Anderson identified developed during what historian George B. Forgie has called the "post-heroic generation." As years stretched out past the War for Independence, the actions of and precedents established by George Washington, and the crafting of a constitution and union, memories altered reality, and politics transformed the historical narrative. In other words, men like the Fains became part of discrete communities that established a dogma about intent. This essay captures the Fains in a moment in American history when men and women like them found themselves paralyzed by forces larger than themselves. They lived in an unforgiving borderland where emotions ran high and loyalty to a cause later determined access to opportunity. Forgie has suggested that those who were born after America's establishment deliberated on all "important political, moral, and personal matters" by referring to what the founders might have done or believed. Hiram Fain's and John Fain Anderson's ideas about what George Washington believed and what he stood for diverged in content and thus diverged in consequence.⁴

East Tennesseans experienced the Civil War and Reconstruction in a way that required outward commitment to imagined communities. In the communities with which Hiram Fain and John Fain Anderson identified, loyalty informed and influenced peoples' daily decisions and interactions, their understanding of history, and their role within it.⁵ As descendants of Revolutionary War veterans, both Fains looked to the father of their country for direction. The narratives of George Washington that guided individual Fain family members were grounded in both historical context as well as personal desires and social identities. Complex histories merged with and informed political and moral beliefs. Benedict Anderson asserts that communities are conceived as a "deep, horizontal comradeship" regardless of demonstrable economic disparities, which certainly existed between the wealthier slaveholding pro-Confederates and poorer upland Unionists in east Tennessee.⁶ Even if the Fains did not know all the other members of the communities with which they identified, they still certainly believed they were part of something larger than themselves. If nothing else, history taught them that. While the Fains' experience in east Tennessee does not fit easily within prevailing tropes of Appalachian exceptionalism, it does demonstrate how effective history can be in determining allegiances. How these two related men, Hiram and John, understood their history directly influenced their identity and their loyalties during both the war and Reconstruction.

HIRAM FAIN CONCERNED HIMSELF, PRIMARILY, WITH THE WEATHER. He was a deliberate man, and the pages of his diary plodded along with the steadfastness of an overworked mule. He wielded his pen as if it were any other tool, without romance or sentimentality. With proverbial blinders on, in January 1851, he remarked, "A white heavy frost this morning, ice." The very next entry was similar: "Last night quite cold, a heavy frost this morning." For Fain, as for any farmer in the Appalachian foothills of Hawkins County, Tennessee, frost held the very real threat of financial hardship. He filled his diary with rainfall estimates and updates on his crops. Even in favorable weather, Hiram Fain kept record of farming conditions. Sitting in the two-story, brick Federal-style home on the land he had inherited from his father, he could glance outside the window of his study and see the mountains. Behind his house, called Springvale, lay the acreage he plowed, and beyond those acres, just a few miles south, flowed the Holston River. The river and the railroad aided his financial interests. Beyond farming, Fain occasionally engaged in the slave trade in local markets with the periodic trip to Charleston and Atlanta. In 1854, his community elected him cashier of the local bank, a position that supplemented his farming income and established his position in the social order of Rogersville. He recorded these activities as well in his diary. Pen and paper served a sensible purpose of cataloging the sort of diligence successful farming required.[7]

He made an exception in February. That month always stood out and elicited reflection, as that was the month in which George Washington was born in 1732. Washington's birthday always merited acknowledgment. For Hiram Fain, the land and George Washington were the warp and woof of his life. Revolutionary men laid the foundation of American government; they defined what it meant to be a citizen of a nation forged in combat and resistant to tyranny. Fain identified with the frontier revolutionaries hell-bent on rebellion. He belonged to the same "post-heroic" generation as Jefferson Davis, united in being "born too late to experience the Revolution, but in time to be raised by the generation that had fought it." Such personal ties to the Revolutionary generation informed how they thought about themselves and their identity. Fain and Davis belonged to a community of shared ideologies; men who read the documents penned by founding fathers like religious texts, reciting chapter and verse to validate their beliefs.[8]

Hiram Fain was the oldest of six. Most were educated at prestigious universities and inheritors of hundreds of acres of family property. In 1851, Fain had the family land appraised; 619 acres was valued at $5,700. The year prior he reported owning three enslaved people to the census: a fifty-year-old black woman, a twenty-seven-year-old black man, and a fifteen-year-old mulatto girl. These advantages gave him the means to become prosperous. Fain's social and economic status may have been taken less seriously in the Lower South's cotton empire, but in the mountain South, Fain's successes and prospects aligned him with men like Jefferson Davis.[9]

The identity residents of the mountain South formed was based on chronicles of George Washington's life rather than on memory. Fain joined this imagined community, leaving behind any memory-based identity that defined older Fain generations. He was not alone in his attachment to Washington. Fain's brother, Richard, and his wife, Eliza, lived nearby and felt strongly about the founding father, too. On February 22, 1861, Eliza Fain rejoiced, "The sun has risen brightly upon our distracted country, ushering in the 129th anniversary of our illustrious Washington.... [H]is name has been transmitted to posterity so familiarly.... [I]t may be said of him more than any human being; he lives always in our midst." Just days before Jefferson Davis's first inauguration to the office of president of the Confederate States of America on February 18, 1861, Eliza Fain recalled her version of American history. In it, the men of Washington's ilk had desired "that we be a free people; that each section of our country might enjoy undisturbed her peculiar institutions; that each should have an equal right in all things pertaining to our form of government and that we would love each other." A southern plantation owner and slaveholder who resisted colonization by a socially rigid monarchy that endorsed impenetrable hierarchies, Washington provided all the justification needed for southern secession. A southern son could model his social and political aspirations on a man who led a successful rebellion.[10]

Hiram Fain agreed with his sister-in-law. In January 1861, he took some time to reflect on southern secession and the future of the nation Washington helped craft. He expressed grief that "this mighty nation of ours, second to none while united, is now dissolved by that hydra-headed monster fanaticism," by which he meant the growing opposition to slavery in the free states. The "black Republican President" wielded a power deemed dangerous in the hands of tyrants, and Fain prayed for God to "save our country from awful calamity." Three days later, he suggested that the American Revolution provided a lesson in how to respond to tyrannical power that sought to destroy "our great American Republic." Secession provided a way to "unloose the shackles that have been put upon the people by tyrants," "the people" here, of course, being white southern slaveholders like himself and his family. The next year, Hiram Fain penned, "This is the birthday of the great and good Washington it is also the day set apart for the inauguration of the President—Jefferson Davis of Mississippi having been unanimously elected he entered upon the duties of his office for six years." In one sentence, Fain tied the first president of the United States to the second inaugural of an unsanctioned office created by the openly rebellious southern states. His understanding of history shaped his worldview.[11]

When the American Civil War broke out, Hiram Fain, fifty-four at the time, declared his allegiance to his home as a devout Confederate sympathizer. He never wore a uniform. Occasionally, he joined local men in defending his land or strategic transportation routes from Union attempts to commandeer materials or blow up bridges, but he left the fighting to younger men like his sons and nephews.[12] His loyalty to the southern cause derived from a historical narrative that encouraged revolution. Washington's likely approval of southern rebellion was indisputable as far as Fain was concerned. Fain's attachment to the land and his identity as a prosperous southern slaveholder led him to revere Washington as an icon of special significance for Confederate citizens. He went so far as to refer to Union politicians and their supporters as "English aristocracy" and to describe the shift in power to Republican northerners as akin to enslavement of white southerners.[13]

White supremacy played a role in Hiram Fain's hero worship of George Washington, whom he hailed as "that greatest of all mortals." He referred to the Union troops passing through his region as the "Abolition Army." By February 1863, he swore that had Washington lived to see the day, he would have been "surprised and mortified" to witness "government making war on the other for the purpose of enslaving the white race to free the Negroes." Washington had created a civilized government, defined by southern characteristics that included mastery. Unionists were "Barbarians." Insults and injuries suffered by occupying "Yankees" led to recollections of the sympathetic Washington, who never would have stood for a "cruel and uncivilized" war as practiced by northern forces.

Fain followed the war through the newspapers, through letters from enlisted family members, and through town gossip and eyewitness accounts. Union forces and Confederate troops or home guards were constantly harassing each other and engaging in skirmishes in and throughout Hawkins

County. Union soldiers attempted numerous bridge burnings throughout the immediate region, some successful and many foiled by local residents. Fain commented on local events as they happened, but he also followed the war beyond the county lines. Whenever he referenced a particularly large battle, he used terms like "bloody fields" and remarked on how Confederates pushed Union forces back "with great slaughter." Though Washington did not take up many lines in Fain's diary prior to secession, the outbreak of civil war quickly transformed Hiram into a patriot, and the slaveholding revolutionary became his muse.[14]

Although Washington owned 317 slaves when he died in 1799, his attitudes had evolved, and he had privately concluded that slavery belied a lack of morality by the end of his life. That did not stop him from rotating slaves from Mount Vernon through the Pennsylvania capital during his presidency. Before the executive mansion was built in the marshes near the Potomac, Philadelphia served as the nation's capital. Washington brought a cadre of enslaved people from Mount Vernon to staff his new abode, but Pennsylvania had strict laws about slavery, and an enslaved person could petition for emancipation if he or she remained in the state longer than six months. Washington's cadre rotated between Virginia and Pennsylvania every five months. He failed to promote a domestic policy of abolition. As president, Washington set the tone of the executive office and established precedents for subsequent generations.[15] As a founding father and slave owner, Washington helped instill racism into the nation's infrastructure and guiding principles. None of this mattered to Hiram Fain. What did matter to Fain was the George Washington he imagined, the one that came with powerful language that excused treason. Fain lost and found himself in the Confederate fray that inspired so many Confederate men and women to defend their home and property from invading enemy forces.

The political zeitgeist fueled the secession crisis with rhetorical power throughout the antebellum South's dance with rebellion. Fire-eaters and secessionists crafted words deliberately to sell ideas of revolution to a white southern citizenry. By the 1830s, George Washington's birthday had been transformed into a reverent holiday. Newspapers throughout the South spoke of parades hosted by "Volunteer Corps and Charitable Organizations" that promoted "the usual demonstrations of respect for the memory and services of that illustrious Patriot." Let no one mistake the devotion to George Washington in southern cities, for their observances proved "sufficiently evident that the 22nd of February did not pass unhonored."[16]

In 1840, the *Charleston Courier* published an opinion piece titled "Revolutionary Reminiscences: Tale of Truth." The author relayed a story about a young and forthright general who sought shelter from strangers on a rainy night during the Revolutionary War. The anonymous young man appeared "above the common rank" of men, possessing a "military air about him." By the time the stranger revealed his identity to the gracious couple who provided safe harbor in a storm, George Washington had already demonstrated his honor and "purpose of transmitting to posterity the treasures we now enjoy." The treasures were not defined, which allowed for contemporary interpretation. The article ended with a message: "Let us acknowledge the benefits received, by our endeavors to preserve therein in their purity." Should the course be altered or the original intent lost, the purity must be preserved, by force if necessary. This sort of rhetoric, over the course of decades, taught a southern population to honor rebellion in the name of defending their way of life. They could look to George Washington for confirmation that their reasons for wanting to start a new nation were legitimate.[17]

In east Tennessee, local newspapers did not wait for national holidays or benchmark anniversaries of Washington's life and achievements to extoll his virtues. An 1850 *Athens Post* front-page article on Washington's family ancestry traced the lineage of "our Cincinnatus of the West," revealing aristocratic blood that tied the founding to the English throne. Washington, however, the *Post* reminded its readers, did not require a pedigree of blue blood to ensure his place in history; he proved himself worthy as "the son of his own actions." Still, the language of the article attached to him a convenient truth: his familial connections and historical ties to his country were not enough to prevent his leading a revolt against tyranny. In 1853, the *Loudon Free Press* described Washington in a Revolutionary history as an "American Chief" that left the red coats "routed, defeated, crushed." Washington's legacy, on this view, endorsed rebellion and offered a precedent of success.[18]

Jefferson Davis chose George Washington's birthday as the date for his second inauguration, honoring the founding father "most identified with the establishment of American independence." Under his presidency, he hoped to "perpetuate the principles of our revolutionary fathers," and Washington's birthday, his memory, "and the purpose seem fitly associated" for the occasion. The Confederacy would be a new and southern form of revolutionary design. Davis recalled how the Revolutionary generation's demand for a representational government bestowed on future generations an obligation to keep the legislative process fair. Tyranny under an unbridled majority demanded action from the southern sons of revolution. Davis recognized the "inheritance bequeathed to us by the patriots of the Revolution" and argued that the Confederacy had to "emulate that heroic devotion" demonstrated by men like George Washington.[19]

Hiram Fain rejected what historian Thomas Bender has called "a political impulse" toward a pure and homogeneous community where national concerns trumped "personal local political units." As the nineteenth century progressed, the southern and northern historical narratives demonstrated a sharp divide in political ideology. In the South, men like Hiram Fain opted into a "fabric of community" in which economic interest and his status as an educated member of the slaveholding class guided his actions. Systems of social life possessed "localized articulations of social organizations" extending beyond geographical borders. Fain's fervent support of the Confederacy represented his identification with a broader community more than with those living in his immediate proximity. Men like Jefferson Davis offered Fain the chance to participate in "new bonds of community" that reached beyond the Hawkins County lines and extended into southern regions more ardent in their desire to maintain the slave system.[20]

Hawkins County residents split almost evenly in the election of 1860 between Democrat John C. Breckinridge and Constitutional Unionist John Bell, with Breckinridge earning 50 percent and Bell earning 46 percent of the total vote, respectively. In February 1861, the county voted against secession. Four months later, 62 percent of voters disapproved of Tennessee's secession again. The county population remained deeply divided on the eve of the Civil War, with the mountain inhabitants favoring the Union position and the foothill farmland populations being what some have called "reluctant Confederates." A decidedly middle-class clan of educated merchants and slaveholding farmers, the Fain family "stood out as zealous Confederates" within their east Tennessee home.[21]

Throughout the Civil War, Hiram Fain cursed the Union forces. He prayed for his "Southern soil" to be cleansed of northern barbarians who "pollute our soil or molest our homes." They were savages who "treated the pople [*sic*] very badly making a cruel and uncivilized war such as a civilized nation would not wage."[22] Fain lost three of his children to diphtheria in the winter of 1863, and amid his grief, a brigade of Yankee soldiers camped on his land, took his grain and his cattle, and burned much of his equipment. Losing family and wealth seems to have broken him, and his diary entries for 1864 took up only half a page.

Fain found his fortunes and prospects depleted as the Civil War ended, and he had difficulty scrounging up the $4 for railroad fare to Knoxville, where he signed the oath of allegiance on July 3, 1865. In the oath, he promised to "faithfully support and defend the constitution of the United States," which, ironically, he felt he had always done in his service to the Confederacy. More pointedly, though, Fain swore in the oath to "support all Laws and Proclamations which have been made during the existing rebellion with reference to the emancipation of slavery." Shortly thereafter, he sent his surviving family to Memphis on a train "crowded with passengers moving away from violence and oppression" in east Tennessee.[23]

The move was meant to be temporary as Fain sought ways to recoup his lost wealth. He also found himself subjected to civil and criminal lawsuits in east Tennessee as the Republican political elite hounded those who continued to voice support for the Confederacy after the Civil War. Historian Susanna Michele Lee argues that during Reconstruction, the former Confederacy "successfully decoupled most aspects of postwar citizenship from wartime loyalty," which "signaled an official policy of forgetting." However, in a decidedly Unionist county, Hiram Fain did not receive the pardon and amnesty most other Confederates did. After the defeat of his imagined community, there was no one to prop Fain up and come to his defense against charges of treason.[24]

While few of the lawsuits against him were successful, the message behind them effectively taught Hiram Fain where his identity betrayed him. George Washington provided Fain with comfort in a world of uncertainty, symbolizing a hopeful what might have been. Washington "did more than any other man to free the American People from the tyranny of the British," and Fain lamented that "the Southern People who did more to sustain the government as formed by Washington and his compatriots are now enslaved by Northern Fanatics and the republic destroyed."[25] Fain looked back to a fledgling republic to reimagine and redeem his South and its place within a reconstructed nation.

According to Fain, it was not his cause that lost; it was rather Washington's intentions that had failed to be realized. Fain grew up in a generation that listened to oral tales about the strength of George Washington's character. The same generation read biographies and pamphlets and knew the legend of the revolutionary spirit of the founding fathers. This generation knew well how to spin a historical tale into something from which they might later profit.

John Inscoe has argued that antebellum east Tennessee inhabitants "perceived themselves and their region in relation to" the entire state and not just the mountain ranges that crossed multiple geopolitical boundaries. Like other communities throughout the United States, this region told its "own stories about the Revolution and emphasized new memories and meanings" until, by the start of the Civil War, a Confederate sympathizer remembered the actions of founding fathers in a meaningful way that allowed a second American Revolution. And as historian Anne Sarah Rubin has posited that southern appropriation of the Revolution represented a generalized and impersonal interpretation of the intentions of the founding fathers, secessionists like Fain prayed for victory and rejected their personal connections to the creation of a new nation in favor of the narrative that endorsed rebellion. That Hiram Fain had direct ancestry to a Revolutionary soldier "was largely irrelevant" in his community; what mattered to him as a Confederate was that the South was separate from the rest of the Union. They "othered" themselves as they connected to a history focused on rebellious and southern founding father narratives.[26]

Hiram Fain had real family connections to Revolutionary soldiers and frontiersmen. From the very mountains on which Hiram Fain looked while he farmed and traded toward an honorable life, great marble slabs had been mined and shipped northeast to the national capital. Andrew Jackson's words "The Federal Union it Must Be Preserved" were engraved and gilded on one block that was contributed in 1850 for the Washington Monument, construction of which had begun in 1848. A decade later, the same foundational landscape attempted to rip itself from the American terrain, and inhabitants of the Appalachian South revised their understanding of Revolutionary history to suit their personal needs. Fain joined the Confederate fray, and he brought George Washington's memory with him, but there was an alternative route he could have taken, a route exemplified in the case of John Fain Anderson.[27]

JOHN FAIN ANDERSON CONCERNED HIMSELF, PRIMARILY, WITH historical accuracy. He was an amateur historian, and the pages of his scrapbooks betray his interest in local and regional histories that he tied to larger national events like the Revolutionary War and the Civil War. The twenty-three scrapbooks in his collection span topics from the Battle of Kings Mountain, the Civil War, and prominent families of east Tennessee to local histories.

Unlike Hiram Fain, John Fain Anderson was young when the Civil War began, only sixteen years old. By 1861, Americans in Anderson's generation learned a national history dominated by what historian Robert Cook calls "grand historical narratives of a country's past" that were carefully crafted by influential men who held a stake in creating "a particular and (they hope) broadly unifying interpretation of their country's history."[28] Like secessionists, southern Unionists drew lessons from the Revolution and subsequent experiment in building a democratic republic. In addition to being exposed to the collective memory of a nation's founding, Anderson also learned about the early history of the American republic from his family. The third son born to Samuel Anderson and Hannah Crawford Fain, he did not stand to inherit much physical property as an adult. He received brief spurts of education at local schoolhouses in the years before and during the Civil War, and his grammar reflected this uneven schooling. His education came from learning his family history. This boy pushed into manhood by the secession of his home state would have to make his own way toward prosperity, and he found that path in his loyalty to preserving the Union his ancestry defended.

As the grandson of John Ruben Fain, brother of Nicholas Fain, and a participant in the legendary Battle of Kings Mountain, Anderson worshiped the Revolutionary generation as much as any other member of the Fain family. During the Civil War, Anderson worked as a messenger boy for the Union and was stationed in both Knoxville and Loudon, Tennessee. When filling out his form for the *Tennessee Civil War Veterans' Questionnaire*, he included an addendum on his family's history. He described family patriarch, Nicholas Fain, who came to "Washington county Tenn in early seventeys" where he gave two sons, John and Samuel, to the "Point Pleasant battle October 4– 1780" and five sons to the Battle of Kings Mountain, proudly owning his heritage by concluding that "this John Nicholas Fain was my great grandfather."[29]

His postwar life provides insight into his understanding of American history in general and of George Washington in particular. He earned a reputation throughout the region as being an able historian and would often use his scrapbooking hobby to "correct" history. One page of the scrapbook features a newspaper clipping titled "Handsome New Courthouse for Ancient Town of Jonesboro." The 1912 article provided a brief history of Jonesboro, Tennessee, as the county seat and described the new courthouse. The paper's headline stated that the courthouse would "Be the Third Temple of Justice in That City Whose History Is So Rich in Historical Lore—The First Built in That Town, Older Than the American Revolution, Was the First Built in the 'New World' West of the Blue Ridge Mountains." The article included pictures of previous courthouses. However, the article placed the images of the courthouses in the wrong order. Anderson cut out the pictures and then renumbered them. The paper also neglected to mention a building used briefly in 1820 that served as a second courthouse. After rearranging the order of the photos, he left a blank space and drew the building that the newspaper left out on the scrapbook paper with a china marker. Only then was history accurately depicted.[30]

An undated clipping titled "States Rights" attempted to place the subject of prohibition into historical context, drawing connections to Patrick Henry's reservations about the wording of the U.S. Constitution, which he felt did not sufficiently safeguard the powers of the state. The article went on to highlight how the Civil War settled the question, putting "the federal government... over and above the governments of the states." In the margins of this entry, Anderson commented on states' rights. He was clear: no state had the right to secede, and laws should be formed only "to protect oranges in the South and cranberrys in the North." For Anderson, states were the sons of the father nation, and "no son has a write [sic] to set aside Fathers command."[31] The founding fathers laid the foundation of American government and, therein, the defining characteristics of what it meant to be a citizen of the republican experiment in democracy. Anderson's devotion to the Union during the Civil War mirrors both his devotion to his family heritage and the region in which he lived. His passion regarding his family's participation in America's creation and his passion for the Union worked in concert.

For Anderson, the strongest feature "in [Washington's] character was prudence." He highlighted how peers hailed Washington for never acting until "every circumstance, every consideration was maturely weighed." For Washington, the Constitution was, as Jefferson reported, "an experiment on the practicality of republican government, and with what dose of liberty man could be trusted for his own good," and he "was determined the experiment should have a fair trial." He encouraged a strong central government in which the states would be subject to the designs of the federal level. In his dealings with the western Pennsylvania rebels during the Whiskey Rebellion, the sitting president donned his military uniform because while "men will not adopt and carry into execution measures the best calculated for their own good," a strong central government with a strong commander in chief could secure compliance. Washington suppressed rebellion in order to preserve the Union.[32]

George Washington served as a player in a regional history of Revolutionary acts. Anderson glued clippings documenting the participation of east Tennesseans in the creation of a new nation next to Civil War biographies and postcards from Abraham Lincoln's grave. He wrote his personal recollections in the margins next to county histories and the obituaries of the dying Civil War generation. George Washington's portrait on a postcard lay underneath a clipping about Knox County's namesake, William Henry Knox, describing how the "hardy and capable pioneers" pushed the fledgling nation westward.[33]

An editorial dated November 14, 1911, recalled how a key crossing of the Holston River had only one Confederate soldier guarding it in November 1861 and suggested that the brave actions of the Confederate soldier, James Keeler, in defending a bridge from a "whole company" of Union men seeking to commit arson and possible assault on Confederate sympathizers in the community most certainly warranted a historical marker at the site. In his scrapbook, Anderson had preserved another article, titled "A Story of a Happening at Strawberry Plains Over Fifty Years Ago," likewise published in 1911, that offered a corrective to this grand Lost Cause recollection of the event. The author of the corrective, W. R. Carter, acknowledged that Keeler's actions forever defined him as a "brave fellow" who deserved credit for defending a bridge singlehandedly. Still, the description of the Union soldiers was inaccurate and needlessly barbaric, and Carter explained how a simple and peaceable plan to ensure a route into east Tennessee for more Union troops resulted in a small group of Union men on a reconnaissance mission encountering a Confederate soldier ready to instigate small-arms fire. Anderson knew this story well and filled the margins of his scrapbook page with comments that agreed with the author and expanded on some issues raised. "This Story is correct," Anderson maintained. "The men who did this atemp[t] ware Good Men They ware Men who desired piece." He insisted they only intended to burn the bridge, "not kill any one." Anderson was pleased to see another defender of the Union cause and the soldiers who served it. He challenged the ever-expanding Lost Cause mythology taking over the mountain South just as fervently as those more closely connected to the former slave economy. Had he ever discussed this event with his second cousin, Hiram Fain, he would have heard a different perspective. Ten days after the attempted burning of the bridge at Strawberry Plains, Hiram Fain joined "some 75 or 80 men pretty well armed," to investigate the "Lincolnites" who had attempted it. The mob was eventually turned away and dispersed: "There were troops enough at the bridge to protect us," Fain recalled, so "I then returned home." Those responsible for the burnings escaped a rather large firing squad.[34]

Anderson found joy in broader great men histories. On February 22, 1920, he clipped out a newspaper feature titled "Lincoln's Tribute to Nation's Founding Father." The article celebrated the seventy-eighth anniversary of Lincoln's memorial speech on George Washington. For Lincoln, George Washington was "mightiest in the cause of civil liberty; still mightiest in moral reformation." Lincoln insisted that "to add brightness to the sun or glory to the name of Washington is alike impossible." Anderson admired Lincoln's assessment of Washington. "I regard Lincons Tribute to Washington," he inscribed next to the article, "greater than his Getysburg Speech. Greatest tribute made by Man to Man." The newspaper articles Anderson chose to preserve stressed the same core values over and over again. Loyalty was a solemn practice, and it called for dismissing hot-headed passions that ended with treasonous secession. In 1914, Anderson added a place card to his scrapbook, a piece of ephemera from a Fourth of July celebration. The wording on the card prayed that the holiday be celebrated "in a way befitting America and Americans—not in foolish frivolity and reckless pleasure—but as a sane people celebrating a national event." Anderson and the Unionists with whom he identified defined their understanding of perpetual union through their histories of Washington. It made siding with the Union the only decision possible.[35]

Here are two members of the same American family with very different outlooks on what the founding fathers intended when they established a republican democracy. Hiram Fain, a member of the "post-heroic" generation, embraced and helped shape a well-crafted version of Revolutionary history commonly espoused by the slaveholding elite. He wanted access to the wealth and opportunity that Confederate politicians had promised. Fain's diary never referred to Nicholas Fain or the life his ancestors fought to preserve. Instead, it offered Fain's musings about what he perceived to be a failed republic. The community with which he identified watched their interpretation of George Washington's America suffer. Family history was diluted within a national narrative where broad strokes make compelling arguments, and Fain drank from a well of apocryphal history that taught values similar to his own. In contrast, John Fain Anderson's scrapbooks not only contain a collection of articles on George Washington but also are filled with local history and stories about the Revolutionary War. Anderson revered his familial ties to the original heroes of this nation as much as he revered the first president and commander in chief. His community helped integrate his family heritage with his interpretation of George Washington's intention. It was that blended community that pushed him to side with the Union and preserving what his founding father had created.

Hiram Fain's and John Fain Anderson's understanding of history informed their opinions on secession, rebellion, and loyalty. Both of their interpretations can be backed by sound secondary scholarship if they are considered separately. They are both buttressed by theoretical foundations soundly explicated by experts in community studies, identity formation, psychohistory, memory history, and Lost Cause mythology. If they are taken together, though, they only present more questions. One man revised his history and one carefully preserved it. One man embraced secession and one rejected it. One man offered his family and support to the Confederacy and one man delivered messages for the Union. One man experienced defeat and one found victory. One man crafted an interpretation of the past to suit his newfound misery and one held fast to the personal ties that defined his life's success. It is striking how the understanding of the Revolution of these members of the same family colored their views on society and politics. More striking, however, is how both were so contradictory to each other in purpose and understanding despite living within miles of each other and being so closely related.

NOTES

1. Augusta Bradford, *Fain of Tennessee: Descendants of Nicholas Fain* (Chattanooga, TN: Lookout Publishing Company, 1930), 7; "A Statement of the Proceedings of the Western Army; Letter to General Gates," *Tennesseans in the Revolutionary War*, www.tngenweb.org /revwar/kingsmountain/formal.html.

2. J. G. M. Ramsey, *The Annals of Tennessee to the End of the Eighteenth Century* (Knoxville: East Tennessee Historical Society Over Mountain Press, 1999), 421–22.

3. The Fains are highlighted in Daniel W. Stowell's "A Family of Women and Children: The Fains of East Tennessee during Wartime," in *Southern Families at War*, ed. Catherine Clinton (New York: Oxford University Press, 2000), 155–73, and the University of Tennessee Press published *Sanctified Trial*, the diary of Eliza Rhea Anderson Fain in 2004. The Fain family women also offered substantive source material for Jennifer Brickey's "The Diary of Fannie Fain of Blountville: Defining Allegiance in Civil War Era East Tennessee" (honor's thesis, College of William and Mary, 2006). Earlier works like Goodspeed's *History of East Tennessee* (Nashville, TN: Goodspeed, 1887) dedicate multiple pages to the progeny of Nicholas Fain. Augusta Bradford's work is reproduced without citation in many genealogy projects online. Hiram Fain's diary and the scrapbooks of John Fain Anderson, however, seem to have escaped critical scrutiny up to this point. The *Journal of East Tennessee History* printed excerpts from Hiram Fain's diary in 1997.

4. George B. Forgie, *Patricide in the House Divided: A Psychological Interpretation of Lincoln and His Age* (New York: Norton, 1979), 8.

5. David M. Potter, "The Historian's Use of Nationalism and Vice Versa," *American Historical Review* 67, no. 4 (1962): 925.

6. Benedict Anderson, *Imagined Communities: Reflections on the Origin and Spread of Nationalism* (London: Verso, 1983), 6–7.

7. Hiram Fain diary, January 1 and 14, 1851, April 11, 1851, March 2, 1854, Archives of Appalachia, East Tennessee State University, Johnson City, Tennessee (hereafter AA); John N. Fain, "The Diary of Hiram Fain of Rogersville: An East Tennessee Secessionist," *Journal of East Tennessee History* 69 (1997), 97.

8. Forgie, *Patricide in the House Divided*, 7.

9. Hiram's brother Richard Gannon Fain attended West Point Military Academy, and some of Hiram's sisters attended all-female academies throughout east Tennessee. There is no evidence that Hiram was formally educated, but his nuclear family was more educated

and possessed more networked wealth than the typical Hawkins County family (Anderson, *Imagined Communities*, 204).

10. Eliza Rhea Anderson Fain and John H. Fain, *Sanctified Trial: The Diary of Eliza Rhea Anderson Fain, a Confederate Woman in East Tennessee* (Knoxville: University of Tennessee Press, 2004), 5.

11. Hiram Fain diary, January 1 and 4, 1861, February 22, 1863, AA.

12. Hiram Fain diary, November 1862, November 1863, AA.

13. Hiram Fain diary, January 4, 1861, AA.

14. Hiram Fain Diary, November 2, 1863, AA.

15. James P. Pfiffner, "George Washington's Character and Slavery," *White House Studies* 1, no. 4 (2001): 457; Erica Armstrong Dunbar, *Never Caught: The Washingtons' Relentless Pursuit of Their Runaway Slave, Ona Judge* (New York: Atria Books, 2017), xvi.

16. "Washington's Birthday," *Charleston (SC) Courier*, February 24, 1830.

17. *Charleston (SC) Courier*, July 10, 1840.

18. *Athens (TN) Post*, November 22, 1850; *Loudon (TN) Free Press*, December 2, 1853.

19. Jefferson Davis, second inaugural address," February 22, 1862, Richmond, Virginia.

20. Thomas Bender, *Community and Social Change in America* (New Brunswick, NJ: Rutgers University Press, 1978), 84, 71, 95.

21. Stowell, "A Family of Women and Children," 156.

22. Hiram Fain diary, July 2, 1862, November 2, 1863, AA.

23. Hiram Fain diary, November 1, 1865, AA.

24. W. Todd Groce, *Mountain Rebels: East Tennessee Confederates, 1860–1870* (Knoxville: University of Tennessee Press, 1999), 181–214; Susanna Michele Lee, "The Antithesis of Union Men and Confederate Rebels: Loyal Citizenship in the Post-Civil War South," in *Creating Citizenship in the Nineteenth-Century South*, ed. William Link, David Brown, Brian Ward, and Martyn Bone (Gainesville: University Press of Florida, 2013), 151.

25. Hiram Fain diary, February 22, 1869, AA.

26. John Inscoe, *Race, War, and Remembrance in the Appalachian South* (Lexington: University Press of Kentucky, 2008), 111; Michael A. McDonnell, Clare Corbould, Frances Clarke, Fitzhugh Brundage, "The Revolution in American Life from 1776 to the Civil War," in *Remembering the Revolution: Memory, History, and Nation Making from Independence to the Civil War* (Amherst: University of Massachusetts Press, 2013), 2; Anne Sarah Rubin, "Seventy Six and Sixty One: Confederates Remember the American Revolution," in *Where These Memories Grow: History, Memory, and Southern Identity*, ed. Fitzhugh Brundage (Chapel Hill: University of North Carolina Press, 2000), 86.

27. National Register of Historic Places multiple property documentation form for the marble industry of east Tennessee, circa 1838–1963, spring 2014, submitted by Carroll Van West and Susan W. Knowles, nps.gov/nr/feature/places/pdfs/64501200.pdf, 4.

28. Robert J. Cook, William L. Barney, and Elizabeth R. Varon, *Secession Winter: When the Union Fell Apart* (Baltimore, MD: Johns Hopkins University Press, 2013), 71.

29. Gustavus W. Dyer and John T. Moore, comps., *The Tennessee Civil War Veterans Questionnaires*, vol. 1, ed. Colleen M. Elliott and Louise A. Moxley (Easley, SC: Southern Historical Press, 1985), 4–8.

30. Scrapbook 10, 1913–14, John Fain Anderson Collection, AA.

31. Scrapbook 10, 1913–14," John Fain Anderson Collection, AA.

32. *The Papers of Thomas Jefferson*, retirement series, vol. 7, *28 November 1813 to 30 September 1814*, ed. J. Jefferson Looney (Princeton, NJ: Princeton University Press, 2010), 100–104; Richard Norton Smith, *Patriarch: George Washington and the New American Nation* (New York: Houghton Mifflin Company, 1993) 211–14.

33. Scrapbook 10, 1913–14, John Fain Anderson Collection, AA.

34. Scrapbook 11, 1912–14, John Fain Anderson Collection, AA; Hiram Fain diary, November 17, 1861, AA.

35. Scrapbook 15, 1919–23, and scrapbook 11, 1912–1914, John Fain Anderson Collection, AA.

An Emotional Rebellion

Wrecking the Old South's Emotional Community

KYLE N. OSBORN

F OR ALL ITS MANY FAILINGS, SECESSION DID PROVIDE EMOTIONAL catharsis. After years of sectional resentment quieted by paeans to the Union, white southerners could finally air their anti-Yankee indignation with full-throated glee. And they did—ad nauseam. It was hardly shocking that southern men, steeped in worlds of masculine honor and patriarchal mastery, lambasted the Yankees in the most contemptuous of terms, their rhetoric providing a feeding frenzy for quote-hungry historians ever since. And while scholars have long since rejected the notion that wily agitators achieved secession by fomenting irrational hatreds, enmity certainly served their cause. No person can speak for an entire political movement like secession, but perhaps Alfred Iverson came close in a harangue delivered before the national Senate in December 1860. Accusing his Yankee counterparts of loathing the South "worse than ever the English people hated France," the Georgia senator proclaimed it was just that implacable hatred that made disunion inevitable (and also that there "was no love lost" among southerners). The "enmity between the Northern and Southern people is deep and enduring," Iverson thundered. "You can never eradicate it—never!" Whether as hate-mongering machinator or the reflector of popular will, Iverson saw his state follow the wave of secession in January 1861, in a sort of culmination to the aggrieved, hypermasculine political culture of the Old South.[1]

Surprisingly, however, (elite) southern women matched the sound and fury of their menfolk, curse for anti-Yankee curse. It was young women, personally confident yet confined by southern gender conventions, who led the charge. Channeling Iverson's ire, Grace Elmore of South Carolina deemed Abraham Lincoln a "long legged, long jawed Oranoutang [sic]" and promised that his victory would prove "the last insult this Yankee nation shall seek to put upon" her downtrodden South. Ella Thomas would have rather seen southern rivers "filled with blood and every mountain covered with the bleached bones of our countrymen" than submit to Yankee rule. "We women are as roused as any one," a young Georgian bragged in a November letter to her brother. She only regretted that southern women could not "fight along with the men," for the mere thought of killing a northern invader filled her heart with "intense satisfaction." In March 1861, Mary Chesnut famously captured the enmity swirling amid the southern air for elite men and women alike: "We are divorced North and South, because we hated each other so."[2]

Yet while their sentiments might have marched in lockstep with their political leaders during disunion, the ferocity of female secessionists violated the norms of antebellum culture. Elite white southerners forged what scholars deem an "emotional community," a distinct and self-conscious collective defined by shared emotional standards and accepted modes of expression. Indeed, in the racially polarized Old South, where the most obvious division was that between white and black, and where class standing at least among slaveholders remained inexact, emotional expression was one of the major demarcations separating elite whites from the poor and middling masses. For elite white men, indignation (even violence) was the expected reaction when one's honor was imperiled or homestead endangered. Men like Mississippi's William Nugent could speak comfortably of his desire to kill Yankee soldiers and see northern farms "desolated, her cities laid waste ... dissipated in the vain attempt to subjugate a free people." Stephen Ramseur in 1856 had deemed the ideal of Christian forbearance—the imperative to love one's enemy—"so beautiful and touching as it must melt every heart not made of stone." And yet the North Carolinian's "blood boil[ed] with indignation" when he reflected on the "Republican hell-hounds" fantasizing of leading a cavalry assault to cut "them down like grass before the mower's scythe." Ramseur felt no need to apologize for his apparent inconsistency.[3]

But the story was vastly different for southern women. Culturally, the elite South had concocted a strange brew of Atlantic Victorianism spiked with the toxins of a slaveholding milieu. Yet regardless of whether southern culture retained its traditional patriarchy of domestic male dominance or had embraced the separate spheres ideology of the antebellum North, neither system tolerated much in the way of female anger. As Virginia's Thomas Dew explained in patriarchal fashion, a southern woman "cannot give utterance to her passions and emotions like a man," for her station demanded that she "suppress the most violent feelings" stirring within and always project "the face of contentment and ease." With inadvertent echo, Victorian writers chided that female anger despoiled the moral sanctuary of the newly enshrined domestic sphere. Maine's Jacob Abbot advised every mother "to control herself, to subdue her own passions. She must set for her children an example of meekness and equanimity," for how "can a mother expect to govern her child when she cannot govern herself?" The ultimate goal was to eliminate "anything like angry contention or contradiction" from the family hearth, another moralist informed. Combining elements of patriarchal subservience and Victorian temperance, the emotional community of the elite South stood pillared on female docility.[4]

The evidence makes clear this was more than moralist hand-wringing—white southerners harshly disapproved of their wives and daughters expressing anger. In a common refrain, Mississippi's Sarah Watkins instructed her school-bound daughter to remain courteous to her classmates, obey her instructors, and above all, "never show your temper at any time." "Be watchful over your temper," a southern father had chided his daughter several years earlier, for "nothing can be more disgusting than to see the female bosom, the seat of tenderness and virtue, agitated by anger." Even well into adulthood southern women were admonished when their sentiments defied the standards of elite society. "Pa says he considers me beyond hope and says he wishes I could hold a few minutes conversation with Christ upon the subject of ill temper," the widowed Ada Bacot groaned after an explosive family spat in 1861. Husbands could prove just as demanding as fathers. From the South Carolina upcountry in 1859, David Harris's journal recorded a pledge from his wife of fourteen years to "*never* to blow me up again." Such outbursts were immoral and unwomanly, the venerable couple apparently agreed; Mrs. Harris dutifully etched her signature below the pledge of emotional equanimity.[5]

Elite women chastised themselves when confessing failure to suppress their scorn. "I lost control of my temper tonight [as] Eliza provoked me very much," Ann Hardeman lamented in reference to her niece. "I will try and regain my balance," for "anger is majestic—but makes slaves of weak minds." From Texas in 1852, Lizzie Neblett feared that her unwieldy temperament would prevent her from becoming a loving wife and nurturing mother—the very ideals of southern womanhood. "I am unfortunate! My temper, my disposition is truly an unfortunate one," she sighed. "I say such angry sinful wicked and ungrateful words[,] ... and all because I am mad to assert my *independence and my pride*."

After firing off an intemperate letter to her father demanding that she be withdrawn from her Maryland boarding school, Tennessee's Cora Ready recorded the incident to ensure she would never "give way to my temper so again." "I did not know I could get so angry," Ready reflected. "Forgive me Lord, and henceforth with thy help my temper shall never rise so high."[6]

Slaveholding itself added a peculiar pressure to suppress emotion, especially for women actively involved in slave management. South Carolina's Keziah Brevard assumed her role as slave mistress following the tragic deaths of her father and husband, who bequeathed a massive enterprise totaling more than six thousand acres of land and over two hundred slaves. Throughout her journals, Brevard painfully struggles to reconcile her desire to live in Christian tranquility with the myriad frustrations provoked by her bondspeople. "I wish I knew what produced anger in the human body," she sighed in 1860. "Lord Jesus[,] ... I ask for help to be more like thee." The self-rebuke became almost incessant. "The sin of anger is a terrible sin to contend with," she recorded again several months later; it causes trifles "to blaze sky high in a twinkling," and "it changes a man or a woman into a demon." To make matters worse, Brevard recognized how the power dynamics of the master-slave relationship required the mask of emotional self-mastery. "Every time I think of Jim's impudence—my spirit boils," she wrote in reference to her capable but irksome slave driver, for she knew that "if I were to shew my feelings they would only devil me the more." The failure of emotional mastery could easily signify weakness, a dangerous dynamic for any slave master. "I do wish I was not such a sinner," she fretted. "Anger—oh what a master you are."[7]

But it was anger's seepage into their white households, especially anger on the part of mothers toward their children, that provoked the greatest distress. The anguished diary of Mississippi's Mahala Roach illustrates the tremendous pressure placed on southern mothers to constrain the expression of their emotions in accordance with the dominant standards espoused by writers like Dew and Abbot. In 1853, she even inscribed a Victorian-sounding passage on the importance of anger suppression (the references to slavery giving it a strong southern accent). "When inclined to give an angry answer," the piece advised, seek the guidance of prayer, retain "a cheerful view of everything and encourage hope, ... speak kindly to the servants and praise them for little things when you can," but most importantly, "remain gentle with the little ones." Throughout the 1850s, however, Roach's entries lamented her self-perceived failure to properly restrain her emotions amid the vexations of parenthood: "Gave Tom three hard slaps today ... [and] was heartily sorry for it afterwards," got "angry with my dear little Sophy for some slight thing," got "vexed with Nora and slap'd her for a trifle." Roach felt "so sorry for these outbursts of temper," deeming herself a "perfect virago."[8]

If it was improper to vent anger before the family hearth, then losing one's temper beyond the household was simply unimaginable, even when the provocateurs were insufferable Yankees. Georgia's Anna King bristled with impotent fury after slogging through an "intolerable evening" at the home of a Connecticut abolitionist during a New England tour in 1852. Southern sojourners took great pains to avoid these odious encounters, yet this Yankee minister proved "perfectly mad" in his antislavery beliefs and interrogated King mercilessly about the religious state and living conditions of her sea island slaves. "I had many tart replies ready," she assured her daughter after escaping his clutches, but "as a guest I was obliged to keep my temper.... I restrained my tongue." For South Carolina's Emily Sinkler, the offending party was a pair of Rhode Islanders touring the Palmetto State in 1852. They were "very banal girls who are paying their first visit to the South" and "think it necessary to be in ecstasy over" every novelty they encounter, Sinkler vented to a sympathetic relative. "I was on the point of giving... a very haughty answer," she recalled, but "I saw two or three pairs of eyes fixed upon me, watching what I would say, so I swallowed my feelings and made a decent and pretty answer about [regional] comparisons."[9]

As these examples attest, elite white women of the South enjoyed what scholars deem an "emotional refuge" in the form of letters (and surely conversations) between trusted female friends and family. The correspondence of many female writers echoes the opening lines of Hattie Harmon to Annie Carleton in 1855: "I am going to have a little social talk with you... and I don't wish" anyone to receive it "other than my warm hearted little Annie." A journal or diary could likewise provide a safe space in which to express the sentiments "of a secret and hidden heart," as Virginia's Amanda Edmonds put it. But these outlets of "emotional refuge" remained less than entirely secure—hostile readers might intercept diaries and letters. Even the reliably outspoken Ella Thomas silenced herself mid-thought in an 1856 journal entry that blasted the depravity of slaveholding men, fearing that some "prying eye of curiosity might scan these pages" in disapproval. But significantly, as these laments demonstrate, even within these largely private writings elite southern women admonished themselves for the sins of indignation and enmity. They had clearly accepted the painful limitations the emotional community of the southern elite imposed, which resulted in clear emotional suffering for those who struggled to conform. "I've always professed to be stoical," wrote Texan Sallie McNeill in describing the torment of habitually bottling her temper.

And "bitter has been my punishment for the falsehood—[for] false I knew it to be."[10]

But the bottle burst in 1860—indeed, southern women shattered it themselves. As southern political leaders, editors, ministers, fathers, and husbands hurled anti-Yankee denunciations with abandon, the boundaries of the Old South's emotional community collapsed and new standards of expression emerged. Southern political leaders constructed Confederate nationalism on the fly, but the new nation lacked the unique characteristics—a different religion, language, ethnic identity—around which nationalist identities traditionally have typically cohered. Yankee society, or at least the southern defamation of it as alien and hostile, provided perhaps the most compelling unifying element for white southerners across state, class, and party lines. The Black Republicans were, in the rhetoric of arch-secessionist Thomas Cobb, a cauldron of John Brown deifiers, "mad preachers, ... free negroes and boot-blacks, coachmen and domestics, infidels and free-lovers, spiritual rappers and every other shade of mania and folly." Mississippi's official statement of secession charged hysterically that a northern majority advocated "negro equality, socially and politically, and promotes insurrection and incendiarism in our midst." With such rhetoric ringing from southern pulpits and raging across southern editorial pages, sectional enmity toward the North was not merely being condoned but actively encouraged. "I hate them with all my soul, the murderers, liars, thieves, rascals!," was how one Louisianan remembered the atmosphere. "You are no true Southerner if you do not hate them as much as I!"[11]

Quite beyond the intention of southern nation builders, elite southern women seized the sentiments of sectional scorn as their own. But in doing so, southern women had to overcome their own deeply internalized disparagement of female anger, and here, a noticeable divergence appeared along generational lines. The diary of Mississippi's Ann Lewis Hardeman (forty years old in 1861) represents well the older generation of women born before 1830, exuding a pained but passive combination of anxiety and fatalism throughout the secession crisis. "My heart is like lead," Hardeman wrote, using one of her characteristic metaphors of paralysis. "I seem to have undergone a petrifying process within the last few weeks," she confessed by the time of Fort Sumter. "I am filled with so many tumultuous emotions which can only be allayed by the grace of God." Likewise, Virginia's Mary Fleet (born around 1820) wondered why "God allow[s] so much misery to befall this once happy land[.] ... I can't think of this awful war with any composure, it haunts me waking and sleeping." Younger women responded quite differently, often echoing and appropriating the vitriol of secessionist leaders. It seems increasingly clear that elite women coming of age in the 1850s deeply (if quietly) resented the restrictions imposed by southern womanhood and strove to challenge those restrictions amid the maelstrom of the Civil War. The anti-Yankee denunciations of young Confederate women emblazoned in diaries and letters represented a landmark rejection of female submissiveness that perhaps helped propel a larger assault against southern patriarchy. In short, it seems tempting to see the revision of emotional standards as providing a prelude for a far grander revision in southern gender roles.[12]

To be sure, young Confederate women fully understood that their emotions violated the norms of elite society, and their initial outbursts of outrage were often countered with apologies and backtracking. Amanda Edmonds, for instance, reacted to the alleged support local slaves showed for John Brown by demanding the offenders be "signed and burnt until the last drop of blood was dried within and every bone smolder to ashes." But she quickly retracted her dreadful utterance: "Ah, but I couldn't." Keziah Brevard would blast northerners as "cut throat Abolitionists, ... the selfish and envious sons of Satan," in one entry, and then pray for the Lord to "let me have right feelings towards [them]," acknowledging that "we should forgive our enemies," in another. "This war has brought out wicked, malignant feelings that I did not believe could dwell in woman's heart," decried Sarah Morgan, an astute social observer who would excoriate her share of Yankees in time. "O! woman! into what loathsome violence you have debased your holy mission!" The emotional turmoil may help to explain why the striking lament—"I wish I was a man"—appeared so frequently in the writings of young Confederate women (including Morgan's) struggling with the internal torment. By comparison, the relative emotional freedom of masculinity represented an appealing chimera.[13]

But these apologies eventually faded from view. By the summer of 1861, Amanda Edmonds openly celebrated the killing of Union officer Elmer Ellsworth as a "good deed," denouncing the "barbarians of the North" who had mobilized at Virginia's border, hoping that "every last one may be slain," and gratefully accepting war trophies taken from killed Yankee soldiers. Though "shocked ... when I think of the wishes which my heart frames and lips utter," Cora Ready ultimately rejected the notion that "God means for me to love [Northerners] when He says 'love your enemies,'" for the Yankees were worse than enemies; they were "implacable foes." Keziah Brevard joined her younger countrywomen in discarding the moral censure connected to female indignation. "We all have legions of bad feelings ever rising—my feelings to those who wish to trample us to earth is wrong," she admitted in the days before the firing on Fort Sumter. "I love God ... but I cannot love those who hate us." Tennessee's Belle Edmonson put the matter much more succinctly by 1863: "May God forgive me if there be sin hating the Yankees."[14]

Nevertheless, these emotional explosions did not necessarily lead to changes in what counted as acceptable behavior for women in southern society. For one, female indignation served the interest of secessionists and the founding fathers of the Confederacy, which was specifically designed to reify the patriarchal relations of the Old South. Anti-Yankee hatred did not just help white southerners rally around secession; its acceleration during the war ("each man we lose," Ella Thompson pointed out, "but serves to render more intense our hatred of the Yankee") provided powerful resolve to maintain the military effort amid repeated military setbacks. If hatred could incite Confederate and Union soldiers to maintain the fight, the same dynamic surely worked for women on the home front. Desperate for manpower, Confederate war leaders would have surely condoned the sentiments of Georgia's Julia Fisher in 1862 (who boasted that northern hatred had become "part of my religion") when she lectured her sister-in-law that "life is little sacrifice" for southern liberty and that she would rather her "boys die in such a cause than live to witness its defeat." It was with pride that postwar southerners recalled General William Sherman's famous lament of southern she-devils amid the March to the Sea: "No one who sees them and hears them but must feel the intensity of their hate."[15]

For another, the fury of female Confederates fell squarely on socially acceptable targets—Yankees and slaves. They often cursed them in the same breath: "What infatuation possesses those Northern ignoramuses," Sallie McNeill emblematically exclaimed in December 1860. "Our worst foes are in our midst. Negro insurrections will be constant and bloody, under the guidance of Abolitionists." Keziah Brevard wished that "abolitionists and Negroes had a country for themselves," and she prayed that God would "separate us in the world to come, let us not be together." For Ella Thomas, an aggrieved sense of racial betrayal emanated from the Yankee decision to forsake southern whites in favor of southern slaves. "Is their love for their Black Brother greater than they experience for their white?" she asked. "Oh they are a miserable set." The Yankees even forfeited full white status in some southern eyes. In 1865, a Union officer encountered a North Carolina woman who "had grown old in her hatred of Yankees." Though considering herself a "pretty good Christian," she declared that "if the Yankees and *white people* were going to be all together in heaven, she believed she'd rather not go to heaven at all." However shocking such sentiments would have appeared by the standards of the antebellum past, they were not subversive barbs aimed at the exposed flanks of southern patriarchy. Southern men said the same thing often in harsher tones. A Tennessee soldier, for instance, had decided "that he who kills the greatest number of abolition thieves and their abettors is the best Christian." Few Confederate men would have taken umbrage with Ella Thomas's declaration at war's end that "I do most honestly despise Yankees, Negroes and everything connected with them."[16]

Finally, some Confederate soldiers actually directed their wives to inculcate their hatred into their children. Teach them to abhor the Yankees "with that bitter hatred that will never permit them to meet under any circumstances without seeking to destroy each other," a Georgian soldier instructed in early 1862. Let the breach widen, he wrote, until "no Yankees are [left] to live in the South." Elijah Petty made a similar request of his wife in September 1862. "Encourage them in a bitter and unrelenting hatred of the Yankee race," the Texan officer commanded, for "I am in eternal hostility to them and I think it but right that my children ... should be indoctrinated with an implacable hatred to so vile and cursed a race." The emotional community of elite male southerners stewed with severe indignation and enmity, and men expected Confederate women to share in the scorching rhetoric of anti-Yankee denunciation. It would have proven more subversive for southern women to reject the violent dehumanization voiced by their menfolk, to make appeals to Christian forbearance, or to display empathy for their erstwhile countrymen.[17]

Female indignation did sometimes venture beyond what southern men had bargained for, leading to patriarchal rebuke. In response to a string of Confederate defeats in early 1862, for example, South Carolina's Mary Leverett vented her rage in a series of letters to her sons, both Confederate officers. She lambasted President Jefferson Davis and his cabinet, wishing she could lift her voice "and blow a trumpet blast in the ears" of the Confederacy's top echelon for their perceived failures of leadership. But Leverett went much further in her critique. "The women are ready to ... suffer any thing—it is the men who are at fault in this war," she fumed in a remarkable diatribe. "I am disgusted with men since this war began, they are not half as honest as women[,] ... slow and stupid, a drinking, swearing, good for nothing set, selfish and unpatriotic. How I hate them!" White southern men "have turned cowards," comparable to a "little puppy dog with the tail between the legs," she concluded. The response of Milton Leverett, her fourth eldest son, was sharp and condescending. "Cease my dear mother and don't indulge in any more warlike demonstrations," he chided. "Get a cow horn ... and you can give a good blast on it all day if you would like." Behind the jest, Milton Leverett was seriously admonishing his mother for her untoward display of emotion on an unacceptable topic and against an unacceptable target. She seemed to receive the message clearly; in her next letter to Milton, she lauded how "our men have behaved grandly, nobly. Such bravery is wonderful." The bellicose demonstrations were quelled for the duration of the war.[18]

Thus, instead of viewing the emotional transformation of elite women as merely presaging a larger renegotiation of southern gender roles, perhaps we should appreciate the importance of the transformation itself—an emotional revolution that broadened the boundaries of the Old South's emotional community and established greater freedom for female expression. The sense of relief afforded Confederate women clearly resonates in the lines of their diaries and letters. "'Tis so refreshing to abuse someone when you've got a heart full of bitterness," Virginia's Lucy Buck exalted after blasting the Yankee bluecoats. "Now that it is done," she noted, "I feel relieved." It was a catharsis southern women shared and even made their own. Indeed, emotional freedom was perhaps the greatest freedom southern women wrested from the Confederate war experience.[19]

But as with all revolutions, there came unintended consequences. "No wonder that our children will dislike the Yankees," Ella Thomas reflected when a toddler in her presence unleashed a profanity-laced curse against northerners and was not censured by an adult for doing so, for "upon their imagination impressions will be made which will grow with their growth and never leave them." It was, after all, the children of secession who blossomed into the generation that violently overthrew Reconstruction, launched Jim Crow, and condoned the heinous lynching wave that haunted the southern landscape. They mythologized the Old South of their parents and the sanctimony of the Lost Cause, maintaining (if sometimes sub rosa) the anti-Yankee enmity of the secessionist movement. "The slaveholder was no criminal," Mildred Rutherford (ten years old in 1861) proclaimed with indignation a half century after Appomattox, "and slavery under the old regime was no crime." In 1891, an unfortunate federal auditor encountered another erstwhile Confederate youth manning the records office in Cobb County, Georgia, and foolishly asked why the documentation ceased prior to 1865. "That was the date General Sherman, the son-of-a-bitch, came through Marietta burning our homes, city buildings, and records," the unreconstructed southerner replied. "He is dead now and in hell and I'm glad of it."[20]

NOTES

1. Alfred Iverson, quoted in Kenneth Stampp, ed., *The Causes of the Civil War* (Englewood Cliffs, NJ: Prentice Hall, 1965), 181. For a discussion of secession as "emotional catharsis," see James McPherson, *Battle Cry of Freedom: The Civil War Era* (New York: Oxford Uni-

versity Press, 1988). For a sophisticated study of the role emotion played in the coming of the Civil War that embraces the recent findings of emotions scholars in various fields, see Michael E. Woods, *Emotional and Sectional Conflict in the Antebellum United States* (New York: Cambridge University Press, 2014).

2. Grace Brown Elmore diary, October 18, 1860, South Carolinian Library, University of South Carolina; Virginia I. Burr, ed., *The Secret Eye: The Journal of Ella Gertrude Clanton Thomas, 1848–1889* (Chapel Hill: University of North Carolina Press, 1990), 185; unknown (probably Mary Fenwick Kollock) to George J. Kollock Jr., November 20, 1860, George J. Kollock Papers, Hargrett Rare Book and Manuscript Library, University of Georgia (hereafter HAR); Ben Ames Williams, ed., *A Diary from Dixie by Mary Chesnut Boykin* (Cambridge, MA: Harvard University Press, 1980), 19–20.

3. William M. Cash and Lucy S. Howorth, eds., *My Dear Nellie: The Civil War Letters of William L. Nugent to Eleanor Smith Nugent* (Jackson: University Press of Mississippi), 42, 46. For more on the theoretical concept of emotional communities, see Barbara H. Rosenwein, *Emotional Communities in the Early Middle Ages* (Ithaca, NY: Cornell University Press, 2006), and Barbara H. Rosenwein, "Problems and Methods in the History of Emotions," *International Journal of the History and Theory of Emotions* 1(2010): n.p. While this sampling of southern women is far from exhaustive, it does appear that the elitist "emotional community" that I have postulated covered the entire antebellum South. There was not, in other words, a noticeable demarcation separating the emotionality of the deep versus upper South.

4. Thomas Dew, quoted in Kathryn Lee Seidel, *The Southern Belle in the American Novel* (Gainesville: University of Florida Press, 1985), 8; Jacob Abbot, quoted in Carol Stearns and Peter Stearns, *Anger: the Struggle for Emotional Control in America's History* (Chicago: University of Chicago Press, 1986), 39. For a discussion on female emotional subservience as a prop for southern patriarchy, see Anya Jabour, *Scarlett's Sisters: Young Women in the Old South* (Chapel Hill: University of North Carolina Press). For an analysis of Victorian culture's assault on the emotion of anger, in a work many see as the genesis of emotions history, see Carol Stearns and Peter Stearns's *Anger*. Historian Jacqueline Glass Campbell has argued that southern women showed general subservience to their husbands, but by choice, not as a result of coercion. Campbell further maintains that female subservience was far less voluntary in the industrializing North. My interpretation of female emotional subservience runs counter to Campbell's argument; I find general similarity in the emotional standards of both sections at least among elites. See Campbell, *When Sherman Marched North from the Sea: Resistance on the Confederate Home Front* (Chapel Hill: University of North Carolina Press, 2003), especially 12–13.

5. David Harris, quoted in Catherine Clinton, *The Plantation Mistress: Woman's World in the Old South* (New York: Pantheon, 1982), 96; Jean V. Berlin, ed., *A Confederate Nurse: The Diary of Ada W. Bacot, 1860–1863* (Columbia: University of South Carolina Press, 1994), 29, 32; Philip N. Racine, ed., *Piedmont Farmer: The Journals of David Golightly Harris, 1855–1870* (Knoxville: University of Tennessee Press, 1990), 92.

6. Michael O'Brien, ed., *An Evening When Alone: Four Journals of Single Women in the South, 1827–1876* (Charlottesville: University Press of Virginia, 1993), 288; Erika L. Murr, ed., *A Rebel Wife in Texas: The Diary and Letters of Elizabeth Scott Neblett, 1852–1864* (Baton

Rouge: Louisiana State University, 2001), 34; C. Alice Ready diary, May 21, 1860, Southern Historical Collection, Wilson Library, University of North Carolina at Chapel Hill (hereafter SHC).

7. John H. Moore, ed., *A Plantation Mistress on the Eve of the Civil War: The Diary of Keziah Goodwyn Hopkins Brevard, 1860–1861* (Columbia: University of South Carolina Press, 1993), 21, 107, 92, 50. A historical analysis of Brevard's remarkable diary is provided in Shearer Davis Bowman, *At the Precipice: Americans North and South During the Secession Crisis* (Chapel Hill: University of North Carolina Press, 2010), 244–49.

8. Mahala Roach diary, August 15, 1853, January 4, 1853, January 17, 1854, April 17, 1860, November 28, 1860, and December 11, 1860, Roach and Eggleston Family Papers, SHC.

9. Melanie Pavich-Lindsay, ed., *Anna: The Letters of a St. Simons Island Plantation Mistress, 1817–1859* (Athens: University of Georgia Press, 2002), 190–92; Anne Sinkler Whaley LeClerq, ed., *Between North and South: The Letters of Emily Wharton Sinkler, 1842–1865* (Columbia: University of South Carolina Press, 2001), 173.

10. Hattie Harmon to Annie Carleton, June 13, 1855, in Letters to Annie Carleton, HAR; Nancy C. Baird, ed., *The Journals of Amanda Virginia Edmonds: Lass of the Mosby Confederacy, 1859–1867* (Delaphane, VA: Nancy C. Baird, 1984), 20; Burr, *The Secret Eye*, 148; Mary Lynn G. Hill and Ginny M. Raska, eds., *The Uncompromising Diary of Sallie McNeill, 1858–1867* (College Station: Texas A&M University Press, 2009), 109. Because correspondence and diaries were often preserved for the specific purpose of posterity, historian Michael O'Brien has classified them as "semi-private" writings comparable to modern-day photo albums. See O'Brien, *Conjectures of Order: Intellectual Life in the American South, 1810–1860* (Chapel Hill: University of North Carolina Press, 2004), 459–63.

11. Thomas Cobb, quoted in Freehling and Simpson, *Secession Debated*, 19; Charles B. Dew, *Apostles of Disunion: Southern Secession Commissioners and the Causes of the Civil War* (Charlottesville: University of Virginia Press, 2001), 13; Charles East, ed., *Sarah Morgan: The Civil War Diary of a Southern Woman* (New York: Simon and Schuster, 1992), 122. The strength, even existence, of Confederate nationalism remains a contested historical debate. For a solid analysis of both Confederate nationalism itself and its scholarly historiography, see James C. Cobb, *Away Down South: A History of Southern Identity* (New York: Oxford University Press, 2005), 34–66.

12. O'Brien, *An Evening When Alone*, 327; Betsy Fleet and John D.P. Fuller, eds., *Green Mount: A Virginia Plantation Family during the Civil War* (Lexington: University of Kentucky Press, 1964), 53–55. See Anya Jabour, *Scarlett's Sisters: Young Women in the Old South* (Chapel Hill: University of North Carolina Press, 2007), especially 239–80. The question of change and continuity in elite southern gender roles remains contentious. For arguments that the patriarchy was weakened during and after the Civil War see, in addition to Jabour, Anne Firor Scott, *The Southern Lady: From Pedestal to Politics, 1830–1890* (Chicago: University of Chicago Press, 1970), and Jane Turner Censer, *The Reconstruction of Southern Womanhood, 1865–1895* (Baton Rouge: Louisiana State University Press, 2003). For arguments that the southern patriarchy sustained its strength despite the Civil War, see LeeAnn Whites, *The Civil War as a Crisis in Gender: Augusta, Georgia, 1860–1890* (Athens: University of Georgia Press, 1995), Drew Gilpin Faust, *Mothers of Invention: Women of the Slaveholding South in*

the American Civil War (Chapel Hill: University of North Carolina Press, 1996), and Laura F. Edwards, *Gendered Strife and Confusion: The Political Culture of Reconstruction* (Urbana: University of Illinois Press, 1997).

13. Baird, *The Journals of Amanda Virginia Edmonds*, 31–32; Moore, *A Plantation Mistress on the Eve of the Civil War*, 65, 97; East, *Sarah Morgan*, 122–23. For a discussion on the "I wish I was a man" phenomenon, see George Rable, "Missing in Action: Women of the Confederacy," in *Divided Houses: Gender and the Civil War*, ed. Catherine Clinton and Nina Silber (New York: Oxford University Press, 1992), 136.

14. Baird, *The Journals of Amanda Virginia Edmonds*, 49, 51, 81, 56; Moore, *A Plantation Mistress on the Eve of the Civil War*, 112–13; C. Alice Ready diary, April 21, 1862, SHC; Loretta Gailbraith and William Gailbraith, eds., *A Lost Heroine of the Confederacy: The Diaries and Letters of Belle Edmondson* (Jackson: University Press of Mississippi, 1990), 18.

15. Burr, *The Secret Eye*, 200; Arch Frederic Blakey, Ann Smith Lainhart, and Winston Bryant Stephens, Jr., eds., *Rose Cottage Chronicles: Civil War Letters of the Bryant-Stephens Family of North Florida* (Gainesville: University Press of Florida, 1998), 209, 118; William Sherman, quoted in Victor Davis Hanson, *The Soul of Battle: From Ancient Times to the Present Day* (New York: Free Press, 1999), 175.

16. Raska and Hill, *The Uncompromising Diary of Sallie McNeill*, 90; Moore, *A Plantation Mistress on the Eve of the Civil War*, 78; Burr, *Secret Eye*, 200, 275; Joseph T. Glatthaar, *General Lee's Army: From Victory to Collapse* (New York: Simon and Schuster, 2008), 235.

17. Bell Wiley, *The Life of Johnny Reb: The Common Soldier of the Confederacy* (Baton Rouge: Louisiana State University, 1994), 309; Norman D. Brown, ed., *Journey to Pleasant Hill: The Civil War Letters of Captain Elijah P. Petty* (San Antonio: University of Texas Press, 1982), 78–79.

18. Frances Wallace Taylor, Catherine Taylor Wallace, and J. Tracy Powers, eds., *The Leverett Letters: Correspondence of a South Carolina Family, 1851–1868* (Columbia: University of South Carolina Press, 2000), 129, 134, 139, 155.

19. Elizabeth R. Baer, ed., *Shadow of My Heart: The Civil War Diary of Lucy Rebecca Buck* (Athens: University of Georgia Pres, 1997), 98–99, 106, 130.

20. Burr, *Secret Eye*, 207–8; Mildred Lewis Rutherford, "Extracts from *Wrongs of History Righted*," *Confederate Veteran* 23, no. 10 (1915), 445; George Montgomery, ed., *Georgia Sharpshooter: The Civil War Diary and Letters of William Rhadamanthus Montgomery, 1839–1906* (Macon, GA: Mercer University Press, 1997), vii.

PART 2
CONFLICTING COMMUNITIES

A Slaveholding Unionist in the Secession Crisis

Reverend Dr. George Junkin and Lexington, Virginia, in Peace and Civil War

BARTON A. MYERS

IN APRIL 1861, THE SITTING PRESIDENT OF WASHINGTON COLLEGE in Lexington, Virginia, Reverend Dr. George Junkin Sr., resigned the office, sold his farm, and left his home of twelve years for Pennsylvania. Since his arrival in the small Virginia town in 1848, the distinguished Presbyterian academic and experienced college president had performed the duties of the demanding leadership position with an imperial sagacity. Meanwhile, his family had established itself in the local community. Junkin's second daughter, Elinor, married Thomas Jonathan "Stonewall" Jackson, the devout but eccentric Virginia Military Institute professor and future Confederate general, with whom George became a close friend prior to the Civil War. Yet in the spring of 1861, Junkin's political views in support of the Union made his position in the Shenandoah Valley community untenable. After Virginia's decision to leave the Union in April, Junkin left his daughter Margaret in Lexington with Confederate friends and family and returned to the state of his birth. After Junkin resigned, the college's presidency was left vacant until October 1865, when Virginian Robert E. Lee took charge of the school.[1]

As an examination of a northern-born, slaveholding, prominent Unionist living in the South who contributed extensive critiques of both secession and abolitionist positions during his life, this piece offers an important view of one brand of hardened American Colonization Society support and principled unionism on the eve of secession and civil war. It examines the intellectual underpinnings of George Junkin's political unionism, his writings on the subject, and its subsequent intersection with his leadership in higher education during the late antebellum period. Junkin's political ideology and life experience present a prism through which to examine the rapidly constricting space for Unionist, public intellectual life in the South in the secession crisis. Dr. George Junkin's interactions with the higher education community in the South, the community of Rockbridge County, and its county seat of Lexington, Virginia, all demonstrate the precariousness of support for both union and anti-abolitionist views as the country moved away from nuanced academic argument and toward violent civil war. Junkin's life acts as a barometer for how fast and high the pressure to secede rose in the Shenandoah Valley of Virginia and the subsequent costs for a man who refused to repudiate his unionism.[2]

Junkin was one of the most important public figures in the small community of Lexington, Virginia, during the years prior to the American Civil War and one of the most politically outspoken. Gradually, Junkin's public reputation and political identity as a staunch Unionist, which reached its apex with the election of Abraham Lincoln to the presidency, became the element that most defined him in the community of Lexington. Eventually, it would cost him his status, his professional life, his farm in Rockbridge County, and even close friends and family. His fall is a study in community dynamics. He lost the support and respect of his students first, young men anxious for war in the *rage militaire* of 1861. Then, the faculty gave up on him, voting no confidence in his presidency and leadership during a time following Virginia's secession. His close friend, son-in-law, and fellow devout Presbyterian, Thomas J. Jackson, came next, abandoning him during the heady days of the secession crisis as well. Finally, he would even split with his own children, especially his daughter Margaret, who married into the Lexington community and stayed behind with her family when her father left Lexington in April 1861. His youngest son, William Finney Junkin, joined the Confederate army, while his oldest son, John Miller, remained loyal and served the Union army in Pennsylvania. Junkin may have retrieved his daughter and son in death, as it was almost certainly them who brought his body back to Lexington to lie beside their mother. Junkin's life during the secession crisis demonstrates how the bonds of southern community were torn away from Unionists as they held to their beliefs. Junkin's other family members had remained in the North and doubtless provided an anchor for him, but he demonstrated the sheer moral strength it took to maintain one's political and intellectual integrity to the Union during the secession crisis. For some people, supporting the continuation of the Union literally meant giving up one's home and happiness as well as career and family ties, even before the hardest fighting of the war began. As a northern-born man deeply immersed in a southern community for more than a decade before the war of '61, his decision to remain loyal revealed the personal price of union and unionism for Americans entangled in the complex web of political loyalty in the American South during the 1860s.[3]

George Junkin was born in Cumberland County, Pennsylvania, in November 1790, during the first term of George Washington's presidency. The precocious youngster graduated from Jefferson College (now Washington and Jefferson College) and then attended Presbyterian Theological Seminary in New York City. After serving as minister to several congregations in the Keystone State, he eventually became principal of Manual Labor Academy in Germantown, Pennsylvania, and then president of Lafayette College, Pennsylvania, in the early 1830s. Over the course of the decade, he became one of the leading intellectual figures in the Presbyterian Church and later one of the leading biblical defenders of slavery. He participated in a highly controversial heresy trial in the 1830s between old and new school theologians within that church body. Junkin, true to form, was an old school theologian and served as principal prosecutor of a new school theologian named Albert Barnes. This event eventually provoked a schism within the church itself over theological differences and regional antagonisms. For most of his career, Junkin used his powerful intellect to address theological issues primarily in his academic work. In 1843, Junkin, then serving as president of Miami University in Oxford, Ohio, published his seminal work *The Integrity of Our National Union vs. Abolitionism*. This speech, delivered in September 1843 in front the Presbyterian Synod of Cincinnati on the biblical interpretation and understanding of slavery, was influential.[4]

Junkin's position was grounded in a mixture of theological and constitutional political interpretation. His adherence to the U.S. Constitution and a position outlined by many Whigs and enlightened Democratic Party members of the period on colonization as a solution to the woes of the master and slave exposed the constricted intellectual space in which other scholars who took up the issue of slavery operated during the antebellum years. A conservative Whig, Junkin both condemned the American abolitionist cause and strongly supported the work of African colonization, especially in Liberia. This position placed him in line with the thinking of Henry Clay, a sponsor of the American Colonization Society, which was founded in 1817. Junkin's speech was polemical. The rock-ribbed, old school theologian strongly defended the national union as unbreakable and vehemently opposed the abolitionist movement, the "Liberty Party," and the political cause of immediate emancipation of enslaved people. Indeed, he was uncomfortable with politicizing the antislavery issue in any way.[5] He valued union and the U.S. Constitution far above any political cause or interpretation and found it second only to the Bible in the worth of its teachings.[6]

Junkin maintained that "the Abolition movement occasions the riveting of the chains of temporal bondage tighter and more tightly upon the colored race" and "the manacles of intellectual bondage and the chains of spiritual and eternal death, to be the more firmly and durably fastened upon this unhappy race." He condemned it in political terms, arguing that "it is a treasonable movement against the Constitution of the United States" and that "it tends to, and aims at a dissolution of this Union." For Junkin, preserving the Union was clearly far more important than ending slavery. As a solution to the problem, Junkin offered an alternative: "the splendid scheme of African Colonization."[7] The old theologian laid out his own biblical understanding of slavery clearly: "I take the distinction before alluded to, that the Bible tolerates slavery. Now, toleration is *bearing with—enduring* a thing; and it implies, that the thing is viewed as an evil." Yet he also offered an equally strong interpretation on the literal understanding as well. "*God has nowhere in the Old Testament Prohibited slavery. There is no command to this amount, 'masters let your servants go free.' The relation of master and slave is nowhere condemned as a sin, and forbidden to exist.*" This was all the room many proslavery advocates needed.[8]

Junkin specifically rebutted the idea that the procolonization society position was a "proslavery" position in his writings. He wrote in his speech that "we are in truth opposed to slavery, and are doing as much in our respective positions to abate its evils. "We differ" from abolitionists, he added, "as to the manner of doing away these evils.... We are much more efficient in the matter of meliorating the condition of the colored race." He angrily rejected the idea that "you are opposed to the Anti-slavery party, and therefore you must be Pro-slavery men."[9] Many individuals, including future President Abraham Lincoln, a devotee of Henry Clay's political ideology, supported the colonization movement as an alternative to a rupture of the Union and as a solution to the moral evil of slavery as an institution. These were commonly held beliefs among southern Whig Party members in the 1840s. It was merely the impracticality of colonization that would eventually convince Lincoln to abandon it as a solution to ending slavery.[10]

In the end, however, Junkin's position left him as a leading biblical interpreter of the historical practices of slavery in the ancient world, and, as a result, his views became a tool of those politicians like South Carolina senator John C. Calhoun, who used Junkin's erudition and understanding of the Bible to promulgate their proslavery argument. Junkin was clearly no George Fitzhugh, the proslavery sociologist, who argued in his works *Sociology for the South* and *Cannibals All!* that slavery was a positive good for all southern laborers and elites, white and black, but his biblical interpretation plainly sustained the institution in antebellum America. Nevertheless, Junkin also specifically rejected the term "proslavery" to describe his own intellectual position on the issue. The northern-born Junkin's political thought placed him firmly among white southern moderates who owned slaves but supported a long, gradual decline of the institution in America. His own actions in 1861 demonstrate that he valued union more than slavery.[11]

After he read the synod speech with what he described as "great pleasure and no little instruction," John C. Calhoun, the vituperative defender and vital intellectual architect of states' rights ideology, wrote in a letter to Junkin in September 1846 that he had read "several able discussions on the same subject, but in none of them have the various passages of the Bible in reference to the subject of slavery been presented in so clear & systematick a manner, and discussed with such thorough knowledge of it, under all its aspects. You have left not a loop hole large enough for the most subtle & sophistical opponent to escape." Calhoun was deeply impressed. "So able & successful an effort, on such an occasion and on so vital a subject, can not fail to be followed by permanent & salutary effects in a religious & political point of view; and you are entitled, for making it, to the gratitude of every Christian & patriot. The argument, by which you vindicate the true interpretation of the Bible in reference to this vexed & agitated subject, will do much to preserve our Union." Calhoun's letter demonstrates the power of Junkin's argument in support of the biblical understanding of slavery, and Calhoun's laudatory and admiring response demonstrates the respect he commanded as an intellectual figure in many circles.[12]

After three largely unhappy years as president of Miami University, Junkin returned to his books, but his powerful intellect would be called on to lead one more institution of higher education by the end of the 1840s.[13] Washington College was not a wealthy school in the antebellum period. The tiny college, nestled in the Shenandoah Valley town of Lexington, Virginia, had originally been called Liberty Hall Academy but then was renamed in honor of George Washington following his large financial gift of $20,000 in James River canal stock in 1796, a sum that shored up the school's finances for a period. The estate of "Jockey John" Robinson also financially supported the school after his demise in 1826. This estate included eighty-four enslaved people as well as land, both of which were used to support the institution. Even its buildings had been built, in part, by enslaved people, a common circumstance at many of Virginia's old, elite institutions of higher education like the University of Virginia and William and Mary.[14] Washington College struggled financially in the antebellum years and ultimately decided to sell the bulk of the remaining Robinson estate slaves in 1836. The school profited from the eventual slave sale from the Robinson bequest, and it also profited by no longer having to keep those enslaved people housed and fed as they grew older.[15]

Junkin was elected by the board of trustees in September 1848 and began his duties in November. The fifty-eight-year-old Junkin officially became president of Washington College on his inauguration day February 22, 1849, and served until his resignation in 1861. Junkin and his wife, Eleanor Cochran Junkin, reared eight children that survived to adulthood: Margaret Junkin Preston (born 1820), John Miller Junkin (1821), Joseph Junkin (1823), Elinor Junkin Jackson (1825), George Jr. (1827), Ebenezer Dickey (1829), William Finney (1831), and Julia Miller Junkin Fishburn (1835).[16] Junkin was not the first prominent leader in Lexington, or even of Washington College, to express beliefs that were not at odds with an acceptance of slavery under the guise of religious teaching and august academic credentials. William Graham, the rector and primary faculty member when the school was still Liberty Hall Academy, consistently expressed these views in academic lectures in the 1780s and 1790s.[17]

College luminaries demonstrated the investment the school had in the enslavement of human beings. In 1855, Junkin presided over the reburial and dedication of an Italian marble monument to John Robinson. After collecting the Robinson remains (twenty-nine years buried), the school put them in a new pine box with a number of mementoes and reburied the benefactor in a place of prominence, the front academic lawn. "How great good has resulted to the world from Mr. Robinson's liberal benefaction! Where are we whilst though readest? Believe in the Lord Jesus Christ and thou shalt be saved," Junkin wrote. The Robinson bequest had been nearly equal in importance to the college as the financial gift of George Washington.[18]

One member of the faculty described Junkin as "short, heavy set, with keen, black eyes, which saw everything without the aid of glasses." He "presented a sharp contrast" to Henry Ruffner, the former president and politically moderate slavery critic, who issued a pamphlet arguing for a gradual emancipation law in the western counties of Virginia, "a man so absorbed in his books that he did not seem to know the students, nor to see them when he passed them on the walks." One of the first orders of business that Junkin and the college took up was scholarships. The practice of "cutting" class was dealt with harshly during these years, as it was a "considerable" problem. During Junkin's administration, the student body size fluctuated between forty-nine and ninety-two students, with the bulk of the young men coming from Virginia. Only a few attended from bordering states, Mississippi, and Ireland. The Presbyterians in Virginia divided their attentions between the University of Virginia, Hampden-Sydney College, and even the Virginia Military Institute. There was plenty of competition for both bright and dim young minds.[19]

Junkin and the faculty monitored the students' moral behavior, and the classical curriculum was undergirded by a strong religious component. All students were required to attend prayers, and "lounging, talking, reading, and being improperly dressed were all considered as offenses in Chapel." The faculty also instituted a policy prohibiting firearms and dueling. The unfortunate, accidental shooting death of a student during a hunting expedition in 1856 further demonstrated the need for this rule. Weapons and immaturity rarely make a good combination on a campus.[20]

While Junkin's presidency did not carry quite the weight of absolute rule, it was the closest thing to it. Faculty members were expected to operate in loco parentis. And that is evident in both the policies and actions of the men who ran the school in the 1850s. Student examinations were "very similar to the old Roman gladiatorial contests or Christian-torture fests, with poor defenseless students being put in the arena to suffer the attacks of innumerable unorganized bursts of questions."[21] The pressure on the young scholars was intense. The school instituted a strong prohibition on alcohol, in line with Junkin's own temperance beliefs. "No student shall bring... into College, gunpowder or intoxicating liquor or use them." Junkin worked his entire administration for the cause of temperance, a "dry" campus, and a sober, greater Lexington community. Despite the best attempts of the faculty and Junkin, the campus witnessed "admonitions, suspension, and expulsions for drinking." In February 1858 two professors felt compelled to enter the dorm room of students who were drinking to intercede. The student revelers were expelled, and consequently, many of their classmates participated in a march through town and the burning of the professors' likenesses in effigy as retaliation for their having interceded. In sum, between the students involved in the first drinking episode and those who participated in the subsequent "riot" during which the students consigned the professors' ectypes to the flames on the front lawn of the college, twenty-five students were expelled. This amounted to roughly half the students in the class.[22]

Lexington benefited from the rich soil and abundant farmland of Rockbridge County, and George Junkin's Presbyterian work ethic gradually paid dividends. George Junkin was also a farmer and a slaveholder, though very little on his role as a master survives in the printed records. Junkin owned one black man aged twenty-eight in 1850. By 1860, he owned eight enslaved people, five women (a thirty-five-year-old woman among them) and three adult men.[23] Junkin's steady, agricultural pursuits in Rockbridge County had almost certainly led to this increased investment in enslaved people over the course of the decade. Junkin may have permitted his first slave to marry and have children; four young girls under the age of ten were part of the group of eight people he owned. Junkin's strong avocation of husbandry techniques and careful investment in both property and enslaved people led to prosperity in Rockbridge County's lush farming environment. Eventually, this region would become the breadbasket for the Confederate Army of Northern Virginia during the Civil War. Junkin's slave ownership was one example of Rockbridge County residents' complex social, cultural, and political support of the institution. The total population of Rockbridge County in 1860 was 17,248, which included 3,985 enslaved people. The percentage of the population that was enslaved was 23.1 percent. In Virginia, the total population of enslaved people in 1860 was 490,865 out of the 1,596,318. There were 36,784 enslaved people in the Shenandoah Valley region during the same year.[24]

President Junkin and his family lived in a house on campus, now known as the Lee-Jackson House, which serves as the current office of the dean of the College of Washington and Lee University. Thomas J. Jackson married Junkin's daughter in the house on campus in August 1853, becoming very close friends with George Junkin during the courtship. She died a little over a year later in October 1854 from pregnancy complications after giving birth to a stillborn child. Junkin's other daughter, Margaret, married Virginia Military Institute founding father John Thomas Lewis Preston. Margaret, a prolific poet, had inherited her father's intellectual ability, if not his politics. Interestingly, in *The Life and Letters of Margaret Junkin Preston*, the woman who was called the "poet of the Confederacy," barely mentions her Unionist father or their relationship.[25]

Tranquility was hard to find anywhere for the opinionated Junkin, even in the beautiful Shenandoah Valley. In 1858, Junkin was involved in a vicious, public argument on the streets of Lexington with Judge John White Brockenbrough, another prominent Lexingtonian, a member of the Washington College Board of Trustees and a staunchly proslavery professor at the Lexington Law School. Brockenbrough would eventually become a member of the Confederate Congress and a Confederate district judge. Junkin's advocacy of the temperance cause influenced his handling of Judge Brockenbrough. "Our little town is in quite a fever of excitement," recounted Mary Davidson to her brother Greenlee, a future Confederate artillery captain killed at Chancellorsville in May 1863:

> Dr. Junkin and Judge Brockenbrough had a fight on the street yesterday evening.... Surely the World is coming to a woful end: when right reverend Doctors are soundly boxed on the ears by dignified judges of the Federal Courts. Judge B—— undertook to make old Junkin apologize for some things, he had said about him. Old Junkin boldly refused. Thereupon, the Judge called him "a vile calumniator" and the Dr. returned the compliment by calling the Judge "a vile rum sucker." That was touching a tender point: or in common parlance, "hitting the nail on the head." The judge couldn't stand it—gets in a great passion and strikes the Dr. in the face. Several law students were standing near the scene of the action, and set up a wonderful shout. Dr. Junkin never said a word, but very calmly walked away. It is an unfortunate and disgraceful affair. I am afraid it will cause trouble. No doubt Dr. Junkin will despise the law class more heartily than ever.[26]

An even more serious incident occurred the next year. In 1859, Junkin's family came to suspect that two slaves were poisoning them after George and several family members had become ill, and later, it was discovered that arsenic was in the "supper cream." The slaves were arraigned, but there was no definitive evidence, and so the case was dismissed. Junkin and the family recovered.[27]

As the 1850s came to a close, Junkin spoke out publicly and wrote often in the local paper about issues related to the Union. At one public meeting in Lexington, Junkin defiantly complained that he "would not dissolve this union if the people should make the devil President." His inflexible unionism would remain a core principle guiding the remainder of his life.[28] Junkin wrote opinion pieces for the local *Lexington Gazette* throughout the late 1850s and into the secession crisis of the early 1860s. The topics he addressed usually had to do with progress in American life, but occasionally he took on economic, labor, and diplomatic policy as well. In the final series of public letters he wrote, he argued against secession, upheld slavery, and also argued against the political theory that American states were sovereign in their own right. The final *Gazette* letter he wrote was published on February 21, 1861, when the Virginia secession convention was in session in Richmond.[29]

The election of 1860 and the secession winter of 1861 saw renewed tension regarding the preservation of slavery and unrest among the heavily prosecession student body of Washington College. Junkin, a lifelong conservative Whig, voted for the Constitutional Union Party ticket of long-time Tennessee senator John Bell and former Secretary of State Edward Everett of Massachusetts in the November 1860 presidential election. This ticket was the heir to the mantle of the Whig Party; this party had fallen apart nationally over the Kansas-Nebraska Act in 1854, but many Americans continued to support the old policies of the party. The Constitutional Unionists took a position that amounted to public neutrality on the slavery question during the election, hoping to prevent discord. Junkin's views on perpetual union were similar to those of both Daniel Webster of Massachusetts and Henry Clay of Kentucky. But his views on slavery and the Bible were attractive enough to proslavery thinkers like John C. Calhoun for them to overlook his strong pro-Union stance. Like Junkin, Rockbridge County strongly supported the Bell ticket in November 1860 with 1,231 votes, while the second-place finisher, Senator Stephen Douglas (a northern Democrat), received 641 votes. Vice President John C. Breckinridge, the southern Democrat, was a distant third with 361 votes. Abraham Lincoln, who was on the ballot in Virginia, received zero votes in Rockbridge.[30] Abraham Lincoln's election and the reaction of white, prosecessionist southerners throughout Lexington, Virginia, and the South to Lincoln's call for troops to put down the rebellion in the spring of 1861 and Virginia's secession, however, would force Junkin into a life-changing decision between slaveholding and Unionism. He chose Union, costing him friends, his farm, and his position as president of Washington College.[31]

The social pressure on Junkin because of his stalwart and caustic pro-Union political views was intense. Junkin's account of the incidents that prompted his resignation in April 1861 detail an escalating series of events between himself and the student body. In February 1861, Junkin's teaching became the focus of student consternation. His lecture on the U.S. Constitution led students in the class to call him a "Pennsylvania Abolitionist," and students wrote on a column opposite his classroom "Lincoln Junkin." Another incident at the end of March also demonstrated the students' prosecessionist views. "A Palmetto flag was placed on the center building of the college [over a statue of George Washington].... This flag I ordered the servants to take down and bring to me," Junkin remembered. "I was asked what I would do with it, and replied 'Burn it after evening prayer.'" Students subsequently crept into his classroom with a ladder and stole the flag back. Students again hoisted the flag aloft a week later, and Junkin took personal action to remove it. "I stepped up and took some matches out of my pocket, set it on fire, and, when it blazed up, told the servants to throw the pole out from the building, and whilst it flamed up, I said, 'So perish all efforts to dissolve this glorious Union!'"[32] During one event on campus, Junkin publicly denounced secessionist William Lowndes Yancey to the students at a chapel reading from the Old Testament Book of Kings, which dwelled on the characteristics of a treasonable person. He exclaimed "That's Yancey!" The youthful college boys hungry for war grew increasingly angry with the stern, septuagenarian Union nationalist serving as their overlord.[33]

On April 17, 1861, the date that the Virginia secession convention delegates passed the secession ordinance, the faculty at Washington College met to deliberate over a student-generated letter endorsing the secession convention's decision and the ordinance. "We have hoisted a Southern Flag over College, as the best exponent of our views. It is now our unanimous desire, that the flag should continue to float; and we, respectfully request, that you will not suffer it to be taken down," the students argued. "There can be no opposition to it from any quarter *now*, save from the enemies of Virginia." Sixty-one students signed the letter.[34] Junkin was absolutely furious. The students responded, rather tongue-in-cheek to Junkin's anger, with their reason for raising the flag. "We, do wholly disclaim any intention whatever of offending [Dr. Junkin] in erecting a Southern Flag.... What we do intend is simply this: an open declaration of our sentiments[,] ... meaning unflinching hostility to the coercive policy of Mr. Lincoln and a firm adhesion to the South."[35]

An apoplectic Junkin threatened to resign over the "Southern Flag" issue. The faculty did not like Junkin's ultimatum and subsequently decided to allow the "Southern Flag" or "red flag" to remain at their discretion. Junkin believed that their placing the "red flag" directly over the building where his lecture room was rather than over the center college building and statue of Washington where they had placed the other flags was a direct insult.[36] Consternation with Junkin over his unionism was evident even among the faculty by this point. As Junkin responded to their decision on the flag, he stated that he would not stand for the student "coercion." "I will not stay where the students dishonor their country's flag!" After Junkin had dismissed the faculty at the meeting, one faculty member—who would be killed at the First Battle of Bull Run about three months later—ran to the door shouting "Thank God for that! Thank God for that!" Junkin resigned in protest, considering the flag an insult and a "personal indignity." In effect, his ultimatum and the students' recalcitrance also forced a no confidence vote by the faculty against him. The board of trustees received Junkin's resignation on April 22, 1861, which effectively severed his relationship with the college. Like his intellectual forbear Henry Clay, Junkin was saying he would "rather be right than President."[37]

Ten days later, on April 27, Virginia offered to join the Confederacy, and the Confederacy subsequently accepted the state's invitation to make Richmond its capital city. Upon paying his debts and selling his property, Junkin drove his horse and carriage 350 miles to Chester County, Pennsylvania, in the state of his birth. He had been given a pass by Governor John Letcher to prevent him from being stopped, but he did not use it. Junkin crossed the Potomac River at Williamsport, Maryland, on May 9, 1861, and settled among his northern family in Philadelphia for the duration of the war.[38]

Old George Junkin continued to write, and he left behind detailed views on the issue of secession and the political history of the United States through his marginal notes in a prosecession book titled *The Sectional Controversy; or, Passages in the Political History of the United States, Including the Causes of the War Between the Sections* by William Fowler.[39] Fowler argued in favor of the right to secession with this logic: "The 'right of the people' here spoken of generally, is applied, in that instrument, to the right of the people of the colonies respectively, who were about to 'alter their former systems of government.' ... Each colony thus became an independent State. Thus each colony, acting for itself, but in concert with others, 'altered its former system of government.'" One can feel Junkin's blood boiling as he read the next passage: "And in the very act of changing the Government from that of the old Confederation, which was established by 'articles of perpetual union,' the several States recognized the right of 'the people of the several States' to change the form of their government." Junkin's response in the marginal notes is concise and destructive. "No: They are independent of Great Britain—not of each other: not each but all in the aggregate unity became independent: [illegible text]. This is called by C. C. Pinckney 'a bind of political heresy.' This conceded the whole question to the South."[40]

Junkin's own published book on the sectional crisis and secession, titled *Political Fallacies* (1863), addressed his views on the national rupture. In it, Junkin dismantled the political interpretations of the Articles of Confederation used by Confederate politicians, specifically President Jefferson Davis, to argue that the states remained sovereign. Davis appealed to article 2 of the Articles of Confederation in his second inaugural speech, delivered on April 29, 1861, to sustain the Confederate states' secession position as legal. "Each state retains its sovereignty, freedom and independence, and every power, jurisdiction and right, which is not by this Confederation expressly delegated to the United States in Congress assembled." Junkin's response highlights his understanding of the Union as perpetual and his willingness to directly revise Davis's interpretation of the Articles of Confederation. "We note the purpose for which he adduces the Article, viz., to prove the absolute independence and sovereignty of the States; whereas it expressly asserts that parts and portions of both are already delegated to the United States in Congress assembled," Junkin asserted. "Yet the whole force of his argument is based on the assumed, but disproved fact, of their absolute sovereignty and independence. These gentlemen all affirm the unqualified and unlimited right of each State to judge and determine, by itself alone, without let or hindrance, whether it will secede from the Union or not, and when it will secede." Junkin's crescendo argument affirmed the opposite interpretation of the article. "That is, they claim for each the highest sovereignty and most absolute independence, and they prove the soundness of their claim by citing Article II., which in most express terms asserts the contrary!"[41]

During the Civil War, Lexington, Virginia, and Rockbridge County became a leadership hub for the Confederacy. The community that had overwhelmingly voted for John Bell in 1860 became one of the most ardent in its support of the Confederate nation. The cadets of the Virginia Military Institute would be a training unit for early Confederate armies, and the two Rockbridge County artillery companies would serve in the Army of Northern Virginia. William Nelson Pendleton, the original commander of the guns Matthew, Mark, Luke, and John, the "cadet battery" of the First Rockbridge Artillery, was not only a confidant of Robert E. Lee but ultimately became overall commander of the Army of Northern Virginia's artillery. Rockbridge County produced no fewer than thirteen companies for Confederate service, including artillery, cavalry, infantry, and home guard units.[42] This was in addition to the Virginia Military Institute Cadet Corps, which in 1864 made up four infantry and one artillery section, a total of 279 cadets.[43]

The war tore through Lexington and its population. The cadet class would fight at New Market, Virginia, in 1864. Many members of the student body Junkin had wrestled with at Washington College over loyalty became the Liberty Hall Volunteers, Company I, Fourth Virginia Infantry, Stonewall Brigade. This brigade was Thomas Jonathan Jackson's original unit from the Battle of First Manassas. In the fall of 1864, Lexington became a battlefield site as Union Army troops burned the Virginia Military Institute barracks, Governor John Letcher's home, and sacked Washington College. It almost certainly was George Washington's connection to the school that saved its buildings from the torch.[44]

Junkin never really escaped Lexington, neither while he was still alive nor after he had died. His family and friendship connections built over twelve years were too deep. In 1863, while ministering to wounded soldiers, he traveled to the battlefield at Gettysburg, Pennsylvania, only to find many of the students he left behind in 1861 no longer boys but battle-hardened veterans of the Army of Northern Virginia. During the war, the Liberty Hall Volunteers saw heavy casualties. Many of the ninety-two enlistees who enrolled when the war broke out died during the war. Eventually, 181 men would serve in the company over the course of the conflict, 60 percent of whom were additional recruits who joined after the initial enlistment. Fifty-six of these soldiers were captured, twenty-seven were killed or mortally wounded, and sixteen died of disease. According to historian Robert K. Krick, "Only eight Liberty Hall Volunteers remained on duty to surrender at Appomattox." Four members of Stonewall Jackson's own wartime staff were alumni of Washington College, including George G. Junkin, a native of Pennsylvania and Dr. George Junkin's nephew.[45] The casualties in this unit alone from Rockbridge were staggering. Today, their roll of honor is affixed to the wall of the narthex of the Lee Chapel on campus at Washington and Lee.[46]

Junkin's sons were divided as well in their military service and political loyalty during the war. His youngest son, William Finney Junkin, a graduate of Washington College and Princeton University's Theological Seminary, joined the Tenth Virginia Cavalry and eventually served as a lieutenant colonel in the Confederate Home Guard. His oldest son, physician John Miller Junkin, served as a surgeon in the Union Army during the war. His brother and later biographer David Xavier Junkin would serve as a Union chaplain on the ship *North Carolina* and frigate *Colorado*. It was his son George who rode off with Stonewall Jackson and served in the Stonewall Brigade. The death of Thomas J. Jackson in May 1863 was difficult for the family, as it still considered him to be a part of it, but it was an event that David Xavier believed was divine intervention to save the Union.[47]

While he was in Gettysburg, Junkin would preach to his former students, now men, who had been captured during the battle and then take out his class roll book and listen to their stories. In June 1864, he traveled to Fort Delaware, sent there by the Presbyterian Church to distribute religious tracts to prisoners of war. There again, he ministered to many of the Rockbridge County boys. He spoke affectionately of Lexington where his daughter Elinor and wife were buried. At one point, in what must have been a difficult, emotional moment, he glanced at his walking cane and said: "This is a gift from 'Stonewall' Jackson, my son-in-law." The costs of war for the community of Lexington came in waves. One private recalled that his visit with Junkin brought back memories of home.[48]

Junkin's resignation in 1861 left Washington College without a chief, and the position remained vacant until General Robert E. Lee accepted an offer at the invitation of Judge John White Brockenbrough and the board of trustees in 1865. During the summer of 1865, Lee was reluctant initially to move to Lexington and accept the position because he had lost his citizenship and was then under federal indictment for treason. He would never be tried for treason in court, and Ulysses S. Grant threatened to resign his commission as lieutenant general of U.S. armies if Lee was arrested on the grounds that the terms of surrender at Appomattox covered Lee's own personal surrender. Lee applied for amnesty from President Andrew Johnson after moving to Lexington, but Secretary of State William Seward pigeonholed his application. His citizenship was not formally restored until the presidency of Gerald Ford in 1975.[49]

In 2003, director Ronald F. Maxwell released a prequel to the successful 1993 film *Gettysburg* titled *Gods and Generals*, based on the book by Jeff Shaara, the son of Pulitzer Prize–winning fiction writer Michael Shaara, who wrote *Killer Angels*. The film closely follows the military life of Thomas J. Jackson and depicts his relationship with his friend and father-in-law George Junkin, as well as their falling out, a deeply painful moment for both men. Jackson would be mortally wounded at Chancellorsville in May 1863, never again having seen his estranged father-in-law after his flight from Lexington.[50]

After the war, Junkin remained a strict conservative. Radical Republican Party politics held no interest to him. By this point, he was in his mid-seventies and unwilling to change his mind on much. The man had always been largely inflexible when it came to his political opinions and his intellectual ideology. Following his death in May 1868, Junkin was buried in Philadelphia, Pennsylvania. He was later exhumed by his family and reburied in Lexington beside his wife and daughter and only yards from his son-in-law "Stonewall" Jackson, former partner in pugilism John White Brockenbrough, and wartime governor John Letcher. His Confederate daughter Margaret Junkin Preston and son William Finney Junkin are also buried near him.[51]

The return of his bodily remains to the Presbyterian cemetery where his son-in-law Jackson rests is the final chapter of a life and death dominated by secession and Civil War. The issues of divided loyalties and ostracism within a Virginia community during the winter and spring of secession can be viewed through the life of Reverend Dr. George Junkin. Indeed, Junkin, a long-time southern resident, was an early casualty of the type of loyalty pressure that most white southern Unionists felt during the war. Even his own family split over the Confederate cause. His gravestone in the old Presbyterian cemetery, now known as the Stonewall Jackson Memorial Cemetery, reads: "The Reverend George Junkin, D.D., LL. D. Son of Joseph Junkin and Eleanor Cochran of Cumberland County, Pennsylvania Born Nov. 1, 1790 Died May 20, 1868 Founder of Lafayette College, Easton, PA and of Miami University, Oxford, Ohio President of Washington College, 1846–1861, Dr. Junkin died and was buried in Philadelphia and later was removed by his descendants to this the spot he had chosen beside his wife." Ultimately, none of Junkin's political arguments, religious beliefs, or moral qualities mattered to the students or citizens of Lexington in 1861. He was a leading Presbyterian clergyman, a pillar of the community's intellectual life, and had even publicly advocated gradual amelioration of the slaves' condition and eventual emancipation over immediate abolition of the institution of slavery, but it was his staunch, unwavering unionism that trumped all of these other qualities, making his position untenable in one of the most Confederate communities of all, Rockbridge County, Virginia.[52]

NOTES

1. David X. Junkin, *The Reverend George Junkin, DD, LLD: A Historical Biography* (Philadelphia: J. B. Lippincott, 1871); Ollinger Crenshaw, *General Lee's College: The Rise and Growth of Washington and Lee University* (New York: Random House, 1969); James I. Robertson Jr., *Stonewall Jackson: The Man, the Soldier, the Legend* (New York: MacMillan, 1997).

2. George Junkin, *The Integrity of Our National Union vs. Abolitionism: An Argument from the Bible, in Proof of the Position That Believing Masters Ought to Be Honored and Obeyed by Their Own Servants, and Tolerated in, Not Excommunicated from, the Church of God: Being Part of a Speech Delivered before the Synod of Cincinnati, on the Subject of Slavery, September 19th and 20th, 1843* (Cincinnati, OH: R. P. Donogh, 1843), 5–15.

3. On community dynamics, see Thomas Bender, *Community and Social Change in America* (Baltimore, MD: Johns Hopkins University Press, 1982), 17–18. The community of Lexington represents an archetypal *Gemeinschaft* community where the deep connections of blood, intermarriage, and intimate social interaction impacted questions of political loyalty during secession and Civil War.

4. Junkin, *Integrity of Our National Union vs. Abolitionism*, 43–55; Junkin, *Reverend George Junkin*, 1–27.

5. On the American Colonization Society, see Harlow Giles Unger, *Henry Clay: America's Greatest Statesman* (Boston, MA: DaCapo, 2015), 79–80, and Carl Degler, *The Other South: Southern Dissenter in the Nineteenth Century* (New York: Harper and Row, 1974), 22–25; on Whig Party ideology, see Harry L. Watson, *Liberty and Power: The Politics of Jacksonian America* (New York: Hill and Wang, 2006), 211–24.

6. On white southern unionism, see John C. Inscoe and Robert C. Kenzer ed., *Enemies of the Country: New Perspectives on Unionists in the Civil War South* (Athens: University of Georgia Press, 2001); for northern-born Unionists living in the South, see Thomas G. Dyer, *Secret Yankees: The Union Circle in Confederate Atlanta* (Baltimore, MD: Johns Hopkins University Press, 1999); on Unionists in the secession crisis, see Daniel Crofts, *Reluctant Confederates: Upper South Unionists in the Secession Crisis* (Chapel Hill: University of North Carolina Press, 1989), and Barton A. Myers, *Rebels against the Confederacy: North Carolina's Unionists* (New York: Cambridge University Press, 2014); for another experience of Unionists in urban Appalachia (Knoxville, Tennessee), see Robert Tracy McKenzie, *Lincolnites and Rebels: A Divided Town in the American Civil War* (New York: Oxford University Press, 2006). A number of the contributions to *The Civil War in Appalachia: Collected Essays*, ed. Kenneth W. Noe and Shannon H. Wilson (Knoxville: University of Tennessee Press, 1997), examine violence and other methods used by Unionists in Appalachia to put pressure on prosecession and Confederate citizens during 1861. A fantastic work that examines the issues of divided loyalty and the pressure put on political dissidents in Appalachian southern communities is Brian D. McKnight, *Contested Borderland: The Civil War in Appalachian Kentucky and Virginia* (Lexington: University Press of Kentucky, 2006).

7. Junkin, *Integrity of Our National Union vs. Abolitionism*, iv, 11.

8. Junkin, *Integrity of Our National Union vs. Abolitionism*, 43.

9. Junkin, *Integrity of Our National Union vs. Abolitionism*, 12.

10. Richard Carwardine, *Lincoln: A Life of Purpose and Power* (New York: Vintage, 2006), 24–26.

11. George Fitzhugh, *Sociology for the South, or the Failure of Free Society* (Richmond, VA: A. Morris, 1854); George Fitzhugh, *Cannibals All! Or, Slaves without Masters* (Richmond, VA: A. Morris, 1857).

12. Clyde N. Wilson ed., *The Papers of John C. Calhoun*, 38 vols. (Columbia: University of South Carolina Press, 1995), 22:450.

13. Elizabeth Preston Allan, *The Life and Letters of Margaret Junkin Preston* (New York: Houghton, Mifflin, 1903), 28–29. A confluence of factors led to Junkin leaving Miami University in Ohio after only three years in 1844, including his Calvinism, his anti-abolitionist views, and his prompt punishment of wayward students. Alfred Brophy, *University, Court, and Slave: Proslavery Academic Thought and Southern Jurisprudence, 1831–1861* (New York: Oxford University Press, 2016), 54–55, argues that Junkin probably lost his Miami position over the speech/pamphlet.

14. Ron Chernow, *Washington* (New York: Penguin, 2010), 803; Crenshaw, *General Lee's College*, 26–34. On the role of slavery in Virginia universities and other institutions, see Jennifer Oast, *Institutional Slavery: Slaveholding Churches, Colleges, and Businesses in Virginia, 1680–1860* (Cambridge: Cambridge University Press, 2016).

15. Crenshaw, *General Lee's College*, 41–44, 93; Working Group on African American History, "African Americans at Washington and Lee," n.d., www.wlu.edu/presidents-office/issues-and-initiatives/timeline-of-african-americans-at-wandl. The trustees tried to keep the families together when they were sold, but Garland violated the terms of this sale. On June 25, 1835, the Washington College trustees met to discuss this breach and how to handle it.

16. "Rev. George Junkin (1790–1868)," n.d., www.frontierfamilies.net/family/junkin/family/C7GJ.htm; Junkin, *Reverend George Junkin*, 496–97; George Junkin, *Christianity: The Patron of Literature and Science* (Philadelphia: Board of Trustees, 1849).

17. David W. Robson, "'An Important Question Answered': William Graham's Defense of Slavery in Post-Revolutionary Virginia," *William and Mary Quarterly*, 3rd ser., 37, no. 4 (1980), 644–52.

18. Claude LaVarre, "Washington College during the Administration of George Junkin," 35, Ollinger Crenshaw Papers, Special Collections, Washington and Lee University, Lexington, Virginia.

19. LaVarre, "Washington College during the Administration of George Junkin," 2–3, 5, 9; [Henry Ruffner], *Address to the People of West Virginia* (Lexington, VA: R. C. Noel, 1847); Ruffner's 1847 pamphlet argued for a emancipation law that would have gradually ended slavery in the western counties of Virginia over a period of years.

20. LaVarre, "Washington College during the Administration of George Junkin," 11–12. On dueling in Virginia during this period, see A. W. Patterson, *The Code Duello, with Special Reference to the State of Virginia* (Richmond, VA: Richmond Press, 1927); on the function of honor and the duel in the antebellum South, see Bertram Wyatt-Brown, *Honor and Violence in the Old South* (New York: Oxford University Press, 1986), 142–43, and John Hope Franklin, *The Militant South* (Cambridge, MA: Beacon Press, 1956), 133.

21. LaVarre, "Washington College during the Administration of George Junkin," 23.

22. LaVarre, "Washington College during the Administration of George Junkin," 12–13, 15–17. The college also prohibited students from chastising the servants employed by the college. It is unclear whether this rule applied to both slave and free servants or just the latter. "The College servants are under the sole direction of the Faculty. A student shall in no case chastise them, or use abusive language to them."

23. W. G. Bean, *The Liberty Hall Volunteers: Stonewall's College Boys* (Charlottesville: University of Virginia Press, 2005), 4; U.S. Census, 1850, population schedule, Rockbridge County; U.S. Census, 1860, population schedule, Rockbridge County.

24. U.S. Census, 1850, population schedule, Rockbridge County; U.S. Census, 1860, population schedule, Rockbridge County; William A. Link, *Roots of Secession: Slavery and Politics in Antebellum Virginia* (Chapel Hill: University of North Carolina Press, 2003), 37.

25. S. C. Gwynn, *Rebel Yell: The Violence, Passion, and Redemption of Stonewall Jackson* (New York: Scribner, 2014), 142–48, 152–53; Allan, *The Life and Letters of Margaret Junkin Preston*, 28–29.

26. Mary Davidson to Greenlee Davidson, February 21, 1858, Rockbridge Historical Society Manuscript, Special Collections, Washington and Lee University, Lexington, Virginia.

27. Stacey Jean Klein, *Margaret Junkin Preston, Poet of the Confederacy: A Literary Life* (Columbia: University of South Carolina Press, 2007), 41. It is unclear what happened to the slaves. Junkin apparently never mentioned the incident after his recovery.

28. Robertson, *Stonewall Jackson*, 208–9.

29. For a selection of Junkin's dry, erudite editorials, see *Lexington Gazette*, May 10, 1860, June 21, 1860, December 6, 1860, January 3, 1861, and February 21, 1861.

30. West Virginia Division of Culture and History, "A State of Convenience: The Creation of West Virginia," n.d., www.wvculture.org/history/statehood/1860presidentialvote.html.
31. Bean, *The Liberty Hall Volunteers*, 5.
32. LaVarre, "Washington College during the Administration of George Junkin," 31–32.
33. Bean, *The Liberty Hall Volunteers*, 6.
34. LaVarre, "Washington College during the Administration of George Junkin," 29.
35. LaVarre, "Washington College during the Administration of George Junkin," 31.
36. Junkin, *Reverend George Junkin*, 522–23.
37. LaVarre, "Washington College during the Administration of George Junkin," 29–30, 31–33; Robertson, *Stonewall Jackson*, 213; Unger, *Henry Clay*, 3.
38. LaVarre, "Washington College during the Administration of George Junkin," 33; Bean, *The Liberty Hall Volunteers*, 7–8.
39. William C. Fowler, *The Sectional Controversy; or, Passages in the Political History of the United States, Including the Causes of the War between the Sections* (New York: Charles Scribner, 1862) 25. This work was housed in the general stacks of the Leyburn Library at Washington and Lee, where it was found in the early twenty-first century by archivists.
40. Fowler, *The Sectional Controversy*, 25 (George Junkin's marginal notes).
41. George Junkin, *Political Fallacies: An Examination of the False Assumptions, and Refutation of the Sophistical Reasonings, Which Have Brought on the Civil War* (New York: Charles Scribner, 1863), 156–57.
42. Robert J. Driver Jr., *The 1st and 2nd Rockbridge Artillery* (Lynchburg, VA: H. E. Howard, 1987); Lee A. Wallace Jr., *A Guide to Virginia Military Organizations* (Richmond, VA: Virginia Civil War Commission, 1964), 321, 334, 340.
43. Wallace, *A Guide to Virginia Military Organizations*, 257–58.
44. William C. Davis, *The Battle of New Market* (New York: Doubleday, 1975); James McPherson, *Battle Cry of Freedom: The Civil War Era* (New York: Oxford University Press, 1988), 738.
45. LaVarre, "Washington College during the Administration of George Junkin," 10; Robert K. Krick, introduction to Bean, *The Liberty Hall Volunteers*, 2 (number of casualties); Bean, *The Liberty Hall Volunteers*, 79 (on Jackson's staff); W. G. Bean, "The Unusual War Experience of Lieutenant George G. Junkin, CSA." *Virginia Magazine of History and Biography* 76, no. 2 (1968), 181–90.
46. Bean, *The Liberty Hall Volunteers*, 201–10; Douglas W. Bostick, *Memorializing Robert E. Lee: The Story of Lee Chapel* (Charleston, SC: Joggling Board Press, 2005), 96.
47. William Finney Junkin, *New York Times*, April 10, 1900; John M. Junkin, alphabetical card index to the compiled service records of volunteer Union soldiers belonging to units from the State of Pennsylvania, M554, RG 94, National Archives and Records Administration, Washington, DC; Junkin, *The Reverend George Junkin*, 539, 551–52; David X. Junkin, case files of approved pension applications of widows and other dependents of Civil War and later navy veterans (navy widows' certificates), 1861–1910, M1279, National Archives and Records Administration, Washington, DC.

48. Bean, *The Liberty Hall Volunteers*, 194–95; on the Washington College connection to Jackson's original brigade, see James I. Robertson Jr., *The Stonewall Brigade* (Baton Rouge: Louisiana State University Press, 1963).

49. Charles Bracelen Flood, *Lee: The Last Years* (Boston: Houghton Mifflin, 1981), 61–65, 171, 276.

50. *Gettysburg*, produced by Ron Maxwell, Warner Video; *Gods and Generals*, produced by Ron Maxwell, Warner Video; Michael Shaara, *The Killer Angels* (Philadelphia: David McKay, 1974).

51. Junkin, *Reverend George Junkin*, 560–67.

52. Carol Hansen Karsch, "Stonewall Jackson Memorial Cemetery" n.d., http://library2.wlu.edu/SJCemetery. Perhaps Junkin's tombstone aimed to redeem him in the eyes of his old community. While he was the first president who helped breathe life into Lafayette College, which was founded before his arrival, he was definitively not a "founder" of Miami University. He was, in fact, its second president. See *The Biography of a College: Being the History of the First Century of the Life of Lafayette College*, chap. 8, and Walter Havighurst, *The Miami Years, 1809–1984* (New York: G. P. Putnam's Sons, 1984).

"In Search of All That Was Near and Dear to Me"

Desertion as a Window into Community Divisions in Caldwell County during the Civil War

JUDKIN BROWNING

ON SATURDAY, APRIL 27, 1861, HUNDREDS OF RESIDENTS OF Caldwell County, North Carolina, flocked to the county seat of Lenoir in "a state of feverish excitement," as twenty-seven-year-old merchant George W. F. Harper put it. In front of the courthouse, a regimental muster called for volunteers to enlist and serve in a company of North Carolina state troops, and ninety-seven young men enthusiastically joined up. Among those eager enlistees was George Harper's seventeen-year-old younger brother, Samuel, who volunteered for the company that called itself the Caldwell Rough and Ready Guards. Though the married slave owner George did not enlist that spring day, he proclaimed that he and other Caldwell men were "in readiness at any and all times... to march in defense of the rights and honors of the South against the aggressions of the North."[1] Meanwhile, Samuel impatiently prepared for departure, "fearful lest our troops in the field would whip the Yankees... before we got there." On June 3, the company marshaled in the town square for its departure. The younger Harper later recalled that "nearly every man, woman, and child was in Lenoir [that] day... to see us off." Some of the leading men in the county gave brief speeches; ladies waved handkerchiefs and shed tears as the men began their journey to Raleigh, where they would become Company A of the Twenty-Second North Carolina Regiment. The enlistment spectacle only created more excitement among the young farmers and laborers in the greater Caldwell community.[2]

Residents throughout Caldwell County, situated in the foothills of the Blue Ridge Mountains, worked and played together, fought and courted each other. Whigs and Democrats argued at election rallies, read partisan newspapers from Charlotte, Asheville, Winston-Salem, and Raleigh, and debated the best methods through which to increase Caldwell's prosperity. While fewer than three hundred citizens lived within its town limits, Lenoir—just a few miles south of the county's geographic center—served as the market entrepôt and hub for social and political engagement for the county's nearly 7,500 residents (which included 1,088 slaves). Planters and yeoman farmers came to town to purchase goods at stores, trade with the merchants, send their sons to Belvoir or Finley High Academy and their daughters to the Methodist-run Davenport College or the Presbyterian-influenced Kirkwood School, conduct legal business at the courthouse, and attend church. Poorer families may have attended the same churches, but did not send their children to school or frequent the stores (although they would demand that planters provide corn and cloth during lean times). When it came to enlisting for the war, however, it didn't matter what class one came from or what one's political affiliations were. The nearly eleven hundred men from this county who enlisted in the Confederate army knew each other's families, kinship networks, social status, and individual strengths and weaknesses.[3]

The *rage militaire* that overwhelmed Caldwell was somewhat surprising given that the community had been Unionist up until that time. In the 1860 presidential election, the politically Whig county voted for the Constitutional Union candidate, John Bell, over the southern rights Democrat, John Breckinridge, by a 499–229 vote.[4] Residents hoped to maintain the integrity of the United States, something they feared would be impossible with the election of the Republican candidate, Abraham Lincoln (who was not even on the ballot in Caldwell County). William Lenoir, a prominent local planter from Fort Defiance in northeast Caldwell and scion of one of the county's foremost families, feared he would see "all the glory for which our forefathers fought, bled, & died buried in eternal shame & ruin." Six weeks later, on December 22, 1860, William's lawyer brother, Walter, led a "Union meeting" in the Lenoir courthouse. While the attendees recognized the right of southern states to secede, they urged a peaceful "final settlement of the issues between the two sections . . . upon principles that were just to both sides." Emphasizing the conditional nature of their Unionism, however, the residents resolved that "if this just demand is not complied with," then the South "must demand, and if necessary, force, a separation of the two sections."[5]

Local leaders earnestly hoped to avoid secession. Calvin Jones, a Caldwell planter and politician, wrote to Representative Zebulon B. Vance in Washington that "North Carolina and especially Caldwell and Wilkes are deeply attached to the Union," and he confessed, "I cant contemplate a disolution of this government without horror and indignation." Walter Lenoir wrote to Vance in February 1861 advocating that North Carolina adopt a position of "neutrality," rather than join the other seceded states. When the state general assembly called for a referendum on whether to hold a secession convention, Caldwell residents cast 651 votes against it and only 186 in favor of it, indicating a strong desire to remain in the Union. The state narrowly rejected the referendum. However, the county and state's Unionism was conditional. If the Lincoln administration took any step to coerce the southern states that had seceded back into the Union, their resolve would break. Calvin Jones admitted, "The nature of southern people is impulsive and sectional feeling contagious."[6]

Indeed, the contagion spread rapidly after April 15, 1861, three days after Confederates fired on Charleston, South Carolina's Fort Sumter, when President Lincoln issued a proclamation calling for seventy-five thousand troops to put down the rebellion. Governor John Ellis indignantly asserted that the call to arms against the seceded states was a "violation of the constitution and a gross usurpation of power." He unequivocally confirmed the state's resistance: "You can get no troops from North Carolina." Within days of Ellis's refusal to supply soldiers to the Union, the regimental muster that inspired Samuel Harper to volunteer met in Lenoir.[7] In neighboring Wilkes County, a crowd gathered in Wilkesboro on April 30 to call their own volunteers for a company. Local planter and merchant James Gwyn noted there was "a great deal of excitement—most everybody now for the South." There was much drinking, rejoicing, and the occasional fight among excited youths in the course of the celebration. The euphoria, however, did not immediately dissipate the people's deeply ingrained Unionist sentiments. On May 2, Gwyn wrote to his brother-in-law Rufus Lenoir of Caldwell that "the people seemed pretty nearly united in the cause of the South—but I think if an influential man had got up and espoused the other side, he would have had a good many to join him," foreshadowing the dissent that would soon emerge.[8]

The martial excitement reached its peak in Caldwell County in July 1861 with the formation of two companies that would become part of the famed Twenty-Sixth North Carolina Regiment. These two companies provide a window through which to view the growing fractures in a community caught up in the whirlwind of secession in 1861. Fully one-third of the men who enlisted that summer came from households that did not own land. Scions of the wealthiest families in the region enlisted with some of the poorest (who were often tenants or laborers on their farms). Similarly, a third of the first enlistees hailed from the commercial hub of Lenoir, but the remainder came from the river valleys, foothills, and mountain slopes throughout the county.[9] While this might suggest unity across class lines, the seeds did not root deeply in secessionist soil. Outside of the county seat, the bonds attaching men to their units were weaker. When the war brought significant suffering to their families, many of these soldiers abandoned their companies to return to the fields and rocky slopes of their homes.

The outburst of enthusiasm that spring and summer following Lincoln's proclamation created a façade of unity in Caldwell County that masked deep-seated divisions, grounded in class, geography, and politics. Cracks in this veneer developed in 1862, as shortages of food and manpower plagued local communities. The façade crumbled altogether in the summer of 1863, when Caldwell soldiers suffered enormous casualties at Gettysburg. Scores of enlistees left their units to return to their families at home, revealing the lack of strong Confederate identity in the county and exposing the various fissures of the community. The fight became one in their own neighborhoods, with deserters, draft evaders, and militant Unionists fighting against Confederate supporters. Few, however, were clairvoyant enough to see those future travails during the war's first exciting weeks.

DURING THE SUMMER OF 1861, CALDWELL'S LEADERS WORKED TO raise companies by giving speeches throughout the county each Saturday. Residents embraced the martial spirit, holding picnics for the speeches and enlistment musters. On July 15, seventy-nine men enlisted in one company, which called itself the Hibriten Guards after the 2,265-foot-high mountain overlooking Lenoir. They elected thirty-two-year-old Nathaniel Rankin, professor of mathematics at Finley High School and son of a local Presbyterian minister, to be their captain. Eleven days later, sixty-four men joined another company, calling themselves the Caldwell Guards and electing local farmer Wilson A. White as captain. On July 31, Rankin's company mustered to leave for Raleigh. In a public ceremony, Laura Norwood (niece to Rufus and Walter Lenoir) led twelve young girls in white dresses and blue ribbons to present a flag to the unit. The blue banner had been made from a silk dress of Rankin's fourteen-year-old sister, Annie, while his twenty-five-year-old sister, Ella Rankin Harper (George Harper's wife), had decorated the flag with the state coat of arms. Norwood presented the flag to Captain Rankin "with few words fitly spoken," according to one of the young girls in the procession. The company then marched to Hickory, where it boarded a train for Raleigh. Two weeks later, White's company followed.[10]

The companies trekked to Camp Crabtree outside of the state capital, where they trained and received their assignments as Companies F and I of the Twenty-Sixth North Carolina Infantry. The thrill of participating in the great adventure animated the men, and some found validation of their entry into adulthood. W. E. "Eli" Setser from Copenhagen, southwest of the county seat of Lenoir, enlisted at age seventeen alongside several cousins. From Raleigh, he boasted to his father, "i am much of a man." Eli spoiled for a fight. In October, he wrote in a letter home, "We think we can whip six thousand yankees, the bois says they can whip five a peace. I think I can whip six myself."[11]

Others were similarly excited about the fight, but less so about their leaders or their comrades. Eli's cousin Thomas W. Setser wrote to his uncle in late August that if Captain Rankin "don't dew beter tha is a bout ten of us going to leav and go som wher els." In the camp, the yeoman farmer Thomas was surprised by behaviors that he had not witnessed in his social world back in Caldwell. "I hav bin in and at meny plases," Thomas wrote, "but this is the god dams plase that i ever Seen. . . . Som Sings, Som gits drunk, Som curses, Som plays cards," and the men generally partake in "all Sorts of devil ment that white men couda think of." Thomas and many of the boys longed for home, especially the girls of Caldwell. In the summer of 1862, he wrote home to "tell the girls not to fancy [others] too mutch until myself and Eli come home, for they never seen good looking men until they see us."[12]

Thomas's service was not the pure lark that he had envisioned. After the Conscription Act passed in April 1862, he tried to hire a substitute to take his place in the regiment but failed. More firmly committed, his cousin Eli wrote in May 1862, "I expet to Stay in this war tele it eaneds." The excitement of military service, along with their conviction that the Lincoln administration would be bad for them, provided motivation to soldiers such as the Setsers, who hailed from modest landholding farms. As the war dragged on, Eli longed for peace but declared, "I never want it made in this world in the yankees favor. I had as Soon live in Africa as to live under A Lincon Government."[13]

After leaving the training camp, the Twenty-Sixth North Carolina moved to the coast near Beaufort, North Carolina, at the southern tip of the Outer Banks. Their first exposure to combat came on March 14, 1862, at New Bern. A Union expeditionary force led by General Ambrose Burnside defeated the Confederate troops defending that port city, and the men of the Twenty-Sixth barely escaped capture. They had been defending the far right flank of the

Confederate line when their comrades' hasty retreat cut them off from the road to New Bern. The regiment had to ferry across a large creek to escape capture, but under the leadership of their colonel, Zebulon Vance, and lieutenant colonel, Henry King Burgwyn Jr., they succeeded.[14]

The regiment then moved to Richmond in June 1862 to help turn back the Union advance on the Confederate capital. It participated in the Battle of Malvern Hill on July 1, 1862, which Eli Setser called a "very hard fite." The main Confederate attack on the formidable Union position, defended by thirty-one cannons and numerous brigades of infantry, began about 4 p.m. and quickly became a slaughter. Burgwyn wrote that upon being ordered into the fight about 7:00 that evening, the regiment marched to the front in confusion through a forest, while enemy artillery shells "were bursting over our heads & cutting down trees & lopping off huge limbs." They attacked in the fading twilight, so that they "judged of the enemy's position solely by the flashes of his cannons & they were fast enough to leave little doubt." Burgwyn counted at least forty-eight artillery discharges each minute. The regiment suffered relatively few casualties because the lateness and confusion of the attack prevented them from getting closer than four hundred yards to the Union line. Eli Setser walked over the battlefield the next day and found it "a terable Sight to see, mens arms and legs and head shot of[f]." He was frankly amazed to have survived: "They haven't got me yet, But they come mity near it."[15]

After the campaign, the regiment transferred to General J. Johnston Pettigrew's brigade and spent the next nine months trekking throughout eastern Virginia and North Carolina in attempts to threaten Union garrisons in the coastal regions of those states. The Caldwell men found the duty disagreeable. After "marching through mud and wading Creeks," Eli Setser wrote in the spring of 1863, "I had Rather be any whear Els." He would soon get his wish; in May, General Robert E. Lee called the brigade to Virginia to join his army for its Pennsylvania invasion, putting it on the fateful road to Gettysburg.[16]

By the time they joined the Army of Northern Virginia, the resolve of many Caldwell boys was weakening. On May 21, Thomas Setser wrote in a letter home, "You donte now how tired I am of this war." Some war-weary soldiers abandoned the regiment on its march north. Members of the Twenty-Sixth North Carolina shamed the Caldwell deserters in their letters home. On June 8, Andrew H. "Dan" Courtney informed his wife that Perk Miller and Slight Shell, both of the Rough and Ready Guards, "has left there company." On June 17, he claimed that Redmond Church, Davis and Thomas Barber, and one other man had left the company during the march north. On June 21, he related that John McCarver and Larkin Coffey had also just deserted the company. The twenty-six-year-old farmer wrote that although life was rough in the army, "I would rather stay here two years longer than to go home dishonestly." Courtney and the rest of the Caldwell men marched toward their fate in Pennsylvania.[17]

In the early afternoon of July 1, 1863, the Twenty-Sixth North Carolina arrived on the western outskirts of Gettysburg and subsequently received orders to drive the Army of the Potomac's Iron Brigade off McPherson's Ridge. The regiment began its charge, with Company F in the center, nearest the color guard carrying the flag. Simeon Philyaw, a twenty-three-year-old farmer from the western Caldwell mountains, rushed out ahead of the unit and fired the first shot during the charge, which "drew the fire from the Federal lines," their initial broadside "striking the ground about 15 paces in front" of the Confederates. The men advanced, receiving volley after volley of destructive fire from the enemy. One of those volleys wounded both Simeon and his twin brother Gideon. The regiment crossed a creek and pushed up the ridge, suffering enormous casualties along the way. A minié ball broke Dan Courtney's left leg below the knee. His comrades carried him to a field hospital, where Union troops captured him three days later. Union doctors amputated his infected leg, saving his life. He was exchanged and returned to Caldwell in October. Marching next to Courtney was his friend Eli Setser, who fell when a ball shattered one of his femurs close to the hip, preventing any successful operation to amputate. Eli lay on the field that night in agony, knowing he would die. His cousin Thomas, who had fortuitously missed the battle, found him that evening and helped him to the same field hospital where Courtney lay. A Caldwell friend who visited was impressed by Eli's resigned acceptance of his fate: "He told me that he was willing to Die and that he hoped to meet me in heaven." Eli died on July 6, leaving behind his parents and six younger siblings on their modest Copenhagen farm.[18]

Even though it had suffered such heavy casualties on July 1, the regiment nevertheless participated in Pickett's Charge on July 3, where more men fell. During the retreat, the regiment suffered additional casualties on July 14, when Union forces attacked while Lee's army tried to cross the Potomac back into Virginia. The campaign was especially devastating for the Caldwell boys. Members of Company F suffered nearly 100 percent casualties in the battle, while Company I fared little better. Of the 194 men present for duty in the two companies, 43 were killed or died of their wounds, 95 were wounded, and 62 were captured. Only seventeen men returned to Virginia unscathed after the campaign. The battle firmly convinced many that there was no point remaining in the army while their families struggled at home.[19]

WHILE THE CALDWELL SOLDIERS OF THE TWENTY-SIXTH NORTH Carolina faced the monotony of marching across eastern Virginia and North Carolina and ultimately saw the devastation of their ranks in Pennsylvania, their families suffered from food shortages, a lack of help on local farms, uncertainty, and loss. In July 1861, the volunteers had been confident that the war would be short, and they expected the community to bond together to take care of their families during their absence. However, scarcity and speculation affected home-front food supplies from almost the moment the men marched out of town. George W. F. Harper noted in his diary as early as September 12, 1861, that groceries were "high and scarce." Coffee was nearly forty cents a pound; two months later, none could be found anywhere in the county. Corn and bacon were selling for much higher than they had at the beginning of the war.[20]

While the wealthier women organized soldiers' aid societies to provide clothing and care packages for their boys in the army, poorer residents struggled to find enough food to survive the winter. To add to the hardship, 130 more men volunteered in the spring of 1862 for the Twenty-Sixth North Carolina. James Daniel Moore, at home recovering from a leg injury, acted as a recruiting agent for Company F, enlisting sixty-four men to follow him to eastern North Carolina to join the regiment. The new recruits included ten members of the extended Coffey family, as well as twenty-four-year-old William McKesson "Keith" Blalock and his brother, Sam, described as "a good-looking boy." Only Moore knew that Sam was actually Keith Blalock's twenty-year-old wife, Malinda. Keith had refused to enlist unless she could join him. They only served for a month before Keith was discharged for disability and "Sam" revealed her identity to gain her discharge as well.[21]

Just after the spring planting season began and these new volunteers had departed with Moore for the front, unwelcome news arrived. The Confederate government had authorized a conscription law. The law required men between the ages of eighteen and thirty-five to enlist in the army, the effect of which would be to remove even more of the prime labor force from the county. The law was universally reviled in the mountains. One resident sarcastically wrote a Raleigh newspaper editor asking that "after they take the next draw of men from this mountain region," could they ask the president "as an act of *great and special* mercy" to send some of his cronies "to knock the women and children of the mountains in the head, to put them out of their misery?" When the Confederate Congress amended the law on September 27, 1862, extending the uppermost draft age from thirty-five to forty-five, residents feared starvation. One western North Carolinian asserted that authorities "can form no conception of the untold deprivation which would be entailed on our women and children by taking off the men from thirty-five to forty-five." Ultimately, sixty-nine more men joined the Twenty-Sixth North Carolina because of the conscription law.[22]

Labor shortages and volatile weather produced poor harvests in the summer of 1862. One Caldwell resident wrote to a Raleigh newspaper on July 7, 1862, "Our corn crops are unusually backward; as far as wheat and oats, it is almost a failure." He admitted that "all the essentials of life are very scarce and dear, and I very much fear many people will be sorely pressed to support their families." He ominously warned about the growing class divide that he saw developing during the crisis: "In this hitherto patriotic and liberal county, the monster avarice has made its appearance among the most wealthy classes." In antebellum days, wealthy planters had always provided surplus food to their tenants and less prosperous neighbors when crops were not as plentiful. In October 1860, William Lenoir had recounted a typical visit of local poor farmers to Fort Defiance: "One wanted lard; another a bushel of corn; another a half bushel of Irish 'taters'; another about a peck of sweet 'taters.'" Indicating the unending nature of it, William wrote, "They all went away satisfied, *until they come again*." But wartime shortages made this traditional largesse less frequent or generous.[23]

Local authorities and men of means began taking steps to redress the grievances of poorer citizens and nip the growing dissent in the bud. In the autumn of 1862, county magistrates appropriated $1,000 to purchase corn and salt for soldiers' families. In December, Samuel Patterson, owner of a cotton factory and tannery, "contributed to the soldiers' families 100 bunches of spun cotton" and agreed to furnish them one hundred bushels of meal at seventy-five cents a bushel. In April 1863, Elkanah Flowers, a farmer who operated a mill in the southernmost part of the county, sold flour to soldiers' families at five cents per pound and salt at $5 per bushel. Joseph Norwood and other large farmers allowed soldiers' wives and widows to tend small garden plots on their lands. "The women begged to retain their rent, expecting to get it at a low rate. I thought it was best to give it to them," he wrote of his tenants. "We find it necessary here to be very liberal with the soldier's families." These noble attempts to live up to the social contract that was implicitly agreed to when the enlistees marched off to war proved insufficient. Charity would never be enough, and many soldiers believed that only they could adequately provide for their wives, children, or mothers.[24]

Volunteers and conscripts alike started to illegally return to their homes to help their struggling families. Local residents snitched on deserters when they appeared. On November 8, 1862, Ella Harper informed her husband, George (then a lieutenant in Company H of the Fifty-Eighth North Carolina), that one of his soldiers, most likely Gordon Morrow, was illegally at home. Morrow, a landless farm laborer, had enlisted in Company I of the Twenty-Sixth North Carolina on March 15, 1862, but transferred to Company H of the Fifty-Eighth North Carolina eight days later. Ella related his excuse for deserting: his wife "sent him word that she could not get provisions for the winter with no one to help her." Morrow decided he would not leave his wife, seven-year-old son, and one-year-old daughter to struggle at their home outside Lenoir. With provisions dear and relief efforts not enough, Morrow was hardly likely to be the only one to forsake his unit for his family. Ella warned her husband that "if there is not something done for the support of the soldier's families, they *will not* stay away when their wives write to them that they are suffering for the necessarys of life, and many of them are doing that now."[25]

More deserters appeared in Caldwell late that year. On December 10, 1862, from Camp French, near Petersburg, Virginia, Thomas Barber and five members of the Braswell family abandoned Company F of the Twenty-Sixth North Carolina. Brothers James and Thomas Braswell ventured home to provide for their elderly parents and twenty-one-year-old sister on their tiny family farm in Copenhagen. They never returned to their unit. Only two of the deserting Braswells did—R. W. and Robert returned in June 1863 just in time to fight at Gettysburg. On the first day of that battle, R. W. received a wound in the breast (and later deserted from a hospital in Danville, Virginia), while Robert fell with a fatal shot to the head. Thomas Barber returned to his wife and four young daughters in Copenhagen to help them through the winter. He rejoined the regiment in February, only to desert for good on the march to Gettysburg.[26]

At least fifty-five Caldwell County men deserted from the Twenty-Sixth North Carolina, and most of them deserted after Gettysburg. More men would undoubtedly have abandoned their unit, but the carnage of that battle reduced the possible numbers of deserters. The war's overall casualty figures for these two companies are revealing. Of the 420 confirmed Caldwell residents who enlisted in the Twenty-Sixth North Carolina, 115 died in service, 35 became POWs, 5 resigned, 46 received discharges for disabilities, 19 retired due to debilitating wounds, and 49 transferred to another unit (and 19 of those eventually deserted from their new units). Thirty-six percent of the remaining 151 men deserted.[27]

Level of financial resources was the major distinguishing difference between those who deserted and those who did not. The average wealth valuation of the 41 deserters who could be positively identified in the 1860 census was only $744, compared to $2,338 for the identified sample of 239 soldiers who did not leave the unit. Other variables reveal slight but illuminating differences between the two groups: 34 percent of deserters were heads of households compared to 39 percent of nondeserters; 32 percent of deserters were married compared to 36 percent of nondeserters; and 7 percent of deserters came from slaveholding households, while 9 percent of nondeserters did so. The average deserter was slightly younger, at 23.6 years of age, compared to 25.5 for nondeserters. These rather similar statistics reveal that slightly younger men returned home to help out their poorer households. They also did not run the first chance they got; deserters served an average of twenty months before leaving their unit. They came from the rural areas of the county as well. Only eight men from Lenoir deserted, out of eighty-three who enlisted. Meanwhile just over 20 percent of the enlistees from the farming valley of Copenhagen, southwest of Lenoir, deserted, while just under 20 percent of the enlistees from Collettsville, in the foothills west of town, and Patterson, along the ridges north of town, did so. As Kevin Oshnock has persuasively argued in his study of two mountain counties, the more geographically isolated a soldier's family was from commercial centers, the weaker his support for the secessionist cause was and the more likely he was to desert.[28]

If soldiers deserted for a variety of reasons, Governor Zebulon Vance did not think treason was one of them. "I do not believe one case in a hundred," he wrote in May 1862, "is caused by disloyalty." Rather, he attributed it to "home sickness, fatigue, and hard fare." Concern for their families clearly was a major factor for Caldwell deserters. Goodwyn Harris, a thirty-eight-year-old husband and father of eight from Lovelady in southeast Caldwell, had been drafted into the army on January 10, 1863, and reported to Company I of the Twenty-Sixth North Carolina. This tenant farmer deserted in June 1863 as the regiment marched north. He explained to Governor Vance that "my better informed Judgment was over ruled by my sympathy for my family and there well fare." He claimed that his wife was "very weakly" and that his family, primarily daughters ranging in age from one to eighteen, were "dependent on my daily labors for their subsistence, knowing that provisions were all most out of the reach of the poor." After he deserted, he began to fear punishment he might face, especially with local militia units seeking out draft evaders and deserters. He begged the governor for a pardon to "escape punishment for I was honestly in search of all that was near and dear to me." Taking advantage of the governor's amnesty proclamation for deserters in August 1863, Harris returned to his unit, and took a bullet in the thigh at the Battle of Bristoe Station, Virginia, in October.[29]

Once they returned home, many poorer soldiers pilfered from their neighbors to improve their own desperate circumstances, further driving a wedge between their personal concerns and those of the community. Dan Courtney, of Company F, wrote to his wife in Copenhagen on May 30, 1863, "I understand the deserters is stealing up there." He declared that those who committed such deeds would rue their fate: "When peace is made, them that lives to get home will show [deserters] where they stand." While not condoning their actions, Courtney and Governor Vance recognized that deserters were just concerned sons and husbands. Vance warned President Jefferson Davis that their terms of enlistment made the men believe that they "*should* have furloughs, which have never been redeemed." He viewed that as a "*principal*" cause of desertion. Men frantic to get home to care for loved ones found their applications for furloughs rejected; Lee needed every man in the army. "Furloughing is stopped," Courtney wrote. "I knot know whether it will commence again or not[;] if they don't I'm afraid there will be a heap of deserters." He was right; fourteen men left the regiment during the march to Pennsylvania. Nearly one hundred other North Carolinians also abandoned the army at the same time. While he did not desert, Courtney admitted on June 14 that even his unit loyalty had a time limit: "I knot think I can stay here longer than till Christmas without I get to see you." His Gettysburg wound meant he got home before the holidays.[30]

Where one lived within Caldwell mattered, as some deserters found that the public shaming made their presence difficult for their loved ones at home. On June 25, while the army crossed the Potomac River on its way north, Harvey Lafevers and Sidney Hood slipped away from Company I and headed back to Lenoir. News of their absconding had reached the community in comrades' letters about a week before they did. The two men finally arrived home on Friday, July 17. That next day, Lafevers went to Nelson A. Miller, captain of a local militia company, and asked for Miller's assistance in getting back to his unit. Lafevers's wife had indicated that he could not stay. The brick mason had married Clementine Hood, Sidney Hood's cousin, on November 1, 1860, and they resided in the county seat. Lafevers had resisted the initial enlistment enthusiasm during the war's first summer and remained home with his pregnant wife, who gave birth to their first child on August 30, 1861. Perhaps succumbing to peer pressure, Lafevers joined James Moore's recruiting party in March 1862. When, after serving for sixteen months without a furlough, Harvey returned home illegally in July 1863, Clementine "told him plainly that he could not live with her if he did not go back to his Co." She told her disapproving town neighbors that when she learned Harvey had deserted, "she was very mutch hurt and said she would not give him one thing to eat, no I will not give him a drink of water." In the face of this pressure at home, Harvey sought to return. Though he was captured at Bristoe Station and spent eighteen months in a POW camp, he survived the war. His friend Sidney Hood returned to the regiment with him but did not fare so well, dying in prison in Maryland in March 1865.[31]

The Lafeverses' story indicates how geographical variations within the county affected both desertion and community cohesion. Clementine likely sent her husband and cousin back to their units not so much because of patriotism as public pressure. No deserter had yet returned to the town of Lenoir. She had to see her neighbors every day, in the street, in the market, and in church. Harboring or sanctioning a deserter would ostracize her from that community, and more importantly, deny her access to public and private relief provided for soldiers' families. Outspoken women like Ella Harper condemned dishonorable soldiers. Reverend Jesse Rankin delivered a sermon on Sunday August 9, 1863, in Lenoir that excoriated deserters. His daughter declared it "pretty severe on the 'croakers' and 'reconstructionists.'" Even President Davis published a public letter calling on women to persuade deserters to return to their units, or if that failed, to shame them into returning. Clementine felt pressure to conform.[32]

Despite these affirmations of Confederate support in Lenoir, ambivalence and Union sentiments prevailed in the rural regions—especially in the mountainous west and among the farmers in the foothills south and west of the county seat. On July 25, 1863, one local woman wrote to Walter Lenoir, who had lost a leg during the war and had moved to his farm in Haywood County, of "the Union sentiment existing in this county, among the women as well as the men." She echoed Ella Harper's warning of the previous fall: "The women write to their husbands to leave the army and come home and that's the reason that so many of them are deserting." In August, a Caldwell planter declared that "the men who have heretofore avoided the fight" exacerbated matters "by crying out for peace which means submission." As a result, he wrote Walter Lenoir, "desertion is rife." Lenoir wrote his brother that same month about this issue: "I hope you are mistaken in saying that many of the Caldwell people say we are whipped, and the sooner we make terms with our enemies the better."[33]

By the war's third summer, many residents had given up the fight and diverted their efforts from the pursuit of a Confederate victory to a bitter struggle to survive. As early as May 1863, deserters had made their presence felt in the county, committing "depredations" around Lenoir. Dan Courtney was angry to learn that his family's plow had been stolen that month from his farm in Copenhagen. He wrote his wife, "I can't tell you what to do about that plow, but if I ever get home he will wish he had never stolen a plow." In August 1863, one resident denounced a "band of robbers and outlaws who are constantly plundering in the night." While some farmers or deserters may have committed such acts because they were desperate to provide relief for their families, there were, according to certain observers, others who had succumbed to the influence of "malicious folks who have their own wicked designs." These residents had no strong attachment to the Confederacy and saw the war as an opportunity to improve their own poor circumstances. One soldier in the Twenty-Sixth North Carolina recalled after the war that "in the western section of Caldwell County along the foothills of the mountains there was a constant dread of depredations committed by lawless bands of bushwhackers and deserters roaming through the mountains."[34]

The leader of one of those bushwhacking bands was former Twenty-Sixth North Carolina soldier Keith Blalock. After leaving the army, Blalock lived on Grandfather Mountain in western Caldwell, where he attracted deserters and draft evaders to his band. Working with Union authorities in east Tennessee, Blalock launched several raids along the western edge of the county. In the spring of 1864, James Daniel Moore of the Twenty-Sixth North Carolina was recovering from his Gettysburg wounds at his home in the Globe, on the slopes of Grandfather Mountain, when a Unionist group of bushwhackers led by his former recruit attacked his father's home. "We had a regular battle with them," Moore remembered, "in which my father was severely wounded, and we wounded two of them," including Malinda Blalock. A few months later, after Moore had returned to the army, the Blalock gang attacked the home again, crippling two of Moore's cousins. But Blalock had his eye shot out in the contest, essentially ending his bandit career.[35]

In neighboring Wilkes County, nearly five hundred deserters, draft evaders, and militant Unionists armed themselves and took shelter in the hills and hollows, battling Confederate troops sent to round up the outlaws. A soldier described in September 1863 the expeditions to catch deserters in Wilkes: "The deserters ambushed us in the mountain gorges." Many of those wanted men crossed the border into the Brushy Mountains of Caldwell. Though his unit caught eighty deserters, one soldier declared, "the mountains are full of them, and it is about impossible to catch them, as they can move from mountain to mountain as we approach." To make matters worse for hungry civilians, the troops hunting deserters commandeered many of the remaining food supplies. One resident assured Governor Vance that "famine is sure and speedy unless they are removed." Such commandeering was not unusual; when some of General James Longstreet's troops came through Caldwell in the spring of 1864 on their way from Tennessee to rejoin Lee's army in Virginia, residents complained that the soldiers were "impressing corn and eating out the country."[36]

In late June 1864, when a Union raiding force from east Tennessee led by Colonel George W. Kirk crossed through western Caldwell on its way to attack Camp Vance in Burke County, George W. F. Harper, home on furlough recovering from a wound, led the militia in pursuit. Nineteen-year-old Columbus A. Tuttle of the Twenty-Sixth North Carolina, who had been wounded in the right arm at Gettysburg, the left arm at Bristoe Station, and severely in the hip at the Battle of the Wilderness on May 5, 1864, was at home recovering from his injuries. On June 28, Tuttle rode into Lenoir simply to pick up the mail and found himself swept up by the militia band. Though Tuttle protested that he "would be of very little service to them" because of his wounds, he nonetheless joined the group. They pursued the Federal force, which included several Caldwell deserters, inflicting only minor damages.[37]

While Tuttle ultimately returned to the army unit after recovering from his wounds, some of his comrades decided to forsake the cause. Simeon Philyaw had enlisted on July 15, 1861, into Captain Rankin's company and served honorably until badly wounded in the thigh and captured at Gettysburg two years later. After being exchanged in October, Simeon had been allowed to recover at home. He undoubtedly encountered his twin brother, Gideon, who had also been wounded at Gettysburg and had deserted from a Confederate hospital six weeks after the battle. Gideon eventually quit hiding and rejoined his unit in the spring of 1864. Perhaps interactions with his wife or brother weakened Simeon's resolve to return. While at home in early July 1864, Simeon asked Columbus Tuttle if he could borrow his horse to visit relatives in Burke County before returning to the regiment. Tuttle consented, recalling later, "That is the last I ever saw of horse or Phillyaw." Philyaw joined Keith Blalock's band of bushwhackers and soon died from an accidental discharge of his own pistol.[38]

Violence only increased as the war dragged on, widening class, political, and geographic divisions. Rufus Lenoir wrote to his brother Walter in November 1864 that "the robbers & bushwhackers in Wilkes & Caldwell are becoming more insolent & aggressive." No one was ever at ease: "We never go to bed without thinking they may come before morning." The increased discontent in the community, combined with the presence of bushwhackers and deserters, prompted many women to stop their social calls in the neighborhoods. It had simply become too dangerous. One lady living in the mountainous western part of the county cautioned her brother not to come home if he got a furlough but to stay in the relative safety of Lenoir. By early 1865, the divisions had become so strong that many left their homes—some fleeing to Lenoir and others abandoning the county altogether. Union cavalry commander General George Stoneman led a raid through the region in March and April 1865, burning buildings, confiscating food, and plundering homes. Long after Stoneman left, bandits continued to raid the county. Home guard units and returning Confederate soldiers fought these raiders for weeks after the war ended.[39] Residents of the county had been forced to limit their interaction with neighbors, the very activity that helped weave the fabric of the community together. The war and the hardships that it brought had rent that fabric apart.

This study of two companies raised in Caldwell County reveals how a community can simultaneously support and undermine military efforts. The martial furor of 1861 galvanized the previously Unionist area to action, motivating its young men to enlist, prompting local women to create aid societies to support those boys in uniform, and inspiring elite farmers, millers, and merchants to promise to look after families left behind. But the hardships of the war proved too much for the tenuous unity within the county. The devastation of the units at Gettysburg dramatically weakened any devotion to the Confederate cause that remained after two years of fighting, especially while soldiers' families faced food shortages at home. Local efforts at charity proved woefully inadequate to deal with the problems of the home front, and soldiers abandoned their regiment to care for loved ones back home.

Returning deserters revealed the long-standing divisions within the community. Poorer, younger farmers and laborers from the rural regions outside the county's commercial center tended to desert at higher rates than those whose families were better off financially or lived within the tight-knit community of Lenoir. Many of these deserters sought to improve their material conditions at the expense of their neighbors. Subsequent efforts to catch deserters and punish home-front foraging tore further at the bonds of society.

Ultimately, a great many Caldwell men chose loyalty to their families over the Confederate cause. Desperation led to discontent and depredations in the county that continued even after the armies surrendered in the spring of 1865. In this way, the story of these two companies is the story of the war; by examining one community in depth, we can better understand the complexities of war and its human implications.

NOTES

1. George W. F. Harper, quoted in W. W. Scott, *Annals of Caldwell County* ([Lenoir, NC]: Caldwell County Genealogical Society, 1996), 127; George W. F. Harper, quoted in John C. Inscoe and Gordon B. McKinney, *The Heart of Confederate Appalachia: Western North Carolina in the Civil War* (Chapel Hill: University of North Carolina Press, 2000), 68; Weymouth T. Jordan Jr., comp., *North Carolina Troops: A Roster*, vol. 7: *Infantry* (1979; repr., Raleigh: North Carolina Office of Archives and History, 2004), 12–25.

2. Samuel Finley Harper, quoted in Scott, *Annals of Caldwell County*, 227; Nancy Alexander, *Here Will I Dwell: The Story of Caldwell County* ([Salisbury, NC]: Rowan, 1956), 128–29; U.S. Census, 1860, free inhabitants schedule, Caldwell County.

3. Scott, *Annals of Caldwell County*, 20–21; "Lenoir—Past and Present," *News and Observer* (Raleigh, NC), July 2, 1911; G. W. F. Harper, *Reminiscences of Caldwell County, N.C., in the Great War of 1861–65* (Lenoir, NC: G. W. F. Harper, 1913), 9.

4. John L. Cheney, ed., *North Carolina Government, 1585–1979: A Narrative and Statistical History* (Raleigh: North Carolina Department of the Secretary of State, 1981), 1330. National Democratic candidate Stephen Douglas gathered only nine votes.

5. William Lenoir, quoted in William L. Barney, *The Making of a Confederate: Walter Lenoir's Civil War* (New York: Oxford University Press, 2009), 43; *Semi-Weekly Standard* (Raleigh, NC), January 1, 1861.

6. Walter W. Lenoir to Zebulon B. Vance, February 5, 1861, and Calvin C. Jones to Zebulon B. Vance, February 4, 1861, in Frontis W. Johnston, ed., *The Papers of Zebulon Baird Vance*, vol. 1 (Raleigh: State Department of Archives and History, 1963), 95, 97; Alexander, *Here Will I Dwell*, 126. See the *Warrenton (NC) News*, March 22, 1861, on the secession vote.

7. John W. Ellis to Simon Cameron, April 15, 1861, telegram, in Noble J. Tolbert, ed., *The Papers of John W. Ellis*, 2 vols. (Raleigh, NC: State Department of Archives and History, 1964), 2:612.

8. James Gwyn, quoted in Inscoe and McKinney, *Heart of Confederate Appalachia*, 68.

9. Jordan, *North Carolina Troops*, 533–48, 573–89; U.S. Census, 1860, population schedule, Caldwell County.

10. Alexander, *Here Will I Dwell*, 132; William S. Powell, *North Carolina Gazetteer* (Chapel Hill: University of North Carolina Press, 1968), 223; David H. McGee, "'Home and Friends': Kinship, Community, and Elite Women in Caldwell County, North Carolina, during the Civil War," *North Carolina Historical Review* 74, no. 4 (1997): 369; U.S. Census, 1860, free inhabitants schedule, Caldwell County; Jordan, *North Carolina Troops*, 7:533–48, 573–89.

11. W. E Setser to W. A. Setser, August [n.d.], 1861, and October 14, 1861, in "The CSA 'Setser Letters,'" pt. 1, http://freepages.genealogy.rootsweb.ancestry.com/~wlsetzer/fam_setzer/csa-letters-part-1.html.

12. T. W. Setser to unknown, August 25, 1861, in "The CSA 'Setser Letters,'" pt. 1, http://freepages.genealogy.rootsweb.ancestry.com/~wlsetzer/fam_setzer/csa-letters-part-1.html; T. W. Setser to W. A. Setser, June 17, 1862, in "The CSA 'Setser Letters,'" pt. 2, http://freepages.rootsweb.com/~wlsetzer/genealogy/fam_setzer/csa-letters-part-2.html.

13. W. E. Setser to W. A. Setser, May 31, 1862, in "The CSA 'Setser Letters,'" pt. 2, http://freepages.rootsweb.com/~wlsetzer/genealogy/fam_setzer/csa-letters-part-2.html; W. E. Setser to family, April 20, 1863, in "The CSA 'Setser Letters,'" pt. 3, http://freepages.rootsweb.com/~wlsetzer/genealogy/fam_setzer/csa-letters-part-3.html. Eli and Thomas each came from households that owned $2500 in real estate (U.S. Census, 1860, population schedule, Caldwell County).

14. Earl J. Hess, *Lee's Tar Heels: The Pettigrew–Kirkland–MacRae Brigade* (Chapel Hill: University of North Carolina Press, 2002), 7–16.

15. W. E. Setser to W. A. Setser, July 16, 1862, in "The Setser Letters," pt. 2, 27; Henry King Burgwyn Jr. to Anna Greenough Burgwyn, July 14, 1862, Burgwyn Family Papers, Southern Historical Collection, University of North Carolina at Chapel Hill (hereafter SHC).

16. W. E. Setser to W. A. Setser, April 20, 1863, and March 24, 1863, in "The Setser Letters," pt. 3, 12, 11; Hess, *Lee's Tar Heels*, 34–118.

17. T. W. Setser to W. A. Setser, May 21, 1863, in "The Setser Letters," pt. 3, 12; A. H. Courtney to Mary E. Courtney, June 8, 1863, June 17, 1863, June 21, 1863, and May 31, 1863, Courtney Letters, Society for the Historical Preservation of the 26th Regiment NC Troops.

18. J. T. C. Hood, "The 26th Regiment at Gettysburg," *Lenoir (NC) Topic*, April 8, 1896; Jordan *North Carolina Troops*, 7:544; Judkin Browning, "Reverberations of Battle," *Civil War Monitor* 7, no. 2 (2017): 61–62.

19. Judkin Browning, "Deconstructing the History of the Battle of McPherson's Ridge: Myths and Legends of the Twenty-sixth North Carolina on the First Day's Fight at Gettysburg," *Gettysburg Magazine* 53 (July 2015): 14–30.

20. George W. F. Harper, quoted in Alexander, *Here Will I Dwell*, 135–36.

21. McGee, "'Home and Friends,'" 369–72; Jordan, *North Carolina Troops*, 7:534–48, 573–89; "Interesting Narrative of the Civil War," *Raleigh (NC) Morning Post*, February 11, 1900.

22. Quoted in Inscoe and McKinney, *Heart of Confederate Appalachia*, 112; *North Carolina Standard* (Raleigh), November 18, 1863.

23. Letter from "Caldwell," *North Carolina Standard* (Raleigh), July 23, 1862; William Lenoir, quoted in Barney, *Making of a Confederate*, 43.

24. Inscoe and McKinney, *Heart of Confederate Appalachia*, 169, 170; *North Carolina Standard* (Raleigh), December 10, 1862, April 18, 1863.

25. Ella Harper, quoted in McGee, "'Home and Friends,'" 374; Ella Harper, quoted in Inscoe and McKinney, *Heart of Confederate Appalachia*, 114; U.S. Census, 1870, population schedule, Caldwell County. Harper refers to the deserter as Nathan Morrow, but he had died three months earlier on August 8, 1862. She must be referring to Gordon Morrow, who de-

serted, stayed home over a year, was arrested, and returned to his unit on March 25, 1864 (Jordan, *North Carolina Troops*, 14:383).

26. Jordan, *North Carolina Troops*, 7:534, 536; U.S. Census, 1860, free inhabitants schedule, Caldwell County.

27. Jordan, *North Carolina Troops*, 7:533–48, 573–89. I cross-referenced every Caldwell County soldier with the 1860 census to confirm residence and build demographic profiles from which I derived the numbers used in the text.

28. Kevin David Oshnock, "The Isolation Factor: Differing Loyalties of Watauga and Buncombe Counties during the Civil War," *North Carolina Historical Review* 90, no. 4 (2013): 385–413.

29. Zebulon B. Vance to Jefferson Davis, May 13, 1863, in Joe A. Mobley, ed., *The Paper of Zebulon Baird Vance*, vol. 2 (Raleigh, NC: Office of Archives and History, 1995), 152; Goodwyn Harris to Zebulon B. Vance, July 13, 1863, Governors Papers, State Archives of North Carolina, Raleigh (hereafter SANC); Jordan, *North Carolina Troops*: 7:579; U.S. Census, 1860, free inhabitants schedule, Caldwell County.

30. A. H. Courtney to M. E. Courtney, May 30, 1863, June 14, 1863, Courtney Letters; Zebulon B. Vance to Jefferson Davis, May 13, 1862, in Mobley, *Papers of Zebulon Vance*, 152.

31. N. A. Miller to Zebulon B. Vance, July 21, 1863, Governors Papers, SANC; U.S. Census, 1860, free inhabitants schedule, Caldwell County; U.S. Census, 1900, population schedule, Caldwell County; North Carolina Marriage Index, 1741–2004, https://search.ancestry.com/search/db.aspx?dbid=8909; Jordan, *North Carolina Troops*, 7:580–81.

32. McGee, "'Home and Friends,'" 374, 380.

33. Julia P. Gwynn to Walter Lenoir, July 25, 1863, Joseph C. Norwood to Walter Lenoir, August 13, 1863, and Walter Lenoir to Rufus Lenoir, August 17, 1863, Lenoir Family Papers, SHC.

34. McGee, "'Home and Friends,'" 379; A. H. Courtney to M. E. Courtney, May 31, 1863, Courtney Letters; C. A. Tuttle, "Incidents Which Happened in Caldwell County in 1864," *Lenoir (NC) News-Topic*, May 4, 1922, box 72, folder 21, Civil War Collection, SANC.

35. Alexander, *Here Will I Dwell*, 136–37; "Interesting Narrative of the Civil War," *Raleigh (NC) Morning Post*, February 11, 1900.

36. *Weekly Observer* (Fayetteville, NC), September 22, 1863; Inscoe and McKinney, *Heart of Confederate Appalachia*, 133–34.

37. Alexander, *Here Will I Dwell*, 138; Tuttle, "Incidents Which Happened in Caldwell County in 1864"; Jordan, *North Carolina Troops*, 7:547.

38. Scott, *Annals of Caldwell County*, 247; Jordan, *North Carolina Troops*, 7:544; Tuttle, "Incidents Which Happened in Caldwell County in 1864."

39. Rufus Lenoir, quoted in Inscoe and McKinney, *Heart of Confederate Appalachia*, 105; McGee, "'Home and Friends,'" 383; Alexander, *Here Will I Dwell*, 139–43.

Fighting the "Laurel War"

The Civil War inside the Henry Household

STEVEN E. NASH

CORNELIA CATHERINE SMITH AND WILLIAM LEWIS HENRY MAY seem a somewhat odd match. Married on April 5, 1855, William was nearly thirteen years older than his almost twenty-one-year-old bride. Perhaps it was for that reason that she routinely referred to him in her diary as "Mr. Henry." They constitute an unusual pair in terms of where they grew up as well. William Henry was raised in mountainous Buncombe County, North Carolina, a far cry from the Cotton Kingdom that Cornelia knew in Union, South Carolina. This nosy historian has not discerned how the couple met. Perhaps they met on one of William's many business trips. Given the popularity of the North Carolina mountains as a getaway for South Carolina planters, it may be that the couple met in Asheville or at the Henrys' Sulphur Springs Hotel in the Hominy Valley west of Asheville. Her journal tells us a great many things, but not how she met her husband. This one detail, at least, does not matter; from all accounts, the Henrys' marriage was one of love, fidelity, and respect.[1]

Family formed the foundation of William and Cornelia's household, their neighborhood, and their community. It is among family that people are most themselves, where people have face-to-face interactions and intimate connections are made, remade, or lost. Led by patriarch Robert, the Henrys were accustomed to drama. No one could accuse Robert Henry, a Revolutionary War veteran, land speculator, lawyer, and adventurer, of squandering his life. His adventures led to his discovery of a sulphur spring—with his slave known as Buncombe Sam—around which he built a profitable tourist destination. A bache-

FIGURE 1. Wedding photo of William Lewis Henry and
Cornelia Catherine Smith Henry, April 5, 1855.
North Carolina Collection, Pack Memorial
Public Library, Asheville, North Carolina.

lor until his forties, Robert eventually married Dorcas Bell Love, a match that amplified his wealth and class standing by wedding his fortunes to those of the Love family in southwestern North Carolina. Robert and Dorcas's daughter Eliza married Reuben Deaver, who became his father-in-law's partner in the Sulphur Springs Hotel. Robert was a suspicious person by nature, and his distrust of those around him only grew after he and Dorcas divorced in the early 1850s. Reuben's death amid a bitter legal struggle with his father-in-law left the family's ownership of the property in doubt. William Henry, Robert's son, solved the problem when he bought it at auction for almost $1,400. The purchase included the hotel and ancillary land holdings, which made Cornelia's husband a significant entrepreneur and landlord in the Hominy Valley.[2]

Sulphur Springs became Cornelia and William Henry's home. Although fertile farmland, the Hominy Valley could not sustain cotton plantations like the one Cornelia's father, William Smith Sr., owned in South Carolina. Still, western North Carolina was home to an elite class akin to that she left behind.

William Henry owned $45,000 worth of real property (including the hotel, the farm where his family lived, and the surrounding rental parcels) and $22,000 of personal property in 1860. But his home was more than that. The Sulphur Springs property also consisted of a mill, a post office, and a school, Sulphur Springs Academy. Collectively, the Henrys' home constituted the central hub of the community not only for the white and black members of the Henry household but for the broader neighborhood as well. Brother-in-law Reuben Deaver had been the community's postmaster, and William assumed that position on June 9, 1853, following Deaver's death. So, the Henry family and household was the foundation for the community surrounding their home.[3]

Household relationships anchored in the family and in labor roles forged those of different races, classes, religions, politics, places, and regions into a community in the fertile Hominy Valley. It was a place like many others in the South, where white people paternalistically viewed their slaves as members of their extended family. Family was therefore both a basis for household relationships and a metaphor for the larger community. But the Civil War and Reconstruction would challenge, break, and rebuild these core relationships. William and Cornelia Henry's experiences reveal how the Sulphur Springs community came to redefine labor and race relations through the Civil War and its aftermath. The transformation of basic relationships makes clear how powerful labor was in defining (and redefining) community bonds and how divided loyalties, internal rivalries, and bitter struggles could destroy even a community's most fundamental relationships.[4]

The Henrys' household benefited significantly from slavery. While the elder Robert kept most of the enslaved people in his name, the members of his family, like the members of many wealthy families in the mountains and the South, broadly profited from the institution even if they did not own slaves themselves. Between 1830, when Robert Henry owned ten slaves, and 1860, the family's fortunes had transformed. In 1860, William owned nine slaves and his brother James owned twelve. Their mother passed away in 1857, which enhanced the standing of Robert and Dorcas's youngest son, James, most directly. Meanwhile, Dorcas's brother James R. Love stood ready to help with his eighty-five slaves in neighboring Haywood County. Wealthy slaveholding families often spread their chattel among the various kinship branches, and the Henrys were no different. Sons Robert, William, and James Henry borrowed, rented, and purchased African Americans from their father, mother, uncle, grandfather, father-in-law, and other relatives. When in need, white family members could reasonably rely on their kin to lend them an extra set of black hands. And in the case of William and Cornelia Henry, her father, William Smith Sr., was a more distant—but large—safety net.[5]

The practice of shifting and sharing enslaved people with family members wreaked havoc on African Americans' relationships. In 1837, an enslaved man of approximately seventeen years named George passed from John Henry to Robert Henry; in 1863, he then passed from Robert to William. George's wife, Ruth, belonged to Dorcas B. Henry, which meant that she and George were also separated when Robert and Dorcas divorced. Ruth remained in the area and moved closer to her husband when James L. Henry inherited her from his mother in 1857. Another enslaved family suffered repeated separations due to the Henrys' wheeling and dealing. Sam and Tena were both under the control of Robert Henry's son-in-law, Reuben Deaver, in the 1840s. Though Sam remained the property of the Henry family patriarch, Tena and their nine children were sold to James R. Love, Dorcas Henry's brother, in 1848. Deaths and sales further shuffled Sam and Tena's family as one daughter, Betsy, passed to James L. Henry in the 1850s.[6]

Hired labor formed another cog in the Henrys' economic machine. William and Cornelia's daily life revolved around work or its management. She sewed, cleaned, and cared for their two young children. He managed the hotel, went to market, and supervised the agricultural workers in the fields. The enslaved performed the bulk of the manual labor with some assistance from hired white labor. The 1860 federal population census provides evidence of this dynamic; beyond the four Henrys, the household included a white farm laborer, Richard Pinkney Allen, and nine people of color. But that is only part of the picture. William Henry hired a white laborer named A. Fullbright and a mulatto boy named Frank Ellison to work the stills. Other whites—George Jones, Carse Wells, and Bill Parker—cultivated the farm. Enslaved George tended the mill while France Corn repaired the hotel. On January 21, 1861, William Henry hired another white worker, J. Snelson, for one year. He further supplemented his workforce by hiring several African Americans from his uncle, James Love Sr., on January 9, 1861.[7]

The hotel was a tremendous asset, but its management caused headaches. William employed C. C. Terry and his family to manage it, but William grew unhappy with their work and attempted to turn them out in late January 1861. Perhaps because the Terrys took the news poorly, William went to Asheville in early February to swear out a complaint against them. He told them to leave on February 6. Ultimately, arbitrators granted the Terrys $500 rent for the house for the coming year, while William Henry received nothing for the previous year. Henry's fortunes took a profound turn for the worse on the night of March 13, 1861, when the Sulphur Springs Hotel burned to the ground. The blaze consumed the hotel, an estimated $12,000 loss, and severely damaged William Henry's financial standing. Already in debt to his father and others, creditors called William to court for roughly $6,000 owed.[8]

William's uncertain finances mirrored the daily declining prospects of the Union. Even before fire consumed the hotel, fire-eating secessionists had gained support in Buncombe County. Although the Henrys supported secession, most white mountaineers adopted a cautious or conditional approach to the crisis. Men of a Whiggish political persuasion condemned extremism on both sides, while other residents, mostly of the Democratic stripe, urged their fellow North Carolinians to secede. William and Cornelia Henry followed events closely. Both sympathized with the nascent Confederacy. On January 7, 1861, Cornelia confessed her anxiety about the future of her native South Carolina. After the "Black Republican" Abraham Lincoln captured the presidency, South Carolina left the Union, and Cornelia worried about the future. As the winds of war swept across the Blue Ridge, Cornelia faced the cold, bracing reality that war meant death and that her husband might join the fight. William's brothers, Robert M. and James L. Henry, quickly joined the Confederate ranks. William was thirty-seven years old, and his soldier talk tormented his wife. Confederate guns outside Fort Sumter in Charleston Harbor had barely ceased firing when Cornelia acknowledged her fears for his life. Following North Carolina's secession on May 20, 1861, William joined a militia company drilling in Asheville. Cornelia knew that war would leave many local families sad and vulnerable once their "[male] protector has been called away." She had no desire for her family to be among them.[9]

Should he go to war, William Henry commanded enough enslaved African Americans to sustain the farm, household, and mill in his absence. Without the hotel, agriculture and milling became the Henrys' economic lifeblood. The Henrys oversaw a mixed labor force of slaves and hired whites. The twenty-four-year-old farm laborer Richard Pinkney Allen worked for the family until he enlisted in the Twenty-Fifth North Carolina Infantry on July 22, 1861. Perhaps Allen was no longer needed after Henry purchased a thrashing machine on July 21. Even with his new mechanized thrasher, Henry depended on his enslaved men—George, Sam, and Andy—to keep the mill and farm going. When he could, he hired additional help. In late July 1863, Henry hired five slaves from a neighbor, agreeing to pay two bushels of grain for one week's worth of work or for eight hours of labor for the month. Even late in the war, he found African American labor available, contracting a black man named

Jim Common in February 1864. William Henry also benefited from his adjacent rental properties, which were occupied through most of the war.[10]

When Henry finally marched to war, he did not go far. By joining a home guard unit, William was able to continue to protect and comfort his wife and family. His localized service allowed him to spend significant time at home, partially preserving his presence as master. Aiding William in managing the farm was Jim Parker. Neither Henry nor Parker proved averse to torture as a means of control. An African American slave named Jim suffered Parker's "discipline" on December 11, 1861. Jim promptly ran away and evaded capture until he returned voluntarily five days later. William Henry evidently got so frenzied "correcting" an enslaved person that he injured his foot in the process.[11]

Cornelia had to assume a greater role in managing the slaves whenever William answered the call of military duty. Raised in the Cotton Kingdom, Cornelia was comfortable with slavery; however, she seemed to be less at ease with a whip in her hand. Enslaved people sensed the difference. Early in the war, Cornelia observed that the slaves "don't like to obey me." Their resistance stoked Cornelia's temper and steeled her commitment to the institution. Within the household, an area generally seen as part of a woman's domain in the antebellum South, her relationships with African Americans appeared steadier. She relied heavily on a small group of enslaved women—Celia, Fannie, Jinnie, Tena, and Atheline—to help with domestic chores. Another vital household function, cooking, demonstrated the volatility within Cornelia's domestic world. Cornelia did not cook, and the Henrys failed to settle on a single enslaved woman to regularly prepare their meals. This was a constant source of frustration for Cornelia. Finding a chicken feather in the family's coffee in September 1861, she denounced her kitchen workers as the "dirtiest cooks" in the world. On another occasion, she threatened to whip Jinnie for making poor coffee. Jinnie ran from the house and wept hysterically when Cornelia came for her. If Jinnie was playing on Cornelia's uncertainty over or discomfort with punishing slaves, it worked. Her mistress confessed that she had a hard time watching the family's overseer, Jim Parker, beat Fannie in late April 1862. Cornelia may have lamented the punishment and shied away from administering beatings herself, but, significantly, she neither intervened on Fannie's behalf nor complained about Parker's brutality. The frustration of dealing with slaves led Cornelia to admit that she "often wish(es) there was not a negro in the world."[12]

Probably no member of the community vexed Cornelia quite as much as George. She never trusted him. One reason for that distrust was a fight that occurred on the night of February 26, 1861. Her husband issued a pass for George to visit his wife, Ruth, on James L. Henry's farm. Around 11 o'clock that night, two patrolmen alerted the Henrys that George was playing the fiddle for the Terrys at the still house. William Henry was livid. He had expressly told George not to go to the still house. Yet the two men managing the hotel had had George come and fiddle for them. The merrymaking lasted well into the night, much to the irritation of George's owner. When Henry confronted the group, a fight broke out. One of the white men suffered a slight puncture wound through his ear. William Henry and George, however, escaped with only minor injuries.[13]

Maybe it was the bitterness from that night that led Cornelia to reflexively suspect George anytime something suspicious happened. Whites blamed George and Andy for the theft of some wheat in the summer of 1861. The relationships between black and white members of the Henry household defy neat categorization; George appeared at various times to be a welcome member of the household and at other times a rogue threatening its very survival. Cornelia did not seem to mind when George played his fiddle for her children's entertainment in 1862. But one suspects that the fiddle's lively tune masked a much more somber beat. George's wife, Ruth, was "confined" in early 1862, likely with the couple's child. Since they lived apart, George could not always be there. Perhaps he wandered and asked for more time away, leading Cornelia to derisively say that George now believed he was free. His owners dispelled that notion forcefully. No matter what George might have said, done, or felt, his owners made sure he knew the whip's sting for allegedly stealing corn in late May 1864.[14]

She may have wished black people away, but reading between her complaints gives glimpses of African Americans' lives beyond their owners' control. At several points in her diary, Cornelia offers narrow windows into African Americans' own community actions. Slaves across the South celebrated Christmas to the fullest of their abilities. The holiday held deep religious meaning and offered a respite from work and time with family. Cornelia noted that George hosted "most of the negroes" at the annual celebration, and she was relieved when the "frolicking" ended on December 30, 1862. A logical conclusion based on the scrutiny leveled against George is that he was something of a leader among the enslaved. He held a position of standing among the local enslaved people as the operator of the Henrys' mill, a position he held despite the fight with the Terrys and his mistress's misgivings. William L. Henry trusted him. So, too, it seemed, did local blacks.[15]

There is no denying the intimacy—wanted or not—that existed between the white and black members of the Henry household. Cornelia noted several occasions during the war when her children found distractions from their troubles by hunting huckleberries, chinquapins, or other natural bounty with members of the enslaved population. Even George could bring joy through his fiddling. Cornelia had an emotional attachment to Atheline, which was made apparent when Atheline became ill. Cornelia visited Atheline in her sickbed and genuinely worried about her. Her expressions of concern, however, demonstrated the distance between them. She remembered Atheline as a "good nurse" who was kind to her mistress and the white children. Almost wistfully, Cornelia recalled how Atheline could keep her children engaged through an entire church service. One suspects that Rose, who Cornelia labeled as "careless," could not do that. Atheline was a constant companion for the Henry children, an occasional cook, and great help to Cornelia in her household responsibilities. When Atheline died shortly after giving birth to a child of her own on July 16, 1864, Cornelia's heartbreak was palpable.[16]

For all that fondness, the Henrys remained committed to the racial social order. When Elvira, another of Tena's daughters, visited on March 13, 1864, Cornelia could not help but view her as a commodity. She described Elvira as a "good negro" and wished "she was mine." While Cornelia dreamed of the comfort that owning Elvira might offer her, she could not find common ground with Tena as a mother. Cornelia could neither see Tena as more than a slave nor her children as much more than assets. The older black woman's family was spread out across several farms. Daughters Elvira, Betsey, and Leizana all lived on different farms. Tena visited Betsey and Leizana when they were sick, but Cornelia gave only passing notice to Betsey's death in June 1864. When Tena's son, Charlie, decided to marry one of Stephen Jones's slaves, Cornelia complained that he was too young and justified her own opposition by recording Tena's displeasure with the match. And for all the closeness and concern for Atheline, Cornelia apparently loved her for loving her kids. Nothing in her diary suggests commiseration with Tena over Atheline's death. Tena grieved for children that Cornelia viewed as capital.[17]

Military service further strained relationships within the household and community. As a member of the home guard, William frequently engaged in countermeasures against local Unionists, deserters, and guerrillas. This regional war within the larger war, which his wife dubbed the "Laurel War," sent Cornelia's husband frequently into Madison County, North Carolina, as well as across the border into Greene County, Tennessee. Dissenters and agents of the state engaged in a reciprocal cycle of violence along the border, which rippled through communities like Sulphur Springs. Due to the prominence of the Henrys' household within the neighborhood, it is not surprising that these disputes sometimes came to their doorsteps. On April 2, 1862, a commotion outside the Henrys' house drew the attention of everyone inside. Nineveh C. Norris of the Thirty-Ninth North Carolina came for a deserter, Dick Night, from the same regiment. William and Cornelia Henry had been in the habit of hiring members of the Night family to do a variety of jobs around their property. According to Cornelia, "all the Night's [sic] were in the yard" presumably protecting their kin from having to go back to the army. Tom Hendrix, whose sister had recently married Night in a ceremony performed by William Henry less than a week earlier, bolstered his new brother-in-law's resistance. In the end, Norris and Night left to return to their regiment but soon became victims in the Laurel War. "The tories on Laurel took them up & treated them very badly," Cornelia noted in her diary on April 13.[18]

Arguably the greatest personal threat to the Henrys emanated from their splintered household. Midway through the war, if not earlier, Richard Pinkney Allen, or "Pinck" as Cornelia knew him, the farm laborer within William and Cornelia's household in 1860, was no longer welcome in their home. Allen had deserted from the Twenty-Fifth North Carolina Infantry Regiment and concealed himself in the mountains. Rumors abounded about his location and his intentions. For William Henry, none of this was good. In Sulphur Springs and the Hominy Valley, the Henry farm was a center of community engagement, a place where people worked, got their mail, attended church, went to school, and visited. People came and went frequently; Cornelia and her husband must have feared what must have seemed like an inevitable confrontation. How could Allen avoid such a central community hub? On November 19, 1862, she denounced Allen as a man of bad character, claiming that he "was no use when at home & now he is no use to his country." She drew a direct connection between Allen's hiding out and reports "of a good many hen roosts being robbed." That following summer, Allen's brother-in-law, John Wilkerson Bryson, apparently deserted from the Sixtieth North Carolina Infantry Regiment. Cornelia felt sorry for Allen's wife, Rachel, who pleaded for leniency to Cornelia's nephew Harrie Deaver. But when Deaver told her he could do nothing, Cornelia no doubt agreed. Matters escalated when Allen threatened to burn the Henrys' mill and kill William Henry. Meanwhile, the home guard did its best to corral Allen and bring him to justice. Whether it was justice or not, Allen met his end when someone shot him through the side in April 1864.[19]

Allen's death failed to bring an end to the Laurel War. As rumors swirled in mid-December 1864 that George W. Kirk's Union raiders were advancing on Asheville, Cornelia's prayers intensified. "Father of mercy," she pleaded, "hasten the glad day when peace will once more smile on my bleeding country." The growing Union military threat likely accelerated slavery's unraveling during the war's final months. Masters and mistresses struggled to maintain their labor amid increasing signs of Confederate defeat. On March 1, 1865, an enslaved woman and her two children came to the Henrys' home seeking refuge and food. The black woman's Confederate owner was a prisoner of war, so Cornelia took them in, but pointedly refused to provide any provision.[20] On the Henrys' farm, none of the slaves deserted the farm, and Fannie, Celia, and Jinnie worked through early March. But trouble loomed. Theft increased. Pinkney Henry's horse was stolen, and "some rogue broke in the back end of the smoke house & stole two sides of meat" in mid-March. By that point, Fannie and Jinnie no longer worked peacefully. Celia was "nicer about things," Cornelia noted, which may have been a result of her recently becoming a mother (and sensing that she and her child might soon be free).[21]

Perhaps unsurprisingly, George stood at the center of the Henry family's difficulties. Reflecting his apparent position of standing within the African American community—and probably experiencing a certain sense of schadenfreude—George notified William L. Henry that the slaves would leave over the coming days. One reason given was the fear of forced military service. The next day, Stephen Jones arrived at the Henrys' door with news that one of his enslaved men had run off with the Henrys' slave, Charlie. Tena and Sam, Charlie's parents, may have known of their son's plans and appeared somewhat vexed by it.[22]

African Americans across Buncombe County fled slavery. On March 27, 1865, Cornelia reported that roughly one hundred African Americans left Asheville and its surrounding communities. She pitied the "poor ignorant things," whom she felt had been duped by the "trash of the country." Nevertheless, Tim and Charlie were gone, and their absence threatened the Henrys' crop. Cornelia anticipated—probably hoped—that George would soon follow. A friend of hers, Till Morris, reported that her slave, John, had recently gone off with her father's slave, Ben. Other women noted the departure of large numbers of enslaved men and women as the Union army passed through Asheville. Most slave owners, it seemed to Cornelia, had lost someone. And it made her vengeful. Rumors that Confederate troops had fired on men and women asserting their freedom gave Cornelia grim satisfaction. "I hope they killed some," she confessed.[23]

The former slaves' assertiveness grew stronger in the spring and summer following the Confederacy's demise. Cornelia blamed trouble at the Henrys' mill, easily attributable to the economic crisis attached to Confederate defeat, on George, who she thought pocketed the toll for himself. Showing her freedom, Tena refused to sew. George further angered his former mistress when he traveled to U.S. Army headquarters in nearby Hendersonville to swear out a complaint against her husband in late June. Everything was fluid. Was George stealing? Collecting money that he rightfully felt was his? Was he leaving? Freedpeople came and went. Tena left but later returned when Fannie departed. Cornelia asked Tena to do the wash, but the freedwoman said no. Celia was still there and working, but Sam was "fixing up" a house of his own. Cornelia did not much care what happened to Sam, as she felt that he and George—with Federal soldiers' help—had stolen from them during the brief Union occupation over the summer. Still, the loss of someone who had been with his family for as long as he could remember left William Henry "looking ten years older." African Americans' freedom threatened to redefine the community and neighborhood.[24]

The rupture was permanent, but the confusion passed rather quickly. For all the handwringing and bitterness in Cornelia's immediate postemancipation diary, things returned to a relative calm by 1866. As they had done for years, the Henrys concluded labor contracts for the coming year in January 1866. A freedman named Boston was hired to work the bucket machine and a black woman named Mary agreed to work for the Henrys as well. Yet so much had changed. African Americans' mobility had a profound effect on the community. One month after starting work, Boston left. No reason was given, and no reason was necessary for a free man to leave. Mary earned twenty-five cents per day for her labor. Such appeared to be the new reality of domestic work. While there was no shortage of women for hire, they turned over frequently and worked only for wages. Former slaves, Celia and Rose, left the Henrys for a fresh beginning in Kentucky. During the summer, a string of women—Lizzie Bentley, Jane Jones, and Ella Lawson—were hired for seventy-five cents per week. Arrangements proved tenuous under these new conditions. The day after Jane Jones was hired, Jinnie left, apparently angry that Jones received more money than she did. Family and friendship bonds could shape the terms of labor. When Cornelia then dismissed Jinnie for good on July 22, Harriet quit and went with her. Neither returned.[25]

The Civil War and the localized Laurel War within that larger conflict strained the bonds within the Henrys' household and the Sulphur Springs community. Emancipation freed the family's slaves, which redefined in fact if not in practice the white family's household. Many of their former slaves left, but others remained as tenants, domestic laborers, or hired hands. Antebellum tenancy sharecropping agreements provided a template that landowners like William Henry could use to negotiate labor contracts with freedpeople. It is striking how quickly Cornelia's anger from the war's immediate aftermath dissipated as she and her family settled into these new arrangements. Prewar sharecropping practices gave a sense of continuity to events following emancipation, somewhat smoothing the Henrys and their community's transition to Reconstruction.

But if family was the foundation for community, then the costs of the war were severe. Arguably the greatest change in the Henrys' community was within their family. During the war, Robert M. Henry initiated a lawsuit against his brother William over the Sulphur Springs and other properties. Robert claimed that he and William had agreed to own jointly any property left to them by either of their divorced parents. William asserted that the apparent deal—solemnized in a contract they signed in 1850—was a fraud. Despite Robert's claims that the agreement reflected his "brotherly affection and sympathy," the legal fight was nasty. Robert accused William of manipulating their elderly father, allowing him to profit off the elder Robert's property and lands in the old man's final years. William was insulted and responded in part by asserting that their father had long concluded that Robert M. was a failure and not his biological son.[26]

In the turbulent times that followed the war, family failed to offer any refuge. Debts and family squabbles threatened to ruin William Henry financially. He remained a Democrat, while his brothers became Republicans during Reconstruction. His brother James was a judge and sometimes presided over his other brothers' legal battle and often ruled against William. Those problems were compounded when other leading Republicans—and former Madison County residents who may have had an ax to grind with William L. Henry from the Laurel War—managed to purchase the Sulphur Springs property at public auction. There is something tragic about the Henry brothers ruining of each other. Their infighting reduced William to a tenant on their father's lands, a status he shared with his former slaves, George and Charlie, in 1870. Familial bonds and labor were quintessential elements of the Sulphur Springs community, and William Henry's household was once a pillar of that community. Various owners tried to rebuild and relaunch the Sulphur Springs resort, but it was not a Henry. Once masters of a vibrant community, William and Cornelia Henry ultimately moved their family from Sulphur Springs altogether.[27]

NOTES

1. U.S. Census, 1860, free inhabitant schedule, Union; U.S. Census, 1860, slave schedule, Union; Karen L. Clinard and Richard Russell, eds., *Fear in North Carolina: The Civil War Journals and Letters of the Henry Family* (Asheville, NC: Reminiscing Books, 2008), 389; *Asheville News*, June 8, 1854, 3. By 1860, Cornelia's father, William Smith Sr., owned $64,200 worth of real property and $134,000 worth of personal property. It is likely that the Sulphur Springs Hotel was well known in Cornelia's native South Carolina community. A cursory look at the guest register for the hotel in the late 1830s and 1840s reveals many South Carolinians among the patrons, including dozens hailing from Union. See Henry Family Papers, North Carolina Collection, Pack Memorial Library, Asheville, North Carolina.

2. Richard Russell, *Robert Henry: A Western North Carolina Patriot* (Charleston, SC: The History Press, 2013), 144–45. For a discussion of family and its place within American community, see Thomas Bender, *Community and Social Change in America* (Baltimore, MD: Johns Hopkins University Press, 1982), 128–42.

3. Record of Appointment of Postmasters, 1832–1971,in Records of the Post Office Department, M841, RG 28, National Archives and Records Administration, Washington, DC. William's assets increased during the decade prior to the Civil War. In 1850, he owned a respectable $5,500 of real property. See U.S. Census, 1850, free inhabitant schedule, Buncombe County. The academy, as it was often referred to by Cornelia Henry, hosted circuit-riding ministers and served as a school. See Russell, *Robert Henry*, 102.

4. In 1860, African Americans constituted 16.2 percent of Buncombe County's total population. Specifically, there were 1,933 enslaved people and 111 free men and women of color living in the county. It is also worth noting that the percentage of African Americans in Buncombe County was higher than the overall regional average, which was 12.6 percent. See Steven E. Nash, *Reconstruction's Ragged Edge: The Politics of Postwar Life in the Southern Mountains* (Chapel Hill: University of North Carolina Press, 2016), 14.

5. U.S. Census, 1830, population schedule, Buncombe County. The 1860 free inhabitant and slave schedules for Cherokee County (where Henry had moved by 1840) shows he had $30,000 in real and $12,000 in personal property. The 1860 slave schedules for Buncombe County show that James L. Henry owned $13,500 worth of real property and $17,138 of personal property including twelve slaves (six men and six women) aged four months to fifty years old, and the 1850 slave schedule for Haywood County reveal that James R. Love owned eighty-five slaves. See also Barbara Sears McRae, "African Americans of Macon County and Surrounding Areas," unpublished manuscript, 2009, copy in possession of author, 108–9. For more on how slaveholders used, treated, hired out, assaulted, and shared their enslaved people, see John C. Inscoe, *Mountain Masters: Slavery and the Sectional Crisis in Western North Carolina* (Knoxville: University of Tennessee Press, 1996), chap. 3, Wilma Dunaway, *Slavery in the American Mountain South* (Cambridge: Cambridge University Press, 2003), Kevin Young, "The Ties That Bind: Slaveholding Kinship Networks in the Toe Valley" (in this vol-

ume); Anthony E. Kaye, *Joining Places: Slave Neighborhoods in the Old South* (Chapel Hill: University of North Carolina Press, 2009); David F. Allmendinger Jr., *Nat Turner and the Rising in Southampton County* (Baltimore, MD: Johns Hopkins University Press, 2017).

6. Clinard and Russell, *Fear in North Carolina*, 395–98; *U.S. Census, 1870, population schedule, Buncombe County*. Sam is likely the same Sam sometimes referred to as "Buncombe Sam" (Russell, *Robert Henry*, 88–89).

7. Clinard and Russell, *Fear in North Carolina*, 1, 7, 8, 11. On tenancy and landownership throughout southern Appalachia before the Civil War, see Joseph D. Reid Jr., "Antebellum Southern Rental Contracts," *Explorations in Economic History* 13, no. 1 (1976): 71–79, and Wilma A. Dunaway, *The First American Frontier: Transition to Capitalism in Southern Appalachia, 1700–1860* (Chapel Hill: University of North Carolina Press, 1996), especially chap. 4.

8. Clinard and Russell, *Fear in North Carolina*, 4–5, 7, 11–12, 14–18; Russell, *Robert Henry*, 146; *Robert M. Henry v. William L. Henry*, 62 NC 334 (January 1868), North Carolina, State Supreme Court Case Files, 1800–1909, Division of Archives and History, North Carolina State Archive, Raleigh. Hindsight may be twenty-twenty, but in 1863 Robert M. Henry accused his brother of leasing Sulphur Springs to "improvident and insolvent persons," presumably the Terrys, and claimed that owing to "mismanagement and neglect, the said farm did not yield a fourth of a fair rental" and that his brother had "permitted said farm and the buildings there to go to decay and become ruinous for the want of ordinary repair." The neglect of both his brother and the "irresponsible man" whom his brother had leased the hotel to culminated in a fire that caused the complete destruction of the "hotel buildings and all the furniture therein," "the same being worth about fifteen thousand dollars."

9. Clinard and Russell, *Fear in North Carolina*, 8–9, 20, 22. On secession in western North Carolina, see Inscoe, *Mountain Masters*, chap. 9. Buncombe County had 1,976 white men of military age (eighteen to forty-five years old) and sent 50 percent of its eligible men into the war. Sulphur Springs sent fifteen men into the ranks, and Hominy Creek yielded eighteen recruits. In total, Buncombe contributed almost one-fourth of all the Confederate soldiers from western North Carolina (Kevin Oshnock, "The Isolation Factor: Differing Loyalties of Watauga and Buncombe Counties during the Civil War," *North Carolina Historical Review* 90, no. 4 [October 2013]: 400–402). Appointed second lieutenant of the First North Carolina Cavalry in May 1861, James L. Henry served with that regiment until he resigned to become captain in the newly formed Fourteenth Battalion North Carolina Cavalry (which became the Sixty-Ninth North Carolina Cavalry and then the Seventh Regiment North Carolina Cavalry) (Louis H. Manarin, comp., *North Carolina Troops, 1861–1865: A Roster*, vol. 2: *Cavalry* (Raleigh, NC: State Department of Archives and History, 1968), 61.

10. Weymouth T. Jordan Jr., comp., *North Carolina Troops, 1861–1865: A Roster*, vol. 7: *Infantry* (Raleigh, NC: State Department of Archives and History, 1979), 437; Clinard and Russell, *Fear in North Carolina*, 31, 151–52, 196, 246. To get a sense of the Henrys' renters and living arrangements, see Clinard and Russell, *Fear in North Carolina*, 7.

11. Clinard and Russell, *Fear in North Carolina*, 47–48, 50, 52, 71, 159. William L. Henry served first as captain of Company B, Fourteenth NC Battalion. His unit was later reorganized as the Sixty-Ninth Infantry Regiment. Clinard and Russell, *Fear in North Carolina*, 391.

12. Clinard and Russell, *Fear in North Carolina*, 34, 52, 75, 84, 102. Cornelia used both

spellings—Jennie and Jinnie—in her diary. It is likely, if unclear, that Jinnie and Jennie refer to the same woman who was Tena's sister. For sake of clarity, I use "Jinnie" throughout. See Clinard and Russell, *Fear in North Carolina*, 327, 395.

13. Clinard and Russell, *Fear in North Carolina*, 16–17, 396.

14. Clinard and Russell, *Fear in North Carolina*, 71, 74, 219–20. The torture inflicted on George in March 1864 likely reflected broader stresses in the community. Roughly three months prior to George's beating, Cornelia complained about deserters stealing from families within her community. Therefore, the thief in question may not have been George (Clinard and Russell, *Fear in North Carolina*, 198).

15. Clinard and Russell, *Fear in North Carolina*, 123.

16. Clinard and Russell, *Fear in North Carolina*, 90, 103, 224–25, 229–31.

17. Clinard and Russell, *Fear in North Carolina*, 200, 223–25, 255, 397–98; *Robert M. Henry v. William L. Henry*, 62 NC 334 (January 1868). Elvira and Leizana were sold to James R. Love in 1848. Betsey was sold to James R. Love in 1848 but passed to James L. Henry in 1856.

18. Clinard and Russell, *Fear in North Carolina*, 46, 62, 71–73, 103, 118, 154; Oshnock, "The Isolation Factor," 400–405; U.S. Census, 1860, free inhabitant schedule, Haywood County. On mobilization in western North Carolina, see John C. Inscoe and Gordon B. McKinney, *The Heart of Confederate Appalachia: Western North Carolina in the Civil War* (Chapel Hill: University of North Carolina Press, 2001), chap. 3. R. H. Night was a private in the Thirty-Ninth North Carolina Infantry. He enlisted in Buncombe County on February 1, 1862, received a furlough February 12, and deserted sometime before May 1, 1862. Nineveh C. Norris of Macon County joined the Thirty-Ninth NC Infantry in October 1861. He was captured in Kentucky on October 10, 1862, paroled, and was absent without leave on February 20, 1863. After returning to duty on March 3, 1863, he fell sick and remained ill for much of the early summer; he then deserted on September 18, 1863 (Jordan, *North Carolina Troops*, 126. Thomas Hendix was a modest farmer ($1370 worth of real property) taking care of his elderly mother and five other family members in 1860. See U.S. Census, 1860, free inhabitant schedule, Buncombe County. Although it is unclear, Hendrix also appears to have been hired by the Henrys for various tasks. In late April 1864, Cornelia suspected Tom Hendrix of killing several of her turkeys and she denounced him as a "rogue." See Clinard and Russell, *Fear in North Carolina*, 213.

19. Clinard and Russell, *Fear in North Carolina*, 114–15, 144, 201, 205, 209, 218. Making a clear identification of the Henrys' overseer, Jim Parker, in the 1860 census is difficult. However, a likely connection shows the ties that once bound some families in the Hominy Valley. Living with a James Parker in Sulphur Springs in 1860 was Rachel Murray who married Richard Pinckney Allen on December 31, 1860. For his part, Allen came and went quite frequently. He first deserted from his regiment on August 21, 1862. After returning to service on January 12, 1863, he went absent without leave again on January 24, 1863. Allen did this dance one last time in 1863, returning from March to August and deserting for good in November. See Jordan, *North Carolina Troops*, 437. About his worth the Henrys said but little. William noted that Allen "worked five days up to Feb. 1 [1861]" and that he lost half a day on February 9. Henry liked Pinck well enough to perform his and Rachel's wedding,

but even that is tainted by the gossipy sense of condemnation behind Cornelia's observation that Rachel had a child out of wedlock in November. See Clinard and Russell, *Fear in North Carolina*, 7, 12, 14. Allen's brother-in-law, John W. Bryson, was a propertyless farmer who signed up for service in the Sixtieth North Carolina Infantry on May 17, 1862. Like Allen, he came and went frequently throughout 1863 and 1864. Unlike Allen, he survived the war. See U.S. Census, 1860, free inhabitant schedule, Buncombe County, and Weymouth Jordan Jr., comp., *North Carolina Troops: A Roster*, vol. 14: *Infantry* (Raleigh: North Carolina Office of Archives and History, 1998), 543. William Harry Deaver was first lieutenant, Company A, Sixtieth North Carolina Infantry, until his comrades elected him major on August 1, 1862. However, he developed a chronic illness, and his resignation was accepted on May 14, 1863. See Jordan, *North Carolina Troops*, 14:502, 505.

20. Clinard and Russell, *Fear in North Carolina*, 260.
21. Clinard and Russell, *Fear in North Carolina*, 261–63.
22. Clinard and Russell, *Fear in North Carolina*, 264.
23. Clinard and Russell, *Fear in North Carolina*, 265; Mary Taylor Brown to John Evans Brown, June 20, 1865, 18–19, W. Vance Brown Papers, Division of Archives and History, North Carolina State Archive, Raleigh; Katherine Polk Gale, "Recollections of Life in the Southern Confederacy, 1861–1865," Gale and Polk Family Papers, Southern Historical Collection, University of North Carolina at Chapel Hill. George didn't leave. He was still there on April 6, 1865, tending to the mill. See Clinard and Russell, *Fear in North Carolina*, 266.
24. Clinard and Russell, *Fear in North Carolina*, 281, 292,298, 301, 303, 307. The military commander that met with George may well have been William C. Stevens, who visited Asheville "at the request of some of the citizens of that place[,] there being some trouble there between the negroes and their former Masters." See William C. Stevens to his sister, June 20, 1865, William C. Stevens Papers, Bentley Library, University of Michigan. On the economic situation in western North Carolina during and immediately after the Civil War, see Inscoe and McKinney, *The Heart of Confederate Appalachia*, and Nash, *Reconstruction's Ragged Edge*. According to the 1883 city directory, Asheville's population grew from 1,100 in 1860 to 1,450 in 1870. Given the unsettled condition of the county and the freedpeople's new freedom of movement, it seems certain that they contributed to this growth. See *The Asheville City Directory and Gazetteer of Buncombe County for 1883–84* (Richmond: VA Baughman Brothers, 1883), 123–24.
25. Clinard and Russell, *Fear in North Carolina*, 314, 320, 326, 329–30, 338, 340, 343, 351.
26. *Robert M. Henry v. William L. Henry*, 62 NC 334 (January 1868).
27. William L. Henry owned $5,000 in real and $3,000 in personal property in 1870 (See U.S. Census, 1870, population schedule, Buncombe County).

Reinterpreting John Noland

Community Coercion Theory and the Black Confederate Debate

MATTHEW C. HULBERT

IN AUGUST 1905, THE REMNANTS OF WILLIAM CLARKE QUANTRILL'S band of Confederate guerrillas assembled for a reunion in Independence, Missouri. Once a source of considerable terror along the Missouri-Kansas border, there was little danger expected from the Quantrill Men on this sun-drenched afternoon. They didn't handle the heat the way they used to; indeed, they bore little resemblance to their wartime selves—to the unruly partisans made notorious by massacres at Lawrence, Baxter Springs, and Centralia. Gone were the wild locks and the flamboyant shirts they'd donned as young men in the bush. And gone were the revolvers—braces of them, loaded with five, six, or even seven Colt Navies—that had been the signature tools of their lethal trade. Now well past middle age, the former bushwhackers were gray, weather beaten, and stooped more by years than iron.[1]

That a unit of aging irregulars, let alone one with a track record so imbrued as Quantrill's, held a public commemoration will perhaps surprise many modern observers. These were men, after all, known the country over for wartime savagery—and yet here they met to reminisce fondly over those lurid exploits. As many historians have illustrated, chief among them David Blight and Caroline Janney, it was not unusual for Civil War veterans to gather to recollect the bloodiest war in American history. And as scholars such as Jeremy Neely and I have previously chronicled, guerrillas frequently got in on the commemorative action too.[2]

Much more jarring to contemporary eyes—and significantly more laborious to explain—was the presence of John Noland at the guerrilla encampment. By nearly every measure, Noland belonged. He was roughly the same age as the other vets in attendance; he'd been born and raised in western Missouri's guerrilla heartland; he had blood kin active in Quantrill's band during the war; and, perhaps most important of all, he himself had taken a hand in the outfit's deadliest operation, the Lawrence Massacre of August 1863. There was, in fact, only one discernible difference between John Noland and every single one of the other Quantrill Men in Independence that day: he was black.

WRITING ON SO-CALLED BLACK CONFEDERATES IS SPARSE; WHAT little has found its way to print is often mistitled, poorly sourced, or highly inconsistent. Despite the stalwart efforts of a few public historians to dispute it, the notion that black southerners consciously sided with the Confederacy—a nation, we must recall, founded for the sole purpose of protecting the interests of African American slavery—thrives among Confederate heritage groups on the internet. The general tendency, both in print and online, is to suggest that black Confederates willingly served in a wide range of wartime capacities—from body servants, cooks, and valets, to teamsters, drovers, and combat troops—while only providing sound primary evidence for the most involuntary roles and for those *not* involving active, armed participation in combat.[3]

On one hand, archivist and historian Ervin Jordan maintains that black Confederates believed demonstrating loyalty might "preserve their freedom and nullify suspicion of them as dissidents" and that "actively supporting the Southern cause" would "lead to expanded privileges and rights" granted them by white southerners. At the same time, however, he asserts that numerous black Confederates "were genuine Southern loyalists, not as a consequence of white pressure." But what could have constituted greater "pressure" than fear of violent reprisal against dissent or of curtailed future freedoms? On the other hand, Paul Petersen, an amateur historian and frequent contributor on the markedly pro-Confederate quantrillsguerrillas.com, proposes that "slaves during the Civil War were occasionally conscripted from their owners to help work on roads and other infrastructure needed by the army." "Southern blacks," he continues, "built bridges, erected fortifications, worked on the docks and offered all kinds of support work to free whites up to go and fight." While never disputing that these conscripted laborers were slaves, forced to work on a daily basis by threat of violence, Petersen somehow still manages to conclude that "the successes of white Confederate troops in battle, could only have been achieved with the support of these *loyal* black Southerners" (my emphasis).[4]

Examples such as these are inherently deceptive because to the general public, the term "black Confederate" implies just the opposite: that blacks had not been hostage laborers but had *voluntarily fought* for the Confederacy because they believed in its merit. The allure of bona fide black Confederates for heritage groups is not difficult to understand. These organizations routinely contend that secession and the war were both carried out in defense of states' rights, and that neither the preservation nor expansion of slavery had much of anything to do with hostilities erupting at Fort Sumter in 1861. Their rationale is rooted in a fallacy of false cause: that if black southerners, many of them slaves to boot, supported the Confederacy, it could not have been founded on a tainted bedrock of white supremacy and black bondage. Along these lines, Petersen opines elsewhere on quantrillasguerrillas.com that "images of slave beatings often negate the true story" and that "the lies surrounding the treatment of slaves was the cause of most of the misunderstanding in the North" as sectional crisis gave way to civil war.[5]

With this in mind, let us now return to John Noland. He's a very popular figure in heritage circles; so popular, as it were, that in the early 2000s, the Sons of Confederate Veterans (SCV) purchased him a new headstone bearing the inscriptions "Black Confederate" and "A Man Among Men." Because he lived in Missouri—technically a Union state—and because he is supposed to have fought as a bushwhacker under Quantrill—independent of the Confederate army's conscription powers—the consensus is that Noland must have done so voluntarily, which made him a true believer in the cause. This argument is often buoyed by the fact that Noland remained in western Missouri after the war and that he attended a few reunions of the Quantrill Men and by his portrayal (as the fictional Daniel Holt) in Ang Lee's 1999 film *Ride with the Devil*.

Not surprisingly, the ideas that constitute the prevailing wisdom on the mythical Noland do not hold up well to scrutiny. The remainder of this essay occupies itself with reinterpreting the historical John Noland and, in a sense, with rescuing him from something akin to what E. P. Thompson famously called "the enormous condescension of posterity." Before I take up Noland's record within the unique wartime circumstances of Missouri's irregular conflict, however, it is necessary to outline a theory of community coercion. This analytical approach takes collective stock of Noland's enslaved status, what we can actually document of his role in the guerrilla war, his postbellum reunion appearances, and his long-term survival strategies as a black man tethered socially and economically to a heavily pro-Confederate community within a Union state; put another way, I attempt to make sense of what choices were available to Noland and hypothesize how the particulars of his situation, which have been as yet so attractive to Confederate heritage enthusiasts, amounted to a crushing form of compulsion via intimidation.

The main tenet of community coercion theory is that until otherwise documented with bona fide primary evidence, scholars should begin historical inquiries into the lives and actions of black men who supposedly sided with the Confederacy (frequently called "black Confederates") from the position that any support rendered to the cause of their own continued enslavement was involuntary, that it was the result of violent, coercive force, or threats thereof wielded by local white communities against the aforementioned slaves and/or their kin, and that it was not based on genuine belief in the underlying principles of the Confederacy. Generally, as historians, we only chart an intellectual course after it has been dictated by archival research and secondary contextualizing because we seek to be objective. In this case, however, beginning with an assumption that apparent black support for the Confederacy was just that is both justified and appropriate due to the rampant misuse of evidence and the obscuring tactics employed by Confederate heritage enthusiasts and white nationalists. In other words, to penetrate the cloak of memory and to achieve something nearer to historical objectivity in the study of black Confederates, it has become necessary to start with a bias. However, community coercion theory *does not* contend that the existence of true black Confederates is an impossibility—it merely dictates where the burden of proof ought to fall given the ulterior political uses and mythologies that habitually surround the topic.

On the one hand, the systemic and often mortal violence that undergirded southern slavery influenced every aspect of slaves' daily lives. It was inescapable and factored into every decision made by slaves. On the other hand, for much of the war, most slaves had no way of knowing the institution would be abolished permanently at conflict's end. In fact, some slaves didn't know of their new status even *after* they'd been legally freed. The waters were especially murky for slaves held in isolated areas or in states that had never seceded from the Union and were thereby not covered under the terms of the original Emancipation Proclamation. This was the case for John Noland. Because of these circumstances, slaves in Confederate territory continued to operate within a behavioral system that Eugene D. Genovese calls "resistance and accommodation."[6] In Genovese's model, slaves resisted as much as possible but balanced their rebellious actions with accommodation designed to avoid incurring more severe or mortal consequences. It is critical to remember, however, that this daily give-and-take played out under the assumption that resistance was never intended to end enslavement, only to survive it and make it as bearable as possible. In short, slaves tempered resistance with accommodation so that they might live to fight another day. (This was because outright rebellions generally failed for a number of reasons, and the consequence of a failed revolt was certain death.) The wartime service that Confederates coerced from their slaves can thus be reasonably understood as an extreme case of accommodation within a version of Genovese's blueprint expanded to include the experiences of slaves as servants not just to southern masters but to military and economic agents of the Confederacy.

BEFORE AND DURING THE WAR, JOHN NOLAND WAS THE CHATTEL of Francis Asbury Noland, a moderately affluent slaveholder in Jackson County, Missouri. The 1860 slave schedule for Jackson County notes that Francis A. Noland—who went by and is hereafter referred to as Asbury to prevent his being confused with his father, Francis Marion Noland—owned two male slaves, aged twenty-three and sixteen years. The twenty-three-year-old, it is important to note, was designated as mulatto by the census taker. Asbury's father, Francis, also owned a mulatto male slave in 1860 (eleven years old) and two female slaves approximately the correct age to be the boy's mother, at forty-five and forty-six, respectively. Moreover, Eli Glasscock, an extended relation of the Noland clan, also owned mixed-race slaves in 1860. All of this information leads to the conclusion that the Noland men had a penchant for taking sexual advantage of their female slaves—which makes it quite likely that the twenty-three-year-old mulatto was not only John Noland but also the biological son of his owner, Asbury Noland. If correct, this blood connection to his master's family would have meant that John Noland had several relations active in Quantrill's band: George M. and George W. Noland would have been John's third cousins, while Edward, James, Henry, and William Noland would have been distant cousins.[7]

The fact that he was a slave greatly diminished John Noland's mobility. That Missouri never managed to secede from the Union equally diminished his choice of allegiance when war broke out in 1861. That the men of his kinship network all chose to fight locally as Confederate bushwhackers in a conflict that unfolded almost entirely on the home front meant that Noland could not simply lay low until war's end and that outward resistance to their cause by a black man—kin or otherwise—would almost certainly be met with mortal injury. The obvious argument that Noland sided with the Confederacy out of loyalty to his kin is difficult to sustain on account of its one-sidedness. That is, the kinship bond was supposedly strong enough to compel Noland to risk his life but *not* strong enough to incite his white "family" to set him free.[8]

Assuming that he had even the most basic awareness of his own circumstances, John Noland would not have had any logical reason to believe that he'd ever live beyond the boundaries of the Noland homestead or the surrounding farms and meadows of Jackson County. Why would he? President Abraham Lincoln's Emancipation Proclamation—which took effect well before the Lawrence massacre of August 1863—did not apply to Missouri. Slave property could not flee to Federal lines and freedom in a Union state. Owing to this immobility and his lack of prospects for freedom, Noland would not have had any inkling during the war itself that he might ever escape the people of his immediate community—the community that begot, reared, and owned him—*regardless* of whether or not the Confederacy succeeded. All of this considered, the most practical assessment of John Noland's options in 1861 is that he really had no choice but to cooperate with Quantrill's men.[9]

The irregulars—pro-Confederate bushwhackers and Unionist jayhawkers—who waged battles along the Missouri-Kansas border were a world apart from the echelons and interior lines of the eastern theater. Guerrillas had little use for Francis Lieber's code or the rules of supposedly civilized, Napoleonic warfare. Rather, their war was hyperlocal and hyperpersonal; it drew women, children, and the elderly directly into the fray. Front porches, barns, corn cribs, living rooms and parlors, muddy fields, and moonlit trails—these were the battlefields of the guerrilla theater, domestic locales where deception, ambush, arson, rape, torture, and massacre all fell within bounds of the status quo. This was the environment John Noland had to navigate.[10]

According to modern proponents of the idea that Noland was a genuine black Confederate, he thrived in it. Patrick R. Marquis submits that Noland "joined up [with Quantrill] because his family had been abused by Jayhawkers" and that "as a hostler and as a spy" he displayed "unstinting loyalty during the Civil War to the guerrilla cause." According to Paul Petersen, during the Battle of Lamar, Missouri, in November 1862, Noland "stood by Quantrill's side shouting more orders than any other of Quantrill's men" and "made three separate charges against the Federal stronghold before withdrawing and continuing into Texas with his fellow guerrillas." Furthermore, he reports that "Federals once offered him [Noland] ten thousand dollars to betray Quantrill and his men, but Noland only replied with scorn." (More on this tale anon.)[11]

What can we actually recover of John Noland's individual wartime experience? Better still, what can we document with primary evidence? Not much on either count, unfortunately. Major John Newman Edwards, the very first historian of Missouri's guerrilla war—and a blatantly pro-Confederate one at that—fails to mention Noland a single time in his magnum opus, *Noted Guerrillas, or, The Warfare of the Border* (1877). William E. Connelley, a diehard Unionist and Edwards's main rival, only remarks on Noland once in *Quantrill and the Border Wars* (1910). Connelley states that Noland had been dispatched to Lawrence, Kansas, as a pre-raid spy; he could not, however, verify that Noland ever reported back to Quantrill before the massacre unfolded (and suggests that Noland himself refused to talk much about his role in the assault).[12]

Memoirs penned by former bushwhackers Cole Younger, Kit Dalton, Hampton Watts, John McCorkle, George Cruzen, and Harrison Trow all included accounts of loyal, Remus-like slaves, but like Edwards, each failed to include John Noland. Of all the known guerrilla memoirists who rode with Quantrill, only Andrew Walker discusses Noland's connection with the group: "John Noland was a negro, and a brave, resourceful fellow." However, he quickly followed this praise with the declaration that "no negro ever fought with us as a regular member of the band, but John would have done so had Quantrill consented." According to Walker, because of his skin color, Noland was more valuable as a spy than a combatant—and that it was in just such a capacity that Noland was sent to Lawrence ahead of the August 1863 raid. (Walker, too, fails to confirm whether or not Noland's intelligence ever reached Quantrill in time to be useful.)[13]

The most tantalizing information comes from William H. Gregg, one of Quantrill's subordinates during the war and a researcher for Connelley. In a November 1904 letter, Gregg reported to Connelley that he'd "finally cornered John Noland," but he was "ticklish about telling his story" for fear it might create trouble for him. According to Gregg, Noland admitted to being sent to Lawrence as a spy, but maintained that he "did not see the Col. [Quantrill] or make any report to him until after his return from Lawrence." Gregg concluded the body of the letter by stating that Noland also told him he was offered $10,000 to betray Quantrill and his men but turned the offer down. Gregg did not disclose when or where the offer was allegedly made, and when examined more closely, the story—which is oft-repeated today—looks increasingly apocryphal. Aside from $10,000 being an exceptional if not downright impossible quantity of money in the 1860s (something like $195,000 in today's dollars), the matter of why Unionists would have let such a known (allegedly) and valuable member of Quantrill's band as Noland walk away freely after he refused to aid them is never addressed.[14]

That John Noland, a black man, would hesitate to broadcast his involvement in a surprise attack that ultimately killed two hundred white men and boys, the vast majority of them unarmed, is understandable. Moreover, although it is likely beyond dispute that William Clarke Quantrill did attempt to use Noland as a spy in the lead-up to the raid, there are more pressing questions. First, if Noland had been involved with Quantrill's band on a more regular basis, possibly even as a combatant, why didn't Edwards (who never missed an opportunity to wax poetic about Confederate guerrillas) or any of the memoirists aside from Walker mention him? Second, to what extent can Gregg's report on Noland be considered reliable? And third, if Gregg's report *is* reliable, what do we actually learn from it?

Walker seems to answer the first question. He is complimentary of Noland but states in no uncertain terms that he was not a regular member of the group. The silence of Edwards and others on the subject does not prove but does strongly imply that Noland's service throughout the war, whatever it amounted to, was considered less than noteworthy. Newspaper coverage of the 1905 reunion seems to back this assessment, stating that Noland was "the only negro who ever had any connection with Quantrell's band" but that his involvement was "rather in the position of a servant than as a fighter." As for Gregg, given his status within the Quantrill Men Survivors Association (the group that organized bushwhacker reunions), there isn't much reason to doubt that he spoke to Noland personally or that he had any obvious reasons to misrepresent whatever Noland told him. Even if we take Gregg's information at face value, though, the fact remains there is no primary evidence that Noland obeyed Quantrill out of voluntary loyalty to the Confederate cause. Conversely, he began his story by reminding Gregg that he was a slave in those days. Simply put, nothing new in John Noland's documented wartime record points to his cooperation having been anything but involuntary.[15]

This observation does prompt another question, however: if John Noland had not been a genuine black Confederate in service of Quantrill's band, why did he attend their reunions? The short answer is he was resorting to the same tactics of self-preservation that saw him through the war. Cultivating the image of a loyal southerner within his Jackson County community undoubtedly afforded Noland a measure of social standing among the white population and helped inoculate him from widespread racial violence in postbellum Missouri. Efforts to maintain this image were evident in Gregg's 1904 letter to Connelley. According to Gregg, Noland initially refused to talk about the war or the massacre because he was afraid it would stir up trouble. Once he relented and decided to tell Gregg his story, Noland walked a razor's edge between loyal service and plausible deniability: he went to Lawrence as ordered but did not deliver Quantrill any information that could have aided the butchery. (Gregg remarked to Connelley that this is not the version of the story he'd heard before, leaving us to infer that other bushwhackers believed Noland *had* delivered intel to Quantrill before the raid.) Perhaps sensing Gregg's confusion and believing it might diminish him in the eyes of white ex-Confederates, Noland then volunteered the story of the $10,000 bribe and claimed to have voted a Democratic ticket. In this light, attending the Quantrill Men reunion a year later in 1905 (and again in 1907) constituted a way for Noland to publicly remind the white community that he wasn't a troublemaker—that he was, and always had been, "on their side."[16]

In spite of its scantiness, John Noland's historical record has been used to construct a disproportionately extensive mythology—mainly based on exaggeration but at times fabrication. As a result, much of what the public thinks it knows about John Noland is derived from a mash-up of history and myth in the form of Ang Lee's *Ride with the Devil* (1999). In the film, Noland is loosely portrayed by the fictional Daniel Holt (Jeffrey Wright), an ex-slave turned bushwhacker who rides with his former master and fights in numerous irregular engagements, including the Lawrence Massacre. According to Holt, he had belonged to George Clyde's father before the war, but when "Old Man" Clyde was killed by jayhawkers, George (Simon Baker)—who had grown up with Holt—bought and freed him. The rest of Holt's family was sold to Texas because George couldn't afford to save them all. At several points in the film, Holt's place among the bushwhackers is questioned, but others defend him by declaring that "he is George Clyde's nigger"—without knowing that Holt is technically free. The tactic works, but it visibly pains Holt more and more with each implementation.

Over the course of the story, Holt befriends Jake "Dutchy" Roedel (Tobey McGuire), a German-born bushwhacker. Initially, Jake doesn't trust Holt— nor does he like the idea of an armed black man in camp. But as a German, Jake can relate to Holt in a way that the other bushwhackers cannot. As their friendship deepens, they grow disillusioned with the guerrilla lifestyle. This disenchantment stems partly from each watching his best friend die a gruesome, war-related death, partly from their guilt over the Lawrence Massacre, and partly from neither man ever being fully trusted or accepted in the bushwhacker ranks on account of his outsider status. To this end, Holt confesses to Jake that he had never been in the war because he believed in the Confederacy but because he believed in George Clyde. With Clyde dead, Holt could be his own man and would never be "nobody's nigger" again. In the end, both survive the war, and viewers are left with the optimistic image of Holt, free and bound for Texas, riding off in search of his long-lost mother.

While *Ride with the Devil* provides a realistic look at the tactics and logistics of bushwhacking during the Civil War, as it relates to the historical John Noland, the film is a disaster. No evidence exists to suggest that Noland was ever given his freedom before or during the war. On the contrary, Asbury Noland was still alive when the war began (not gunned down by jayhawkers), and John Noland himself admitted to being a slave during this time. In turn, the three jayhawkers Holt kills while defending his master's family are based on nothing from the historical record. Likewise, while the film at least avoids presenting Holt as espousing ideological allegiance to the Confederacy, his being depicted as participating in numerous firefights leading up to the raid on Lawrence and in the Lawrence Massacre itself contradicts Noland's and other bushwhackers' statements after the fact.[17]

Most problematic of all, however, is the film's final scene in which Holt sets out for Texas. It's a hopeful ending—one that signals a new beginning framed by freedom. It's also a major blow to the historical John Noland. Unlike Holt, we know with certainty that when the war ended, Noland stayed put in Jackson County and lived among the people of that community until his death in 1908. He did not ride off into the proverbial sunset to start life anew. This fact notwithstanding, the two figures have begun to fuse in popular memory. As Civil War buffs and online heritage enthusiasts enlist the details of Holt's story to fill the myriad lacunae in Noland's, the details of the fictional man inevitably become those of the historical one. This retroactive introduction of mobility and choice where they did not exist has the effect of obscuring the true, coercive nature of Noland's relationship with Quantrill and company both during and after the war.

As a general rule, bushwhackers who survived the guerrilla theater returned home to their houses and farms. The end of slavery made them no less dedicated to white supremacy, and their tendency to use terror and violence coercively was not diminished. After all, Missouri was one of just two non-Confederate states with racial violence so rampant as to require the presence of Freedmen's Bureau agents. Much like in slavery days, whites in western Missouri maintained a strict racial hierarchy and codes of behavior that triggered severe, even mortal, consequences when blacks violated them. Whites still expected deference and labor from Noland—and so, lacking a better alternative, Noland (along with other ex-slaves) had to arrange and live his daily life around the preferences of his white neighbors.[18]

More simply put, though technically covered by the terms of the Thirteenth Amendment, the basic conditions within John Noland's community—the conditions that had prompted him to cooperate with Quantrill's men—did not change all that much after the war. He still lacked social and economic mobility. He still lacked the freedom to choose how to behave without fear of violent repercussions. A gun was not literally held to Noland's head at all times during and after the war to pressure him; nevertheless, it's a drastic oversimplification to assume one needed to be. The implied threat that the gun symbolized always loomed large, and Noland appears to have acted accordingly.

This is of course not to argue that the existence of a genuine black Confederate is a historical impossibility. The past is well stocked with inexplicable figures and equally inexplicable examples of self-abnegation.[19] The few available sources and a pragmatist's read of circumstantial evidence, though, suggest that John Noland is simply not one of them. The manipulation of his story does, however, underscore the necessity of a community coercion theory for understanding black Confederates and Civil War history more broadly. In cases lacking direct evidence of black Confederate loyalty, we should default to the position that black southern men's participation in white Confederate enterprises (regular or irregular) was the result of overwhelming (white) community pressure and therefore necessary for survival, informed by a belief that slavery would not end in the near future or at war's end and motivated by a lack of mobility or opportunity to escape from proslavery/pro-Confederate communities without risking grave injury or death to themselves or kin, communities that had exhibited a track record of wielding violence against southern black men (and women and children) to maintain white supremacy. In other words, when it comes to determining whether or not African Americans consciously fought on behalf of communities—or a nation—bent on subjugating them, we ought to assume that they did not until incontrovertible proof of the opposite is brought forward. For whatever reason John Noland attended the Quantrill Men reunion in 1905, we owe him this benefit of the doubt.

NOTES

1. B. James George Collection, State Historical Society of Missouri, Columbia; Warren Welch Collection, Jackson County Historical Society, Independence, Missouri.

2. On Civil War memory, see Dwight W. Blight, *Race and Reunion: The Civil War in American Memory* (Cambridge, MA: Harvard University Press, 2001), and Caroline Janney, *Remembering the Civil War: Reunion and the Limits of Reconciliation* (Chapel Hill: University of North Carolina Press, 2013). On guerrilla reunions, see Matthew C. Hulbert, *The Ghosts of Guerrilla Memory: How Civil War Bushwhackers Became Gunslingers in the Amer-*

ican West (Athens: University of Georgia Press, 2016), chap. 4, and Jeremy C. Neely, "The Quantrill Men Reunions: The Border War, Fifty Years On," in *Bleeding Kansas, Bleeding Missouri: The Long Civil War on the Border*, ed. Jonathan Earle and Diane Mutti Burke (Lawrence: University Press of Kansas, 2013), 243–58.

3. Through their blogs, *Civil War Memory* and *Crossroads* (respectively), Kevin Levin and Brooks Simpson have been admirable critics of attempts by Confederate heritage groups to fabricate black Confederate history. See also Sam Smith, "Black Confederates: Truth and Legend," https://www.battlefields.org/learn/articles/black-confederates. For examples of misleading scholarship, see various essays in Richard Rollins and Arthur W. Bergeron Jr., eds., *Black Southerners in Gray* (Redondo Beach, CA: Rank and File Publications, 1994), but especially Richard Rollins, "Black Confederates at Gettysburg," and Thomas Y. Cartwright, "Better Confederates Did Not Live." For a standard academic take on black camp servants and laborers, see Joseph T. Glatthaar, *General Lee's Army: From Victory to Collapse* (New York: Free Press, 2008), specifically chap. 24, "Blacks and the Army."

4. Ervin L. Jordan, "Different Drummers," in *Black Southerners in Gray*, 57, 59, 62–63, 64, 69; Paul Petersen, "Go Back Jack and Do It Again," available at quantrillsguerrillas.com. To be fair, Jordan does not write with the motives of heritage/neo-Confederate groups, though his work on African Americans during the war is highly contradictory when it comes to black Confederate combatants. See also Ervin L. Jordan, *Black Confederates and Afro-Yankees in Civil War Virginia* (Charlottesville: University Press of Virginia, 1999). My categorization of quantrillasguerrillas.com as a neo-Confederate website is based on both content and the group's mission statement, in which it notes that "we will promote and commemorate Southern heritage and education by advancing the awareness of the contributions of the Missouri Confederate partisan service." Elsewhere, the site states that "we are a pro-Confederate website" and that "our goal is to present the stories history books don't tell you because they were written by the Yankees."

5. In spite of overwhelming evidence to the contrary, Petersen also suggests that southern laws prevented the breaking up of slave families, that slaves were allowed to keep any wages earned in their spare time by default, and that most slaves were "given wide latitude of freedom" by their benevolent masters. See Paul Petersen, "Slavery in the South," quantrillsguerrillas.com.

6. See Eugene D. Genovese, *Roll, Jordan, Roll: The World the Slaves Made* (New York: Vintage, 1974).

7. *Independence Examiner*, August 22, 1908, in Donald R. Hale, *The William Clarke Quantrill Men Reunions, 1898–1929* [Independence, MO: Blue and Gray Book Shoppe, 2001], n.p.); Hulbert, *The Ghosts of Guerrilla Memory*, 132–33.

8. U.S. Census, 1860, slave schedule, Jackson County; registers of births and deaths, Noland family Bible. On Quantrill's last ride into Kentucky, see Albert Castel, "Quantrill's Missouri Bushwhackers in Kentucky: The End of the Trail," *Filson History Club Quarterly* 38, no. 2 (1964): 125–32.

9. For a better understanding of the role kinship played in guerrilla warfare and might have played in Noland's experiences, see Joseph M. Beilein Jr., *Bushwhackers: Guerrilla Warfare, Manhood, and the Household in Civil War Missouri* (Kent, OH: Kent State University Press, 2016), 81–83.

10. On guerrilla war, see Beilein, *Bushwhackers*; Hulbert, *The Ghosts of Guerrilla Memory*; Andrew William Fialka, "Controlled Chaos: Spatiotemporal Patterns within Missouri's Irregular Civil War," in *The Civil War Guerrilla: Unfolding the Black Flag in History, Memory, and Myth*, ed. Joseph M. Beilein Jr. and Matthew C. Hulbert (Lexington: University Press of Kentucky, 2015), 43–70, and Daniel E. Sutherland, *A Savage Conflict: The Decisive Role of Guerrillas in the American Civil War* (Chapel Hill: University of North Carolina Press, 2003).

11. Petersen, "Go Back Jack and Do It Again"; Patrick R. Marquis, "The Third Greatest Myth of the Civil War," quantrillsguerrillas.com.

12. John N. Edwards, *Noted Guerrillas, or, the Warfare of the Border* (St. Louis: Bryan, Brand, 1877); William E. Connelley, *Quantrill and the Border Wars* (Cedar Rapids, IA: Torch Press, 1910), 310.

13. J. C. Eakin, ed., *Recollections of Quantrill's Guerrillas, as Told by A. J. Walker of Weatherford, Texas, to Victor E. Martin in 1910* (Independence, MO: Two Trails Publishing, 1996), 56–57. On racial stereotypes and guerrilla memoirs, see Hulbert, *The Ghosts of Guerrilla Memory*, chap. 3.

14. William H. Gregg to William E. Connelley, November 26, 1904, Quantrill Research Collection, McCain Library and Archives, University of Southern Mississippi (hereafter QRC).

15. "Frank James Was Missing," *Kansas City (MO) Times*, August 26, 1905.

16. William H. Gregg to William E. Connelley, November 26, 1904, QRC.

17. Even though the film embraces the black Confederate myth, that doesn't stop Patrick Marquis from contending that Holt's on-screen loyalty is in fact "watered down" compared to Noland's in real life ("The Third Greatest Myth of the Civil War").

18. On racial violence in Missouri, see Kimberly Harper, *White Man's Heaven: The Lynching and Expulsion of Blacks in the Southern Ozarks, 1894–1909* (Fayetteville: University of Arkansas Press, 2012).

19. Harvard English professor John Stauffer has argued that the fact that blacks owned black slaves in the Old South means true black Confederates existed (he claims these numbered to between three thousand and six thousand). However, he does not provide any credible primary evidence to verify that blacks voluntarily served as Confederate combat troops. See John Stauffer, "Yes, There Were Black Confederates. Here's Why," January 20, 2015, TheRoot.com.

"Full of Danger to the Community"

Driving the Mormons from Brasstown in Late Nineteenth-Century North Carolina

MARY ELLA ENGEL

IN AUGUST 1879, THE *RALEIGH OBSERVER* ISSUED A WARNING TO North Carolina readers. Only recently made aware that Mormon missionaries actively sought converts in the mountains of north Georgia, the newspaper felt it necessary to alert readers that Mormons had now slipped over the border. "They have broken out in this state, too," the *Observer* warned, and "begun to multiply to an extent that is very gratifying to them and full of danger to the community." What the *Observer* intended in its use of the word "community" is unclear, but it is likely that writers hoped to conjure the image of a tight-knit and cohesive social structure jeopardized by the divisive potential of Mormon proselytizing. For the purposes of this essay, "community" simply establishes the boundaries of a highland mission field on which competing ethnicities—Protestant clergy and Mormon missionaries—battled for the souls of mountain folks.[1]

The community at risk lay approximately three hundred miles west of the state capital, in Cherokee and Clay counties. Ancient mountains—the Great Smoky Mountains and Blue Ridge Mountains—dominated the landscape there. The U.S. government forcibly removed the area's first residents, the Cherokee Indians, in 1838, paving the way for further white settlement of the territory bordering Tennessee and Georgia in North Carolina's westernmost corner. Formed in 1839 and 1861, respectively, Cherokee and Clay counties comprised the state's southwestern edge. Still, local leaders benefited from North Carolina's slave-based economy. Although African Americans constituted slightly more than 6 percent of Cherokee County's population in 1860, local slaveholders dominated society. One of the wealthiest men in the county, William Holland Thomas, owned more than fifty slaves, ran a vibrant mercantile business in the county seat of Murphy, and emerged as a strong advocate for secession. In many ways, Thomas was a typical "mountain master" employing his slaves in a variety of enterprises, since no staple crops were produced in the region.[2]

The Civil War tested those mountain communities. Western North Carolinians did not escape "the internal divisions... that emerged as early as the secession crisis and intensified as the war progressed," and though the region was spared the "full-scale military conflict that tore apart other parts of Southern Appalachia," it did suffer from the bloody guerrilla warfare that often pitted neighbor against neighbor. While infrequent, military raids into the southwestern corner of the state disrupted long-standing community relationships. Confederates, for instance, crossed from Georgia into Cherokee County and abducted eight suspected Unionists—later released—in March 1863. Unionists proved equally dangerous in the divided region, murdering William Walker, a prominent slaveholder in Cherokee County, in October 1864. His body was never recovered. When a riot erupted in the Clay County seat of Hayesville in the war's immediate aftermath, it took a bipartisan posse of sixty men to effect a fragile peace.

During Reconstruction, Carolina highlanders faced the severe social and economic dislocations that characterized the period and sought to restore the "traditional community system as they had known it before the war." That goal—only partially realized—depended, to some extent, on the region's churches. Estimates suggest a doubling of church membership after the war, a religious resurgence that both reflected America's "discovery" of Appalachia in the postwar period and posed a potential threat to those renewed community bonds.[3]

The proselytizing of Mormon missionaries in the late nineteenth-century mountain South coincided with the nation's new awareness of Appalachia as a distinct and unusual place, populated by needy people who only required "education, religion, and civilization" in order to "advance with the rest of the nation." Prompted by concerns for the unchurched souls of Appalachia, Protestant churches rushed to offer relief in the form of home mission societies and settlement houses. In the spirit of competitive Christianity that characterized the last quarter of the nineteenth century, the Presbyterians, Methodists, Baptists, and Episcopalians turned their attention to the mountains. So did the Church of Jesus Christ of Latter-day Saints.[4]

The Mormon missionaries who provoked such concern among Raleigh observers represented a new effort by the church to seek southern converts. Established in 1875, the Southern States Mission sent dozens of Mormon elders into the region. Church authorities directed these lay preachers to share the "first principles," the major points of the Latter-day Saints' restored gospel—faith, repentance, baptism by immersion for the remission of sins, and the gifts of the Holy Spirit. By the time missionaries reached North Carolina, the church had already established a headquarters and prosperous mission field in the mountain counties of Georgia; from there, President John Morgan directed the elders' southern labors. In fact, Morgan's mission journal and letters suggest that he favored the southern mountains for proselytizing. Georgia newspapers marveled that Mormon elders "stick to the mountainous districts," a preference that alarmed North Carolina correspondents, who noted that "the Mormons appear to have chosen the mountains of Georgia as an eligible field of labor, and it is said they have not been unsuccessful in making converts to their peculiar faith." Indeed, Mormon converts in north Georgia provided introductions for Mormon elders as they moved into the highlands of North Carolina, which suggests that cohesive kin and neighbor relationships survived the Civil War.[5]

Considered within the context of this powerful religious push into the mountain South, the work of Mormon missionaries seems to fit neatly within a larger movement dedicated to cultural uplift and determined to propel mountain folks back into American society. In fact, the Mormon Church did not intend a mission dedicated to Appalachia and would not—at this particular time—have supported a program that encouraged cultural assimilation. Indeed, the church firmly set itself apart from America's dominant culture at midcentury when church officials acknowledged the practice of plural marriage (or polygamy) among its members, a revelatory belief viewed by many in the nineteenth-century United States as the social construction of sexually insatiable men. "The Mormon Question" asked Americans to consider the limits of religious freedom but also raised important questions about government's role in defining marriage and family that defied quick or easy resolution. Mormon missionaries who labored in this time period understood that they would likely face serious, often violent, opposition from those people intent on maintaining cultural norms and willing to resolve the national issue on local battlegrounds.[6]

For Elder Joseph Hyrum Parry, the challenge of laboring in a volatile mission field proved irresistible. Parry was nineteen years old when he was first called to mission on behalf of the Latter-day Saints. A devout and obedient saint, he left behind his Salt Lake City home to travel to England in the fall of 1874. He was assigned to labor in the Liverpool conference but preached little there; instead, he devoted most of his time to assisting the emigration of converts to America. Whenever possible, Elder Parry traveled from Liverpool to North Wales, the birthplace of his father and mother. His father, a stonemason, had abandoned the Episcopal Church for Mormonism in the 1840s and transported the family to Brigham Young's new Utah Zion that same decade.[7]

Two years of faithful service in Liverpool culminated in an honorable release to return home, but in 1877 Elder Parry was called to a second European mission, this time to Wales. When he left Salt Lake City for this second mission, he left behind Parthenia Parry, his wife of ten months. If heartache accompanied the separation, it did not diminish his dedication. By January 1879, with new Welsh converts safely delivered to America and only months remaining of his successful second mission, Elder Parry considered his options. Letters from home confirmed that his wife was anxious for his return—according to Parry's journal, she was "not well" when he left Utah and "feared to be left alone." Further, Parry had left her "nearly destitute," he wrote, "trusting that the kind and merciful Father would protect and preserve her, and supply her wants" until his return.[8]

Marital concerns aside, Elder Parry chafed at the thought of returning home without serving the duration of his mission. According to his journal, the missionary felt obligated to put the remaining months of his second mission to good use. Parry regularly received copies of the *Deseret News*, a Salt Lake City newspaper that served as the mouthpiece for the Mormon Church. In that periodical, he read avidly the reports from fellow missionaries in distant mission fields. He particularly looked forward to the "stirring letters" written from Georgia by his former college headmaster and president of the Southern States Mission, John Morgan. In them, he followed the establishment of Mormon branches in the mountainous counties of northwest Georgia, an especially fertile mission field that locals had dubbed "Utah." He celebrated the bravery of Morgan and others who reported to Salt Lake City that "despite opposition," much of it from local ministers, "a general spirit of inquiry has sprung up throughout all this mountain country."[9]

From his European vantage point, Joseph Parry saw an opportunity to further assist his church. He described himself as excited by the possibility of service in the volatile but vibrant Southern States Mission. "In this field," he wrote, "I felt that I should get some real old-time missionary experience." Parry requested and was granted a transfer. It was a decision that would soon place him squarely at the center of a violent confrontation with western North Carolinians intent on resisting Mormon efforts in order to preserve religious norms. Upon receiving permission to labor in the Southern States Mission, Elder Parry booked passage to New York City, arriving in mid-February 1879. He immediately purchased a train ticket for Rome, Georgia. John Morgan's letters to the *Deseret News*, he reasoned, usually originated from that city, and "this was the only address I had." When he disembarked in Rome, he set out to locate his friend and mission president. According to his own account, Parry "wandered about" Rome for several hours in a fruitless search, before finally encountering two men who had once heard Elder Morgan preach. They directed Parry to travel out into the "woodsey" country of Beech Creek in Floyd County. He complied, following a "rough, muddy, and tortuous road as directed," but found "no President there." To his distress, he learned that John Morgan had recently left north Georgia for western North Carolina, a trip intended to open a new mission field in that state.[10]

While Elder Parry awaited his return, John Morgan preached to sizable audiences at Notla in Cherokee County and Brasstown in Clay County, both in far western North Carolina and on the border with Georgia. To readers in Salt Lake City, he reported an initially hospitable welcome from local ministers, describing "the rather novel sight of different denominations holding service together under the same roof" and asking them to imagine "a couple of Baptist ministers uniting with a minister of the Methodist church in inviting a Mormon elder to preach to their congregation." That hospitality would prove short lived. On a chilly day in late February, Morgan dammed a little creek, and baptized his first North Carolina converts. It is likely no coincidence that a warning arrived two days later. The letter, written by a local Methodist farmer-preacher named Henry Green, ordered Morgan "out of the country." Morgan ignored the warning and continued to put the creek to good use. By the first week of March, the area numbered eleven converts, enough to merit the organization of the Brasstown branch of the church.[11]

When Joseph Parry and John Morgan reunited in Georgia in mid-March, Morgan assigned his former student to the new Brasstown branch, along with young elders Thomas S. Higham and Edlef B. Edlefsen, both of whom had recently arrived from Utah. The dedication of three missionaries to a branch consisting of eleven members seems excessive; perhaps Morgan was concerned about sending missionaries into a dangerous field, or possibly he believed that the field would be a fruitful one. Still, an expedition of three Mormon elders guaranteed that they would not slip into the area unnoticed. Indeed, the young missionaries resolved to share their message with all they met along the way, believing that "by discreetly following this course the Elders can do much in spreading the truth." As Joseph Parry explained, "A chance word will often go far afield like thistle-down and find lodgment in some fertile ground." So as they passed from north Georgia into Tennessee and along Ducktown road into North Carolina, they attracted attention. Elder Parry later recalled that although "we didn't know it at the time," this proselytizing strategy "made our coming into North Carolina as widely known throughout the whole countryside as though we were accompanied by a brass band, stirring up both friends and foes, as we were made aware almost immediately." Later, Parry learned that "the enemy" followed their every step. They "dogged our footsteps from the hour we first crossed the state line," Parry said, and "they knew every move and call we made, and arranged to give us a 'public reception' upon our arrival."[12]

Sure enough, the missionaries encountered opposition on their first day in Brasstown. It was early in the morning when a group of three men confronted elders Higham and Edlefsen to order them out of the state. Later that evening, a "committee" of nine armed men, headed by Methodist preacher Henry Green, called on the three missionaries to deliver a written "resolution" which gave the saints twenty-four hours to leave town: "We, the undersigned have decided that we will not put up with doctrines of a certain class of men called Latter Day Saints, and it is decided that if they do not get out within twenty-four hours of this date, we will put them out. Given under our hands and seals this first day of April, 1879." Though the missionaries were told that twenty-one individuals signed (and that the document represented the opinions of three hundred), they were not allowed to read the signatures for themselves. Locals provided the names of the nine-man "committee": Henry Green, Henry Green Jr., John Stephen Bell, Marion M. Webb, John Ditmore, Jefferson J. Bell, Harrison Hampton, Zebulon Allaway, and Robert Coffee. An examination of census records for Clay County confirms that most resided in the Brasstown Township (although Marion Webb lived in the county seat of Hayesville). Henry Green, who considered himself the leader of the committee, appears to have been the oldest. Forty-five years old at the time and identified on the census as a farmer, Green also signed his teenaged son, Henry Green Jr., up for the cause. Except for John Stephen Bell, who was a Brasstown merchant, the men were identified as farmers, although the extent and value of their property was not determined. All were married, most had children, and they were relatively young, the majority under the age of thirty. Whether or not the men were Methodists or members of Henry Green's congregation is unknown.[13]

When asked about their grievances, Reverend Green spoke on behalf of the group:

> You men come in here preaching strange doctrines, the doctrine of laying on of hands for the Gift of the Holy Ghost, and belief in prophets, apostles, and revelations; we do not believe these things, and will not put up with them. You are raising such a disturbance among the people with your doctrines that we hear nothing else but Mormons and Mormonism in everybody's mouth. We are Christian people and want to be left alone in peace, and you must leave in the specified time. We give you this warning for we don't wish to hurt you if you will leave, for leave you must.[14]

It is interesting that polygamy was not specifically listed as a grievance, although the reference to prophets and revelations may suggest that plural marriage was among the practices considered abhorrent. However, it appears that as both the intensity and success of the church's efforts accelerated, so did the threats against Mormon missionaries in North Carolina. A few months later, the *Raleigh Observer* celebrated the local resistance: "The people turned on these Latter-day Saints and threatened to make it hotter for them than the thermometer indicated if they didn't shut up and put out. They were kindly allowed thirty days in which they might arrange their North Carolina affairs previous to their departure to the head of the Saline Lake."[15]

The elders, possessed, Parry said, by "the courage of ignorance," presented an earnest defense, sprinkled heavily with scripture references, but ultimately refused the invitation to leave, at least not before "God's work was done" in the area. Infuriated by the response, the locals dedicated the rest of the night and the next day to "stirring up blind passion and hate," calling a mass meeting of Brasstown residents to address the Mormon problem. A day later, during a meeting at the home of convert Leander Teems, the elders were startled to see a group of approximately fifty men on horseback, gathering on a hillside overlooking the Teems' home. After a time, a "friendly" delegation of five men, including one justice of the peace, broke away from the larger group and rode down to the house. They asked the missionaries whether they intended to disrupt the government there and whether it was their goal to break up the existing churches. The elders responded that their only goal was to preach the gospel in peace. The North Carolinians—described by elders as the "class of better men," so presumably possessing the highest social and economic status—promised to do what they could to avert violence.[16]

Elder Parry targeted local ministers as the chief sources of opposition, describing them in his journal as "jealous" and "slandering," but he also believed the resistance served more to publicize the mission of the Latter-day Saints than discourage it. In June, two more Mormon elders, driven out of northwest Georgia by a mob, arrived to labor in the Brasstown branch, which swelled the missionary force to five elders in the small mountain community. They could have used many more, Parry said, as the Mormon message seemed to be falling on receptive ears. "They would come miles through the woods, day or night to hear us," Parry wrote of the North Carolinians, "and then would remain two or three hours after meeting to listen to us sing the favorite songs of Zion. And in our visits they frequently had us copy words of the songs and teach their children to sing them, with marked success."[17]

Parry believed it was their success that sparked new threats. At midnight, on July 20, an organized mob of armed men raided the homes of the new Mormon converts in Brasstown. After rousing the new saints from their beds, members of the mob proceeded to beat them with fists and clubs. Neither advanced age nor gender deterred their efforts. Seventy-year-old "Pappy" James Harrison and his sixty-year-old wife, Mary, apparently suffered most severely. As the elderly couple lay helpless after the beating, they were warned to give up either their new faith or their homes and property, for they could not continue to practice Mormonism and live in Brasstown. Harrison, a poor farmer who had once commanded "the respect and confidence of the entire community," never recovered from the abuse suffered at the hands of his neighbors. He lingered a few months then died. According to Mormon accounts, Mary Harrison survived but carried the marks from her whipping. No assailants were named, and no charges were filed. Rather, North Carolina converts resolved to leave the state. The new saints who could travel hurriedly tossed belongings into satchels and wagons then deserted their homes and property to flee into north Georgia. North Carolina convert and Brasstown branch president Leander Teems abandoned a farm valued at more than $1,000 in order to protect his wife and seven children from potential abuse.[18]

Elder Parry appealed to North Carolina authorities for help. In a letter to Governor Thomas Jordan Jarvis, he recounted in detail the Brasstown mobbing and his fears for both missionaries and converts, asking the governor to "take steps to protect our people." Although the governor addressed the issue by directing letters to the solicitor general of North Carolina and the sheriffs of Clay and Cherokee Counties, the *Raleigh Observer* accused Parry of "parttruths and exaggerations," arguing that the missionary "in the name of liberty of worship, coolly asks for license of conduct that is not of North Carolina growth or liking." The newspaper also advised that "people with Mormon ideas had better go to Utah, and until they get there, bless Joe Smith that they don't live in Georgia, where a Mormon Elder has been recently found not on the earth nor yet in the heavens—but sorter betwixt and between." Elder Parry reported in disgust that "nothing was done to redress the Saints or punish their assailants."[19]

It was true that Mormons could find little comfort in Georgia. On July 21, the day after the attack on Brasstown converts, elders Joseph Standing and Rudger Clawson had been confronted by an armed mob in northwest Georgia. It is not clear that the mob intended murder—they claimed that they intended only to whip the elders and drive them from the state—but Elder Standing was shot and killed. Though disheartened and sorrowful, the Georgia converts welcomed their North Carolina brethren into their homes.

From as far away as Winston-Salem, journalists reported on growing tensions to the west. "Mormonism has broken out in Cherokee and Clay Counties, and some trouble is anticipated." The Mormons anticipated trouble, too. They now avoided Brasstown. Instead, Elder Parry held meetings at William L. Webster's home in Notla, which he said were well-attended by an attentive and enthusiastic audience. But he found no permanent peace there. On August 3, 1879, he concluded a meeting at the Webster home then retired there for the night, only to be awakened around midnight to find that a mob of men had surrounded the house. Webster attempted to placate the mob, but to no avail. The "ruffians," as Parry described them, continued to demand the surrender of the Mormon elder. When threats were made against the Webster home and family, Parry thought it best to give himself up.[20]

"I was immediately escorted by them into the woods about a quarter of a mile," he recalled. There, they halted, "and began to wrangle as to what they should do with the Elder now they had him in their power." Some argued for physical punishment while others argued for death. As the deliberations continued, Parry reported that he "preached to them what will always be my most earnest and eloquent sermon." He defended Mormonism but also argued his legal rights, pointing out that the U.S. Constitution and the laws of North Carolina "gave me the right to preach the Gospel to them and to their neighbors." The missionary believed that his words "softened the hearts of some of the band," although the leaders of the group became even more enraged. They determined that he should be flogged then expelled from the state, but he was given the right to choose his assailants, a move that Parry deemed, under the circumstances, a "privilege." The mob likely viewed his participation as tacit agreement that he, in fact, deserved punishment.[21]

Parry deliberated for a time, circulating in the moonlight among the assembled men, surreptitiously examining musculatures for signs of weakness. Some of the younger men, he recounted, whispered to him: "Choose me; I'll not hit ya hard." He selected those who promised to go easy to administer his flogging, and they were true to their word, despite putting on a show of energetic punishment. When the leader of the mob (unnamed, but described by Parry as a profane and vicious former Civil War guerrilla) concluded that the Mormon elder had not suffered enough, he stepped in to deliver blows with a stout hickory cane, only stopping when his associates finally cried "enough."[22]

Once recovered from his beating, Elder Parry sought protection from local authorities. Unsuccessful, he turned his back on North Carolina and followed his converts to Georgia. An appeal to church authorities in Utah produced money sufficient for Joseph Parry to deliver the North Carolina saints to the new Mormon settlement of Manassa, located in southern Colorado. Parry lingered among them long enough to assist in the construction of a fine log meeting house before returning to his home in Utah.[23]

It may come as no surprise that local ministers like Henry Green—men who likely viewed themselves as protectors of church, family, and community—took the lead in encouraging opposition to religious outsiders. The violence against Mormon missionaries and converts may be seen as an effort by local religious authorities to establish cultural boundaries beyond which community members could not easily go. It also reflects the disorder created when rival religious groups targeted the human resources of the Appalachian South, as denominational rivalries could incite violence against both unfamiliar religious representatives and their followers. Finally, this incident of anti-Mormonism in North Carolina reveals the attendant loyalties and stresses that accompany community relationships and thus challenges descriptions of community as a mechanism that fosters unity and order. Instead, community is revealed as a location where both disagreement and agreement take place.

NOTES

1. Though there were very few newspapers operating in western North Carolina at this time, periodicals in the east did provide some coverage of the event. See *Raleigh (NC) Observer*, August 10, 1879, and *Union-Republican* (Winston-Salem, NC), August 28, 1879.

2. John C. Inscoe and Gordon B. McKinney, *The Heart of Confederate Appalachia: Western North Carolina in the Civil War* (Chapel Hill: University of North Carolina Press, 2000), 14–15, 18; John C. Inscoe, *Mountain Masters: Slavery and the Sectional Crisis in Western North Carolina* (Knoxville: University of Tennessee Press, 1989), 27, 43, 65–66, 70; Richard B. Drake, "Slavery and Antislavery in Appalachia," in *Appalachians and Race: The Mountain South from Slavery to Segregation*, ed. John C. Inscoe (Lexington: University Press of Kentucky, 2001), 16–26. In 1860, Cherokee County had a total population of 9,166. Of that num-

ber, 520 were enslaved and another 38 were free blacks. We do not have population data for Clay County when it was created in 1861, but voter registration data from 1867–68 is suggestive. At that time, Cherokee's registered voters were 96.3 percent white. Clay County's percentage was slightly higher at 96.9 percent. See Steven E. Nash, *Reconstruction's Ragged Edge: The Politics of Postwar Life in the Southern Mountains* (Chapel Hill: University of North Carolina Press, 2016), 14, 100.

3. Inscoe and McKinney, *The Heart of Confederate Appalachia*, 7–9, 120–21, 143, 150, 196, 270, 284–85.

4. Henry David Shapiro, *Appalachia on Our Mind: The Southern Mountains and Mountaineers in the American Consciousness, 1870–1920* (Chapel Hill: University of North Carolina Press, 1978); Allen W. Batteau, *The Invention of Appalachia* (Tucson: University of Arizona Press, 1990); Mary Beth Pudup, Dwight B. Billings, and Altina L. Waller, eds., *Appalachia in the Making: The Mountain South in the Nineteenth Century* (Chapel Hill: University of North Carolina Press, 1995), especially the editors' introduction, "Taking Exception with Exceptionalism: The Emergence and Transformation of Historical Studies of Appalachia," 1–24; John Alexander Williams, *Appalachia: A History* (Chapel Hill: University of North Carolina Press, 2002); David C. Hsiung, "Stereotypes," in *High Mountains Rising: Appalachia in Time and Place*, ed. Richard A. Straw and H. Tyler Blethen (Urbana: University of Illinois Press, 2004), 101–13; S. Marc Sherrod, "The Southern Mountaineer, Presbyterian Home Missions, and a Synod for Appalachia," *American Presbyterians* 71, no. 1 (1993): 31–40; Loyal Jones, *Faith and Meaning in the Southern Uplands* (Urbana: University of Illinois Press, 1999); Deborah Vansau McCauley, *Appalachian Mountain Religion: A History* (Urbana: University of Illinois Press, 1999); James C. Klotter, "The Black South and White Appalachia," *Journal of American History* 66, no. 4 (1980): 841; Nina Silber, "'What Does America Need So Much as Americans?': Race and Northern Reconciliation with Southern Appalachia, 1870–1900, in *Appalachians and Race: The Mountain South from Slavery to Segregation*, ed. John C. Inscoe (Lexington: University Press of Kentucky, 2001), 245–58.

5. *Atlanta (GA) Constitution*, August 5, 1879; *Raleigh (NC) Observer*, August 6, 1879.

6. Leonard J. Arrington and Davis Bitton, *The Mormon Experience: A History of the Latter-day Saints* (Urbana: University of Illinois Press, 1992); Claudia Lauper Bushman and Richard Lyman Bushman, *Building the Kingdom: A History of Mormons in America* (New York: Oxford University Press, 1999); Richard L. Bushman, *Joseph Smith and the Beginnings of Mormonism* (Urbana: University of Illinois Press, 1984); Eric A. Eliason, ed., *Mormons and Mormonism: An Introduction to an American World Religion* (Urbana: University of Illinois Press, 2001); Jan Shipps, *Mormonism: The Story of a New Religious Tradition* (Urbana: University of Illinois Press, 1985); Kenneth H. Winn, *Exiles in a Land of Liberty: Mormons in America, 1830–1846* (Chapel Hill: University of North Carolina Press, 1989); Patrick Q. Mason, *The Mormon Menace: Violence and Anti-Mormonism in the Postbellum South* (New York: Oxford University Press, 2011).

7. Joseph Parry, "Missionary Experience and Incidents in the Life of Joseph Hyrum Parry, Written By Himself," www.welshmormonhistory.org.

8. Joseph Parry, "Missionary Experience and Incidents in the Life of Joseph Hyrum Parry, Written By Himself."

9. Parry, "Missionary Experience and Incidents in the Life of Joseph Hyrum Parry"; conferences established by John Morgan in the Organization of the Southern States Mission, box 3, folder 5, John Hamilton Morgan Papers, Manuscripts Division, Marriott Library, University of Utah, Salt Lake City (hereafter JHM Papers); John Morgan, letter to the editor, *Deseret News*, December 4, 1876, transcript in vol. 1 of Letters and Articles on the Missionary Labors of President John Morgan, 1872–1879, box 1, book 1, JHM Papers. For the history of the Southern States Mission of the Church of Latter-day Saints, see LaMar C. Berrett, "History of the Southern States Mission, 1831–1861" (MA thesis, Brigham Young University, 1960), Heather M. Seferovitch, "History of the LDS Southern States Mission, 1875–1898" (MA thesis, Brigham Young University, 1996), Rex Thomas Price, "The Mormon Missionary of the Nineteenth Century" (PhD diss., University of Wisconsin-Madison, 1991), Devon H. Nish, "A Brief History of the Southern States Mission for One Hundred Years, 1830–1930," box 8677.5, Special Collections, Harold B. Lee Library, Brigham Young University, Provo, Utah, "Southern States Mission," box 5, folder 27, JHM Papers, and Arthur M. Richardson and Nicholas G. Morgan Sr., *The Life and Ministry of John Morgan* (privately printed, 1965).

10. Record of elders in the Southern States Mission, 1877–1898, Southern States Mission, Manuscript History, reel 1, Church Archives, Salt Lake City, Utah; Parry, "Missionary Experience and Incidents in the Life of Joseph Hyrum Parry."

11. John Morgan, letter to the editor, *Salt Lake Herald*, February 6, 1879, box 1, book 1, JHM Papers; John Morgan to John Taylor, February 13, 1879, box 1, book 1, JHM Papers; John Morgan to President John Taylor, 15 March 1879, Box 2, Folder 3, JHM Papers; John Morgan journal, January 24, 1879, January 25, 1879, January 30, 1879, February 3, 1879, February 8, 1879, February 15, 1879, February 25, 1879, February 26, 1879, February 28, 1879, March 1, 1879, March 4, 1879, March 5, 1879, JHM Papers.

12. Joseph Hyrum Parry, letter to the editor, *Latter-Day Saints' Millennial Star* (Liverpool, UK), March 17, 1879, in Journal History of the Church, Church Archives, Salt Lake City, Utah.

13. Parry, "Missionary Experience and Incidents in the Life of Joseph Hyrum Parry"; U.S. Census, 1870, population schedule, Clay County, Brasstown Township; U.S. Census, 1880, population schedule, Clay County, Brasstown Township; U.S. Census, 1870, population schedule, Clay County, Hayesville; U.S. Census, 1880, population schedule, Clay County, Hayesville.

14. Parry, "Missionary Experience and Incidents in the Life of Joseph Hyrum Parry."

15. *Raleigh (NC) Observer*, August 10, 1879.

16. *Raleigh (NC) Observer*, August 10, 1879.

17. *Raleigh (NC) Observer*, August 10, 1879.

18. Parry, "Missionary Experience and Incidents in the Life of Joseph Hyrum Parry."

19. Parry, "Missionary Experience and Incidents in the Life of Joseph Hyrum Parry"; *Raleigh (NC) Observer*, August 10, 1879.

20. Parry, "Missionary Experience and Incidents in the Life of Joseph Hyrum Parry"; *Union-Republican* (Winston-Salem, NC), August 28, 1879.

21. Parry, "Missionary Experience and Incidents in the Life of Joseph Hyrum Parry."

22. Parry, "Missionary Experience and Incidents in the Life of Joseph Hyrum Parry."

23. John Morgan to John Taylor, September 17, 1879, box 2, folder 3, JHM Papers; John Morgan to John Taylor, September 22, 1879, box 2, folder 3, JHM Papers; John Morgan to John Taylor, October 2, 1879, box 2, folder 4, JHM Papers. For North Carolina converts living in Manassa, see U.S. Census, 1880, population schedule, Manassa, Conejos County; records of Old Manassa Cemetery, Manassa, Conejos, CO.

Community and the Commons

*Richmond Pearson and the Buncombe
County Stock Law Revolt of 1885–87*

LUKE MANGET

ON THE MORNING OF JUNE 8, 1885, ONE OF THE MOST CONTENtious commission meetings in Buncombe County history was brought to order. In addition to more than a dozen commissioners and justices of the peace, citizens from Black Mountain, Upper Hominy, Sandy Mush, and other communities across the county packed the meeting room. Some carried petitions with hundreds of signatures on them that called on commissioners to exempt their respective districts from the operations of a countywide stock law passed a few months earlier by the Democratic legislature in Raleigh, North Carolina. This law would have effectively closed the county's open range by requiring livestock owners in most of Buncombe County to fence in their animals. However, it also included a clause that allowed certain districts to opt out of the law if a majority of registered voters in those locales petitioned to do so at the county commissioners' meeting in June 1885. Having acquired enough signatures, the attendees now waited anxiously for the commissioners to address their petitions and reject the proposed fence law.

The commissioners ultimately proved unwilling to cooperate. Though promising the audience that their concerns would be heard at the end of the day, the commissioners abruptly adjourned the meeting in the early afternoon before doing so, prompting a cacophony of shouts and jeers. "We have our stock law," one of them reportedly yelled, while others cried, "Shame."[1] This meeting marked the beginning of the stock law revolt in Buncombe County that would make Richmond Pearson, a relative newcomer to the county and a young independent Democrat, an unlikely leader in the movement to protect the commons.

The Buncombe County stock law revolt was one chapter in a series of violent and nonviolent disputes over new fence laws that swept across the American South during the late nineteenth century. Prior to the Civil War, laws required southern farmers to fence in their crops, thereby shielding livestock owners—whose stock remained free to roam—from liability for damages to those crops. After the war, states began a piecemeal shift away from this open-range system in favor of legislation mandating that livestock owners fence in their animals. By the 1880s, much of the Piedmont South had adopted such laws. There, conservative Democrats successfully pushed through the stock law, in part, by capitalizing on racism and the need for black labor to unify landowning whites against the open range.[2]

In western North Carolina, however, rural opposition to enclosing the open range continued well into the twentieth century.[3] This was partially due to the region's relatively small African American population, which likely caused stock law proponents' fearmongering against "negro rule" to resonate less with mountain whites.[4] Perhaps more importantly, many rural mountaineers remained dependent on the open range to earn a living. In the Carolina highlands, nature and culture had created a strong commitment to a system of land use characterized by overlapping networks of commons, or resources that were widely accessible to both whites and blacks. Local custom recognized all community members' right to access the forest for livestock forage, as well as game, fish, medicinal herbs, nuts, and more.[5] Consequently, many rural residents viewed fence laws as a threat to their livelihoods and communities.[6] The stock law controversy in Buncombe County channeled this commons culture into partisan politics and benefited the Republican Party, which by opposing the law, garnered the support of white voters—Democratic and Republican alike—who sought to preserve and protect the local community from outside interference.

The southern range was established in the earliest days of Euro-American settlement, when abundant land and forage and a relatively sparse human population made fencing in livestock unprofitable and undesirable. Though many owned a few head of cattle, virtually all farmers, including tenants, owned hogs, which they turned loose in the forests for much of the year, notching their ears to identify them during the fall roundup. It required little capital or manpower to keep livestock in the mountains. Hogs fed themselves on chestnuts and other mast, while cattle browsed on grass and other plants. Meanwhile, farmers fired the woods annually to stimulate new growth.[7] Whether they owned land or not, all livestock owners' shared use of the mountains to nourish their animals strengthened their ties to the forests. As Edward King remarked about southwestern Virginians in 1875, "Their love for the peaks, among which they range their droves of cattle, horses, and hogs, amounts to devotion."[8]

Livestock forage was only one way in which rural southerners interacted with the commons. Throughout the eighteenth and nineteenth centuries, residents of all ages, genders, and backgrounds utilized unimproved spaces for subsistence and recreational purposes. They used these spaces to hunt, fish, and gather berries, nuts, mushrooms, ginseng (or "sang"), and other resources. In the higher altitudes, people sought out groves of sugar maples, or "sugar orchards," tapping them in the late winter to make sugar, molasses, and syrup. The forested mountainsides, the streams, and the grassy balds were all treated as commons by local inhabitants. The commons allowed farmers to supplement their incomes and provided land-poor residents with the opportunity to earn a living without having to depend on "public work" or charity. It was also a space for recreation, where neighbors bonded during hunting, fishing, and ginseng hunting, or "sanging," trips. One West Virginian recalled the role that "sanging" played in creating and maintaining friendships: "A day of sanging had all the fun of gambling with no risk of losing any of your own nickels."[9] Indeed, the commons was part of the social, cultural, and economic fabric of mountain communities. It was woven into their identity.

The existence of vast forests in the mountains may have fostered this system of land use, but the idea that people should have access to resources on unimproved land predated European colonization of the New World. Indeed, common rights were rooted deep in European, Native American, and African pasts.[10] Some Anglo-Americans believed that their rights derived from English common law, while others clothed their rhetoric in the Enlightenment discourse of natural rights.[11] Many eighteenth- and nineteenth-century Americans, in particular, believed that a person did not really own the land until he mixed his labor with nature. Although this labor theory of ownership served as an early rationale for dispossessing Native Americans of their land, it also had implications for ongoing land use, namely, that if a person could not improve the land with his (or his slaves') labor, then he owned too much land, and thus, for the public's welfare, anyone could use his land.[12] Of course, these beliefs were not unique to southern Appalachia, but the highland landscape fostered and reinforced them. Due to the relatively small acreage suitable to monocrop agriculture and the fact that outside individuals and companies owned some three-quarters of the land, "commoning" became as much a part of subsistence patterns as agriculture in the mountain region.[13]

Over time, common rights became intimately bound up in Appalachian community identity. Landowners had a legal right to post no trespassing signs, and some of them did, but to "do so unneighborly a thing" often drew the ire of local residents.[14] As Fred Burnett, a famous hunter from eastern Buncombe County, explained about life in the late nineteenth century, "Where we lived, no man set himself above his neighbor nor was he another's servant."[15] In threatening both of these tenets, new fence laws rent holes in the fabric of community. In the 1880s, for instance, Chattanooga businessman John T. Wilder constructed a fence around the grassy balds that surrounded his hotel on top of Roan Mountain in eastern Tennessee. The fences, however, were burned repeatedly by locals, who had long used the balds to graze their livestock. Wilder eventually gave up trying to build fences, and "victory remained with the upholders of primeval communal privileges."[16] A similar confrontation occurred in the early 1870s when James Bailey of Yancey County, North Carolina, attempted to fence in a deer herd on his fifty-acre property, infuriating local hunters who—viewing Bailey's act as an affront to their rights—"flatly refused to believe that there was such a thing as the Posting Law."[17] Such anecdotes reveal the tension that fences evoked in communities built around equal access to resources.[18] Allowing access to one's unimproved spaces was part of being a member of a community, and the community often compelled landowners to accept that conventional practice by destroying property.

Richmond Pearson was an unlikely champion of common rights. Born in Yadkin County in 1852 to a wealthy judge and North Carolina Supreme Court chief justice with the same name, Pearson graduated from Princeton at age twenty, valedictorian of his class, and spent the next several years working as a diplomat in the U.S. State Department before returning to North Carolina in 1879. By 1882, he had married a wealthy debutante from Richmond, Virginia, and moved to Asheville to practice law. Within a few years, he had accumulated forty-nine tracts of real estate in Buncombe County worth more than $230,000.[19] Pearson was not a stock law partisan when he decided to run for the North Carolina House of Representatives in 1884, but he demonstrated an independent streak that eventually enabled him to embrace the issue. Influenced by his Republican father, he ran as an independent Democrat.

By the early 1880s, the Republican Party was resurgent in western North Carolina. In the late 1860s and early 1870s, widespread anti-Confederate sentiment and an active Freedmen's Bureau translated into early, albeit limited, support for the party among mountain whites who hoped to challenge the economic and political dominance of former Confederates. However, the end of the Freedmen's Bureau in 1868 and intensified violence from the Ku Klux

Klan weakened mountain Republicanism and brought conservatives back to power across North Carolina. Democrats aggressively pursued a vision of a "New Mountain South" based on railroads, agricultural reform, and industrial development, leaving Republican leaders searching for a new set of issues that could turn their fortunes around. Disentangling itself from the contentious racial politics of Reconstruction, the party focused instead on issues that protected local autonomy, and by the early 1880s, white North Carolinians—especially those in the mountains—began to defect from the Democratic Party in large numbers.[20] As an independent who flirted with Republicanism, Pearson was poised to ride the wave.

The stock law emerged as the most important issue to Buncombe County voters during the 1884 campaign. In particular, voters in rural communities demanded to know where candidates stood on the "fence question." At an October meeting in Avery Creek, Pearson and Johnstone Jones, another Democratic candidate, reportedly opposed changes in the fence laws.[21] For the most part, however, the two politicians tried to avoid the topic, as the stock law had increasingly become a divisive issue, especially around Asheville. Instead, Pearson focused on public education and manufacturing.[22] Buncombe Democrats similarly devoted most of their attention to the subject of the pending completion of the Asheville and Spartanburg Railroad and the creation of a railroad commission.[23] With minimal Republican opposition, Pearson and Jones were the top two vote getters, and in January 1885, they took their seats in Raleigh as Buncombe's delegation in the house of representatives.

A former state adjutant general and editor of the *Charlotte Observer*, Johnstone Jones was also a relative newcomer to the county, having moved to Asheville in the early 1880s to practice law. In the years following the Civil War, he oversaw the rebuilding of the state militia and later served as secretary to the state constitutional convention in 1875, which successfully rolled back many of the democratic reforms of the "radical" constitution of 1868. Upon taking office in 1885, he quickly angered many Buncombe County residents by introducing a bill that required all livestock owners in the county to fence in their animals. Like other "stock law men" throughout the South, Jones claimed that the bill would boost agricultural production, improve stock-raising methods, and reduce the costs of fencing. Though many southern planters saw the stock law as a way to control black labor, this was not the case in Buncombe County because large-scale agriculture did not dominate its economy.[24] By the 1880s, however, timber had emerged as a valuable commodity in the region, encouraging some landowners to become timber speculators and—no longer wanting commoners to set fire to the woods and potentially damage their investment—to support the fence law. Other stock law proponents were conservationists also concerned about damage to trees and farmers who felt it was unfair that they had to protect their property from the intrusions of wandering stock.[25] Jones drew on a discourse of progress to defend his bill, telling the *Asheville Citizen* in 1886 that the law "teaches the great lesson that we must respect each other's rights of property.... Let our shibboleth be progress— People everywhere are quitting old, effete methods, and are taking to new improved ones, better adapted to existing conditions, and reaching out and upward, climbing higher and higher towards more elevated planes of civilization and enlightenment."[26]

Pledged to oppose the stock law, Pearson voted against the bill and convinced Jones to include an exception clause that would allow several rural districts in Buncombe County to opt out by petitioning county commissioners at their June meeting.[27] He also attended the commissioners' meeting that June and, like many in attendance, was shocked when the board adjourned before considering the petitions. Though not a stock law partisan when he first went to Raleigh, Pearson—recognizing an opportunity to harness voter anger—immediately embraced the anti–stock law crusade. That following week, he helped to organize a mass meeting and wrote and presented a petition of grievances to the board of commissioners. In it, Pearson claimed that the commissioners adjourned "accidentally or inadvertently" and demanded that the citizens of Buncombe County be allowed to vote on the proposed stock law. He further argued that Democrats had abandoned the principle of local self-government by imposing a law on citizens who were not ready to accept it. "To force any law upon a people, in the face of their express and overwhelming protests, is to follow the methods of a Czar or a Sultan," Pearson warned, pointing out that—unlike residents elsewhere in the state—western North Carolinians heavily depended on unimproved land to earn a living. "As the law is an experiment in a mountainous county, let its merits be tested by the townships in which it is absolute," he concluded.[28]

Meanwhile, angry residents mobilized against the stock law. From the summer through the winter of 1885, stock law opponents held several mass meetings across the county.[29] Pearson was a visible and vocal figure at most of these meetings. Other leaders included Captain Nathaniel Atkinson, a Democrat, former Confederate officer, attorney, and fruit grower from Swannanoa; Robert Patterson, a forty-two-year-old Swannanoa farmer and landowner; Thomas J. Candler, a landowning farmer and Republican from Lower Hominy; and Grady Howell, a landowning farmer from Upper Hominy. Each meeting produced a series of resolves trumpeting the same message: shame on the members of the legislature and the board of commissioners and a pledge that "we will never support any candidate for the Legislature who is not known to be in favor of the repeal of the aforesaid 'no fence law.'"[30] Some attendees even called for the creation of a third party around the issue. They all asserted that the stock law was not suited to the "unfencible and untillable mountain lands" and that it violated the "material interests and protection of the most sacred rights of the people of this county."[31] They also advocated for the eradication of the "undemocratic system of county government" that Democrats had established after Democrats successfully regained control of state politics in the early 1870s. Under this system, the state legislature rather than local voters selected the county commissioners.

Unfortunately, few letters from stock law opponents to the editor of the *Asheville Citizen* in Buncombe County have survived, as the pro–stock law newspaper refused to publish anything that might help the opposition. In order to understand the law's critics, therefore, we must turn to accounts in other newspapers in western North Carolina where similar disputes occurred in the 1880s and 1890s. As numerous letters to the editors revealed, some mountain people worried about the cost of the fencing, while others expressed more concern with maintaining local control of their institutions than protecting the commons. However, most Carolina highlanders opposed the law because it represented a threat to their community identity, which had always been bound up in the land and access to it. The mountains were "a paradise for the poor man, and a delightful abode for all who live within her borders," Leander Green wrote to the *Watauga Democrat* when Watauga County began considering a stock law in 1892. "Deprive our people of [the range] and in a few years you look upon this lovely land, the boasted paradise of the poor man, converted by the stock law into a wilderness of distress and poverty.... The stock law is not a native of Watauga and will never do well if transplanted in our soil."[32] Viewing the stock law as part of a general enclosure attempt, rural mountain residents defended the open range by appealing to a broader commons ethos. "I think they have the same right to turn their stock on our lands, as they have to dig roots, gather herbs and skin our timber, which has always been the custom of our country," John Winebarger informed the *Watauga Democrat* in 1892. "Suppose we were to post our land and deprive the people the liberty of digging roots and gathering herbs. Would it not be a great disadvantage to our people here in the mountains?"[33] These stock law opponents were not concerned with agricultural progress or state politics. To them, the law threatened to overturn community customs that determined who had access to what resources.

Some western North Carolinians believed that the stock law, like other enclosure schemes, was a plot by wealthy landowners to control the poor and dominate the community. The law would be particularly hard on tenants, critics argued, because they would have to rent pasturelands, thereby making raising livestock prohibitively expensive. "By bringing [the stock law] in, in that way [the rich] will soon have the whole of everything at their command," a Caldwell County man wrote to the editor of the *Lenoir Topic* in 1885. "The poor man must work at their price, then give their price for meat, milk, and butter, or let his children starve. In doing so they root the poor man out further and further, stamp him lower and lower, till at last he will have to depend on the unmerciful rich man for everything, and at last he will become his slave."[34] Indeed, slavery was on the minds of many commons defenders as they attempted to forestall other enclosure attempts. During statewide discussions in West Virginia over an 1873 bill prohibiting the digging of ginseng on private property, for example, one man claimed that the proposed law would be a "step towards enslaving the industrious poor people and placing them in the power of the wealthier class of landowners.... God created all men free, and He intended the uncultivated hills and hollows for their heritage."[35] Mobilizing this kind of commons rhetoric and equating enclosure with slavery, mountain people generated widespread opposition to the Buncombe County stock law.

In the summer of 1885, anti–stock law sentiments spilled over into the courts. James McNair, a property owner in Black Mountain, hired Asheville attorney (and Pearson protégé) Foster A. Sondley to file a lawsuit on behalf of "himself and all other resident tax-payers and property holders" of Black Mountain. Accusing the county commissioners of violating the rights of petitioners granted in the stock law bill, McNair asked for an injunction against the enforcement of the act until their petitions could be heard. Some 90 percent of Black Mountain taxpayers had signed a petition for exemption from the law, he asserted, which commissioners had illegally ignored.[36] Avery Creek farmer John Ingram issued a passionate plea to the court for his community. "The woods are full of valuable food for stock, our people live largely by raising stock for sale and it is almost their only source of income," he wrote, "and I am confident that the enforcement in our township during the coming winter of the Stock law will produce great loss and even great suffering among its people."[37] Nearly every commissioner submitted affidavits defending their actions, and while they focused primarily on the details of the commissioners' meeting, most took the liberty to argue for the necessity of the stock law. Commissioner George Whitson, a Swannanoa dentist and farmer, claimed that he was "well acquainted

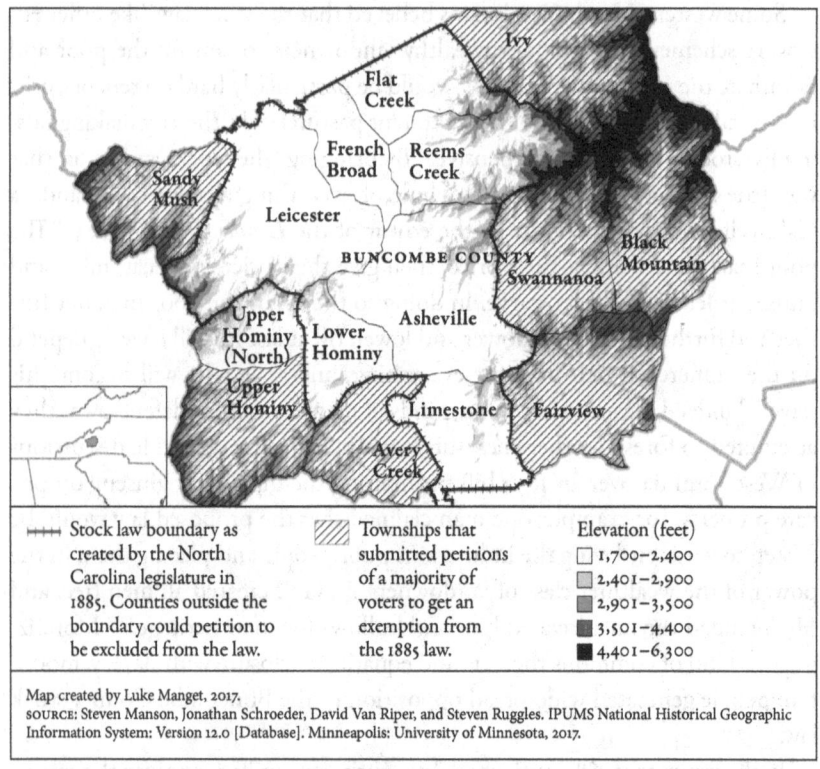

MAP 2. The Buncombe County Stock Law, 1885

with the wants and needs of the agricultural population of Buncombe County" and "well satisfied in his own mind that the stock law while it may prove injurious to some individuals here and there will be of great benefit to the public generally."[38] The superior court sided with the commissioners, but McNair appealed his case to the state supreme court. At the October session, the state's high court reversed the lower court's decisions, issued a temporary injunction, and ordered the commissioners and justices of the peace to hold another joint meeting in February 1886 to receive the petitions.[39]

At the much-anticipated February joint meeting of the board of commissioners and justices of the peace, Pearson personally presented the petitions to the board for consideration, and Johnstone Jones and others spoke in support of the stock law. A committee was then appointed to review the petitions, and by the evening, it announced the results. The petitions included the signatures of some 80 percent of Black Mountain's registered voters, 63 percent of Swannanoa voters, 72 percent of Fairview voters, 65 percent of Avery Creek voters, 51 percent of Upper Hominy voters, 56 percent of Sandy Mush voters, and 65 percent of Ivy voters. Petitioners were elated, as the law required only a majority of registered voters to exempt a particular township from the law. But the justices and commissioners now had to vote on whether each district would be exempted. To the dismay of petitioners, the board exempted only Black Mountain and Avery Creek. Additionally, the members somewhat arbitrarily divided Upper Hominy, a community in the western part of the county, into two sections—North and South Hominy—and declared the more mountainous South Hominy exempt from the law.[40] Once again, stock law opponents felt that the board had silenced their voice.

Following the February meeting, the "fence question" showed no signs of resolution. Pearson published an "open letter to the voters of the 'outside townships'" in local newspapers. In his diatribe, he excoriated Jones for his undemocratic bill and accused commissioners of inflating the voting rolls with dead people and refusing to count the votes of nonlandowners. He also continued to argue against the necessity of the stock law:

> There are parts of this county, such as the great ranges on Black Mountain, on Craggy, and on Pisgah, where there are fifty acres of wild land to one acre in cultivation, where a man can take his stand on a commanding point and look for miles around without seeing a single field, or the smoke of a human habitation, where the wild mast and herbage are abundant and rich, where the lands are too rugged for cultivation, where tillage is unprofitable, where cattle raising is the only remunerative employment of the people, and where fencing is entirely unnecessary for cattle raising—for such sections as these, a cast iron law prohibiting stock from running at large is not a benefit but an intolerable hardship.[41]

Promising to work in Raleigh to repeal Jones's law, Pearson then urged disgruntled residents not to resort to violence and instead to turn to "the tribunal of last resort—the ballot box."[42]

Pearson failed to follow his own advice. Throughout the spring of 1886, he was embroiled in a public feud with Jones, and Asheville's newspapers took sides. The *Asheville Advance*, a Republican paper, backed Pearson and the anti-stock law men, while the *Asheville Citizen* supported Jones and the stock law. In April, the *Asheville Citizen* published a seven-column, two-page open letter from Jones to the "People of Buncombe County," defending the necessity of the law and criticizing Pearson's behavior. Jones maintained that most of the county was no longer made up of "wild ranges" and had been settled by people who farmed for a living. He then accused Pearson of ignoring the will and the desire of property owners, who he claimed found it too expensive to pay for both the cost of fences and the taxes to support landless residents. "If [Pearson] will inquire," Jones wrote, "he will find that nearly all the owners of the wild ranges mentioned are friends of the stock law and would be pleased to have the exclusive enjoyment of their property."[43] He also labeled Pearson a demagogue, attacked his personal character, and questioned his courage.

Livid, Pearson fired off a letter to Jones in which he declared that such a slight to his honor could not go unanswered. "I feel satisfied that you will not deny me the opportunity of vindicating it," he wrote.[44] News that Pearson had challenged Jones to a duel spread rapidly through newspapers across the state. Jones publicly declined to take up the gauntlet; he not only cited his principled opposition to dueling but also claimed that the stakes were unequal. If he were to die, his family would be left destitute, whereas if Pearson were killed, his family would remain wealthy.[45] To many Americans, including North Carolinians, affairs of honor seemed at best quaint and at worst illegal. The *New York Times* satirized the incident as a fight between "two colonels" that demonstrated the "progress happening in North Carolina."[46] But honor, although weakened by the events of the mid-nineteenth century, remained a strong social force in the South, and Pearson had many supporters who recognized him as a firebrand critic of Bourbon democracy. Pearson was brought up on charges of conspiring to start a duel, but despite having the handwritten letter from Pearson challenging Jones to a duel, the grand jury refused to indict him.[47]

Running for reelection during the fall of 1886, Pearson campaigned on the promise that he would work to repeal the stock law and reform the system of county government. Nominated by Buncombe Republicans in their September convention, he quickly became the target of vicious Democratic attacks in the local press. The *Asheville Citizen* waged a relentless campaign against him, attempting to stoke whites' racial fears by claiming that Pearson's support was mostly from "negroes, most of whom live in Asheville township" and "not ten percent" of whom "own any property."[48] Pearson's reelection, the newspaper warned, would "vitally injure the white people of the east and the white property-holders and regular tax-payers of Buncombe."[49] The editors of the *Citizen* predicted he could never win, but they underestimated the opposition to the stock law in the county. Attracting enough support from Republicans and anti–stock law Democrats, Pearson won the election by a majority of around eleven hundred votes and credited his convincing victory to his stand on the issue.[50]

Pearson's reelection was part of a surge, as Republicans and independents took control of the House of Representatives in the fall of 1886. Disenchanted white farmers and workers from across the state bolted from the Democratic Party. Many of these voters were drawn to third parties, such as the Greenback-Labor Party, the Prohibition Party, and the People's Party, and so state Republican leaders situated the party to attract the protest vote. In addition to adopting positions against using convict labor for road construction and against the county government system, the state Republican Party—well aware of the power of stock law opposition in the west—also demanded that local communities be able to vote on the stock law. Although Democrats remained in power in the Senate, the Republican platform attracted enough of these disaffected voters to win over the House of Representatives.[51]

Pearson followed through on his promise to repeal and replace the Buncombe stock law, introducing a bill in January 1887 that allowed each township to vote on whether the stock law would apply to their districts. In a well-executed plan of subversion, Democrat and stock law man H. A. Gudger introduced a companion bill in the senate that also replaced the existing law but provided for elections in only four townships. As the general assembly debated the bills, two delegations from Buncombe County—one in favor of the repeal, the other against it—visited Raleigh to lobby legislators. Both bills passed their respective houses, but when the Democratic conference committee hashed out the disparities between the bills, it included most of the senate's version to the consternation of Pearson, who then attempted unsuccessfully to amend it. Buncombe's new law did protect the open range in Black Mountain, Avery Creek, and South Hominy where voters had already rejected the stock law, but it allowed only the voters of Ivy, Swannanoa, Fairview, and Sandy Mush townships to vote on the stock law if they could produce new petitions with the signatures of a majority of registered voters in four months.[52] As these four townships included some of the highest mountain ranges and the fewest cultivated acres in the county, Democrats successfully protected the existing stock law in the loamy bottomlands of the French Broad river valley. By the August deadline, only Swannanoa and Fairview had submitted petitions. Ivy took no action, and Sandy Mush residents, for reasons that remain unclear, submitted and then withdrew their petition.[53] In November, Swannanoa and Fairview voted against the stock law by a solid majority, adding their lands to Black Mountain, South Hominy, and Avery Creek as the last places in Buncombe where the open range persisted.[54]

The stock law continued to generate controversy in the mountains as residents and politicians wrangled for decades over the fate of the livestock commons. A patchwork of overlapping laws passed by the general assembly reflected the renegotiations taking place. In 1885, a year after the state prohibited people living inside stock law territory to run stock outside of the territory, the North Carolina legislature exempted the counties west of the Blue Ridge from the operations of the law, protecting access to the open range there. This law took effect before any mountain county adopted the stock law, which suggests that the law's supporters wanted to maintain access to the mountains for people residing in stock law territory in the Piedmont. Apparently, nonmountain residents ranging their stock in the mountains had become a problem, for in 1889 and 1891, the state passed laws making it unlawful for nonresidents to range livestock in Graham and Swain counties, effectively creating an exclusive open range for locals. In 1887, the state made it a felony to kill livestock on the range in southwestern North Carolina.

These protections of the open range proved short lived. In 1891, when Pearson was no longer a house delegate, the general assembly passed another law adding all of Buncombe County outside of Black Mountain to the stock law territory.[55] From 1895 to 1915, portions of every mountain county fell under the stock law, either by popular vote or by legislative fiat. In 1895, the state laid out the election process for southwestern counties of Jackson, Graham, Swain, Clay, Macon, and Cherokee, requiring petitions from a majority of voters in a district to force a vote. Subsequent decades saw large sections of these counties adopt the law. In 1903, Ashe County simply removed legal protections of livestock owners for damages to growing crops. In 1921, state legislators passed a stock law that applied to all counties in eastern North Carolina, but pockets of open range persisted in the mountains for decades until the general assembly enacted a statewide stock law in 1971.[56]

Pearson and the Republican Party remained popular in western North Carolina for more than a decade after the revolt. In 1894, voters in what was then the Ninth District elected Pearson to Congress over Waynesville Democratic incumbent William Crawford. As it did in upcountry Georgia, the stock law issue galvanized voters in Buncombe County and other parts of western North Carolina and paved the way for populism.[57] This time running as a Republican on a fusion ticket, Pearson received support from populists, who willingly overlooked his commitment to protective tariffs because he supported free silver, an income tax, and honest elections. Although the stock law was no longer a campaign issue, the revolt helped launch Pearson into statewide political leadership and mobilized his base of Republican voters. Pearson would go on to serve three terms in the U.S. House before President Theodore Roosevelt appointed him U.S. consul in Genoa, Italy.[58]

The closing of the open range did not upend the commons ideal in mountain communities, but it was a severe economic blow to users, as livestock was one of the principal ways in which they procured food and earned extra income from the forest. The stock law was part of the opening salvo that would lead to the gradual erosion of the de facto commons, the commons created by local custom. Between the 1880s and the 1920s, as much of the mountains fell under the new stock law, states took aim at other common rights with new fish and game regulations that required, for example, landowners' permission to hunt and fish on private lands. Some states also passed laws prohibiting the digging of ginseng on private lands without the landowners' permission. This placed corporate and government landowners in the position of commons managers, and they generally worked to curtail subsistence uses of the forest.[59] In addition, as increasing numbers of outsiders moved into the mountains following World War II, they brought with them different ideas of property rights that were often at odds with community norms. Watauga County native Juanita Jones lamented in 1993 that when these newcomers came into the community, "the first thing they do is put up a No Trespassing sign and they don't want anything to do with the community."[60] Council Main, who grew up in Watauga County in the 1940s, recalled the commons as a "way of life" in the mountains. "If I found something on your land, I could get it. Or if they found it on ours, they could get it. You didn't have these 'no trespassing' signs... The tops of the mountains were just for everybody."[61] In the 1880s, such a defense of community access to the commons informed the opposition to the stock law and generated support for the Republican Party.

NOTES

1. Details of the commissioners' meeting are gleaned from the North Carolina Supreme Court case *James McNair et al. v. Commissioners of Buncombe County*, 93 NC 364 (NC, 1885).

2. Most historiographical debate over the stock law centers on the motives of stock law proponents and opponents. Steven Hahn sees the stock law controversy as an ideological and class conflict in which opponents of the law sought to protect their vision of a cooperative commonwealth against large landlords who hoped to use stock laws to control white and black laborers. According to Hahn, this vision translated into support for populism in the 1890s. Hahn's critics, most notably J. Morgan Kousser and Shawn Kantor, argue that the stock law was neither a class nor ideological conflict. Rather, it was an economically rational response to the growing population and the increased costs of fencing during the late nineteenth century. The stock law controversy in Buncombe County was not entirely about class or labor control, as supporters and opponents often came from the same economic station. However, stock law opponents there seemed to be motivated by a precapitalist sense of

egalitarianism rooted in a commitment to the protection of common rights. And the story of Richmond Pearson suggests that opposition to the stock law translated into support for populism. See Steven Hahn, "Hunting, Fishing, and Foraging: Common Rights and Class Relations in the Postbellum South," *Radical History Review* 26 (1982): 37–64, Steven Hahn, *The Roots of Southern Populism: Yeoman Farmers and the Transformation of the Georgia Upcountry, 1850–1890* (New York: Oxford University Press, 1983), Shawn Kantor, "The Economic and Political Determinants of Fence Reform in Postbellum Georgia," *Journal of Institutional and Theoretical Economics* 150, no. 3 (1994): 486–510, Shawn Kantor, *Politics and Property Rights: The Closing of the Open Range in the Postbellum South* (Chicago: University of Chicago Press, 1998), Crawford King, "The Closing of the Southern Range: An Exploratory Study," *Journal of Southern History* 48, no. 1 (1982): 53–70, Brian Sawers, "Property Law as Labor Control in the Postbellum South," *Law and History Review* 33, no. 2 (2015): 351–76, Drew A. Swanson, "Fighting over Fencing: Agricultural Reform and Antebellum Efforts to Close the Virginia Open Range," *Virginia Magazine of History and Biography* 117, no. 2 (2009): 104–39, Matthew Walpole, "The Closing of the Open Range in Watauga County, NC," *Appalachian Journal* 16, no. 4 (1989): 320–35, and Shawn Kantor and J. Morgan Kousser, "Common Sense or Commonwealth? The Fence Law and Institutional Change in the Postbellum South," *Journal of Southern History* 59, no. 2 (1993): 201–42.

3. Buncombe, western North Carolina's most populous and commercialized county, was the first in the region to adopt the stock law in the mid-1880s, and it did so against the wishes of a majority of its voters. Most other counties in the western part of the state would not adopt the law for another decade or more. Buncombe's population was over fifteen thousand in 1870. The next most populous county in the western part of the state was Ashe at ninety-five hundred. The level of commercialization of a given area can be gauged by the amount of real estate and personal property, which in Buncombe was assessed at nearly $2 million in 1870, over twice that of the next highest western county (Ashe at $830,000). For these statistics, see U.S. Census Bureau, *Report of the Ninth Census*, vol. 1: *The Statistics of the Population of the United States* (Washington, DC: Government Printing Office, 1872), 52–54, U.S. Census Bureau, *Report of the Ninth Census*, vol. 3: *The Statistics of The Wealth and Industry of the United States* (Washington, DC: Government Printing Office, 1872), 49–51.

4. For more on the racial views of mountain whites after the Civil War, see Steven E. Nash, *Reconstruction's Ragged Edge: The Politics of Postwar Life in the Southern Mountains* (Chapel Hill: University of North Carolina Press, 2016), and Gordon B. McKinney, *Southern Mountain Republicans, 1865–1900: Politics and the Appalachian Community* (Knoxville: University of Tennessee Press, 1978).

5. For more on commons culture in western North Carolina, see Kathryn Newfont, *Blue Ridge Commons: Environmental Activism and Forest History in Western North Carolina* (Athens: University of Georgia Press, 2012).

6. Because southern states typically empowered local districts to vote on the issue, the stock law controversy played out in a thousand different contexts. Several historians have effectively utilized the lens of community studies to explore the southern fence laws, focusing primarily on explaining the motivations behind them. However, to fully explain opposition to the Buncombe County stock law, we must expand the scope of community studies beyond its traditional concern with questions involving social relations, economic inequality,

and political opinions on a local level. From this perspective, the stock law was more than a question of torts or a mere change in property law; it represented a fundamental change to the relationship between nature and culture in the mountain communities. Few scholars have attempted to recreate the intricate and dynamic relationships between rural communities and nature. These relationships remained part of what Ivan Illich has called the "vernacular" landscape, which were undocumented and visible only on the local level. Hahn and Walpole have come the closest, and since their publications, new scholarship on rural communities and their environments has enhanced our understanding of these relationships. See, for example, Newfont, *Blue Ridge Commons*, and Karl Jacoby, *Crimes against Nature: Squatters, Poachers, Thieves, and the Hidden History of American Conservation* (Berkeley: University of California Press, 2001).

7. Donald Edward Davis, *Where There Are Mountains: An Environmental History of the Southern Appalachians* (Athens: University of Georgia Press, 2000), 100–107.

8. Edward King, "The Great South: Among the Mountains of Western North Carolina," *Scribner's Monthly*, March 1874, 513–44.

9. John Nuttall, *Trees above with Coal Below* (San Diego, CA: Neyenesch Printers, 1961), 18.

10. Peter Linebaugh, *Stop, Thief! The Commons, Enclosures, and Resistance* (Oakland, CA: PM Press, 2014); Eric T. Freyfogle, *On Private Property: Finding Common Ground on the Ownership of Land* (Boston: Beacon Press, 2007).

11. Stephen Aron, *How the West Was Lost: The Transformation of Kentucky from Daniel Boone to Henry Clay* (Baltimore, MD: Johns Hopkins University Press, 1996); Jacoby, *Crimes against Nature*; Harry Watson, "'The Common Rights of Mankind': Subsistence, Shad, and Commerce in the Early Republican South," *Journal of American History*, 83, no. 1 (1996): 13–43.

12. Freyfogle, *On Private Property*, 47–49.

13. Wilma Dunaway, "Speculators and Settler Capitalists: Unthinking the Mythology about Appalachian Landholding, 1790–1860," in *Appalachia in the Making: The Mountain South in the Nineteenth Century*, ed. Dwight Billings, Mary Beth Pudup, and Altina L. Waller (Chapel Hill: University of North Carolina Press, 1995), 53; John Sherwood Lewis, "Becoming Appalachia: The Emergence of an American Subculture, 1840–1860" (PhD diss., University of Kentucky, 2000).

14. Arthur Spalding, *Men of the Mountains* (Nashville, TN: Southern Publishing Association, 1915), 172.

15. Fred M. Burnett, *This Was My Valley* (Ridgecrest, NC: Heritage Printers, 1960), 16. Several scholars, most notably Altina L. Waller and Patricia Beaver, have found that an egalitarian ethos rooted in independence formed the bedrock for social relations in the mountains. See Altina L. Waller, *Feud: Hatfields, McCoys, and Social Change in Appalachia, 1860–1900* (Chapel Hill: University of North Carolina Press, 1988), and Patricia D. Beaver, *Rural Community in the Appalachian South* (Long Grove, IL: Waveland, 1992), 8.

16. Before the Civil War, Wilder lived and owned businesses in the Midwest, where the open range was quickly disappearing. Ohio, for example, passed statewide fence laws in 1840 and 1859. See *The Fence: A Compilation of Facts, Figures, and Opinions from National and State Agricultural Reports, Agricultural Journals, and the Public Press for the Past Sixty Years*

(Worcester, MA: Noyes, Snow, 1879); For Wilder's incident on Roan Mountain, see E. W. Bemis, "In the Tennessee Mountains," *Christian Union* (New York), September 10, 1892.

17. Muriel Earley Sheppard, *Cabins in the Laurel* (Chapel Hill: University of North Carolina Press, 1991), 78–80.

18. See Luke Manget, "Root Diggers and Herb Gatherers: The Rise and Decline of the Botanical Drug Industry in Southern Appalachia" (PhD diss., University of Georgia, 2017).

19. Statement of the financial condition of Richmond Pearson, December 1, 1890, Richmond Pearson Papers, Southern Historical Collection, University of North Carolina, Chapel Hill (hereafter RPP).

20. Nash, *Reconstruction's Ragged Edge*, 88–95, 118–68; McKinney, *Southern Mountain Republicans*, 30–123. For more on the Republican Party in North Carolina after the Civil War, see Deborah Beckel, *Radical Reform: Interracial Politics in Post-Emancipation North Carolina* (Charlottesville: University of Virginia Press, 2011).

21. "The Book of Doom!" *Asheville (NC) Advance*, October 20, 1886.

22. "West N.C. News and Notes," *Biblical Recorder* (Raleigh, NC), July 2, 1884.

23. "Buncombe Democracy in Convention," *Asheville (NC) Weekly Citizen*, June 26, 1884; "Railroad Meeting in Asheville," *Charlotte (NC) Observer*, January 18, 1883. The Asheville and Spartanburg Railroad was chartered in 1873 and completed in 1886, linking the upstate of South Carolina to western North Carolina via the French Broad River corridor.

24. This is the contention of Hahn, *The Roots of Southern Populism*, and Sawers, "Property Law as Labor Control in the Postbellum South."

25. Manget, "Root Diggers and Herb Gatherers," 243–60.

26. Johnstone Jones, "Buncombe Stock Law: Reply to Richmond Pearson," *Asheville (NC) Citizen*, April 24, 1886.

27. "The Buncombe County Stock Law: History of Its Passage; Review of the Big Meeting," fol. 19, vol. 2, RPP.

28. Richmond Pearson, T. J. Candler, and W. Y. Porter, "A Petition," *Asheville (NC) Advance*, July 7, 1885.

29. "Anti-Stock Law Meeting Saturday," *Asheville (NC) Citizen*, June 5, 1885; "The No-Fence Question," *Asheville (NC) Citizen*, December 9, 1885; "The Anti-Stock Law Meeting," *Asheville (NC) Citizen*, December 20, 1885.

30. "Anti-Stock Law: A Large Meeting Yesterday," *The Asheville Advance*, 14 June 1885.

31. "The Anti-Stock Law Meeting," *Asheville (NC) Citizen*, December 20, 1885.

32. *Watauga Democrat* (Boone, NC), March 24, 1892.

33. "From Meat Camp," *Watauga Democrat* (Boone, NC), April 28, 1892.

34. [D. W.], "A School of Laziness," *Lenoir (NC) Topic*, September 30, 1885.

35. [Tomahawk], "Charleston," *Wheeling (WV) Daily Intelligencer*, November 11, 1873.

36. *James McNair et al. v. Commissioners of Buncombe County*, 3.

37. *James McNair et al. v. Commissioners of Buncombe County*, 24.

38. *James McNair et al. v. Commissioners of Buncombe County*, 34.

39. *James McNair et al. v. Commissioners of Buncombe County*, 1–43.

40. "The Stock Law Case: Meeting of the Justices and Commissioners," *Asheville (NC) Citizen-Times*, February 16, 1886.

41. "The Buncombe County Stock Law: History of Its Passage; Review of the Big Meeting," fol. 19, vol. 2, RPP.

42. "The Buncombe County Stock Law: History of Its Passage; Review of the Big Meeting," fol. 19, vol. 2, RPP.

43. Johnstone Jones, "Buncombe Stock Law: Reply to Mr. Richmond Pearson," *Asheville (NC) Citizen*, April 24, 1886, supp.

44. Copy of indictment, Buncombe County Superior Court, July term 1886, fol. 19, vol. 2, RPP.

45. Richmond Pearson to Johnstone Jones, October 28, 1886, RPP.

46. Pearson filled forty pages in a scrapbook with newspaper clippings on the entire stock law controversy (fol. 19, vol. 2, RPP). Most do not include citation information.

47. *Lenoir (NC) Topic*, August 4, 1886.

48. "Come Down to Business, Mr. Pearson," *Asheville (NC) Citizen*, September 29, 1886.

49. "Come Down to Business, Mr. Pearson," *Asheville (NC) Citizen*, September 29, 1886.

50. "Post-Election Points," *Statesville (NC) Record and Landmark*, November 11, 1886.

51. Beckel, *Radical Reform*, 125–28; "Meeting of the Republican State Convention," *Goldsboro (NC) Messenger*, September 27, 1886.

52. *Laws and Resolutions of the State of North Carolina, Passed by the General Assembly at Its Session of 1887, Begun and Held in the City of Raleigh on Wednesday, the Fifth Day of January, A.D. 1887* (Raleigh, NC: Josephus Daniels, 1887), 689.

53. "Election on the Stock-Law Question," *Asheville (NC) Citizen-Times*, August 2, 1887.

54. "No Stock Law for Swannanoa and Fair View Townships," *Asheville (NC) Citizen-Times*, November 10, 1887.

55. *Laws and Resolutions of the State of North Carolina Passed by the General Assembly at its Session of 1891, Begun and Held in the City of Raleigh on Wednesday, the Eighth Day of January, A.D. 1891* (Raleigh, NC: Josephus Daniels, 1891), 158.

56. This survey of stock law legislation is based on a thorough perusal of the *Acts and Resolutions of the State of North Carolina*, 1885–1971, found at Session Laws of North Carolina, North Carolina State Government Publications Collection, Government and Heritage Library, State Library of North Carolina, Raleigh, http://ncgovdocs.org/guides/sessionlawslist.htm.

57. Hahn, *The Roots of Southern Populism*, 56–64.

58. McKinley Pritchard, "A Tribute to Richmond Pearson," fol. 1, RPP.

59. Manget, "Root Diggers and Herb Gatherers," 259–60; Newfont, *Blue Ridge Commons*, 3–5.

60. Leland R. Cooper, *The Pond Mountain Chronicle: Self-Portrait of a Southern Appalachian Community* (Jefferson, NC: McFarland, 1998), 188.

61. Patricia Beaver, Sandra Ballard, and Brittany Hicks, eds., *Voices from the Headwaters: Stories from Meat Camp, Tamarack (Pottertown), and Sutherland, North Carolina* (Boone, NC: Center for Appalachian Studies, 2013), 200–201.

PART 3

RE-CREATING COMMUNITIES

Too South of the South

A Louisiana Family Searches for Community in Cuba

ROBERT C. POISTER

THE EARLIEST RECORDS OF JAMES MCHATTON'S INTEREST IN Cuba reveal two of his most impressive traits. A friend of McHatton's wrote a letter of introduction to a Mr. D. Butts Morris of Havana in which he announced that "my friend James McHatton Esq is visiting your island for the purpose of locating himself or to purchase a Refinery," placing McHatton's hunger for business opportunities front and center. The second trait, his foresight and ability to plan, was slightly less obvious. Written in November 1862, this note—and a second introduction to the same Mr. Morris—anticipated McHatton's arrival in Cuba by a full three years. It would have been unlikely for him to seek two letters of introduction had he not been looking ahead to relocating there. For the McHatton family, the three years between when the letters were written and when James would introduce himself to Mr. Morris of Havana were years of almost constant motion.[1]

James and Eliza McHatton decided to abandon their plantation near Baton Rouge and escaped Union-occupied Louisiana following a circuitous route to a new home in 1862. Making their way from Louisiana to south Texas, James traded in contraband across the Rio Grande. In the fall of 1864, as business prospects in Texas dwindled, the McHattons crossed the border into Mexico, interacting with the thriving business community of Matamoros as both brokers and consumers. In March 1865, they once again emigrated, this time to Cuba, purchasing a plantation on which they resided until after Reconstruction. While striving to re-create a brutal economic system and the life it afforded them, the McHattons failed to re-create the culture and community they had left behind.²

This failure weighed more heavily on James's wife, Eliza, than on James himself. Economically, Eliza's first thoughts on entering Havana followed a similar line as her husband's. "How prosperous and rich Cuba was in those days!" she later remembered. "We arrived when it was at the very acme of its opulence," she wrote, describing a place so affluent it was "fairly drunk with the excess of wealth and abundance." It seemed exactly the kind of economic environment she and her husband had spent the last three years searching for, one that presented ample business opportunities and held the potential to compensate handsomely for their risk and knowledge. If any place could reward James for his entrepreneurial schemes, Cuba seemed to be it.³

At first glance an ostensibly ideal spot for a business venture, Cuba proved less than ideal for a home. The importance of economic opportunity was, to James, greater than his desire to be part of a familiar community. He spent much of the period during which the family resided in Cuba involved in international ventures, often visiting the United States and maintaining a steady international business correspondence. Eliza, who had always aligned herself more closely with the South and the Confederacy than had her husband, was left in Cuba to fulfill her role as a southern plantation mistress on foreign soil. She found Cuba less like the South than had been reported to her, a poor substitute for home, and she mourned "the last resting spot for my weary feet on my own, dear, native soil," the loss of "the last American home I shall ever have."⁴

Perhaps due to what she felt she had lost, Eliza never allowed Cuba to become her "home." Transient groups of southerners and ex-Confederates provided her with short-term communities based on familiarity and commonality of language, experience, and values. Correspondence with friends and family still in the South similarly helped maintain ties with the life she had left behind. The first of these groups was impermanent, the second nearly intangible. In a new country, she fought to surround herself with the voices, news, and personalities of the old. James lacked this same cultural allegiance. His home, his community, was the market where he found excitement and meaning in the wheeling and dealing of business.⁵

While husband and wife had two different ideas of community, both failed to find their ideal in Cuba. It was their very lack of a community—whether in the domestic or business realm—that underscored its importance to them and raised doubts regarding a fraternal order of slave masters in which "apparently shared cosmopolitan interests could triumph over the various linguistic, racial, national, and historic chauvinisms that otherwise fractured the Hispanaphone and Anglophone Caribbean."[6]

JAMES'S DECISION TO MOVE HIS FAMILY TO CUBA IN 1865 REPREsented the culmination of a search for better economic prospects that began long before the war. Both James and Eliza came from wealthy, politically connected families that expected their offspring to be successful and that afforded a lavish lifestyle. Family lore was that James's grandfather, John McHatton, had been a Revolutionary War soldier from Scott County, Kentucky, and had made the acquaintance of the famous aristocrat the Marquis de Lafayette, who recognized John as a good friend on his tour of Kentucky in 1825. John's son Robert McHatton fought with Andrew Jackson and was known as an excellent stump speaker and congressman. James spent his boyhood in Kentucky, moved to Illinois for a short time as an adult, and eventually ended up in Louisiana with his young wife Eliza in search of the same wealth and reputation his ancestors enjoyed.[7]

Born Eliza Chinn in Kentucky, his young wife was raised in New Orleans in a family with an equally impressive heritage. One grandfather, a Pennsylvania transplant to Kentucky named Ash Emmerson, according to his descendants, "was said to be one of the best men ever in Kentucky." One of Emmerson's daughters married Richard Chinn, a talented lawyer whose expensive interests included fine cigars. Chinn was close friends with Henry Clay and named one of Eliza's brothers Henry in his honor. According to Eliza, Clay was the only person close enough to Richard Chinn to call him Dick.[8]

As a child, Eliza enjoyed the high culture of the Louisiana planter elite. One historian called her marriage to James in 1852 "a union of dynasties," and, considering their social inheritance, this is fairly accurate. Together they moved into what they and their contemporaries deemed a beautiful plantation home on the banks of the Mississippi, in East Baton Rouge Parish. Eliza described it as "a spacious mansion ... with deep verandas supported by fluted columns" and "a broad lawn, dotted here and there with live-oak and pecan trees." To meet both the economic and cultural expectations of their social status that accompanied such a lifestyle, James pursued several business ploys. In these, he displayed an aptitude for schemes, if not for business.[9]

McHatton owned hundreds of slaves, multiple plantations, and traded his sugar upriver himself rather than through a broker in Baton Rouge or New Orleans. Yet his most unusual antebellum business venture displayed the kind of entrepreneurial approach to risk, investment, unorthodox thinking, and state-sanctioned cruelty that would propel him to Mexico and Cuba. He was one of the first convict lessees in Louisiana, contracting with the state to use prisoners for levy construction and maintenance, showing that innovation and brutality went hand in hand in the antebellum South in more arenas than slavery. In October 1844, James entered into a five-year lease of the state penitentiary's convicts and set them to work building levees. The terms of the lease were "modest indeed"; according to one source, McHatton, Pratt, and Company "were required to pay nothing for the privilege of working the state's convicts." Initially, Louisiana advanced the company substantial sums of money, and in return McHatton and his business partners paid for the convicts' food, clothing, and necessities out of the company's profits. In 1855, McHatton again signed a five-year lease with new partners, consolidated as McHatton, Ward, and Company. Louisiana charged McHatton and his partners a fee of one-quarter of their profits. That they set the minimum rent at $1,000 suggests they thought that McHatton, Ward, and Company would do very well.[10]

Having spent his antebellum years growing both wealthy and accustomed to a wealthy lifestyle, McHatton and his family were not ready to concede either when the Civil War began in 1861. A year later, New Orleans had fallen to the Union, Yankee ironclads patrolled the Mississippi, and James and Eliza's neighbors busied themselves with destroying their sellable cotton. None of this fit into James's business model of making profits regardless of where he had to go, who he had to partner with, or who he had to subject to back-breaking labor. He and Eliza thought it prudent to move to Texas for both their safety and their livelihood. Once there, James smuggled cotton across the Rio Grande into Mexico, avoiding the Union blockade around the coast. When he could, he moved his cotton onto boats that would break the blockade out of Galveston, utilizing a state-sanctioned position as a cotton agent to sell bales for both the state of Louisiana and himself.[11]

Just as McHatton arranged for letters of introduction three years before his family emigrated to Cuba, he planned ahead for their trip to Texas, sending his slaves ahead of him. With Cuba already on his mind, however, Texas was never considered a final stop. Eliza explained both the cultural and economic reasons for moving years later. "We were going to Texas for many reasons," she wrote. "A loving brother, and our slaves were there at peaceful work on land cultivated on shares." The primary reason remained escape. "Above and beyond all," she admitted, "we could take refuge in Mexico if the worse came to the worst."[12]

By May 1864, after perhaps a year buying, moving, selling, and smuggling cotton, James found that the Yankees were not the only force standing in the way of his membership in an economic community. After being stymied in an attempt to move his cotton by sea, he let Confederate officials know in no uncertain terms his dismay with their management. "The Government exercised such exclusive control of the Boats that the owners were unable to fulfill their pledges to take the cotton and after being for months subjected to a series of disappointments and a large expense for storage I determined to procure teams and haul to the Rio Grande," he fumed. "The expenses that have accumulated on this cotton are enormous and a large amount of it will not sell today on the Rio Grande, for a sufficient sum to cover the actual disbursements made upon it." Eliza, as a consumer, lamented her access to a tangible business network, while maintaining her more ethereal connection to those closest to her through correspondence. Items as simple and common as hats and garden seed were now scarce and coveted. Sending a package of handkerchiefs, stamps, and envelopes to her niece and nephew, she instructed that the paper "must come back to me neatly scribbled over. I find it so difficult to get paper that I could not get it, and so have to divide my small supply with you."[13]

Moving to Mexico in October 1864 temporarily solved their economic woes. Eliza, who had a child, Annella, on the trip, was so impressed by the availability of goods that she pushed her recovery and went shopping with her eighteen-day-old daughter. In Texas, she had searched for scarce material. In Mexico, she reeled under the choices, debating not how to find material for dresses but which material to buy. For his part, James continued to sell cotton into Matamoras and Piedras Negras. Even outside the country they did not trust the Confederate government. "You must all be very careful what you write to us about *specie* and *leaving the country* etc," Eliza warned her family, "for all the letters to doubtful individuals are opened in Brownsville before delivered." Of all the letters she mailed her brother in Laredo, she claimed, there was not one "that was not opened on the Texas side first."[14]

Culturally, Mexico left much to be desired. For a woman used to fluted columns and high verandas, living out of a wagon proved quite an adjustment. The population was of little consolation, and years later Eliza described them as "little, half-naked *muchachos* who never had seen an ambulance [wagon], never had seen anything but themselves and the muddy river." She openly mocked their isolation with a sense of humor. "If they had ever heard of Queen Victoria," she claimed, "they might have thought she was coming to town, for I was the first *white* woman and my attendant the first *black* one the generation had ever seen." Despite the vigorous border trade and business potential, socially and culturally, Mexico was not a suitable place for the McHattons to settle.[15]

There was likely no single incident that propelled the McHattons from Mexico to Cuba; rather, their momentum seems to have carried them there from the moment they first made plans to leave Baton Rouge. That money could be made and goods purchased along the way may have slowed their departure, but it never eliminated its possibility. Cuba had been on James's mind for three years, but it had been in southerners' thoughts and the political aspirations for far longer. An island buzzing with agricultural promise and thick with slavery, southerners saw it as a ripe opportunity for an expanding nation in need of both land and slaves. President James K. Polk had offered Spain $100 million for the island in 1848, while then Senator Jefferson Davis avowed that "Cuba must be ours" to "increase the number of slaveholding constituencies." James Buchanan renewed efforts as chief executive in 1858, when southern and northern Democrats found that Cuban annexation was the only item they could agree on. In 1860, Lincoln worried that the South would demand annexation in return for abandoning secession.[16]

It was not annexation that was on Eliza's mind when she arrived in Havana in March 1865 but hyperbole. "No pencil can give an adequate picture of Havana as one enters its harbor," she wrote. "It is the loveliest gem of the ocean." Compared to Texas and Mexico, "it was as a bit of fairyland, where everybody was happy." Transient white southerners staying at the Hotel Cubano, which was "kept by a true rebel woman," provided her with familiar conversation. The cultural connection led Eliza to recommend the hotel to anyone else who might come to Cuba, though she knew of no one in particular who was planning to come, nor did she explicitly invite anyone. She had minimal interaction with the locals, however, and instead enjoyed an ever-changing retinue of southern guests, who stopped in to bring news from Louisiana, slander the Union, and discuss potential business. The most stable community the McHattons had took the form of their business and family correspondence between Cuba, England, and the United States.[17]

This made Cuba more of a substitute for home than a home itself, a headquarters for an international community that was isolated from the local community. As a substitute, however, it was certainly better than Mexico. Even if it could not be a re-creation of Baton Rouge, Cuba was far more similar to Louisiana than Louisiana was to Mexico. Louisianans like the McHattons *felt* they had much in common with Cuba, even if the reality of life in Cuba would prove their feelings misplaced. Planters from both sides of the Gulf of Mexico had long kept tabs on each other, for their shared commodity and life built around sugar cane ensured economic entanglement. Sharing a crop, however, like sharing a labor system, did not provide a seamless transition for southern expatriates, though Eliza and James's disillusionment was delayed by comparisons to their vanished South. As Eliza's transient friends and news from home reminded her, the Louisiana she thought of as home was likely gone forever. Eliza claimed many years after Lincoln's assassination that when it happened, General John C. Breckinridge had announced, "Gentlemen, the South has lost its best friend"; the South, he recognized, would subsequently be treated as a defeated enemy.[18]

The economic news that flowed in following this historic turn was bad, and James and Eliza were likely torn as they realized that their economic fortunes were closely tied to the destruction of the home they once knew. Even before the assassination, the fortunes of cotton had been dwindling. "Our cotton market has been in a very unsatisfactory condition ever since 1st January, prices having steadily declined and stock accumulated largely," R.C. Curd and Company wrote from Liverpool in April 1865. "One cause of the decline has been a belief in peace being brought about by defeat of the Confederates and as a matter of course as long as this belief prevailed nothing short of peace prices were looked on as safe for cotton."[19]

Cotton was not selling, though it seemed the material would sell were the war to end. "It would appear that we have now about reached this point, for we have news of Richmond captured and Gen Lee's army almost destroyed," the same company told James, though in reality Lee had already surrendered and the news simply traveled slowly across the ocean. "Yet for the first time this year," they explained, "the market has shown more animation after the receipt of the bad news. Prices gave way at first but under the active demand they are improving." Unfortunately for the Confederacy, "It looks now as if peace would not do cotton any harm and if peace should not ensue we may again have much higher prices." Days later James's cotton brokers repeated their predictions, which much have caused him angst. "If we have immediate peace prices will not go down much," they wrote, though "if we have war they will go up immediately to a much higher figure." His fortunes were, quite literally, tied to the war.[20]

Social and political news from this network was likewise negative, making life in Cuba all the more familiar and appealing. "Annie wrote very cheerfully, but they all, every one of them, write us not to come back. The country is terrible," Eliza's friend had warned her, urging her, "as long as we have a cent, to stay away." Her brother sent her "a fearful account of things in New Orleans."

Apparently, a Union general was using their Baton Rouge plantation as his headquarters to begin the reconstruction. Eliza's most virulent criticism was reserved for her old slaves, however, who she denigrated as "perfect *leeches*," an ironic remark from someone who had made a handsome living by taking advantage of the uncompensated labor of those same men and women. Slavery remained legal in Cuba, which was an economic and a cultural bonus for James and Eliza, evidenced by their purchase of a plantation and enslaved laborers and by Eliza's repeated racial remarks.[21]

More bad news followed a few months later. Writing again to her brother and sister-in-law, Eliza was "mighty sorry to hear how the tax collectors have been serving you." The situation sounded so bad that Eliza predicted that the South "will soon get to be like they were in France in the time of Louis XVIII, when... people 'sold their beds and lay in the straw' so they could pay the government taxes." Louis XVIII had been made king by the French Revolution, though he had to rule in exile. To Eliza, the U.S. government had taken the Civil War as a signal that it was now a monarchical dictatorship rather than a republic. It was ruling the South as a king ruled his subjects. "Were not for some of my own precious blood in the country," she admitted, "I would wish the whole concern would go to the dogs. It looks like things did have a tendency that way." Though Eliza had been able to leave the South, her family and everyone she cared about remained there, keeping her, like her memories, tied to a place other than where she lived.[22]

Reports of repeated sorrows back home made Cuba seem idyllic in the moment. "I am more thankful daily that I am here," she wrote. "If there's any political disturbance in this lovely land or any oppression we do not find it out," she averred, referring only to her own freedom and blissfully ignoring the enslaved African and Chinese laborers toiling on her new plantation, Desangaño. She and James remained unengaged with the locals. "The more we see of the Cuban character the more are we convinced that a military government is what they need. They are totally unfit for freedom and the pusillanimous puppies will never have it unless some strong nation fights for it, for them." Even as Eliza decried the military government—or king, as she represented it—controlling her beloved homeland, she saw no irony in calling for just such a measure in Cuba. Despite their similarities, she began to accentuate the differences between the two regions. Whereas the South needed freedom, Cuba needed control. In contrast to friends and family back home who suffered through four years of war, however, she enjoyed the quiet and sedentary life at Desangaño. "We lead such a quiet life out here that I scarcely have anything to write you," she claimed. Yet her future and that of the South remained uncertain. "Three years ago we were all so happy in Matagorda—when will we meet again?" she wondered. "God only knows."[23]

Two years after the war ended, having reentered the sugar business with his new plantation in Cuba, James took the opportunity to return to the United States to settle some financial issues. "Don't be disappointed if you don't get a cent," his brother-in-law warned him. "No one in the states will pay a dollar on the past—the war settled all claims so they seem to think." Still, James made the trip to see for himself. His conclusion was that the South was a cultural and economic disaster. Explaining the situation to Eliza, he wrote from New Orleans that "nearly all the [state] house are negroes and I really assure you things look gloomy here and everyone I have conversed with appear to be down hearted." Their familiar racial caste had been inverted, and, what was more, James informed Eliza, one of their friends whom he thought was doing "big business" had assured him that, unfortunately, "he is not making any much." With no home or community to return to, Eliza and James settled into life in Cuba, finding its rhythms closer to that of their antebellum years than anywhere else, including the very place where they had spent those years.[24]

Reports of a devastated, severely changed South made the McHattons emphasize the wealth, safety, and racial boundaries of Cuba all the more. Conversely, when Cuba proved less lucrative and safe than they had anticipated, James and Eliza's opinion of the South rose. Eliza's claims of a peaceful and calm countryside were challenged when two highwaymen attacked James in 1868. As he brandished his umbrella at them in self-defense and refused to relinquish his property, the brigands shot him in the neck, the bullet "narrowly escaping the jugular vein." Eliza admitted that "for months past the whole neighborhood has been harassed by thieves and desperadoes. Cattle and horses and hogs are nightly stolen." What was incomprehensible to the McHattons was that James's assailants were well known to everyone in the area and could be easily identified.[25]

Despite the McHattons' earlier perception and misrepresentation of the peacefulness of Cuba, this sort of banditry and violence was far from uncommon at the time. Around the time James was attacked, a nationalist insurgency was building in eastern Cuba that would, one month later, become an armed call to end Spanish rule on the island. The first act of the white leaders of this rebellion was to free their slaves, something inconceivable to the McHattons. Although the rebellion was primarily confined to the eastern side of the island, not all the violence was contained by geography. The concentration of land on the western side, where Matanzas and Desangaño lay, was attractive to the social bandits that Eliza claimed frequented their plantation. Perhaps due to this shattering of their mythological Cuba, the next time James visited the South after he healed, he reported enthusiastically to Eliza, if without specifics, "I am so glad I came.... [Y]ou have no idea of the number of our old friends I meet here." Having recently been brutally attacked on an island that supposedly lacked problems and oppression, McHatton said of the South, "The place has improved very much."[26]

Taking every opportunity to add to his difficulties, James sank increasingly into debt. As he had been in the Mississippi plantation partnership, James was perpetually behind with his creditors. Rather than repay them with earnings, he began borrowing additional funds to pay off the capital he already owed. Despite the size of his operation, he, like many of his fellow plantation owners, placed his faith in the crop of the coming year. For funding, he uncharacteristically turned to local banks, perhaps because his international creditors knew him too well. On one trip into Havana, James borrowed $12,000, which he figured "will be sufficient to take us through I think until we commence to grind." The profit from his sugar would have to help pay for two other debts he mentioned to Eliza. His lender, a Señor Sainz, "did not want sugar shipt him only molasses," and thus the $12,000 "advance is on our molasses only I could get no advance on our sugar." The uncertainty of the market made it difficult for James to guarantee his loans, much less pay them back.[27]

Cuba fed James McHatton's appetite for economic schemes, and that he never ignored his business responsibilities while traveling speaks to the fluidity of his family's move. This likewise reinforces that his business community was an international one of letters and agreements rather than one based on geography. His cotton brokers in Liverpool sent business correspondence concerning cotton sales out of Matamoros, Mexico, to the McHattons in Cuba well before they arrived there, more confirmation that James and Eliza knew well in advance that their travels would ultimately lead them to the island.

James returned to America multiple times for business reasons, though none of these ventures worked out well for him. Creditors tried to collect antebellum debts, and while James and Eliza were still certainly living the lifestyle of wealthy antebellum aristocrats, cash flow was an eternal problem. While staying with his brother in St. Louis in 1871, James petitioned for bankruptcy and was "duly adjudged a bankrupt." The court gave him a certificate "for all purposes as a Protection in Bankruptcy," absolving him from his American debts. Though this can be viewed as a business failure, it was also a rational decision. Saddled with American debts but lacking American assets, James had every reason to petition for bankruptcy. His Cuban property would be safe, and, in the event that he and Eliza moved back to New Orleans or Missouri, the wealth he brought with him would be protected as well.[28]

Constant travel and his bullet wound took their toll on James's health but perhaps not as much as the unyielding strain and stress he experienced from his business ventures aimed at maintaining a luxurious lifestyle. On March 3, 1872, at fifty-eight years old, he was pronounced dead of "nervous exhaustion." At the time, he was chasing one last scheme, helping the Unionist sons of his Mississippi plantation partner file for recompense with the Claims Commission. Union soldiers had reportedly stolen their cotton during the war, and they sued the American government for repayment of that debt. They promised McHatton a potentially lucrative 20 percent of any settlement they were awarded, though such an arrangement would certainly have been illegal given that his testimony would form the crux of their argument.[29]

Eliza remained at Desangaño with her daughter after James's death, though she would eventually marry another southerner and move to Brooklyn, New York, a place far different from the antebellum South of her memory and imagination or the Cuban substitute she inhabited for almost a decade. While Eliza adjusted well to life in the North, raising her family and writing her memoirs, it was not so for all the McHattons. Her son, Henry, named after Eliza's brother (the one who was a namesake of their father's friend Henry Clay), provided an interesting cultural contrast.

Though he had been fairly young when his family left the South, Henry knew of his father's vast landholdings, his elite family history, and the social expectations that went along with being a southern aristocrat. When James and Eliza attempted to re-create this in Cuba, for Henry, it worked all too well. Whereas Cuba had been a substitute for the Old South for his parents, it was, culturally, the only Old South Henry actually knew. His parents raised him to assume a role that the Civil War had made both obsolete and illegal in the American South. It was still possible to assume such a role in Cuba, and Henry longed to return to it to live the lifestyle that he felt was in his blood: that of the elite slave master and aristocratic southern sportsman.[30]

Eliza, however, had been educated in the North and expected the same thing for her son. He hated it. "Have made arrangements to go on a grand fishing party on Saturday," Henry wrote his mother from New Haven Collegiate and Commercial Institute in Connecticut. The ugly northern weather ruined his plans. "This A.M. got up to find about three inches of snow on the ground," he explained, sarcastically proclaiming Connecticut a "Splendid place to live. Yesterday 72, today 31." More complaints about the weather followed. "I will never live in this country," he vowed. "We have frosts every night and rain all day. Beats our rainy season [in Cuba] all to nothing."[31]

The personalities he interacted with in the North offered little consolation for the terrible climate. Once, when Henry learned he would miss a visit by some family friends, he was openly disappointed. "I should enjoy our evening with them better than 100 evenings with these Yankee girls that only know what pork and beans is and don't know what this is when it is rain, poor girls." His mind was constantly on the hunting he had done as a southern youth and his longing to return to it. "How I wish Charley [his uncle] could express Frank [his hound] over. How I would make these Yankee hunters open their eyes."[32]

Henry's biggest fear was that his mother would sell their Cuban plantation and he would be unable to return. "Old Desengaño [sic], how I wish I were there and not coming north again. I hate this country.... I should be very sorry for you to sell Desengano," he informed her. "I do not think there is any safer thing to put the money into." Whatever her decision, Henry felt it important to make clear that "I never want to live in Yankee land. I have been here three years now. I think that is long enough to try the place and I hate it more now than I did the first day I set foot on it and hate it more and more every day." While claiming to hate the cold and the people, it was likely something engrained deeply in Henry's southern upbringing that caused him to gripe. His parents had brought him up with their particular interpretation of the South, the interpretation that came through in Eliza's letters and the books she later authored. Henry knew only the legends and what he had lost, and he knew the myth far better than the reality. He did return to Desangaño to live the gentlemanly sporting life he envisioned, but he was so preoccupied with it that the plantation's productivity suffered. As with his father before him, the lucrative opportunities Henry envisioned merely disappointed him.[33]

Culturally and economically, Cuba represented different things to different members of the same family. To James, it was an escape, an opportunity, wealth. To Eliza, it was an isolated economic headquarters; not a home, but a place where she could be comfortable with her lifestyle if not part of a community. Henry saw in Cuba the South as he had learned of it, a land of sugar and slaves that could sustain the last of the southern gentlemen. They all ignored the worst aspects of Cuba as long as they had something to compare it favorably against. For James and Eliza, the New South provided this comparison, with its poor business environment and racially inverted politics. For Henry, it was the North. For all of them, it was more the idea of something better than anything tangible.

To each of them, too, Cuba was not an extension of the South, but a substitute for it. As the McHattons' experience reveals, as interconnected as the two were, they were far from interchangeable. James would never find the wealth he sought there, never find the economic opportunities he had made for himself before the war. Eliza would not lament her departure from Desangaño with the same lifelong sense of loss she—and much of her home region—would feel for the mythologized Old South. Henry could not live his father's life, nor the lives of his storied ancestors. Cuba allowed him a brief glimpse into such a life, but the end of American slavery and Union victory in the Civil War demolished the life he expected to live and broke the chains of those he expected to master. Cuba represented the hopes and failures of each of these people as they learned that the Caribbean was not an "American Mediterranean," not an extension of the lower South. It provided a brief escape and refuge, but in the end, even a mythologized Cuba could not provide the same community as a mythologized South.[34]

NOTES

1. Letters of introduction to D. Butts Morris, ms. 2855, box 10, folder 22. McHatton Family Papers, Hargrett Library, University of Georgia Libraries (hereafter MFP).

2. While the McHattons' coping mechanism of escape was not unusual—Daniel Sutherland estimates that "a reliable, probably conservative, count" numbers the citizens of Louisiana roaming or vacating their state during the Civil War was in the thousands ("Looking for a Home: Louisiana Emigrants during the Civil War and Reconstruction," *Louisiana History* 21, no. 4 [1980], 343—there are not many studies of escape as a long-term individual move; rather existing studies on Mexico and Brazil accentuate the communal nature of exile by focusing on *groups* of people who moved together, often using the terminology of "colonies." Conversely, biographical studies of prominent ex-Confederates after the war, including Robert Toombs, Judah P. Benjamin, and John C. Breckinridge, emphasize that exile for these *individuals* was impermanent. Cuba was a stop rather than a new home. The McHattons were, in many ways, alone: they neither brought their community with them, nor did they have one in mind to which they would return. Whereas the communities attempted a long-term relocation, often the individuals of biographical focus were short-term exiles. The McHattons (in the historiography, at least) were atypical: individuals who sought a long-term home on foreign soil. To compare and contrast their experiences as typically told, however, may not be as revealing as rereading older texts with the McHattons' economic aspirations in mind, which might reveal that an intractable Confederate pride was directly linked to the desire to accumulate wealth. For "traditional" scholarship on Confederate expatriates, see Lawrence F. Hill, *The Confederate Exodus to Latin America* (Columbus: Ohio State University, 1936), Alfred Jackson Hanna, *Confederate Exiles in Venezuela* (Tuscaloosa: Confederate Publishing Company, 1960), Eugene C. Harter, *The Lost Colony of the Confederacy* (Jackson: University Press of Mississippi, 1985), William Clark Griggs, *The Elusive Eden: Frank McMullan's*

Confederate Colony in Brazil (Austin: University of Texas Press, 1987), Cyrus B. Dawsey and James M. Dawsey, eds., *The "Confederados": Old South Immigrants in Brazil* (Tuscaloosa: University of Alabama Press, 1998), Donald C. Simmons Jr., *Confederate Settlements in British Honduras* (Jefferson, NC: McFarland, 2001), and Anthony Arthur, *General Joe Shelby's March* (New York: Random House, 2010). For a popular representation, see *The Undefeated*, directed By Andrew V. McLaglen, 20th Century Fox, 1969. Biographical studies focusing on the individual experience include Robert Douthat Meade, *Judah P. Benjamin: Confederate Statesman* (Baton Rouge: Louisiana State University Press, 2001), Mark Scroggins, *Robert Toombs: The Civil Wars of a United States Senator and Confederate General* (New York: McFarland, 2011), and William C. Davis, *Breckinridge: Statesman, Soldier, Symbol* (Lexington: University Press of Kentucky, 2010).

3. Eliza McHatton-Ripley, *From Flag to Flag: In the South, in Mexico, in Cuba* (New York: Appleton, 1896), 126.

4. Eliza McHatton to unknown, undated, ms. 2855, box 13, folder 7, MFP.

5. For familial studies see Stephen Berry, *House of Abraham: Lincoln and the Todds, a Family Divided by War* (Boston: Houghton Mifflin, 2007), Keith Bohannon, "They Had Determined to Root Us Out: Dual Memoirs by a Unionist Couple in Blue Ridge Georgia," in *Enemies of the Country: New Perspectives on Unionists in the Civil War South*, ed. John Inscoe and Robert Kenzer (Athens: University of Georgia Press, 2001), 97–120, and Tom Dyer, *Secret Yankees: The Union Circle in Confederate Atlanta* (Baltimore, MD: Johns Hopkins University Press, 1999).

6. Matthew Pratt Guterl, *American Mediterranean: Southern Slaveholders in the Age of Emancipation* (Cambridge, MA: Harvard University Press, 2008), 6, 9. Guterl focuses on what the McHattons had in common with the inhabitants of their various destinations, particularly Cuba, the traits these locales shared that predisposed them to embracing the institution of slavery, and an inherent racial bias at the fore. As their correspondence reveals, however, the McHattons themselves felt bitterly the differences in these regions and populations. A focus on broad systems paints a different picture than an exploration of individual experiences. In this case, the systems reveal commonalities, while the experiences of James and Eliza McHatton better illuminate differences. Laura Jarnagin likewise explains that a complex international community made exile easier. "Networks that had been fortified by centuries of interplay among familial, business, religious, political, ideological, and ethnic connections," she contends, "came to intersect and comingle in ways that promoted and facilitated this elite migration" (*A Confluence of Transatlantic Networks: Elites, Capitalism, and Confederate Migration to Brazil* [Tuscaloosa: University of Alabama Press, 2008], 2).

7. "Information Concerning Revolutionary McHattons and the Descent of T. H. McHatton Therefrom," ms. 2855, box 13, folder 4, MFP; "Henry McHatton Diary, April 1870," ms. 2855, box 10, folder 91, MFP.

8. "Information Concerning Revolutionary McHattons and the Descent of T. H. McHatton Therefrom," ms. 2855, box 13, folder 4, MFP; "Henry McHatton Diary, April 1870," ms. 2855, box 10, folder 91, MFP; Guterl, *American Mediterranean*, 86; Eliza Ripley, *Social Life in Old New Orleans: Being Recollections of My Girlhood* (New York: Appleton, 1912), 169. Eliza remarried after James's death and published her memoirs as Eliza McHatton-Ripley and Eliza Ripley. While bibliographically it is necessary to refer to her as Eliza Ripley, I have chosen in

the text to use the name she went by at the time: Eliza Chinn as a girl, Eliza McHatton after her marriage to James.

9. Ripley, *Social Life in Old New Orleans*, 9, 14; Guterl, *American Mediterranean*, 88; Ripley, *Flag to Flag*, 7–8.

10. Receipts for sugar sales to E. B. Kimball and Company, ms. 2855, box 10, folder 10, MFP; U.S Census, 1860, population and slave schedules, Provo; Mark T. Carleton, *Politics and Punishment: The History of the Louisiana State Penal System* (Baton Rouge: Louisiana State University Press, 1971), 9.

11. Special order no. 78, March 2, 1863, and addendum to special order no. 78, March 10, 1863, ms. 2855, box 10, folder 26, MFP. While James McHatton may not have left at the same time as Judah P. Benjamin and John C. Breckinridge, his motive for leaving might have been the same: fear of arrest. As Confederate leaders, both Benjamin and Breckinridge feared indictment and punishment for treason. Eliza, at least, claims that a warning of arrest caused James to flee Arlington plantation, despite his lack of participation in the secession effort.

12. McHatton-Ripley, *Flag to Flag*, 66.

13. James A. McHatton to W. J. Hutchins, May 20, 1864, ms. 2855, box 10, folder 28, MFP; Eliza McHatton to Anna, March 11, 1864, ms. 2855, box 10, folder 30, MFP.

14. Eliza McHatton to Anna, February 22, 1865, ms. 2855, box 10, folder 38, MFP; Eliza McHatton to Anna, October 10, 1864, ms. 2855, box 10, folder 30. MFP (emphasis in original). While most international exiles, and particularly the communal groups in Brazil and Mexico, left after the defeat of the Confederacy in 1865 and 1866, the McHattons had left more than a year earlier both owing to where they had settled and to forethought.

15. McHatton-Ripley, *Flag to Flag*, 83.

16. Quoted in James McPherson, *Battle Cry of Freedom: The Civil War Era* (New York: Oxford University Press, 1988), 104, 194–95, 253.

17. McHatton-Ripley, *Flag to Flag*, 125; Eliza McHatton to Tim, January 25, 1866, ms. 2855, box 10, folder 42, MFP.

18. Ripley, *Social Life in Old New Orleans*, 288. Rebecca Scott explains the connections between Cuba and places like New Orleans without describing them as one entity. "A record-breaking harvest in Cuba could mean lowered profits in Louisiana," or "a new tariff in the United States could be a blow to Cuban producers," but, she emphasizes, they were not a single, aligned region (*Degrees of Freedom: Louisiana and Cuba after Slavery* [Cambridge, MA: Harvard University Press, 2008], 2).

19. R. C. Curd and Company to James A. McHatton, April 19, 1865, ms. 2855, box 10, folder 40, MFP.

20. R.C. Curd and Company to James A. McHatton, April 19, 1865, ms. 2855, box 10, folder 40, MFP; R. C. Curd and Company to James A. McHatton, April 22, 1865, ms. 2855, box 10, folder 40, MFP.

21. Eliza McHatton to Tim, January 25, 1866, box 10, folder 42, MFP.

22. Eliza McHatton to Robert and Anna, August 26, 1866, ms. 2855, box 10, folder 42, MFP.

23. Eliza McHatton to Robert and Anna, August 26, 1866, ms. 2855, box 10, folder 42, MFP.

24. R. H. Chinn to James A. McHatton, July 19, 1867, ms. 2855, box 10, folder 48, MFP;

James A. McHatton to Eliza McHatton, November 12, 1867, ms. 2855, box 10, folder 44, MFP.

25. Eliza McHatton to F. Fessir, September 21, 1868, ms. 2855, box 10, folder 51, MFP. The attack on McHatton was an odd reversal of paramilitary violence in the South.

26. Ada Ferrer, *Insurgent Cuba: Race, Nation, and Revolution, 1868–1898* (Chapel Hill: University of North Carolina Press, 1999), 15, 22; Louis A. Perez, *Lords of the Mountain: Social Banditry and Peasant Protest in Cuba, 1878–1918* (Pittsburgh, PA: University of Pittsburgh Press, 1989), xv–xvii; James A. McHatton to Eliza McHatton, November 15, 1870, ms. 2855, box 10, folder 82, MFP.

27. James A. McHatton to Eliza McHatton, June 17, 1869, ms. 2855, box 10, folder 65, MFP.

28. Certificate of protection, ms. 2855, box 10, folder 89, MFP.

29. Death certificate, ms. 2855, box 10, folder 106, MFP; memorandum agreement, July 21, 1872, ms. 2855, box 10, folder 104, MFP.

30. Nicolas W. Proctor, *Bathed in Blood: Hunting and Mastery in the Old South* (Charlottesville: University of Virginia Press, 2002), illuminates the similarities between mastery of the home and mastery of the field, contending that social standing dictated that in the Old South, any gentleman was by definition a sportsman.

31. Henry McHatton to Eliza McHatton, May 4, 1872, and October 13, 1872, ms. 2855, box 10, folder 112, MFP.

32. Henry McHatton to Eliza McHatton, October 18, 1872, ms. 2855, box 10, folder 109, MFP.

33. Henry McHatton to Eliza McHatton, November 24, 1872, ms. 2855, box 13, folder 7, MFP.

34. For an interesting comparison of sons' expectations before and after the Civil War, see Stephen Berry, *All That Makes a Man: Love and Ambition in the Civil War South* (New York: Oxford University Press, 2002), and Peter S. Carmichael, *The Last Generation: Young Virginians in Peace, War, and Reunion* (Chapel Hill: University of North Carolina Press, 2009).

"Yankees Invade the South Again"

Race, Reconciliation, and the 1913 National Grand Army of the Republic Encampment at Chattanooga, Tennessee

SAMUEL B. McGUIRE

Early morning mists blanketed Chattanooga, Tennessee, on September 17, 1913, as thousands of Grand Army of the Republic (GAR) members from across the nation made their way downtown. The blue-clad veterans met at the corner of Georgia Avenue and High Street and prepared to parade through the Mountain City. Intermittent rain showers failed to dampen either the veterans' spirits or the anticipation among the throngs of onlookers lining the streets. The parade marked the formal opening of the Forty-Seventh National GAR Encampment and fiftieth anniversary of the battles of Chickamauga and Chattanooga.

As the rain clouds lifted at ten o'clock, the parade began. Columns of roughly ten to fifteen thousand Union veterans, organized by home state, marched past downtown buildings adorned with red, white, and blue bunting. The Sons of Union Veterans acted as official escorts of the gray-haired veterans, while standard-bearers carried post and state department flags. Bands played popular wartime ditties—including "Yankee Doodle," "The Girl I Left Behind Me," and even "Dixie." The *Chattanooga News* reported, "The spectacle of aged marchers, tattered flags and fifes and drums playing the tunes that stirred the hearts of the boys in blue fifty years ago, though enthusiastically received, carried with it a touch of pathos, visible on every countenance."[1]

Black veterans marched alongside their white comrades.[2] Whereas "the first colored man seen in the parade" was the New York department's color bearer, the first contingent of "colored troops was seen in the Kentucky division."[3]

FIGURE 2. GAR encampment parade on Broad Street, September 17, 1913. Chattanooga Collections, Chattanooga Public Library.

The black and white comrades from the Bluegrass State drew loud cheers from spectators as they sang "My Old Kentucky Home." Close behind them marched "the Louisiana-Mississippi department, composed mostly of negroes," representing their home states by carrying "stalks of sugar cane, topped with cotton balls."[4] As encampment hosts, the large contingent of 350 black and white Tennesseans brought up the rear of the parade.[5] According to local reporters, many of the estimated thirty-thousand spectators "frequently interrupted the progress of the parade," and policemen found it difficult to restrain the "hundreds who rushed into the ranks of the marchers to shake hands with the veterans."[6]

Though white and black Union veterans marched side by side, some white GAR members spontaneously coaxed a few former Confederate bystanders to take part in the demonstration. Three gray-clad Confederate veterans "received a great demonstration in the parade as they marched arm in arm with veterans in blue."[7] In the spirit of fraternalism and reconciliation, the Grand Army men had disregarded a strict organizational policy that prohibited all non-GAR members from participating in encampment parades.

The parade lasted a mere two hours; however, participants, spectators, and Americans across the country recognized that the parade marked a truly historic occasion. An *Asheville Citizen* editorial remarked that the reunion in

Chattanooga "is the first time in history that such an encampment is held in the real south. It is true, one national encampment was held in Louisville [in 1895], but that city was really too far north... to be considered as part of the real south."[8] Others compared the Chattanooga encampment to the famous Blue-Gray reunion at Gettysburg a few months earlier, as the symbolic end of any lingering sectional animosities. The *Boston Post* noted, "The Gettysburg reunion beautifully typified the reunion of the Union. This Chattanooga encampment of the G.A.R. adds a sort of benediction to the former event."[9]

The Forty-Seventh National GAR Encampment that took place September 15–20, 1913, encapsulates a critical moment in history. This reunion in a southern Appalachian community would be the first and only time the GAR would hold a national meeting in the former Confederacy. An estimated thirty-one thousand to thirty-five thousand Union veterans and guests attended the event in Chattanooga.[10] Recently, historians have brought into sharper focus the role of veterans, reunions and commemorations, memory, and reconciliation as integral parts of the Civil War's aftermath in both the North and South.[11] Yet historians have too briefly touched on the GAR in the South, and no one has studied a single Union veterans' reunion.

Examining the 1913 Chattanooga reunion—especially controversies before and during the encampment—provides fresh insight into Civil War veterans, memory, and reconciliation. Official GAR documents, published post rosters, the descriptive records of the Department of Tennessee GAR, and fourteen volumes of encampment scrapbooks form the foundation of this study. Unique to Tennessee's GAR, the descriptive records include original rosters that provide demographic information about GAR members—including birthplace, age, residence, occupation, wartime service and rank, and admission date into the GAR.[12] The rosters provide an accurate snapshot of the community of veterans who joined the order from its establishment in 1884 through its height in 1890. The scrapbooks include an exhaustive number of national, regional, and local newspaper articles that comprehensively chronicle events before, during, and after the reunion.[13]

Employing these sources, this essay chronicles how communities of Civil War veterans and residents of a southern Appalachian town grappled with race, sectional tensions, and reconciliation. GAR officials and encampment promoters hoped to showcase Chattanooga as a New South city and attract northern capital to the region by touting sectional reconciliation. But a number of controversies that received national attention speak to the limits of the nation's collective memory of an imagined national American community reunited after the Civil War.

The GAR was the largest Union veterans' organization in post–Civil War America. The organization experienced enormous growth nationally in the 1880s and peaked in 1890 with a membership of over four hundred thousand veterans nationwide. Members wielded considerable political influence; they led Civil War commemorations, held Memorial Day observances, and handled veterans' pensions. Comrades also hosted local post meetings as well as annual state and national encampments. Annual encampments were typically multiday reunions that included official and semiofficial GAR meetings. Throughout the late nineteenth and early twentieth centuries, Tennessee's GAR boasted the largest membership in the former Confederacy. At its height in 1890, the Grand Army in the Volunteer State boasted nearly thirty-seven hundred members. Members included local mountaineers, transplant Yankees, southern blacks, and European immigrants of urban and rural backgrounds. As wartime Unionist and postwar Republican sentiment permeated many east Tennessee communities, mountain residents quickly came to dominate the state organization. Thirty of the thirty-four state leaders resided in highland communities. Additionally, 75 of the 132 local posts in the state were in the eastern highlands.[14]

Chattanooga was home to two large all-white GAR posts (Lookout Post 2 and Mission Ridge Post 45) and one more modest all-black post (Chickamauga Post 22). These posts were unique in east Tennessee. Most GAR members in the region were native southerners, especially native Tennesseans. But, reflecting Chattanooga's postwar growth and diversity, most of the members of the city's two all-white posts were northern transplants. Most had moved to Chattanooga from Ohio, New York, and Pennsylvania. White Tennesseans and southerners were in the minority of both posts, making up nearly one out of every four members. A few were foreign-born immigrants—mostly born in the British Isles and modern-day Germany. Members' occupations also set them apart from their comrades in more rural posts in the region. Many took an active role in the town's diversified and booming industrial, manufacturing, commercial, and railroad industries throughout the 1880s and 1890s. Quite a few were skilled and semiskilled tradesmen such as carpenters, brick and stonemasons, blacksmiths, mechanics, and boilermakers. Others were middling businessmen and entrepreneurs, such as merchants, grocers, druggists, and hotelkeepers. Still others were white-collar professionals—clerks, bookkeepers, manufacturers, engineers, lawyers, and physicians. Also among the veterans who joined Chattanooga's local GAR posts were some of the city's wealthiest and most notable residents—including John T. Wilder, Andrew J. Gahagan, Zeboim and George Patten, and Hiram S. Chamberlain.[15] Paralleling GAR membership trends in northern communities, most business executives and white-collar professional GAR members in east Tennessee resided in city centers and surely benefited from the networking opportunities and social contacts that urban posts provided.[16]

Though the Tennessee GAR's black membership ebbed and flowed throughout the late nineteenth and early twentieth centuries, Chattanooga's Chickamauga Post 22 was one of the most active and largest all-black posts in east Tennessee. Unlike many of their comrades in local white posts, nearly all of Chattanooga's black GAR members were native Tennesseans or southerners and a part of Chattanooga's black working class. Many were common laborers, but others were skilled or semiskilled workers, like blacksmiths, stonemasons, and tanners. A few were ministers.[17] While quite a few posts in the Tennessee highlands disbanded over time, members of the Chickamauga post remained active well into the twentieth century.[18] The GAR in Chattanooga certainly provided its diverse members with an inviting community to network with fellow veterans.

By 1913, the GAR in Tennessee, like the national order itself, was in its twilight. Whereas 171,335 members of 5,572 posts made up the national body, Tennessee's department included 966 members and 32 posts in good standing.[19] Death, old age, declining health, and waning interest in the order accounted for the membership loss.[20] Regardless of their declining numbers, Tennesseans remained the most active GAR members in the former Confederacy. Only members from the border South states of Kentucky, Missouri, and West Virginia had greater numbers of members and posts.[21] East Tennessee mountaineers continued to dominate the state order. In 1913, members of highland posts monopolized every elected and appointed leadership position in the state organization.[22] As of that December, 84 percent of GAR members in the Volunteer State belonged to mountain posts.[23]

For years, GAR members in the Volunteer State had actively campaigned to host a national encampment; only in 1913 did officials finally select Chattanooga. Veterans and newspapermen across the nation were ecstatic with the selection because the encampment would coincide with the fiftieth anniversary of the battles of Chickamauga and Chattanooga and symbolically reunite the country.[24] An editorial in a New York newspaper deemed Chattanooga an ideal southern host city, claiming many former Rebels and Federals resided peacefully together there. "The population of Chattanooga is made up of both Southern and Northern men, who are members of the same churches, neighbors, partners in business, and all of them are united in the work of entertaining the survivors of the Union army and their friends," it read. "No such thing as sectional prejudice exists in Chattanooga."²⁵ An article in Georgia's *Athens Banner* echoed the reconciliationist rhetoric, predicting that, like the Gettysburg reunion, the GAR encampment "on Southern soil of the men who wore the blue will help wonderfully to make all forget the bitterness. This can be done, too, without giving up a whit of the loyalty to tradition and truth."²⁶

Throughout the summer, while members of the encampment committee and residents of Chattanooga worked tirelessly to prepare for the encampment, promoters also attempted to attract northern visitors to east Tennessee by amalgamating New South boosterism with the myth of Appalachian Unionism. Proponents hoped to encourage northerners to immigrate to and invest in the southern highlands by brushing mountaineers' divided wartime loyalties and the twenty thousand to thirty thousand east Tennesseans who served in Rebel regiments under the carpet; they portrayed the region as home to a lily-white citizenry who universally despised slavery and remained zealously devoted to the Union.²⁷ An editorial in the *Erie Times* claimed that Knoxville "lies in the center of a region that within the next few years will be the scene of the country's greatest development. It is situated in the very heart of the greatest hardwood timber belt in the country; it lies in the very heart of a district rich in minerals of all kinds; it lies in the heart of a great agricultural and live stock section." The article went on to embellish east Tennesseans' wartime unionism by asserting that the region "furnished more soldiers to the Union armies than there were votes in that section of state at the time and it furnished more soldiers to the Union army than any other section of the country in proportion to its area." The editorial concluded by highlighting the homes of famous east Tennessee Unionists and Federal soldiers—including those of William G. Brownlow, Andrew Johnson, and Admiral David Farragut—and the National Soldiers' Home for Union Veterans in Johnson City as tourist attractions.²⁸

Regardless of boosters' and veterans' welcoming and reconciliationist rhetoric, several controversial incidents suggest that that rhetoric rang hollow and illustrate veterans', Chattanooga residents', and the nation's ambivalence toward race and reconciliation. One squabble concerned displays of the Confederate flag. As locals decorated the city in America's national colors, a few residents unfurled Rebel flags. Some argued that they were not doing so maliciously, but boosterish local newspapers censured the residents. One editorial demanded that only Old Glory should be displayed, because some northerners may feel the Rebel flags were "a breach of hospitality, if not a show of disrespect.... [T]hey are our guests and hospitality and southern chivalry demand that we display none but their flag."²⁹ Even W. E. Brock, chairman of the

United Confederate Veterans (UCV) reunion that took place in May, agreed that encampment week was no time to display the Confederate flag. He asserted that northerners "are our guests and I trust everybody will feel most keenly the responsibility that rests upon all Chattanoogans.... [E]verybody, of course, realizes the town should be properly decorated, and I trust that at least every home that was decorated for the confederate reunion will demonstrate the same patriotic spirit in decorating for the G.A.R. encampment with American flags."[30] The Confederate banners were eventually taken down, but the public quarrel portended sectional tensions to come during the encampment itself.

In addition to sectional animosities, segregated accommodations for black veterans stoked racial tensions. Before the encampment opened, preparations had been made for local members of the Colored YMCA to receive African American guests and direct them to segregated quarters with black hosts. However, some African Americans unknowingly made reservations at local whites' houses. Tempers flared when whites refused to board black visitors. A local newspaper article recalled one such incident and showed little sympathy for the black visitors who were an affront to Jim Crow. The editorial began, "Civil war was very nearly started again between some of the old [black] 'vets,' and one of our [white] Chattanooga men, and . . . had war started, our sentiments would have been entirely with the Chattanoogan." It recalled that an anonymous white Chattanooga resident—under the pseudonym "Mr. Citizen," had unwittingly agreed to house twenty-six black veterans. According to the article, once the veterans arrived at the house, "'Mr. Citizen' hurried to the door, threw it wide open in true southern style, but somehow his greetings were never given—for the regiment was of negroes."[31] Newspapermen did not elaborate on the situation or any similar incidents, but white veterans' public silence over segregated housing is deafening. White Grand Army men made no public outcry in defense of their black comrades. Though the GAR was officially an interracial organization, this did not necessarily prompt criticisms of Jim Crow or endorsements of racial equality at organizational functions.

Two other incidents at the encampment parade suggested that racial and sectional tensions simmered just below the surface of public claims of reconciliation and fraternalism. Racial tensions boiled over on the downtown streets as black and white GAR members made final preparations for the encampment parade. As the veterans were queuing up, white members of an unaffiliated band from Alabama refused to march alongside black Union veterans from Mississippi and Louisiana. Band members and their leader, Professor D. P. Barber, vehemently refused to march ahead of "the Louisiana department, composed in front ranks exclusively of negro veterans." A white GAR leader came forward to defend his black comrades. He reprimanded the musicians and gave them a curt ultimatum: either march with the black veterans as directed or forgo participating in the parade. As tempers flared, a white GAR bandmaster interceded. But he acquiesced to the white band members' objections and reassigned them to march with a contingent of white veterans.[32] The episode and veterans' conflicting reactions reveal white GAR members' ambivalence toward their black comrades.

Another incident immediately preceding the parade brought lingering sectional feelings to the fore. The seeds of the episode were planted days before the procession. Ohio GAR member Henry Hansen invited members of Chattanooga's Nathan Bedford Forrest UCV camp to march at the head of the Ohio delegation. While many lauded the impromptu invitation, the proposition violated a strict GAR policy prohibiting anyone, except Union veterans and assigned escorts, from marching in encampment parades.[33] Hansen also allegedly failed to inform his superiors about the invitation. This led to an incident that would receive national attention.

On the morning of the parade, roughly twenty to twenty-five local UCV members, donning their Confederate uniforms, made their way to Fountain Square to meet the Ohio delegation. As the old Confederates plodded past the forming queue, GAR members all along the line began cheering loudly. As the old soldiers in gray and blue fell into formation together, just minutes before the parade was to begin, GAR officials abruptly ordered Hansen to bar all non-GAR members from the parade, including the UCV men. Hanging his head, Hansen apologetically informed the old Confederates that they would not be permitted in the column and expressed his deepest regrets over the embarrassing situation. Though visibly distressed by the news, the former Confederates quietly withdrew.[34]

The day after the parade, reports of the alleged snub made headlines across the nation.[35] The hiccup unleashed sectional venom that had been lingering below as well as above the Mason-Dixon Line. In particular, the fallout from the parade incident revealed veterans' and contemporary society's ambivalence toward reconciliation.

In the immediate aftermath of the parade incident, GAR leaders attempted to publicly downplay it and tender an olive branch to insulted white southerners. Hours after the parade, Commander in Chief Alfred B. Beers justified the GAR's exclusionary parade policy, stating, "The grand parade at each encampment is intended to be reserved for the Grand Army of the Republic and its official escort.... In the past we have been troubled with all sorts of organizations which wanted to march in the parade." He asserted, "I want it emphasized that members of the Forrest camp were not excluded because they were confederate veterans. The Ohio officer's procedure was in violation of every military rule of the Grand Army.... [W]e deeply deplore the affair brought on by the officer of the department which had received my orders and then allowed them to be disregarded."[36]

The next day, UCV adjutant Colonel Dickinson also attempted to disarm the scandal, stating publicly that "we [Confederates] do not attach blame either to the Toledo post or any member of the rank and file of the Grand Army of the Republic, for the orders served yesterday that we could not march in the parade." He went on to add, "We will remember with only the kindliest feeling the receipt of the invitation to participate in the parade. I am glad we accepted it, and showed them that we have the most brotherly feeling for each and every man in the rank and file of the Grand Army of the Republic and for the officers of the Ohio posts."[37] He concluded by inviting members of the GAR to attend a special town-hall meeting at the N. B. Forrest meeting hall for an open dialogue on the incident.

The next night, hundreds of GAR and UCV members attended the "open campfire" at the local Confederate veterans' meeting hall. By the time the meeting began at eight o'clock, every seat in the building was occupied and many in the overflowing crowd had to either stand along walls or listen through windows outside. While newspapers claimed it was a "meeting of goodfellowship," both GAR and UCV leaders chose not to tackle the issue at hand. Only Colonel Samuel W. Burroughs, a GAR member from Detroit, briefly touched on the parade incident. He insisted that "the wounds of the war were not healed at Gettysburg last July as has been insisted by many," and deemed the order barring Confederates from the parade a mistake. Major Thomas M. McConnell, a Confederate veteran from Chattanooga, then addressed the crowd. Though he lauded the Union soldiers' martial prowess during the war, he unapologetically claimed, "I believed in the doctrines of the confederacy. What I believe today is nobody's business." He concluded by referencing the Reconstruction-era Ku Klux Klan, defiantly implying he was a former member by telling the crowd, "Whether I was member of the Ku Klux doesn't concern anyone but me."[38]

In subsequent days and weeks, many northerners and ordinary Union veterans, including members of the National Association of Union Ex-Prisoners of War, vented their frustration over the incident and expressed concerns that it would undermine reconciliation efforts.[39] Claiming to speak for his fellow prisoners of war, George A. Todd, former member of the Thirty-Second Iowa volunteers and POW, asserted, "We all feel that an outrage has been committed against a body of gentlemen who represented in their person and particularly their uniform the chivalry and bravery of the south.... Once we were mad at the south ... [but] we have learned that there is nothing in resentment and if the south can obliterate from mind the bitterness of the defeat in the sixties, we hold that we can afford to forget any wrongs we may have suffered." Todd concluded that "lessons were learned [at the Gettysburg reunion] from the proud southern gentlemen that should have prevented the affront offered to the veterans Wednesday.... I and my comrades are ready to take their hands in token of forgetfulness so that the last days of the veterans of both sides may yet see the entire obliteration of Mason and Dixon's Line."[40] Union POW association members and many of the GAR rank and file advocated for a formal policy inviting Confederate veterans to participate in all future Grand Army functions.[41]

Disregarding GAR and UCV members' reconciliationist overtures, a number of southern presses claimed the incident exposed Yankees' lingering spitefulness. The editor of the *Orlando Reporter and Evening Star* suggested that former Confederates should refuse to take part in joint reunions with Union veterans. He maintained that "it will be well to omit these fraternizing reunions and let each side enjoy its own," resentfully claiming that Rebel veterans "are willing to shake hands across the bloody chasm and to do everything to prove that their bitter memories of the late conflict have been obliterated, but they are not ready to truckle or bend the knee that thrift may follow."[42] Echoing the Orlando editor's invective, the editor of the Mobile, Alabama, *Register* alleged that GAR leader Beers enforced the policy to its letter because of personal animosity toward Confederates. He claimed, "We remark that he discovered the rule, and applied it, after the Confederate veterans were in line and the parade was ready to start. We suspect that he discovered the veterans and saw it was time to apply the rule."[43] An editorial in the Paducah, Kentucky, *New Democrat* rejected Beers's claim to be following a strict parade policy as an alibi and instead blamed a cabal of malicious GAR members for barring the Confederates: "It is clear, however, the small act is to be placed at the door of a faction within the G.A.R. management which was in Chattanooga—guests of the men to whom they offered the insult—and not the main body, and only the faction, if it can be uncovered, is to be held responsible."[44]

While some southern newspapers spouted sectional venom, Chattanooga's boosterish newspapermen continued to maintain the host city's reputation by downplaying the episode. The editor of the *Chattanooga Sunday Times*, for example, predicted that the incident "will be forgotten very soon," while the editor of the *Chattanooga News* reprinted an article from the *Birmingham Ledger* censuring those who employed the incident to stir up sectional animosity. It noted that the blunder "is unfortunate because it gives an opening for bloody shirt wavers on both sides to do a lot of imprudent talking, which has some tendency toward reviving sectional feeling. It appears that the incident was in no way intended as any kind of a slight to Confederate veterans, and a few of them will so regard it.... Many of the rank and file of the Union veterans expressed regret over the matter because they realized that it might result in unkind sectional feeling and unwise criticism." It concluded, "The men who really contributed to the promotion of either cause are willing to bury the sectional spirit for good and discourage anything that tends toward its revision. Happily, only a few bloody shirt wavers continue to stir up feeling, and even they have less influence with either side as the years go by."[45]

As the press continued to harp on the parade incident, issues debated at the formal encampment sessions on Thursday and Friday further illustrated GAR members' ambivalent feelings toward former Rebels. As at every encampment, GAR members at Chattanooga held closed meetings in which the veterans debated major issues confronting the order, elected new officers, and discussed the order's membership and financial standing. During Friday morning's session, debate became quite heated over a resolution supporting federal pensions for Confederates. Former GAR commander in chief from Minnesota, Ell Torrence, put forward the resolution, which called on GAR members to formally support congressional legislation that provided Confederate Soldiers' Homes with federal funds. In particular, the proposal called for indigent former Rebels residing in Confederate Homes to receive $100 annually. Torrence implored his fellow GAR members to support the statute. He appealed to his fellow Union veterans' "good judgment, to your fraternal spirit, and to your sympathetic soldierly hearts. There is no old Confederate soldier today, who, if he approached your home hungry, you would not feed. There is not an old Confederate soldier today, who, if he stood at your door helpless, you would not gladly take in and shelter from the storm. To refuse to do either would do injustice to both."[46]

Other veterans staunchly disagreed with Torrence. New Jersey's Frank O. Cole adamantly rejected the notion that former Confederates should receive federal aid, because former Rebels remained guilty of treason. He determinedly claimed,

> I will give the last dollar I have got to any man who needs food or drink, but I will not put a Confederate soldier on the Pension Roll with my vote as

long as I live. I believe there is a difference between patriotism and treason, and I believe that treason is odious, and I believe when we say that no one shall come within our ranks on whom there has been a stain of treason, we mean business.

Cole suggested that GAR leaders table Torrence's resolution "until the crack of doom." Officials agreed with Cole and voted to table the motion indefinitely.[47] D. Minor Steward, resident of Chattanooga and past Tennessee Department commander, commended the leaders' decision. Though Steward sympathized with his ex-Confederate neighbors, he, too, rejected any resolution that equated former Rebels with Union veterans. He claimed that GAR members in Tennessee ungrudgingly paid state taxes to support residents of Confederate homes, "but we forever protest against placing them in a position where they are before the law equal with the men who spent four years and shed their blood in the cause of preserving the Union.... [W]e will take care of our late enemies, but we will not rest if you place them on an equality with us."[48]

GAR officials' rejection of federal aid to Confederates pleased some Union veterans; however, local newspapermen perceived it as yet another stumbling block to genuine reconciliation. A *Chattanooga Daily Times* editorial implied that critics of the resolution were guilty of continuing to wave the bloody shirt. It railed that the "defeat of action on the [Torrence] resolution was due to the unmerciful attacks on it made by the 'uncompromising' Union veterans attending the encampment.... Speakers attacked the resolution from the standpoint that its adoption might induce Congress at a later time to grant pensions to Confederate veterans and in that way place them on par in the eyes of the government with the federal veterans already enjoying pensions."[49] Despite criticism from the press, Confederate veterans also differed over the idea of receiving federal pensions, which speaks to the limits of reconciliation. According to the *Atlanta Constitution*, infighting among UCV members in Rome, Georgia, arose after George W. Fleetwood forwarded a letter urging GAR members to support Torrence's resolution. Though Fleetwood's letter listed the names of several old Confederates who welcomed government annuities, "many members of the camp indignantly assert that they do not want and would not have federal pensions, and repudiate the action of their comrade as not representing the real sentiment" of the UCV.[50] Nearly fifty years after Appomattox, some former Confederates remained unreconstructed.

In the wake of the formal encampment sessions, Friday night's entertainment suggests that although the GAR was officially a "color-blind" organization, members did not advance this notion outside the post door. White GAR members remained ambivalent on race. The local Sons of Union Veterans camp hosted a barbeque for northern visitors at Chamberlain Field—the University of Tennessee at Chattanooga's stadium—that lasted into the night. Though encampment boosters had sought to undermine pejorative stereotypes of a benighted Dixie by showcasing a fully modernized and industrialized South, the barbeque entertainment included a reproduction of an antebellum plantation scene and a "real negro cake walk." A log cabin was constructed on the field, which served as the centerpiece for the plantation scene. To provide a veneer of authenticity to the scene, organizers hired local African Americans to perform. One editorial claimed the entertainers were not "a troupe of blackfaced minstrel men" but rather "real negroes.... Care is being taken to get those with the best voices and those most familiar to the old plantation songs and manners."[51] The black entertainers opened the show by singing "Massa's in de Cold, Cold Ground" and "Old Black Joe" in a minstrel half circle.[52] In addition to singing, the performers acted out "characteristic negro amusements and jokes."[53] Following the minstrel show, the black entertainers took part in a "watermelon feast, and a regular crap game, in which the participants are old timers who are thoroughly familiar with the idiosyncrasies of the ivory bones and know just how to talk to them."[54]

The white audience members then enjoyed the grand finale: the cake walk. One editorial broadcast that "it is to be a real cake walk, something seldom seen north of the Mason Dixon line." Several local black couples "who claim the championship of graceful dances" entered the contest and performed for the northerners.[55] Not only did the show provide northerners with idyllic imagery of slavery in the antebellum South, but white members' attendance at this spectacle and their lack of public criticism of it illustrate their ambivalence, at best, and implicit acceptance of patronizing racial stereotypes at worst.

Neither white and black GAR members nor Chattanoogans publicly criticized either the plantation scene or the men and women who were put on display as specimens of an exotic culture; however, it is telling that African American members of the local First Baptist Church hosted an emancipation jubilee for black veterans at the same time as the barbeque. As with the meeting of black veterans at Wiley Memorial Church the night before—during which black members of the Women's Relief Corps and GAR spoke—the jubilee celebrated those African Americans who served in a war for black emancipation. Noted black clergyman, orator, and NAACP corresponding secretary Dr. Madison Charles Butler Mason's speech titled the "Heroes of '63" was

FIGURE 3. "Wiped Out," *Chattanooga News*, September 20, 1913.

the principal feature of the evening. Additionally, the host church's choir entertained visitors by singing "plantation melodies" and "national airs."[56] It is unclear how many whites attended the jubilee, though all veterans and guests were welcome. Yet the topic of Mason's address and the timing of the jubilee itself most certainly challenged the racial stereotypes disseminated at the barbeque, as well as symbolized black autonomy and served as a reminder of black service in a war that brought about "a new birth of freedom."

The next day, Union veterans and their visiting families boarded trains for home and bid adieu to the Mountain City. Local boosters and northern visitors publicly proclaimed that the encampment was a stupendous success in its contribution to mending sectional wounds and symbolically reuniting the nation. A cartoon printed in the *Chattanooga News* captured this sentiment. The cartoon pictured a white GAR veteran on a train—dubbed the New South Express—bidding farewell to a beautiful white Miss Chattanooga, a female personification of the city. The caption accompanying the sketch read, "Goodbye, you've proved to us there's no Mason and Dixon Line to cross as we go back."[57] Welthea Miller, a tourist from Akron, New York, who visited the encampment and later published her observations in a pamphlet, agreed with the cartoon's message. She dismissed the parade incident as a minor disappointment and crowed that "on account of the Chattanooga Encampment we are much nearer the realization of that remark than ever before."[58] However, the controversies that arose during encampment week were not so easily resolved. Regardless of their public rhetoric and niceties, GAR members remained ambivalent about reconciliation with former Rebels. Sectional animosities remained just beneath the surface in the communities of Civil War veterans, Chattanooga residents, and citizens of the wider nation. At the same time, white GAR members vacillated on race. White GAR members did not publicly criticize Jim Crow segregation, rebuke southern whites who refused to associate with African Americans in the parade, or condemn patronizing racial stereotypes displayed at entertainment programs. However, black Union veterans' participation in GAR activities reminded white comrades and contemporary society of black military service and remained an affront to the Lost Cause. Though white and black GAR members marched side by side during the encampment parade and former Rebels and Federals claimed lingering war wounds had fully healed, it was unclear to perhaps many concerned how far the nation had yet to travel for both of those idyllic gestures to be fully realized.

NOTES

1. "Grand Army Veterans in Mile-Long Parade," *Chattanooga (TN) News*, September 17, 1913.
2. The order of march was based on departmental seniority, except for members from Tennessee who were encampment hosts. Seniority in the GAR was based on the date each department formally joined the national organization. See especially, GAR, National, *Forty-Seventh National Encampment* (1913), 148–52, and "Blue Army on Parade," *Chattanooga (TN) Times*, September 17, 1913.
3. "Long Line of Veterans," *Chattanooga (TN) Times*, September 18, 1913.
4. "South Applauds Big G.A.R. Parade," *Plain Dealer* (Cleveland, OH), September 18, 1913.
5. GAR, Tennessee, *Thirty-First Encampment* (1914), 13.
6. GAR, Tennessee, *Thirty-First Encampment* (1914), 13.
7. "Long Line of Veterans," *Chattanooga (TN) Times*, September 18, 1913.
8. "G.A.R. Veterans Meet First Time in the Real South," *Asheville (NC) Citizen*, August 31, 1913.
9. "No Enemy's Country," *Boston Post*, September 16, 1913.
10. "Thirty-One Thousand Attended Encampment," *Chattanooga (TN) News*, September 20, 1913; "Rain Failed to Halt G.A.R.," *Houston (TX) Post*, September 16, 1913. Guests included GAR members and their families as well as members of auxiliary organizations of the GAR and other Civil War veterans' organizations that held concurrent meetings during the week.

11. For a sample of this scholarship, see especially, Stuart McConnell, *Glorious Contentment: The Grand Army of the Republic, 1865–1900* (Chapel Hill: University of North Carolina Press, 1992), David W. Blight, *Race and Reunion: The Civil War in American Memory* (Cambridge, MA: Belknap Press of Harvard University Press, 2001), Barbara Gannon, *The Won Cause: Black and White Comradeship in the Grand Army of the Republic* (Chapel Hill: University of North Carolina Press, 2011), James Marten, *Sing Not War: The Lives of Union and Confederate Veterans in Gilded Age America* (Chapel Hill: University of North Carolina Press, 2011), Caroline E. Janney, *Remembering the Civil War: Reunion and the Limits of Reconciliation* (Chapel Hill: University of North Carolina Press, 2013), and M. Keith Harris, *Across the Bloody Chasm: The Culture of Commemoration among Civil War Veterans* (Baton Rouge: Louisiana State University Press, 2014).

12. GAR, Tennessee, descriptive records, Calvin M. McClung Collection, Knox County Public Library, Knoxville, TN (hereafter CMM Collection). The McClung collection houses two bound volumes of the original rosters, which provide information on 131 posts from across Tennessee. These volumes have been microfilmed and indexed by post name, number, and location. Multiple rosters have been transcribed by Raymond A. Sears and published in various issues of the East Tennessee Historical Society's *Tennessee Ancestors*. See also *Roster of Ed. Maynard Post, No. 14, Department of Tennessee GAR* (Knoxville, TN: Department of Tennessee GAR, 1890, 1909), and *Roster of Mission Ridge Post, No. 45, Department of Tennessee GAR* (Chattanooga, TN: Department of Tennessee GAR, 1888). For each individual listed in the GAR post rosters, I correlated their biographical information with the information listed in the population schedules of the 1880 and 1900 U.S. censuses.

13. Grand Army of the Republic Scrapbooks, 1913, Chattanooga Public Library. The fourteen massive, leather-bound scrapbooks exhaustively chronicle the encampment. Clippings inside the scrapbooks include editorials from newspapers across the nation that range across the ideological spectrum and that express both positive and negative views of the encampment and the controversies surrounding it.

14. McConnell, *Glorious Contentment*, xiv; Mary R. Dearing, *Veterans in Politics: The Story of the D.A.R.* (Baton Rouge: Louisiana State University Press, 1954), 219–66; Robert B. Beath, *History of the Grand Army of the Republic* (New York: Bryan, Taylor, 1899), 634; Gordon B. McKinney, *Southern Mountain Republicans, 1865–1900: Politics and the Appalachian Community* (Chapel Hill: University of North Carolina Press, 1978); Department of Tennessee, Grand Army of the Republic, records, 1893–94, CMM Collection; *Journal of the Proceedings, Eleventh Encampment, Greeneville, March 21, 1894*, 70, CMM Collection. Department of Tennessee and Georgia posts were established in Tennessee, Georgia, and Alabama. For a complete list of posts comprising the Department of Tennessee, see GAR, Tennessee, descriptive records, CMM Collection.

15. The northern and midwestern members of the Lookout and Mission Ridge posts, included men from Ohio (ninety-five), New York (seventy), Pennsylvania (forty-six), Indiana (twenty-nine), Michigan (fourteen), Massachusetts (six), Vermont (six), Maine (five), Illinois (five), New Jersey (three), Rhode Island (three), New Hampshire (three), District of Columbia (two), Minnesota (one), Iowa (one), Wisconsin (one), Connecticut (one), and Delaware (one). Whereas Ohioans accounted for 18.1 percent of members, New Yorkers and Pennsylvanians accounted for 13.4 percent and 8.8 percent of members, respectively. See especially

Lookout Post 2 and Mission Ridge Post 45 rosters in GAR, Tennessee, descriptive records, CMM Collection.

16. Stuart McConnell, "Who Joined the Grand Army? Three Case Studies in the Construction of Union Veteranhood, 1866–1900," in *Toward a Social History of the American Civil War; Exploratory Essays*, ed. Maris A. Vinovskis (New York: Cambridge University Press, 1990), 139–70.

17. See especially, Chickamauga Post 22 roster in GAR, Tennessee, descriptive records, CMM Collection.

18. Though post membership was not reported every year, Chickamauga Post's reported membership from 1890 to 1917; see especially GAR, Tennessee, *Eighth Encampment* through the *Sixteenth Encampment* (1891–99), *Twenty-Seventh Encampment* (1910), *Twenty-Eighth Encampment* (1911), *Thirty-First Encampment* (1914), *Thirty-Second Encampment* (1915), *Thirty-Fourth Encampment* (1917).

19. GAR, National, *Forty-Eighth Encampment* (1914), 61.

20. GAR, Tennessee, *Thirtieth Encampment* (1913); "Commander's Address," n.p.; *Thirty-First Encampment* (1914), 13.

21. GAR, National, *Forty-Eighth Encampment* (1914), 61. Southern states with active posts in 1913 included Alabama (6 posts, 116 members), Arkansas (22 posts, 405 members), Florida (22 posts, 656 members), Georgia and South Carolina (9 posts, 170 members), Kentucky (64 posts, 1,061 members), Louisiana and Mississippi (42 posts, 728 members), Missouri (219 posts, 5,046 members), Tennessee (32 posts, 966 members), Virginia and North Carolina (28 posts, 381 members), Texas (20 posts, 399 members), and West Virginia (34 posts, 1,057 members).

22. For a list departmental officers, see especially "Officers for 1912–1913," in GAR, Tennessee, *Twenty-Ninth Encampment* (1912), n.p., and "General Orders No. 1," in *Thirtieth Encampment* (1913), n.p.

23. According to state GAR membership reports, Tennessee had thirty-four posts with a total of 1,005 members. Of those 1,005, 845 belonged to posts in east Tennessee. See especially GAR, National, *Forty-Eighth Encampment* (1914), 15–23, 30.

24. "How Chattanooga Was Selected," *Chattanooga (TN) News*, July 29, 1913.

25. "G.A.R. Will Meet in Chattanooga: First National Encampment in the South," *Times* (Watertown, New York), July 10, 1913. This article was reprinted in a number of other newspapers across the North. See especially, "South Will Be Host to G.A.R.," *Star* (Newark, NJ), July 11, 1913, "The Grand Army Encampment," *Transcript* (Holyoke, MA), July 11, 1913, and "Boys in Blue Will Meet in the South," *Dispatch* (Moline, IL), July 11, 1913.

26. "Yankees Invade South Again," *Banner* (Athens, GA), August 28, 1913.

27. Appalachian historians have found throughout the late nineteenth and early twentieth centuries, various individuals and organizations cultivated a "monolithic Unionism" mythology. See especially James C. Klotter, "The Black South and White Appalachia," *Journal of American History* 66, no. 4 (1980): 4, Shannon H. Wilson, "Lincoln's Sons and Daughters: Berea College, Lincoln Memorial University, and the Myth of Unionist Appalachia, 1866–1910," in *The Civil War in Appalachia: Collected Essays*, ed. Kenneth W. Noe and Shannon H. Wilson (Knoxville: University of Tennessee Press, 1997), 242–64, Kenneth Noe, "'Deadened Color and Colder Horror': Rebecca Harding Davis and the Myth of Unionist Appalachia,"

in *Confronting Appalachian Stereotypes: Back Talk from an American Region*, ed. Dwight B. Billings, Gurney Norman, and Katherine Ledford (Lexington: University Press of Kentucky, 1999), 85–97, John C. Inscoe, *Race, War, and Remembrance in the Appalachian South* (Lexington: University Press of Kentucky, 2008), and Tom Lee, "The Lost Cause That Wasn't: East Tennessee and the Myth of Unionist Appalachia," in *Reconstructing Appalachia: The Civil War's Aftermath*, ed. Andrew L. Slap (Lexington: University Press of Kentucky, 2010), 293–322.

28. "Loyal to the Union," *Times* (Eire, PA), September 23, 1913, reprinted in *Russellville (OH) Advocate*, n.d.

29. "A Matter of Good Taste," *Chattanooga (TN) Daily Times*, September 12, 1913.

30. "Chairman of U.C.V. Reunion Urges All to Decorate," *Chattanooga (TN) Daily Times*, September 13, 1913.

31. "Echoes of Encampment," *Chattanooga (TN) Daily Times*, September 22, 1913.

32. "Alabama Band Declines to March with Negroes," *Chattanooga (TN) Times*, September 18, 1913. The band was one of several ensembles hired to perform in the GAR demonstration.

33. "The Blue and the Gray," *Chattanooga (TN) Times*, September 17, 1913. See also "Former Foes Arm in Arm," *Chattanooga (TN) Times*, September 16, 1913.

34. For a detailed account of the incident, see especially "Southern Troops Barred by G.A.R. from Big Parade," *Register* (Mobile, AL), September 18, 1913, and "Who Issued the Orders That Excluded Forrest Camp from Grand Parade?," *Chattanooga (TN) Times*, September 18, 1913.

35. The story was related in newspapers across the country. See especially "Bars 'Rebs' from Parade," *Chicago Tribune*, September 18, 1913, "No Grey Uniforms and No Old Confederates in G.A.R. Parade at Chattanooga Yesterday," *Raleigh (NC) Observer*, September 18, 1913, "Gray Uniformed Men Are Barred from G.A.R. Parade," *Asheville (NC) Citizen*, September 18, 1913, "Confederate Veterans Barred from the G.A.R. Parade," *Times* (Savannah, GA), September 18, 1913, "Bar Confederates from G.A.R. Parade," *New York Times*, September 18, 1913, "Boys in Blue March, but Bar the Gray," *New York World*, September 18, 1913, "Southern Veterans out of G.A.R. Parade," *Public Ledger* (Philadelphia, PA), September 18, 1913, "G.A.R. Bars Gray Ranks," *Boston Herald*, September 18, 1913, and "Gray Veterans Barred by Blue," *Atlanta (GA) Constitution*, September 18, 1913.

36. "Who Issued the Orders That Excluded Forrest Camp from Grand Parade?," *Chattanooga (TN) Times*, September 18, 1913.

37. "Who Issued the Orders That Excluded Forrest Camp from Grand Parade?," *Chattanooga (TN) Times*, September 18, 1913.

38. "Order Was a Mistake," *Chattanooga (TN) Daily Times*, September 19, 1913.

39. "Col. Watrous Expresses Veterans' Indignation," *Chattanooga (TN) News*, September 18, 1913; "Making Amends," *News* (Dayton, OH), September 27, 1913.

40. "Ex-Prisoners Are Red Hot," *Chattanooga (TN) Times*, September 19, 1913.

41. "Confederates Wanted in All Future Parades," *Chattanooga (TN) News*, September 19, 1913.

42. "The Chattanooga Incident," *Orlando [FL] Reporter and Evening Star*, September 25, 1913.

43. "Chattanooga Incident," *Register* (Mobile, AL), September 19, 1913.
44. *News Democrat* (Paducah, KY), September 23, 1913.
45. "A Mere Incident Soon Forgotten," *Birmingham (AL) Ledger*, reprinted in *Chattanooga (TN) News*, September 22, 1913.
46. GAR, National, *Forty-Seventh Encampment* (1913), 243.
47. GAR, National, *Forty-Seventh Encampment* (1913), 243–44.
48. GAR, National, *Forty-Seventh Encampment* (1913), 244–45.
49. "Hot Bloods Defeat It," *Chattanooga (TN) Daily Times*, September 20, 1913.
50. "Floyd Veterans Are Angered at Request of Federal Pensions," *Atlanta (GA) Constitution*, September 16, 1913.
51. "Genuine Cake Walk for Daughters' Benefit," *Chattanooga (TN) Times*, September 5, 1913.
52. "Entertainment by Sons of Veterans," *Chattanooga (TN) News*, August 30, 1913.
53. "Plantation Program for Northern Visitors," *Chattanooga (TN) Times*, September 7, 1913.
54. "Genuine Cake Walk for Daughters' Benefit," *Chattanooga (TN) Times*, September 5, 1913.
55. "Genuine Cake Walk for Daughters' Benefit," *Chattanooga (TN) Times*, September 5, 1913.
56. "Patriotic Meeting of Colored Veterans," *Chattanooga (TN) News*, September 19, 1913; "Entertainment for Colored Veterans," *Chattanooga (TN) News*, September 19, 1913.
57. "Wiped Out," *Chattanooga (TN) News*, September 20, 1913.
58. Welthea Miller, *The National Encampment At Chattanooga* (Akron, NY: J. G. Childs and Son, 1913), 26.

The Lucy Cobb Institute

Mildred Lewis Rutherford and Her Mission to Preserve an Idealized Southern Community

KATHERINE E. ROHRER

IT WAS EARLY SEPTEMBER, AND THINGS WERE ABUZZ ON STATELY North Milledge Avenue in Athens, Georgia. The year was 1930. The Lucy Cobb Institute and its principal James Brooks were welcoming students to its campus in that historic northeast Georgia college town. Lucy Cobb had opened its doors each September to the elite daughters of Georgia, the South, and areas beyond for seventy-one years.[1] Later in the afternoon, shortly before the dinner hour, as their "sisters" had done before them, the young women and their families gathered for the opening convocation of the new academic year. Sitting in the octagonally shaped Seney-Stovall Chapel, they listened as Principal Brooks invoked the virtues of education, celebrated school traditions, introduced the assembled faculty, and announced plans for the upcoming session.

Upon leaving the chapel, those assembled took a moment to admire the dignity of the campus. The mansion, the focal point of the Lucy Cobb Institute, was a three-storied Greek revival structure, resplendent in stuccoed brick and boasting a hipped roof and parapet. A dramatic flight of steps led to the wide, one-story verandah adorned with locally famous ironwork that, fittingly, had left Philadelphia on the last train to the South before the fall of Fort Sumter in 1861 and looked inviting with its black wicker furniture complete with rose chintz-covered cushions.[2] A popular spot, this porch, in the tradition of the nineteenth-century South, had served as a gathering place for the duration of the institute's history. Abutting the verandah was the façade of the mansion, striking in appearance with its row of large windows ornately decorated with cast-iron cornices and its imposing front door framed by pilasters and flanked by sidelights. Annexed to the rear were Margaret Hall and Alumnae Hall, which housed residential quarters, meeting rooms, and classrooms. Close by stood the kitchen, separated for safety's sake from the main structures of the campus. A dense hedge distanced the property from the town, connoting Lucy Cobb's position as a community "apart."

At twilight, many of the young Lucies—as Lucy Cobb students had always been known—took respite from the heat on the verandah. The porch was the ideal place to socialize with both old friends and new arrivals that first evening. In those fading moments of daylight, the young ladies took in the sights, sounds, and smells of their surroundings, which included the gracious Greek revival, Queen Anne, neoclassical, colonial revival, and Tudor revival residences standing in both directions along Milledge Avenue; the tinkling of the bells on the street cars that trolled by; and the wafting of the fragrances emanating from the season's last blooms on the magnolias on the school's lawn.

It would thus appear that everything was properly in place for Lucy Cobb to carry on just as before. It was not. For decades, the institute remained unwilling to learn, let alone study, those lessons that might have ensured this community's future; its ultimate demise was less than a year away. Yet as its "death" became imminent, administrators at the Lucy Cobb Institute refused to seriously consider any alternative identity than the one that had defined the school since its founding.

For longtime Lucy Cobb administrator Mildred Lewis Rutherford, the institute functioned as a microcosm of the Old South, an enduring legacy of a region in which racial and sexual subordination was de rigueur.[3] At the same time, this institution offered Rutherford opportunities to embrace and promote the conservative values of an idealized Old South while she steadily expanded her intellectual and professional capacities, the latter ironically suggestive of a more progressive era. In Rutherford's eyes, the Lucy Cobb Institute served as a community—perhaps, more appropriately, a factory—in which she and her like-minded colleagues helped to produce well-educated southern women who would go on to hand down this romanticized memory of the antebellum South to future generations; perhaps in the best case scenario, and in her vision, such alumnae would partially control the historical narrative of the Old South. Rutherford's community—her factory—could not and did not stand the test of time. Ultimately, Rutherford's refusal to jettison the educational philosophies of and gendered ideas from the antebellum era contributed to the institution's closure in 1931.

THE CITIZENS OF ATHENS ESTABLISHED THE LUCY COBB INSTITUTE in 1858 via charitable contributions.[4] The campaign for it was inaugurated by Thomas R. R. Cobb, who realized the need for a female institution of higher education in northern Georgia. The Cobbs ranked among the most distinguished families in antebellum Georgia, and Thomas R. R. was a particularly noteworthy family member. He was an ardent southern nationalist, a prominent attorney and legal scholar who helped establish what became the University of Georgia Law School, a short-time member of the Confederate Congress, and a Confederate general who gave his life at Fredericksburg in 1862.[5]

In 1854, Laura Cobb Rutherford, Thomas R. R. Cobb's sister, appealed for a female institution of higher learning in Athens through an article that she published—under a pseudonym—in the *Southern Watchmen*.[6] By 1858, the Georgia legislature had passed an act incorporating such an institution of higher learning there. When completed, it was initially to be called "Athens Female Seminary." Sadly, shortly before the opening day, Thomas's thirteen-year-old daughter, Lucy, died unexpectedly. This prompted the renaming of the school as the Lucy Cobb Institute, forever a memorial to the child and a tribute to the commitment of her father. On January 10, 1859, its first students arrived.[7]

Dozens of schools similar to the Lucy Cobb Institute opened between 1830 and 1900.[8] In fact, nearly one hundred female colleges of some description operated across the South during those decades. In contrast, before 1830, girls' schools, at any level, were uncommon, while, at the same time, institutions for boys flourished and were promoted and funded by state legislatures. However, beginning in the 1830s, both state legislatures and religious circles increasingly promoted the education of women.

"College" is a tricky term that was not easily definable during much of the nineteenth century. Depending on the place and time, the terms "college," "seminary," "institute," and "academy" were used interchangeably. Most such schools offered a curriculum that was more comparable to one offered by a high school or its equivalent. The curricula at these institutions were in no way standardized, but literature, composition, foreign language, and the ornamental arts dominated. In contrast to their northern counterparts, such southern female institutions offered a more intellectually rigorous curriculum. The South educated elite women to become cultured ladies; the North educated women across a wider class spectrum, particularly those who intended to enter the workforce. Although southern women's schools emphasized greater intellectual achievement than northern ones, the diplomas granted by southern institutions were "memorable mementos, not credentials to a new world of work."[9] In this regard, Lucy Cobb was typical of other nineteenth-century southern academies and colleges. Without a doubt, the school placed high importance on elocution, drawing, music, and other allegedly feminine subjects. That said, the school also offered advanced classes in such subjects as analytical geometry (calculus), Latin, chemistry, and physics.[10]

After an inauspicious start, the Lucy Cobb Institute flourished during the final two decades of the nineteenth century. The school underwent a significant transformation during the tenure of Mildred Rutherford—Thomas R. R. Cobb's niece—as its principal between 1880 and 1895. Rutherford possessed the attributes of an able administrator, including enthusiasm, social position, and intellect. Admired by students, graduates, instructors, and the Athens community, Rutherford remained at Lucy Cobb, in various capacities, until her death in 1928.[11] Nonetheless, while she may have been an effective leader of the institute in the nineteenth century, she was far less effectual in the twentieth. Quite simply, Rutherford refused to adjust to the changing times; she was incapable of burying the Old South at a time when her region was just beginning to shed its anachronistic identity.

To appreciate why Rutherford and her fixation with the preservation of the Old South significantly contributed to Lucy Cobb's demise, one must first understand the institution's evolution at the turn of the twentieth century. By the late 1880s, Lucy Cobb offered a growing array of advanced courses, and the faculty had increased to fifteen instructors, several of whom also taught at the University of Georgia (UGA). Furthermore, George I. Seney, a New York philanthropist and donor to Emory College and Wesleyan College, donated $10,000 for a chapel. In the 1890s, Lucy Cobb added an elementary school, intended to prepare young girls for the demands of the institute's secondary and postsecondary curricula.[12] In praise of Mildred Rutherford and Mary Rutherford Lipscomb—a later Lucy Cobb principal—and the school's ascendance, one Athenian remarked in the early 1890s that "under the wise guidance of these two remarkable women Lucy Cobb has steadily prospered until it is now one of the best known and popular schools in the South."[13] The parents of girls and young women from across the South and beyond selected the institute, attracted by its esteemed academic standing as well as its role as a highly respected finishing school.

By 1900, the Lucy Cobb Institute advertised that its graduates could matriculate at traditional women's four-year colleges and seminaries—specifically naming Smith and Mount Holyoke—where they could enter as upperclassmen. During Mildred Rutherford's tenure, the curriculum expanded—though the "feminine" arts continued to be stressed—and many of the instructors held master's degrees. During these years, young Lucies typically enrolled in a program that included English composition and literature, higher-level mathematics, religion, ethics, biology, chemistry, physics, and modern and/or ancient languages, supplemented with art, music, and elocution.[14] Thus, by 1910, Lucy Cobb—although it had not achieved the official status as a traditional women's liberal arts college—legitimately offered a curriculum consistent with those found at what would soon become junior colleges.[15]

Aside from academics, Rutherford stressed extracurricular activities—notably those tied to religion, civic service, music, art, and literature—that reinforced Old South femininity. Perhaps most important to Rutherford was the spiritual development of the Lucies. Rutherford was a self-avowed evangelical and required students to enroll in weekly Bible classes and urged them to participate in extracurricular religious activities. She also oversaw the establishment of a chapter of the Young Women's Christian Association and other religious organizations, including the King's Daughters, which promoted work in home missions.[16] Likewise, Rutherford fostered civic and social relationships between her students and the United Daughters of the Confederacy and the Children of the Confederacy. Evidence of this tie includes generous scholarships available to Lucies who were "the descendants of Confederates and whose mothers were loyal to the cause."[17] Many Lucy Cobb alumnae shaped by Rutherford's conservative worldview would later assume leadership positions in these organizations in the years well after World War II.

Aside from urging participation in these religious and civic outlets, Rutherford encouraged students to form clubs that supported the arts and literature. The subsequent creation of the Poets' Corner, the Thalians, and other clubs attested to the school's broad conceptualization of an education and its support for the arts, especially music and drama.[18] Many students, for example, availed themselves of private voice and/or instrumental music lessons and performed at regular recitals. Several of the music instructors, including the renowned Hugh Hodgson, were imported from the University of Georgia. Dramatics were yet another artistic outlet. The Lucies performed Shakespearian and other plays for both the school and the community.[19] Semiregular excursions to Europe underscored these ideals of elite womanhood. As early as the late 1880s, Mildred Rutherford guided small parties of students on the Grand Tour, visiting such destinations as Great Britain, France, Germany, Switzerland, Belgium, Italy, and even the Holy Lands.[20] Meanwhile, Rutherford deemphasized physical education, which she likely considered a threat to southern femininity; her choice stood in contrast to that made by many other female academies and colleges that had already incorporated athletics into their curricula.

By the turn of the twentieth century, Mildred Rutherford, in partnership with faculty, students, alumnae, and the board of trustees, had turned Lucy Cobb into an elite institution.[21] The school had established an excellent academic reputation, offered a curriculum that prepared its graduates to enter the world possessing both intellectual prowess and the social graces found only in elite environments, attracted a group of well-regarded and well-trained instructors, and boasted outstanding facilities. However, between 1900 and Lucy Cobb's demise in 1931, Mildred Rutherford and the institute—her idealized community—changed exceedingly little, while the world around them changed exponentially. Ideas and practices in secondary and postsecondary education—and women's place with relationship to them—underwent profound redefinition. Once a bright star, the institute began to fade into obscurity.

After stepping down as principal in 1895, Mildred Rutherford served several terms as president of Lucy Cobb throughout the next three decades. Rutherford thus remained involved in nearly all aspects of the institute as evidenced by her voluminous collection of personal and institute papers. Newspaper clippings, institute programs, catalogs, and alumnae newsletters all bear her imprint. Quite simply, Rutherford remained the real power behind the throne at Lucy Cobb until her death in 1928. She defied conventional female behavior by virtue of her continued embrace of a public life as a spinster, yet she did so in ways that preserved the priorities and values of the antebellum South.

Concurrent with her new roles at Lucy Cobb, Rutherford committed herself to two conservative causes: (re)writing the master narrative of the Old South and the Confederacy and advocating traditional societal roles for women. Relative to the former, Rutherford assumed leadership positions in the Ladies Memorial Association of Athens, the Southern Memorial Association, the Confederated Southern Memorial Association as well as the United Daughters of the Confederacy at the local, state, and national levels. For these organizations, she prepared papers, pamphlets, histories, and speeches on a multitude of topics in southern history. Such publications and speeches reflected a decidedly white supremacist, pro-Confederate, anti-women's suffrage message. Similarly, the tireless southern patriot encouraged fellow ideologues to follow in her footsteps and to corroborate this worldview. For example, while serving as general historian of the United Daughters of the Confederacy during the 1910s, Rutherford chaired the committee that selected the recipient of the Loving Cup, a prize for the best essay submitted on a given subject connected with the South's history. Representative topics included "The Misrepresentation of Jefferson Davis in History and Fiction" and "The Ku Klux Klan."[22]

In addition, Rutherford beseeched publishers to correct textbooks that, in her opinion, not only misrepresented the South but also got the facts wrong. In one very personal example, Rutherford recalled the "indignation" felt by her mother when she discovered in a textbook she was using to educate her grandson that "her own brother Howell Cobb [was] named among southern traitors and rebels that should have been hanged."[23] While Rutherford made a formal complaint to the publisher, "the only redress was a promise to have that particular leaf cut from the book."[24] Innumerable other pieces of correspondence between Rutherford and publishers across the country substantiate her mission to control the historical narrative of the South.

Mildred Rutherford's second cause—advocating traditional societal roles for women—was reflected in a number of her actions, memberships, and ideas but particularly those that intersected with the field of education. Not surprisingly, this is seen in those instances in which the viability of Lucy Cobb was at stake. An active member in the Georgia Association Opposed to Woman Suffrage, Rutherford affirmed her increasingly outmoded conceptions of southern femininity when two additional postsecondary institutions—State Normal School in Athens and the University of Georgia—opened their doors to young women in 1891 and 1918, respectively.[25] Quite simply, these institutions and the type of women graduates they produced challenged Rutherford's idealized image of the Old South. Transformations in higher education reflected acceptance of new pedagogies and impacted how society in general perceived women and how women perceived themselves. Most notably, such institutions offered ample opportunity for women to interact with men in social as well as academic environments, the latter in which they experienced relative parity. Similarly, female students at both State Normal School in Athens and UGA enjoyed a degree of independence that Rutherford purposely and protectively denied to the innocent and impressionable Lucies. Throughout its existence, for instance, the Lucy Cobb Institute adhered to the strict rule that students could not leave the campus without a chaperone.[26] Yet even in the Deep South—far removed from the suffragette activities centered in northern urban areas—women at UGA and State Normal School in Athens developed new aspirations and embraced new societal roles that would take them out of the home. Mildred Rutherford's conceptions of female education were nearing their expiration date.

Despite an inauspicious beginning in part due to limited funding, State Normal School in Athens expanded via generous support from the community, private organizations, philanthropists, and the Georgia legislature as the need for better-trained teachers became acute.[27] Between 1880 and 1920, normal schools, including the one in Athens, increasingly outpaced private institutions like Lucy Cobb. The former offered students a solid curriculum that included English, French, history, civics, geography, music, and art. Students who enrolled in the "advanced course" typically took higher-level classes, such as physiology, chemistry, physics, advanced mathematics, philosophy, and ancient languages.[28] In addition, and in contrast to students at Lucy Cobb, where tradition trumped practicality, normalites pursued courses in child and adolescent psychology, history and philosophy of education, and methods of teaching.

By 1908, State Normal School in Athens had matured into a sizable institution with over a thousand students—both men and women—studying there during any given academic year. A surviving architectural plate from 1908 illustrates that the campus included two academic buildings, two dormitories, a library, a dining hall, the Muscogee Practice School, a chapel, an infirmary, and miscellaneous outbuildings.[29] One cannot deny the advantages that the State Normal School in Athens provided for its students. In particular, it offered an extensive variety of advanced classes, afforded women a greater degree of independence, gave women the opportunity to socialize with men, and educated women for a specific vocation. Undoubtedly, the popularity of the normal school was one factor in the Lucy Cobb Institute's slow demise, but it certainly was not the only one.

Mildred Rutherford wanted Lucy Cobb to remain a place "where girlhood ripen[ed] into the acme of Southern womanliness and the perfection of sacred womanhood." Harkening back to a romanticized version of the Old South, she waxed nostalgically of the institute as possessing an "atmosphere of refinement, of gentle, sweet dignity, of natural and easy culture" that "was cultivated ... in the days when the grandmother was receiving the training that made her the type and the queen of womanhood of the world."[30] Even as the United States emerged from World War I, Rutherford described the physical environment in which such idealized girls and young ladies were created in equally sanguine, yet conservative, terms. More than subtly reinforcing a racial hierarchy indicative of the antebellum era, Rutherford referred to the gracious parlor at Lucy Cobb, where students and visitors alike were greeted by a painting of Aunt Dot, Rutherford's "black mammy" who had faithfully served her family for decades.[31] Rutherford's sentimentalized rhetoric upheld the superiority of antebellum southern society while simultaneously reinforcing her definition of the ideal Lucy Cobb graduate: an articulate, cultured, intellectual, and religiously devout lady who would enter the public sphere only when needed to defend the racial, gender, and class hierarchy of the Old South.

It is impossible to determine the extent to which alumnae accepted Rutherford's views regarding gender and race. That said, Rutherford routinely invited graduates who shared her worldview—and whose words could influence current students—to speak at the alumnae banquet and other institutional events. For example, in 1917, Rutherford praised alumna Mrs. Jones whose "utterances" at the banquet "were strong and forceful, emphasizing the fact that woman is needed more than ever before in her own peculiar sphere of usefulness."[32] That Rutherford invited Mrs. Jones—and other like-minded women in the late 1910s—to speak at alumnae events reflected her discomfort with evolving gender roles. Lucy Cobb students might be reluctant to accept the words of an aging administrator but more likely take seriously those of a young alumna who, just a few years before, had published articles in the *Lucy Cobb Magazine* that simultaneously celebrated a sexist, white supremacist Old South and mocked "Negro minstrels."[33]

Especially threatening to Rutherford and her gendered ideals as they pertained to women's education was the University of Georgia's proposal to appropriate the junior college portion of Lucy Cobb.[34] By 1916, UGA had increasingly become interested in such a merger, and its trustees appointed a committee to consider the terms, legal and otherwise, of such an arrangement. Rutherford vociferously opposed the institute's incorporation into UGA. It is impossible to assess whether Rutherford's opposition influenced the personal views of faculty, students, alumnae, and the board of trustees. Nevertheless, it would appear for the short term that Rutherford got her way. In 1917, with no further mention in the Lucy Cobb minute book of merger plans, Rutherford—at age sixty-six—again took the helm as president of Lucy Cobb on a five-year contract.

Despite significant developments in the field of education—both locally and nationally—as well as the recent threat of a merger with UGA, Rutherford and like-minded administrators remained reluctant to modernize the Lucy Cobb collegiate curriculum.[35] Most of the course offerings in the late 1910s and 1920s were scarcely different from what they had been at the end of the nineteenth century. The school did, however, begin offering domestic science, a course typically found at the burgeoning junior colleges and normal schools. But this was the extent to which the institute embraced any curricular change. Ironically, inclusion of domestic science into the curriculum could be interpreted as a gesture to securely attach women to the home rather than to prepare them for the world at large. One could ask if the Lucy Cobb Institute—which for decades had stressed ancient languages, Shakespeare, philosophy, and physics and offered stimulating lectures on Islam and the role of electricity in society—was experiencing a crisis of identity.

The composition of the student body at Lucy Cobb by the 1920s should have also served as a wake-up call to Rutherford that her teaching philosophies were seriously outdated. By then, the social and economic identities of the Lucies had changed little from what they had been decades before. However, and quite significantly, the majority of the enrollees were then either Athens or Clarke County residents. During the institute's final years, exceedingly fewer young women from outside the immediate geographical area selected Mildred Rutherford's school as their academy or junior college. Parents perhaps felt the institute would not prepare their daughters for a more modern, progressive society but instead for the anachronistic one of the Old South. As a result, the Lucy Cobb Institute—without a formal endowment or significant financial support from the community or religious denominations—suffered profoundly from the loss of tuition and other fees that in the past had been generated from the boarding students who had disproportionately funded the school.[36]

Exacerbating Lucy Cobb's situation was the grim financial picture that defined the South during the 1920s. The boll weevil—with its devastating effects on the South's cotton economy—significantly contributed to the long-lasting depression that plagued the region. Consequently, fewer families, especially those whose financial interests were tied to cotton, could afford the luxury of sending their daughters to schools such as Lucy Cobb. The fiscal situation at Lucy Cobb had become so grave that Rutherford had to use her personal funds to keep the school afloat.

Meanwhile, numerous other elite women's academies and colleges in the South, many of which shared Rutherford's "unreconstructed" worldview, faced a similar bleak future. At the same time, these institutions—all idealized Old South communities in their own right—confronted futures incompatible with their pasts. Some lingered on briefly in their more or less original form, a number closed, a few found new institutional-rescuing financial backing, and still others merged with similar institutions. For example, Cox College—a women's institution in College Park, Georgia, originally founded as the LaGrange Female Seminary in 1842—closed its doors in 1923. Mary Sharp

College in Winchester, Tennessee, one of the earliest and best-known schools for female higher learning, shut down in the late 1910s, and Mount Hermon Female Seminary in Clinton, Mississippi, closed in 1924. Other female institutions of higher education merged with other (mostly male) colleges or simply became coeducational in last-ditch efforts to survive.[37] Each female institution had its unique reasons for closing, merging, or becoming coeducational, but they all experienced many of the same profound educational and societal changes and challenges as the Lucy Cobb Institute. As the institute's final days approached, its administrators recognized ever more so clearly that the lack of an endowment would deliver the fatal blow.[38]

Mildred Rutherford chose to resign from the presidency for the final time in 1923, bequeathing the position to her niece, namesake, and ideological heir, Mildred Rutherford Mell. Also a conservative, Mildred Mell was well qualified to fill this office. An alumna of both Lucy Cobb and the University of Wisconsin, she had received a master's degree from the University of Georgia in 1925.[39] Mildred Rutherford, however, did not absence herself from the institute, and she continued to shape it in important ways, particularly by actively soliciting financial support from alumnae.

In 1925, T. J. Woofter, the dean of education at UGA, approached the board of trustees of Lucy Cobb. In a well-argued yet gentle and even complimentary letter, Woofter outlined in considerable detail a realistic plan for the incorporation of the institute into the university. By way of introduction, the dean identified the reasons why the institute was deteriorating, especially relative to its more successful peers in and beyond Athens. In particular, Woofter noted that the Lucy Cobb Institute had failed to sufficiently modernize:

> The conditions have changed and are still diverging more widely from the environment that made the old Lucy Cobb. College plants today demand more extensive buildings and grounds, more of laboratories and libraries, higher salaried instructors with advanced degrees, and other expensive factors such that no college can live and rank as first class without large endowment. Many colleges have been forced out of existence or now eke out a precarious existence, only a few having been able to secure the necessary endowment or the increased appropriations in lieu of endowment.[40]

Woofter further acknowledged the much-improved state of public education—both secondary and postsecondary—in the South. By his estimation, over 90 percent of high school pupils in the United States attended public schools. The rate was likely lower in the South, but it was considerably higher than what it had been in the late nineteenth and early twentieth centuries.

Woofter remained convinced that collegiate education would follow the same evolutionary path that the high school had. While only a mere handful of the old collegiate institutions under private control had succeeded in amassing substantial endowments, Woofter concluded that "the marvelous increase in numbers, in incomes, and in widening influence is to be found in recent years in a growing number of State Universities counting their students by the thousands, and their annual incomes by the millions."[41]

Woofter strongly believed that Lucy Cobb could become an "integral college" at the University of Georgia, and he made efforts to make such a plan—a veritable lifeline—sound both appealing and viable to the Lucy Cobb community. The university had been offering universal admission to women since 1918, yet Woofter acknowledged that women's education had not yet become a significant priority among his fellow administrators. Thus, in Woofter's eyes, the Lucy Cobb Institute—with its dormitory space, classrooms, and gymnasium—would present UGA the opportunity to more fully embrace women's education. In particular, the institute would provide a much needed and desirable physical space for the increasing number of female UGA students.

Woofter outlined some of the specific roles that Lucy Cobb would play as a part of the University of Georgia. In keeping with Lucy Cobb's curricular emphases, Woofter promised that a newly evolved form of the institution would be part of the general arts (and sciences) division of the university.[42] Mildred Rutherford categorically vetoed Woofter's proposal for consolidation. Although she was not officially in a position to accept or reject UGA's lifeline, she designated her cousin, Judge Andrew Cobb—chairman of the Lucy Cobb Institute Board of Trustees—to speak in her place.[43] The demise of the Lucy Cobb Institute stemmed directly from the nepotism of the Cobb and Rutherford families. No archival material remains to suggest that there was further communication between the Lucy Cobb Institute and the University of Georgia relative to a merger.

In place of a merger, Mildred Rutherford—then seventy-four years of age—took it on herself to organize a mammoth fundraising drive to secure the school's accreditation as a junior college, which she believed to be the last best hope for the school and her idealized community. A huge obstacle, however, lay in her path. The Southern Association of Colleges and Secondary Schools (SACSS) required that any institution applying for junior college accreditation present proof of an endowment of no less than $500,000.[44] Lucy Cobb, although still in operation, had virtually no endowment. Many, if not most, administrators in Rutherford's situation would have likely concluded that acquiring such a hefty sum would be impossible. Rutherford, in contrast, enthusiastically accepted the challenge and directed an ambitious and far-reaching appeal. An *Athens Banner-Herald* editorial promoted the fundraising campaign and tried to aid the school in shoring up financial support:

> Let Athens and Georgia show their faith in Lucy Cobb in a substantial manner and the fight is won. And it is as much a Georgia undertaking as it is an Athens project, for what town or city is there in the State that does not enjoy the distinction of being the home of one or more alumnae of Lucy Cobb? The *Banner-Herald* esteems it as a privilege to command this movement to the people of Georgia, and invites the press of the State to join it in getting the matter before the public, to the end that Georgia may prove her faith in the type of educational training that is being fostered by Lucy Cobb Institute.[45]

Rutherford courted potentially useful individuals and organizations both within and outside the state, but her fundraising campaign fell far short. Complicating matters, many prospective donors would only provide support once a minimum amount had been raised. Despite its bleak prospects, the Lucy Cobb Institute continued to soldier on for about five years more.

MILDRED RUTHERFORD—APTLY DESCRIBED AS A STEEL MAGNOLIA—tightly clung to the ideals of the past, yet one cannot deny that she was a remarkable and steadfast leader. Symbolically, when she passed away in 1928, an idealized community died with her. The closure of the Lucy Cobb Institute was also emblematic of the collapse of the Old South or at least spoke to Mildred Rutherford's refusal to consider a South that had begun to transcend its nineteenth-century identity. After Rutherford's death, the institute tried to remain a viable educational option, but such efforts were too little and too late. The last high school and college classes graduated in May 1931. In an *Atlanta Journal Constitution* article announcing the closing of the Lucy Cobb Institute, reporter Sadie Myers wrote: "Lucy Cobb, Beloved School for Sixty [*sic*] Years, Would Write 'Finis' on Her Scholastic Scroll."[46] The sun had set on the Lucy Cobb Institute, as it would eventually on other "sister institutions" still clinging to the Old South.

NOTES

1. Lucy Cobb Institute (hereafter LCI) Photographs, Hargrett Rare Book and Manuscript Library, University of Georgia Libraries (hereafter HAR); Mary Ann Rutherford Lipscomb Family Papers, HAR.

2. See www.cviog.uga.edu/about/lucycobb.php.

3. For general works on Mildred Lewis Rutherford, see Fred Arthur Bailey, "Mildred Lewis Rutherford and the Patrician Cult of the Old South," *Georgia Historical Quarterly* 78, no. 3 (Fall 1994): 509–35; Sarah H. Case, "The Historical Ideology of Mildred Lewis Rutherford: A Confederate Historian's New South Creed," *Journal of Southern History* 68, no. 3 (2002): 599–628, and Grace Elizabeth Hale, "Some Women Have Never Been Reconstructed: Mildred Lewis Rutherford, Lucy M. Stanton, and the Racial Politics of White Southern Womanhood, 1900–1930," in *Georgia in Black and White: Explorations of the Race Relations in a Southern State, 1865–1950*, ed. John C. Inscoe (Athens: University of Georgia Press, 1994), 173–201.

4. LCI Collection, HAR.

5. Thomas Watson Brown, "The Military Career of Thomas R. R. Cobb," *Georgia Historical Quarterly* 45, no. 4 1961): 345–62; William B. McCash, "Thomas Cobb and the Codification of Georgia Law," *Georgia Historical Quarterly* 62, no. 1 (1978): 9–23; William B. McCash, *Thomas R. R. Cobb (1823–1862): The Making of a Southern Nationalist* (Macon, GA: Mercer University Press, 2004).

6. Phinizy Spalding, ed., *Higher Education for Women in the South: A History of the Lucy Cobb Institute, 1858–1994* (Athens: Georgia Southern Press, 1994), 12.

7. Minutes of the Lucy Cobb Alumnae Association, 1908, 7, LCI Collection, HAR.

8. Christie Farnham, *The Education of the Southern Belle: Higher Education and Student Socialization in the Antebellum South* (New York: New York University Press, 1994).

9. Farnham, *The Education of the Southern Belle*, 140.

10. LCI Collection, HAR.

11. LCI Collection, HAR.

12. At its peak between 1890 and 1910, Lucy Cobb averaged approximately 15 students per class (approximately 125 students enrolled in the elementary school, academy, and junior college).

13. Augustus Longstreet Hull, *Annals of Athens, Georgia, 1801–1901* (Danielsville, GA: Heritage Papers, 1978), 204.

14. LCI Grade Books, 1904–10, HAR; Joan Marie Johnson, *Southern Women at the Seven Sister Colleges: Feminist Values and Social Activism, 1875–1915* (Athens: University of Georgia Press, 2008), 21.

15. At least by the 1907–8 academic year, the institute officially called itself the Lucy Cobb Institute for Women Academy and Junior College. According to historian Joan Marie Johnson in her study of southern women who attended the Seven Sister colleges, as late as 1911, only seven southern women's colleges were accredited by the Association of Colleges. These were Agnes Scott, Goucher, Converse, Florida State College for Women, Randolph-Macon, Sophie Newcomb, and Westhampton.

16. LCI Collection, HAR.

17. According to various Lucy Cobb catalogues from the first decade of the twentieth century, the national United Daughters of the Confederacy offered $500 scholarships, the Georgia United Daughters of the Confederacy offered $200 scholarships, and the Children of the Confederacy offered $100 scholarships (Mildred Lewis Rutherford [hereafter MLR] Scrapbooks, HAR).

18. Other student organizations were the Brush and Palette Club, the Mandolin Club, the

Schubert Club, the Glee Club, the Browning Club, the Sketch Club, the Symphony Club, the Cicero Club, the Kodak Club, and the prestigious Almathean Society, an invitation-only honors society.

19. Carolyn Cobb Papers, HAR; LCI Collection, HAR; MLR Scrapbooks, HAR.

20. MLR Scrapbooks, HAR.

21. Although the Lucy Cobb Institute had attained academic and social stature, it was almost always financially strapped. There were brief exceptions. For example, the school declared itself as fiscally viable at the turn of the century via a 1902 report prepared for the board of trustees. In six of the years around the turn of the century, the Boarding Department alone had grossed $50,000 (see LCI stock books and minutes, HAR).

22. MLR Scrapbooks, box 2, folder 2, HAR.

23. Friends of the Lucy Cobb Manuscript Collection, box 1, folder 8, HAR.

24. Friends of the Lucy Cobb Manuscript Collection, box 1, folder 8, HAR.

25. By the early 1910s, the doors at the University of Georgia opened to women, albeit only in specific instances. At first, some females were allowed to attend summer school. Beginning in 1916, other women received graduate student status in a few select fields. Despite the presence of these women on the campus and the support for their universal admission by the Georgia legislature, the University of Georgia Board of Trustees continued to block the universal admission of women. Finally, in 1918, President Andrew M. Soule announced the official recognition of the right of women to attend the university as full-time students with privileges and opportunities equal to those of men in both undergraduate and graduate programs. See Thomas G. Dyer, *The University of Georgia: A Bicentennial History, 1785–1985* (Athens: University of Georgia Press, 1985), 172.

26. LCI Collection, HAR.

27. During the first session, there were substantial enrollments totaling 112 men and women. The institution operated as only a summer school in 1892, 1893, and 1894; the State Normal School added a year-long program beginning in 1895. See Dyer, *The University of Georgia*, 141.

28. The vast majority of normal school attendees did not enroll in an enriched curriculum. Christine Ogren estimates that approximately 10 percent of normalites opted for the "advanced course" (*The American State Normal School: "An Instrument of Great Good"* (New York: Palgrave Macmillan, 2005), 38). Nonetheless, this was a great educational opportunity for both men and women, but particularly for women, who were denied admission at all-male colleges and universities.

29. Ogren, *The American State Normal School*, 155.

30. MLR Scrapbooks, box 1, folder 5, HAR.

31. MLR Scrapbooks, box 1, folder 5, HAR.

32. MLR Scrapbooks, box 1, folder 6, HAR.

33. MLR Scrapbooks, box 1, folder 6, *Lucy Cobb Magazine* (1905), HAR.

34. In May 1910, the Lucy Cobb Board of Trustees—then composed of five men—had authorized a committee to confer with a similar committee appointed by the trustees of the University of Georgia to investigate such an arrangement. Neither party, however, took serious action on the issue at that time. See LCI stock books and minutes, HAR.

35. Transformations in precollegiate education also affected Lucy Cobb in significant, and

ultimately negative, ways. When Lucy Cobb opened its doors in the late 1850s, public education in Athens (Clarke County) was virtually nonexistent. Education—at any level—was the purview of the middle class and elites who could afford to send their children to one of the more than thirty private schools in Clarke County. In 1885, Athens finally appointed a school board, and public schools there opened in the fall of 1886 with 1,085 students. By the first decade of the twentieth century, the Washington Street School offered a high school curriculum. In most cases, elite families continued to send their daughters to more socially exclusive private academies—evidenced by the enrollment data at private schools such as Lucy Cobb—but Athens' growing middle class now had the option to seriously consider a public education, particularly for high school, over a private one. See Frances Taliaferro Thomas and Mary Levin Koch, *A Portrait of Historic Athens and Clarke County* (Athens: University of Georgia Press, 2009), 129.

36. I traced the changing composition of the Lucy Cobb student body via an analysis of student names and hometowns as recorded in the institute's yearbook, *Nods and Becks*, Friends of Lucy Cobb Manuscript Collection, box 2, folder 1, HAR.

37. Some of the schools included Due West Female College in Due West, South Carolina, Tillotson College in Austin, Texas, Hartshorn Memorial College in Richmond, Virginia, Virginia Intermont College in Bristol, Virginia, and Greensboro Female College in Greensboro, North Carolina. See Florence Fleming Corley, "Higher Education for Southern Women: Four Church-Related Colleges in Georgia, Agnes Scott, Shorter, Spelman, and Wesleyan, 1900–1920" (PhD diss., Georgia State University, 1985).

38. T. J. Woofter to the Lucy Cobb Board of Trustees, February 1925, LCI Collection, HAR.

39. Spalding, *Higher Education for Women in the South*, 46.

40. T. J. Woofter to the Lucy Cobb Board of Trustees, February 1925, LCI Collection, HAR.

41. T. J. Woofter to the Lucy Cobb Board of Trustees, February 1925, LCI Collection, HAR.

42. At that point in time, the School of Education was part of the arts division. The education division would include not only academic classes but ones in teacher administration and supervision; health would include not only physical education but health and hygiene classes and classes in social hygiene and sanitation of home and community; citizenship was broadly defined and would include classes in economics, ethics, political science, history, sociology and social service; and the fine arts would include both music and art classes. See T. J. Woofter to the Lucy Cobb Board of Trustees, February 1925, LCI Collection, HAR.

43. Spalding, *Higher Education for Women in the South*, 47.

44. The Southern Association of Colleges and Secondary Schools set other requirements, but the endowment was the biggest hurdle. This $500,000 requirement is equivalent to over $7 million in 2017 (*Lightning Bug* 1, no. 6, 87, LCI Collection, HAR).

45. LCI Collection, HAR. Included in this collection is the original editorial. Unfortunately, the date has been cut off, and "*Athens Banner-Herald* 1926" has been handwritten on the clipping.

46. LCI Collection, HAR.

Rocks in a Whirlwind

Protest and Alienation in Southern Autobiography

GEORGE W. JUSTICE

O**N THE FIRST DAY OF MY FRESHMEN SURVEY CLASSES, I LIKE TO** give a rehearsed speech that I have used for many years on the importance of history. The purpose is to get students invested in the course, even if they have not always enjoyed history. It is an "appreciation" speech for nonhistory majors. In brief, I ask them to imagine that they suddenly develop amnesia. What would be the personal consequences of such a drastic episode? You would not know your family, friends, or community, to say nothing of your accomplishments, goals, and ambitions. More importantly, you would have no memory of your medical history, allergies, or other susceptibilities. How would this affect you? What immediate decisions would you have to make to move forward? I then proceed to explain how history is the means by which we get to know ourselves. Those who do not know it have a kind of collective amnesia and must rely on others to tell them who they are. History, in a fundamental sense, is getting to know ourselves in relationship to our communities—global, national, and local.

One of the effective ways to learn about ourselves relative to the past is through autobiography. John Inscoe has suggested that "autobiography and memoir are history at its most humanistic."[1] Autobiography and memoir are perhaps the most accessible forms of history for students with no, or little, interest in the past. Because they relay intimate experiences and particular interpretations of those experiences, students reading them encounter emotionally charged stories of individuals growing and learning within their communities.

The joys and pains of life can be expressed in autobiographies in ways they cannot in monographs and textbooks; thus, they provide a human connection to the past for students. Three books, in particular, exemplify this: Lillian Smith's *Killers of the Dream*, Richard Wright's *Black Boy: A Record of Childhood and Youth*, and William Alexander Percy's *Lanterns on the Levee: Recollections of a Planter's Son*.

All of these books appeared in the 1940s, in the era of the Jim Crow South. Each provides unique personal insights into a southern culture that was both continuous and changing. They reveal a southern community at large in flux, desperate for its traditions but trying to cope with the consequences of modernization. There is much pain, anguish, and anger in the stories of these southerners. They lived in a regional community largely defined by white supremacy and sought to explain it, with diverse aims, in personal terms. Smith, Wright, and Percy were native members of their southern community who refused to embrace its 1940s culture. Nevertheless, they had internalized southern society and carried their emotional scars like a birthright with them wherever they went.

Louis Rubin Jr., a scholar of southern literature, provides insight into the influence of the southern community on its people. In a brief book of essays based on a series of lectures, Rubin relates the story of a trip to John Donald Wade's home in Marshallville, Georgia, for dinner with a literary scholar from the North. Wade had been one of the Nashville Agrarians who produced the classic southern apologia *I'll Take My Stand: The South and the Agrarian Tradition* in 1930, a book often considered an important contribution to the southern renascence. Two other unnamed University of Georgia faculty also attended the dinner; one was "a noted southern historian" and the other "an economist also distinguished in his field." All, with the exception of Rubin's northern friend, were southerners. When they arrived, they were soon "sipping Jack Daniel's from silver cups" and "swapping stories" of their southern upbringings in a regional vernacular "with lots of drawling and contracting of syllables" to the amazement of the visiting northerner. Upon leaving later in the evening, the friend consulted Rubin about what he had witnessed: notable scholars, among the top in their fields, who had seemingly retrogressed to the behavior and language of southern "crackers." Rubin explains this apparent contradiction by pointing out that while these men had left home to become academics of some repute, home had never left them. Their character was an organic consequence of a peculiar southern culture that imbued in them a reverence for regional manners and traditions. What Rubin's guest had witnessed was the power of communities over their members. That power, according to

Rubin, was informed by a sense of belonging and the "real-life identity it had afforded its members." This had been foreign to the northerner, whom Rubin described as "baffled."[2]

Rubin's story gets to the heart of the South as a community. As diverse as the region might be, the fact remains that, certainly in the early twentieth century, the American South had a coherency that regions in other parts of the nation did not. Its defeat in the Civil War at that point in time was not that distant; in fact, a number of veterans from the Confederacy were still alive. At the same time, the South as a community was undergoing some dramatic changes. Agrarian life was giving way to a growing industrial culture. This included a new materialism that made modern conveniences such as refrigerators, radios, and automobiles quite enticing and within the reach of the southern urban middle class. Such items were typically inaccessible to an ever more envious and depressed rural population. Change brought opportunities, but also anxieties. The Nashville Agrarians certainly tapped into these anxieties. The transformations happening around them threatened their sense of belonging to a community and therefore their past. The age-old historical conflict between change and continuity became a central element in the work of twentieth-century southern writers, including the three authors examined here.[3]

When historians speak of communities, they often imply certain unifying features, for example, the bondage that unified slave communities, which in turn suggest common characteristics like shared spaces, social practices, political culture, and purpose. Certainly, communities form around these and other elements of social cohesion. Communities also produce affective experiences like feelings of belonging and personal commitment to ideas and traditions. At the same time, there can be a dark underbelly to these affective experiences that fosters the social opposite to unity, leaving members subject to apartness and alienation. While the condition of apartness can be a choice, alienation suggests an imposed separation. Such distance may be not only physical but also emotional and psychological.

Autobiographies can be soul-searching efforts to grapple with one's place in society. Southern autobiographies, in particular, often highlight the effects of apartness and alienation on blacks and whites in the South as a community. This is especially evident in literature from the Jim Crow era. Lillian Smith, Richard Wright, and William Alexander Percy starkly describe Jim Crow as southern tradition and its impact on racial identity and community kinship. These autobiographies are valuable because they explore the personal feelings of individual community members in ways that scholarly treatments cannot.

The autobiographies of Smith, Wright, and Percy provide students with valuable insights into communities as bastions of tradition and as agents of change. They highlight the contentious relationships among members of a community who have competing claims on it. They afford students the opportunity to ask questions about society and self. How are one's values and beliefs shaped by community culture as well as by the family? What happens when one begins to find oneself at odds with those social and family values? What happens when social values and beliefs begin to change and challenge traditional norms? What responsibility does one have to perpetuate or challenge traditions? Each taking a different approach, these authors reveal their struggles with such questions, often in dramatic fashion. By comparing and contrasting their stories, students are exposed to the conflicting currents of tradition and transformation within their communities.

In the 1961 reprint of *Killers of the Dream*, Lillian Smith notes that the book "is personal memoir, in one sense" and that "in another sense, it is Every Southerner's memoir." She readily admits that she could "snip off a little of the pain" from the text, but "it may be the most real part of the book." Pain, it seems, is the point of the book. For Smith, the prejudice and social injustices associated with racial hatred had infected the Jim Crow South, and even the nation at large, with a sickness that was painful to both whites and blacks. "Even its children knew that the South was in trouble," she begins the book. From the outset, *Killers* is a call to action against "the sins and sorrows of three hundred years" of racial inequities in the South. Smith is tormented by the "edgy blackness and whiteness of things... the breathing symbols we made of the blackness and the whiteness... the metaphors we created and watched ourselves turning into... the shaky myths we leaned on even as we changed them into weapons to defend us against external events." White southerners had created a system and a language to justify white supremacy based on their myths about African American intellectual inferiority, greater tendencies toward criminal behavior, and lust for white women.[4]

In reading Smith's autobiography, students learn about a southern white woman who was indoctrinated with all of the same racially charged values as other white children. There was an etiquette surrounding race relations that defined the South by the early twentieth century. Smith's middle-class family and community effectively instructed her on its rules and behaviors. Sometimes speaking through her child's mind, Smith questions these values in passing but generally accepts them as children are prone to do. Christianity, the sexual purity of white women, and the inferiority of African Americans were mile markers for asserting racial control, what she calls "first lessons." She comes to believe "that a terrifying disaster would befall the South if I ever treated a Negro as my equal" and "that God so loved the world that He gave His only begotten Son so that we might have segregated churches." An inner conflict, however, becomes palpable: "I learned it is possible to be a Christian and a white southerner simultaneously; to be a gentlewoman and an arrogant callous creature in the same moment[,] . . . and to glow when the word *democracy* was used, and to practice slavery from morning to night."[5]

Smith grew into a defiant daughter among Jim Crow architects, experiencing what Fred Hobson has termed a "racial conversion" or a determination to express guilt for racial transgressions. Smith had found racial liberalism within the gates of racial oppression. She became an unwelcome reformer. Her unabashed assault on Jim Crow portended the liberal white support for the civil rights movement of the 1960s. Seemingly a lone voice in the wilderness, she relentlessly recounts the racial sins of her family, her race, and her southern community. "Every little southern town is a fine stage-set for Southern Tradition to use as it teaches its children the twisting turning dance of segregation."[6]

Smith challenges the need of white southerners to control race relations that developed after the Civil War freed more than four million slaves. With the onset of the South's "redemption" from the grips of Republican Reconstruction, whites conflated Lost Cause defeatism with white supremacy to ensure the longevity of a peculiar community below the Mason-Dixon Line. Jim Crow emerged when "a kind of gentlemen's agreement came about that a state of emergency existed within the areas of race and money and politics which necessitated a suspension of morals in these fields." Reconstruction and the courting of the black vote by the Bourbon Democrats and populists were threats to white supremacy. A new racial order began, and many white southerners "dissolved their scruples by substituting for a personal conscience and a clear brain this thing politicians call 'loyalty to southern tradition.'" The complicity of the rest of the nation was necessary to cement this order, but, that, as it turned out, was not an obstacle after Reconstruction. Smith denounces such complicity as offending her sense of justice.[7]

Students who read Smith's autobiography witness an individual conscience at odds with community values and discover how hard it is to overcome established traditions. In Smith's case, the tensions are fueled additionally by her sexuality. Not only was she an outspoken southern liberal on race, rare enough indeed, but she was also a gay woman who lived with her partner, Paula Snelling. Together, they ran the family's camp for girls established by Smith's father in the Georgia mountains. Although she was closeted, her sexual identity was another source of Smith's feelings of injustice. Moreover, as Jennifer Jensen Wallach has suggested, this frustration could have contributed to Smith's own feelings of alienation within her community and perhaps contributed to her persistent defiance. Throughout her book, Smith provocatively compares white racial guilt to the guilt of sexual self-exploration, describing it as "the same overwhelming guilt we felt when we crept over the sex line and played with our body." Crossing the racial and sexual "line" was deviant behavior and in the community's eyes "deserved punishment."[8]

Smith's autobiography is atypical in another way that is beneficial to students. At the same time that she effectively portrays the racial injustices in the South through her personal stories, she also offers a sociological explanation of the South. The moral repression of Christian revivals, the suppression of women's agency that resulted from notions of white women's sexual purity, and the more violent forms of racism like lynching that sharecropping and rural poverty paved the way for were all related to maintaining southern traditions.[9] Richard King has pointed out that Smith's racial critiques are also symbolic of other deficiencies in the South. For example, many southerners were marginalized by modernization. "Segregation became a metaphor for the estrangement and dehumanization of modern life." Dissecting racial oppression also meant addressing economic and social problems in a community still trapped in the past. This makes Smith's book a rich source for understanding a range of southern problems during the era of Jim Crow.[10]

One popular story among critics of *Killers* sheds light into the power of collective perception on children. A young white girl who was found living in a black residence was brought to live with Smith's family. Little Janie shared Lillian's room and the two grew rather close. Later, authorities abruptly removed Janie from the house when they learned that she was actually a light-skinned African American. The suddenness of the episode and the compliance of Lillian's parents shocked and confounded Smith, as well as Janie. It was an early lesson for Smith in the racial etiquette of Jim Crow. Despite her protests, Lillian's mother explained that "a colored child cannot live in our home." Unable to offer any satisfactory explanation to her daughter, the mother finally declared, "You're too young to understand. And don't ask me again, ever again, about this!" Understanding is often more difficult than complying with social norms. Reflecting on this incident, Smith reveals her disappointment in her parents. At the same time, she excuses them because of "something Out There that was stronger than they" and that made them act the way they did. "Out There" was southern tradition embodied as community. Smith came to understand that even adults were often powerless in the face of the authority of the past. Unless there was a change in the hearts of individuals, "Out There" would perpetuate racial injustices. Challenges to the established order, however, constituted deviant behavior unbecoming of a "true" southerner.[11]

Smith was an outlier among liberal white southerners in the early twentieth century. Much like Katherine Du Pre Lumpkin, another liberal white Georgian, she underwent a conversion in racial attitudes after leaving the South as an adult and then returned as a crusader against its entrenched racial practices. Smith, however, was less patient and more unforgiving with the pace of change than fellow moderates. James Cobb notes that Smith was, in fact, a "notable exception" compared to other southern liberals such as journalists Ralph McGill and Hodding Carter. "Smith's unrelenting attacks on the injustice and hypocrisy of the Jim Crow system and her forthright explorations of the repressed guilt and sexuality that festered within the southern white psyche," Cobb writes, "had taken her well beyond where any but a very few whites were willing to go on the race issue in the 1940s." Only during the civil rights movement did her voice earn credibility among the mainstream of liberal colleagues.[12]

One of the criticisms of *Killers* is that Smith cannot speak as a white woman for African Americans but that she sometimes tries to do just that. Although her empathy with southern blacks is genuine, she at times seems overly eager to convey their racial plight to her white audience and ends up describing them in paternalistic terms that resonate with conservative southerners. As Wallach points out, "Smith appears caught between what her conscience dictates and what her culture has taught her to believe." African Americans, in Smith's view, had "a psychosexual vigor" and their "lying, deceit, and flattery became almost second nature to many of them." Unaware of her own racist predispositions, Smith, like her parents, had been a victim of the "Out There," subject to the indiscernible influences that often mold attitudes and behaviors. Social structures can determine the kinds of people who live in the community, as Smith was quick to acknowledge of others if not herself.[13]

Smith's vitriol against racial inequalities and injustices are matched by Richard Wright's popular narrative of black youth in the Jim Crow South. Wright's *Black Boy* is an autobiographical novel of his experiences as an African American child. According to Ralph Ellison, the dramatic license afforded by fiction allows Wright to infuse his writing with "a near-tragic, near-comic lyricism" much like that which characterizes the improvisational musical tradition of the blues. It is "an autobiographical chronicle of personal catastrophe expressed lyrically." Wright seeks to embody the injustices of Jim Crow in himself as a child. Born into a poor black family in Mississippi, he provides a different perspective on community than Smith.[14]

While Smith's formal style contrasts sharply with Wright's vernacular approach, *Black Boy* effectively reflects the same concerns as Smith's autobiography. It describes the disenchantment of black youth caused by limited opportunities for them in a racially controlled environment. It traces Wright's progressive awakening to these limitations and his growing frustration with the apathy he perceives among his family and peers. The story is compelling and grips students from the first pages, in which Wright introduces himself as a four-year-old who burns down his family's home after setting fire to the curtains. Every turn of the page seems to offer a new lesson in Jim Crow etiquette for him, lessons often defied. Wright intended his story to be the black story writ large in this era of institutional racism, and as Inscoe has noted, "the searing account he left us of the traumas he endured in Jim Crow Mississippi does indeed reveal a reality endured by so many other southern African Americans as well."

Wright also explores the theme of alienation, which, for him, was a product of both racial segregation and established racial etiquette. He not only longed for social inclusion in the community but also struggled with alienation from his family. Wright's family persistently scolded him for his defiant personality. "I had already begun to sense that my feelings varied too far from those of the people around me for me to blab about my feelings." They scoffed at his desire for more learning and berated him for his lack of religious spirit. These rebukes sometimes turned violent. His Uncle Tom and Aunt Addie, for instance, physically accosted him as well as chastised his cousins for associating with Wright. "I could recall no innocent intimacy, no games, no playing, none of the association that usually exists between young people living in the same house." Even his friends attempted to coach Wright on how to navigate peacefully within the Jim Crow culture. His principal would not let him write a graduation speech because whites would be in attendance. Wright rejected any "technique that snared black young minds into supporting the southern way of life." He questioned how one could "live in a world in which one's mind and perceptions meant nothing and authority and tradition meant everything."[15] This feeling of not belonging only intensified his hunger to escape his family and the South.[16]

These episodes convey the ways in which belonging and not belonging often affect identity and purpose. The conflicts that Wright witnesses among whites and blacks were so intense that by the age of twelve, he had developed "a conviction that the meaning of living came only when one was struggling to wring meaning out of meaningless suffering." Fighting back against the pressure to conform, he carved out an isolated and lonely existence and dedicates himself to a journey of emotional and intellectual fulfillment. He despised the seeming compliance of African Americans with their oppression. And he struggled with his own betrayal when he was forced to suppress his resentment to find jobs that would allow him to escape. In one such moment, he recounted his difficulties in meeting the racial expectations of working in a white world. "My preoccupation with curbing my impulses, my speech, my movements, my manner, my expressions had increased my anxiety." Wright found racial accommodations an unrelenting burden. This, in part, informed an identity apart from his community and family that haunted him but that fed his determination for a just existence."[17]

Wright effectively links his alienation to that of the broader African American population. African Americans suffered collective alienation in a society that embraced white supremacy that mirrored the personal insignificance he experienced in his community. Undemocratic practices that limit minority communities can fracture them in ways that can make them appear estranged. Wright speaks of this as another type of alienation. Stories of racial violence and lynching swirled around Wright during his childhood and affected him greatly. "Nothing challenged the totality of my personality so much," he wrote, "as this pressure of hate and threat that stemmed from the invisible whites." As a child without much interaction with whites, he experienced this race as merely an abstraction, but one with powerful effects. This social invisibility and the "hate and threat" informing the violence perpetrated on African Americans inspired fear and hatred in Wright.[18]

Wright's community was both a product and a producer of racism. He recounts how in order to gain acceptance among his peers in school he had to "subscribe to certain racial sentiments." What secured him "admittance to their company" was "my feelings toward white people, how much hostility I held toward them, what degrees of value and honor I assigned to race," he recalled. "None of this was premeditated, but sprang spontaneously out of the talk of black boys who met at the crossroads." Wright's racism seemed to grow organically as well as out of his direct encounters with whites. The lynching of a friend's brother was only confirmation of this hatred. Although Wright had not yet witnessed much racial violence, this event had a profound effect on him.

> What I had heard altered the look of the world, induced in me a temporary paralysis of will and impulse. The penalty of death awaited me if I had made a false move and I wondered if it was worthwhile to make any move at all. The things that influenced my conduct as a Negro did not have to hap-

pen to me directly; I needed but to hear of them to feel their full effects in the deepest layers of my consciousness.... I was compelled to give my entire imagination over to it, creating a sense of distance between me and the world in which I lived.

Under Jim Crow, racism grew out of the community culture and had isolated Wright emotionally as well as physically, undermining his chances for any upward mobility. Throughout *Black Boy*, students learn the consequences of community norms and traditions on marginalized groups. Central to the book is acceptance, tolerance, and equality of opportunity and Wright's hunger for them.[19]

Hunger in its many dimensions is one of the prominent themes in *Black Boy*. Wright explores his physical, emotional, and intellectual hunger as he grapples with his place in society. Food, affection, and validation are lacking for him. At an early age, after his father abandoned the family, there was not enough food in the house. This led to a persistent anxiety about not having enough to eat that remained with him into adulthood. Even as an adolescent at his grandmother's home in Jackson, Mississippi, Wright's diet was so meager that he was forced to fill himself with water to temporarily ease his hunger. Out of desperation, he sought after-school jobs to feed himself. This led him into direct contact with whites. While he believed most whites were not to be trusted, he set out "to find the exceptions." Here, he reflects, "I was quickly learning the reality—a Negro's reality—of the white world," where he was mistreated and ostracized because of the color of his skin.[20]

It was also at his grandmother's house that Wright began to feel another kind of hunger more acutely. From his point of view, Wright's family and friends were willing accomplices to Jim Crow because of their submission to its rules. Moreover, he resented their efforts to force him to submit. He dreamed of joining those whose response to Jim Crow was to leave the South in the Great Migration. Stories of Chicago as some racial Eden, which captured and then never let go of his imagination; there, he would be an equal to whites. "The North symbolized to me all that I had felt and seen; it had no relation whatever to what actually existed," he writes. "Yet, by imagining a place where everything was possible, I kept hope alive in me."[21]

Wright's racial sensitivities drive his narrative. One vignette after another in the book demonstrates his quest for fulfillment, an end to his hunger. Even after leaving the South for Chicago, satisfaction never comes. In many ways, Wright left his community for another but unwittingly took the South with him. As Rubin's story of southern professors suggests and Wright's story confirms, community is internal as well as external. No autobiography expresses this better than William Alexander Percy's *Lanterns on the Levee*.

Percy's autobiography provides a dramatically different view of Jim Crow than either Smith's or Wright's. It presents a nostalgic defense of southern tradition in the face of mounting criticism of Jim Crow by liberal activists such as Smith and Wright. Percy's autobiography is a defense of the Old South legacy, including white supremacy; however, it is not a defense of the violence, such as lynching, that characterized Jim Crow. Rather, Percy seeks to highlight the decline of a paternalistic culture in the South that had been dedicated, according to his views, to caring for and protecting African Americans. *Lanterns* is, in many ways, a swan song to southern aristocracy.

Percy recalls a family with aristocratic pretensions, a common aspiration among nineteenth-century planters across the South. The setting is Percy's hometown of Greenville, Mississippi, in the delta region, where he owned a three-thousand-acre plantation, Trail Lake. His father had a profound impact on Percy's perceptions, although he was unlike his father in most ways. He described his father, whom he admired "boundlessly," as a "dazzling" and towering figure who "could do anything except drive a nail or a car."[22] In contrast, Will Percy, a lifelong bachelor and homosexual, calls himself a "sissy" with a "feebleness of spirit." The son never believed he could earn the same admiration and respect from the community as his father. LeRoy Percy was the personification of the aristocratic tradition in the South, and Will Percy, inadequate as he felt, was duty bound, he believed, to carry the mantle of that class into the modernizing world, even if that world had turned against him.[23]

Smith and Wright focused on bringing about changes to the South that Percy found disturbing but unfortunately inevitable. Students quickly discover that Percy was a lone voice in the wilderness. His values and perceptions were born out of the Old South, even as his community was abandoning that past. A relic, he was determined to leave a record of the existence of his kind, "while the world I know is crashing to bits." In many ways, he viewed those of his class as the real victims, not African Americans who were suffering the injustices of Jim Crow. He describes his community as bereft of proper leadership; legitimate leaders were vanishing from a world ungrateful to Percy's kind.[24]

Throughout his life, Percy fought many battles to prove he was worthy of his family's legacy, including opposing a Ku Klux Klan chapter in his county, serving as an officer in World War I, and leading recovery efforts after the great Mississippi flood of 1927. Percy insists that it was these great conflicts that made his life a "purposeful adventure." Part of his purpose, he felt, was the enforcement of class, as well as racial, boundaries. Class issues are a paramount concern for Percy throughout the book. While he regards African Americans paternalistically and sympathetically, he has nothing but disdain for lower-class whites. The South, he claims, is divided among three types of people: "the governing class" or those descended from the slaveholding gentry, poor whites whose possessions include, at most, "small unproductive holdings," and blacks. Overlooked are any middling classes such a yeomen or urban professionals, as Percy treats all white classes other than the governing class as singular. This conflation is revealed in his account of his father's campaign for the U.S. Senate in 1910.[25]

James K. Vardaman, a popular demagogue in Mississippi, was LeRoy Percy's rival. The Percy faction contended that it was the responsibility of the ruling class, which occupied "the world of honor," not only to care for their black servants but to protect their community from the grips of the ruffians and crooks of the lower class. After all, it was his father's fellow aristocrats who had been the bulwark against "scalawaggery and Negro domination during reconstruction." Vardaman was a champion of these troublemakers and the Percys could not allow his victory. It was a contentious campaign in which all manner of white southerners participated. These were the people who "lynch Negroes, that mistake hoodlumism for wit, and cunning for intelligence, that attend revivals and fight and fornicate in the bushes afterwards." It was a bitter contest that LeRoy Percy won by five votes in the state legislature and that confirmed Will Percy's views of poor whites as "the bottom rail."[26]

It is the chronicling of race relations that critics of the book find most compelling in *Lanterns*. Percy had a higher opinion of blacks than of poor whites. In most ways, poor whites were "inferior to the Negro." Although they were, he suggests, childlike, their "good manners" endeared them to their white benefactors. For this reason, whites and blacks in the South "live side by side with so little friction, in such comparative peace and amity." Percy's perceptions were framed by noblesse oblige. African Americans were incapable of caring for themselves, so it was necessary for the ruling class to "protect and defend" them. This was a burden unacknowledged by outsiders and understood only within the community. These white caretakers were "worthy not only of sympathy but of pity" for this was, indeed, the "white man's burden."[27]

The best and most mutually beneficial mechanism for creating an effective biracial community, Percy believed, was sharecropping. He rejects all the criticisms leveled at this economic arrangement. Although he confesses that the system was ripe for abuse by "a landlord on the make," sharecropping was "profit-sharing" and "the most moral system under which human beings can work together." Capitalism, in Percy's view, would be better served if other industries adopted such a mutually beneficial program. One critic claims that, like Smith, Percy "does not understand the inner workings of black people" and yet assumes to speak for them through his own privileged, white voice. He refuses to acknowledge the exploitation rampant in the sharecropping system or else is unaware of it; instead, he speaks of the cheating and abuse of sharecroppers by landowners as mere exceptions.[28]

Percy's racial views also become apparent in his description of Fode, pronounced by Percy as "Ford." Fode was a black man who served him in several personal capacities, such as chauffeur (Percy could not drive an automobile) and house servant. Percy's description speaks to the paternal burden the planter class often lamented when discussing African Americans in the South. "In the South," Percy remarks, "every white man worth calling white or a man is owned by some Negro, whom he thinks he owns, his weakness and solace and incubus. Ford is mine." The complaint is obvious. Percy and Fode "own" each other. Although Ford is at Percy's beck and call, Percy feels compelled to rescue him repeatedly after he suffers various tragedies and engages in criminal acts, persistently rehiring him after firing him on several occasions. Even after Fode permanently leaves for Chicago, Percy insists on his duty to care for him. "I hope the government supports him as long and as loyally as I did, because if it doesn't, I must. I must because Ford is my fate." African Americans, Percy contends, are "people whom imagination kills and fantasy makes potent, who thieve like children and murder ungrudgingly as small boys fight." They should be forgiven because such was their nature. These misguided ideas informed paternal racism. No one articulated this view better than Percy.[29]

From these autobiographies, students gain certain insights into the atrocities of Jim Crow and their effects on communities of the era. First, both Smith and Percy were indoctrinated by their exposure to their community's traditional southern mores that included racial stereotypes. Their stories present, in differing ways, the power of tradition in shaping behavior and beliefs. Smith battled against her racially charged legacy and advocated for radical changes. Her greatest frustration was the slow pace of change or even the lack of recognition of the need for it. Percy, on the other hand, fully embraced the persistent nostalgia of the Lost Cause and the racial order it protected. His greatest frustration was that the Old South seemed to be crumbling around him. Thus, Smith bemoaned the continuity of the past as Percy bemoaned its discontinuity. In reading these autobiographies, students come to appreciate the often-conflicting forces of change and tradition within communities.

As an African American, Wright is an outlier in his assessment of community values and traditions. His story reveals a personal revolt against his family and community from the outset. Even as a child, he refused to accept the racial indoctrination of whites and blacks, believing it anathema to all that was just. He is not an agent of reform like Smith or a melancholic victim like Percy. Rather, by escaping, he assumes a position in between. For Wright, there is no hope in the South, only pain and injustice for blacks. The community is too rooted in the past to be saved. His salvation, and by extension the salvation of all southern blacks, is to leave it. Neither Smith nor Percy experiences the oppression of being black in the Jim Crow South. This is all Wright knows. Moreover, also unlike them, he does not have any standing in the community that would enable him to be heard. Only through his escape does he eventually find a voice.

Another lesson learned from these accounts involves the individual's quest for meaning within the community. None of these authors finds fulfillment. Smith's fulfillment hinges on her role as a reformer and her receiving acknowledgment for playing that role. Initially, she was a lone voice in the wilderness among whites. She ascertained what her mission was via her critical analysis of race relations in the South. She spoke of "ghosts" that haunted the region from the past and the need to exorcise them like demons. She was a ghost hunter in the cause of racial equality who, like Wright, felt a keen sense of alienation from her community.

Wright's search for meaning came with many more difficulties. His cause célèbre was educating himself. He had discovered that ignorance was the key to oppression, and he abhorred it. It was a lonely journey, as the community around him, family included, refused to support any efforts that did not conform to the racial etiquette demanded of African Americans in the period. Most whites and blacks considered his pursuits too prideful or "uppity" and therefore attempted first to dissuade and then to sabotage his goals. What stands out in his autobiography is the determination to triumph over oppression in a community saddled with traditions created to ensure that oppression. Unfortunately, escape seemed the only path to freedom for Wright. Even then, Wright carried alienation with him.

Southern tradition, in contrast, anchored Percy's identity. He perceived a tradition under siege, an "enemy at the gate." His role was unquestionable to him; he was the last defender of noblesse oblige. In many ways, Percy felt as unfulfilled in his community as Smith or Wright. He failed to live up to the expectations of his father and his cultural legacy. He did not encounter the same struggles, however, on his journey as did Smith and Wright. In the end, he resigned himself to his enemy—change. His autobiography was meant to be an epitaph to southern tradition. Will Percy was a man both within and without the community in which he spent his life. As one biographer has indicated, "Percy's life story, then, becomes a window onto two cultural identities, 'southern' and 'homosexual,' that were contested and in flux during his lifetime." As provincial as his racial attitudes were, he was otherwise cosmopolitan, even liberal. He was a world traveler, open to all that literature, whether classical or contemporary, symphonies, and art offered one toward self-improvement. As a gay poet whose quest was to learn all he could of the mysteries of the human experience, he was an oddity in his hometown of Greenville, Mississippi. He seems to have experienced a double alienation: from the cultural conservatism of the southern community and from the changing race relations that threatened to place the "bottom rail on top." The melancholy tone of *Lanterns* speaks to this conflict.[30]

All three authors were marginalized figures in their communities; Smith as a radical liberal and gay woman, Wright as a black child in a Jim Crow culture, and Percy as a dying breed of southerner, as well as a gay man. All of them died frustrated idealists. Although Smith lived to see many of the gains of the civil rights movement, she continued to feel underappreciated and unfulfilled. Wright eventually left the United States for Paris, where he felt a greater belonging but experienced a lingering resentment toward his country. The end of Percy's memoir, on the other hand, suggests he finally came to peace with the end of his kind, even as he remains melancholy. These were exemplary lives that demonstrate the importance of communities in establishing a sense of belonging and identity and in providing meaning. All three writers were like rocks in a whirlwind; even as tradition swirled around their hopes and ambitions, they were steadfast. Smith, Wright, and Percy were fire bells signaling that communities sometimes fail their members. The consequences of such failure plague us today, as recent headlines make clear. White nationalists, neo-Nazis, and ISIL are the manifestations of the disconnections between individuals and their society, whether born from cultural, religious, or racial distinctions. The difference, of course, is that Smith, Wright, and Percy used their stories as a way to convey their social criticisms, not to destroy their communities. The challenge to tradition requires a balancing of history with the present, and sometimes is a dangerous endeavor. Lillian Smith, Richard Wright, and William Alexander Percy illuminate the difficulties involved in such endeavors. Change is difficult. Smith might have said it best: "People find it hard to question something that has been here since they were born."[31]

NOTES

1. John Inscoe, *Writing the South through Self: Explorations in Southern Autobiography* (Athens: University of Georgia Press, 2011), 15. My interest in and whatever expertise that I bring to the topic of southern autobiographies is due to the mentoring of John Inscoe as my major professor years ago. It is a debt that will remain impossible to settle. Any deficiencies revealed in that expertise here are solely, of course, my own.

2. Louis D. Rubin Jr., *The Writer in the South: Studies in a Literary Community* (Athens: University of Georgia Press, 1972), 83–86.

3. The most prominent example of the continuity versus change debate in southern history remains C. Vann Woodward's criticism of W. J. Cash's *Mind of the South*. Woodward notes that Cash's narrative has "a skewed interpretation" that emphasizes "the fundamental continuity of Southern history" ("White Man, White Mind," *New Republic*, December 9, 1967, 28). Cash, in this view, downplays secession, Civil War, and Reconstruction. James C. Cobb has written insightfully on this and has concluded that history, especially southern style, is more complex that a mere assessment of the transformative or the persistence of culture can do justice to ("Does 'Mind' Still Matter? The South, the Nation, and the Mind of the South, 1941–1991," in *Redefining Southern Culture: Mind and Identity in the Modern South* [Athens: University of Georgia Press, 1999], 44–77).

4. Lillian Smith, *Killers of the Dream* (New York: Norton, 1961), 21–22, 25–26, 12.

5. Smith, *Killers of the Dream*, 84, 28–29. See Joel Williamson, *The Crucible of Race: Black-White Relations in the American South since Emancipation* (New York: Oxford University Press, 1984).

6. Fred Hobson, *But Now I See: The White Southern Racial Conversion Narrative* (Baton Rouge: Louisiana State University Press, 1999), 1–2. Smith, *Killers of the Dream*, 95.

7. Smith, *Killers of the Dream*, 66, 63. For fuller discussions of national cooperation with the reordering of southern race relations after the Civil War, see Nina Silber, *The Romance of Reunion: Northerners and the South, 1865–1900* (Chapel Hill: University of North Carolina Press, 1993), Edward J. Blum, *Reforging the White Republic: Race, Religion, and American Nationalism, 1865–1898* (Baton Rouge: Louisiana State University Press, 2005), K. Stephen Prince, *Stories of the South: Race and Reconstruction of Southern Identity, Stories of the South* (Chapel Hill: University of North Carolina Press, 2016), and Jackson Lears, *Rebirth of a Nation: The Making of Modern America, 1877–1920* (New York: HarperCollins, 2009).

8. Jennifer Jensen Wallach, *"Closer to the Truth Than Any Fact": Memoir, Memory, and Jim Crow* (Athens: University of Georgia Press, 2008), 114. Smith, *Killers of the Dream*, 84.

9. Smith, *Killers of the Dream*, 103–10, 138–55, 163–74.

10. Richard King, *A Southern Renaissance: The Cultural Awakening of the American South, 1930–1955* (New York: Oxford University Press, 1980), 173.

11. Smith, *Killers of the Dream*, 34–39.

12. See Katharine Du Pre Lumpkin, *The Making of a Southerner* (New York: Knopf, 1947), and James C. Cobb, *The South and America since World War II* (New York: Oxford University Press, 2011), 12–13, 235–36.

13. Wallach, "*Closer to Truth Than Any Fact*," 118. Smith, *Killers of the Dream*, 118.

14. Ralph Ellison, "Richard Wright's Blues," *Antioch Review* 5, no. 2 (1945): 199.
15. Wright, *Black Boy*, 98, 175, 164.
16. Richard Wright, *Black Boy (American Hunger): A Record of Childhood and Youth* (New York: Perennial Classics, 1998), 173.
17. Wright, *Black Boy*, 195, 100.
18. Wright, *Black Boy*, 73. Scholars from Eugene Genovese to Steven Hahn have deliberated the issue of black nationalism. Still, none of the scholarly views fully capture what Wright meant by espousing it. As well as graphically detailing the personal effects of Jim Crow on African Americans, Wright also sought to fulfill a charge he earlier gave to his contemporary black writers. Although much of *Black Boy* documents his own desire to escape his racial oppression, Wright knew that to focus only on his personal situation was to ignore the problem of alienation for other black Americans in the South. In a 1937 essay, he argues that black nationalism was necessary to achieve social, economic, and political equality. It was not an attempt "to propagate a specious and blatant nationalism." There were certainly "nationalist aspects of Negro life," Wright argues. He locates these in the black institutions of the "Negro church, a Negro press, a Negro social world, a Negro sporting world, a Negro business world, a Negro school system, Negro professions," but it was the oppression of whites, he points out in dismay, that called these into existence. "This special existence was forced upon them from without by lynch rope, bayonet and mob rule." African Americans suffered the inequality of these institutions because of Jim Crow. Here, Wright illuminates black alienation within Jim Crow. For him, black nationalism must be nurtured in the mind first "to clarify his consciousness and create emotional attitudes which are conducive to action." The foundations of this nationalism lay primarily in the black church and the legacy of black folklore. These were at the heart of the African American mind. Wright charged his contemporary black writers to join him in raising the nationalist consciousness of African Americans and lead them out of twentieth-century oppression. His was an appeal to capture the intellectual and emotional character of a unique black history so that collective action could be successful. *Black Boy* is, in many ways, reflective of the writing Wright expects of his contemporary black authors. See Wright, "Blueprint for Negro Writing" *New Challenge* 2, no. 1 (1937): 53–61, Eugene Genovese, *The Legacy of Slavery and the Roots of Black Nationalism* (Boston: New England Free Press, 1969) and *Roll, Jordan, Roll: The World the Slaves Made* (New York: Vintage, 1976), 280–84, and Steven Hahn, *A Nation Under Our Feet: Black Political Struggles in the Rural South from Slavery to the Great Migration* (Cambridge, MA: Harvard University Press, 2003).
19. Wright, *Black Boy*, 78, 172.
20. Wright, *Black Boy*, 148.
21. Wright, *Black Boy*, 168.
22. William Alexander Percy, *Lanterns on the Levee: Recollections of a Planter's Son* (Baton Rouge: Louisiana State University Press, 1973), 57.
23. Percy, *Lanterns on the Levee*, 141, 126, 348.
24. Percy, *Lanterns on the Levee*, foreword.
25. Percy, *Lanterns on the Levee*, 169. See Hobson, *But Now I See*, 286–87.
26. Percy, *Lanterns on the Levee*, 148, 68, 149, 153.

27. Percy, *Lanterns on the Levee*, 20, 298.

28. Percy, *Lanterns on the Levee*, 278. Wallach, *"Closer to the Truth Than Any Fact"*, 132.

29. Percy, *Lanterns on the Levee*, 287, 296, 305.

30. Benjamin E. Wise, *William Alexander Percy: The Curious Life of a Mississippi Planter and Sexual Freethinker* (Chapel Hill: University of North Carolina Press, 2012), 9. Wise finds Percy a man who was alienated from many of those in his community but seemingly at home with all of the constant visitors, boarders, and close circle of friends who surrounded him in his later years.

31. Smith, *Killers of the Dream*, 57.

AFTERWORD

The Inscoe Connection

STEPHEN BERRY

> A relationship in which a person, thing, or idea is linked or associated with something or someone else.
> —*OED*, s.v. "connection"

> Relative(s); usually treated as a collective noun ... as in "I hope I will get to see you all a gain So nothing more At present Give my Respects to All of the Cornection [*sic*]."
> —Private Voices, Corpus of American Civil War Letters (CACWL) project, s.v. "connection"

IN A PARTICULARLY INSIGHTFUL PASSAGE OF *WRITING THE SOUTH through the Self*, John Inscoe tells one story three times, Rashomon-style, about the exact moment when boxer Joe Louis beats the ever-loving Christmas out of German Max Schmeling in 1938. In the first version, we hear the story from the perspective of a ten-year-old Maya Angelou, crammed into her grandmother's grocery store with the rest of the black community of Stamps, Arkansas, all of them staring down a staticky radio. "Champion of the world," Angelou remembers thinking as the radio crackled out confirmation of Louis's first championship. "A black boy," "some Black mother's son," was "the strongest man in the world." We then see the same scene through the eyes of thirteen-year-old Russell Baker, who sits on a stoop in Baltimore in 1938 amid his white-trash-talking neighbors pondering a "cruel theological mystery": "How could faith in the universal order be justified so long as Louis, a black man, was allowed to pound white men senseless with so little exertion?" And in the same moment we see a future president arriving at his own vague and ambivalent racial consciousness—James Earl Carter Jr., only fourteen, hardly knowing what to think when the tenants and laborers of his daddy's farm come hat in hand to ask if the Big House would be willing to place the radio on the windowsill. In a Georgia June the "hands" listen respectfully from outside and down below, while the whites listen comfortably from inside and up above. One hundred and twenty-four seconds later Joe Louis devastates everything white supremacy stands for. The blacks tip their hats and pay their respects, then go quietly back to their tenant shacks to raise a ruckus so loud Jimmy Carter remembers it seventy years later.[1]

The preoccupying concept that animates all of Inscoe's work is community as manifested in the different versions of the Joe Louis story: blacks from Baltimore to Arkansas to Georgia are a community, reveling in those singular moments when American culture produces a level playing field and the better person wins. The whites and blacks of the Carter farm also form a community, sharing an instant when the local form of race wobbles on its axis. For Inscoe, community is neither static nor singular but dynamic and multivariate; it tugs at our heartstrings while simultaneously tying us to our social role. We are simultaneously members of communities that abuse and sustain us, communities we love and hate, because what defines us as a community is *whatever is shared*, whether good or bad.

This takes us immediately into the heart of Inscoe's work and the reason it is so important. Much of the latest work on the South focuses not on community but on the household as the constituent element of nineteenth-century southern life. This makes sense: the household was the organic center of power relations—of family, gender, capital, and race relations—all of which remain historiographical preoccupations. Community, as the introduction notes, can sometimes seem less conflicted or contentious or methodologically sophisticated; we think, for instance, of Blassingame's slave community, which is a culture of resilience but not a culture conflicted with itself. There is no such community for Inscoe. Inscoe is (in)famous for nothing so much as for dragging Appalachia out of its Edenic exceptionalism and into the mainstream of the slaveholding South. Think of the irony: the mountain South had waited so long for its modern historical champion, but when he finally came, he completely decimated the white South's final holdout and idyll, reclaiming Appalachia for the South precisely to taint it with the South's many sins. Inscoe rescued Appalachia from its insulting backwaterism only to bury a dagger in its precious exceptionalism on the subject of slavery and race. Everything that Inscoe writes about Appalachia smacks not of paradise lost but of a pretense to innocence stripped away to expose the only real possibility for redemption—a deep owning of the past and the humble quest for forgiveness. This is community as it really is, reflected in the pressure to conform and the occasional willingness to set another person free. Wherever these forces operate, you have a community.[2]

Inscoe's definition of community, then, emphasizes *shared* internal conflict. "As easy as it is to romanticize [the] attachment to home, to land, or to community," he writes, "those linkages between self and place were often precarious or uncomfortable ones for southerners, both black and white. Many found themselves at odds with their communities or with the region as a whole." What motivated southern autobiographers to write, then, was "an attempt to understand what it was they felt alienated from, marginalized by, or hostile toward." Elsewhere Inscoe applauds James Watkins's observation that "*place* can denote a fixed position in a racial or social hierarchy as much as a geographical locale, and as such, many southern autobiographers chronicle their efforts to reject the place he or she has been assigned." Acts of negation thus become acts of belonging and acts of literary power. In Inscoe's work, southernness itself inheres in *this* sense of "place"—the sense that the gravity of the place is too strong, creating a deeper longing to be free.[3]

Community for Inscoe, then, is not a place but a system of "placedness," a sort of social gravity. There is no sense in Inscoe's community that anyone can be *in* but not *of*. We are all of us all in, each the sum of the forces that pull and push us and pin us down and hold us up; community is what we orbit and what orbits us, the sum total of who has claims on us and whom we have claims on. We long to feel fully inside our role or, failing that, to be free of the community forever, cutting all cords, as if we might escape gravity itself. But we can't, and so we must deal.[4]

There is, finally, an ecology to Inscoe's writing; his people grow out of and into their environment as into an ecological niche. His people have choices, to be sure, but a staggering amount has already been decided for them by the "natural" forces that fix them in place; the only question is how they will react to their sliver of a chance to be better. "The political questions in North Carolina," noted University of North Carolina geologist Collier Cobb in 1896, "have always been questions of east and west, of up-country against lowlands, of crystalline schists and granites against unconsolidated clays, sands, and gravels." Inscoe would never go so far toward geographic determinism. Certainly he was an environmental historian before we even knew there was such a thing (just as Bertram Wyatt-Brown was a gender historian before he ever knew there was such a thing). Certainly Inscoe's characters are *organic*, created of, by, and for the land they are buried under to become the mead for each other's bones. And yet there is no romanticism in Inscoe's sense of place; he writes, as I say, not of place but of placedness, of fixed laws that are occasionally broken to produce something close to grace.[5]

This brings me to my second-favorite piece of Inscoe's writing, the preface that reintroduced his masterpiece *Mountain Masters* when it appeared in paperback. It is rare that a scholar gets to take stock of his own work, and Inscoe undertakes the task with his characteristic humility, quoting only his worst review: This is "solid, old-fashioned, elite history," he quotes his critic, "constructed from the top down from the kinds of records that lawyers, merchants, land owners, travelers, and politicians generate." For all his esteemed gentleness, Inscoe quotes this colleague only to turn the tables. In this he reminds me of no one so much as Abraham Lincoln. "He was wise as a serpent," remembered a fellow lawyer who'd been on the losing side of Lincoln more times than he cared to remember. "Any man who took [Abe Lincoln for] simple-minded... would very soon wake up with his back in a ditch." Inscoe follows on his critic with one of his most trenchant lines: "Where other than Appalachia does historic revisionism consist of shifting attention *onto* its ruling class?" No line ever did more work to so justly wreck a tranquil paradise.[6]

Inscoe is rightly proud of the undergraduate classes he taught for twenty years on southern lives. But it may have been his graduate class on southern community studies that made the more indelible impression. "Especially evident among current works in progress," he notes in his first methodological meditation on community, "is a surprising number of richly detailed and strikingly varied community studies, which are exploring these issues in even more innovative ways." He was thinking here, yes, of *Cades Cove* but also of *Victims: A True Story of the Civil War*, Phillip Shaw Paludan's gorgeous classic, the only American microhistory worthy of the European tradition.[7]

Paludan's first chapter, appropriately and simply titled "The Place," begins, "for almost three generations the valley had sustained and sheltered them." Before we know who "they" are, we know one thing irreducibly: that "they" are the product of the environment and the abuses and graces that it makes possible: "Nevertheless, Americans were a people connected to the soil.... They marched to a cadence set not by the drum or the hum of the machine, but by place, and the time of year, and techniques and habits followed for generations.... People did not just reside in Shelton Laurel; they were a part of it.... The place and the people were almost one."[8] Inscoe admired this, but he would never have written it. Community, for him, is too conflicted for an account such as this to suffice—a man's placedness fixed him in time and place, but he was synonymous with nothing; he still had a chance to *belong* to the right side of history.

As a child I remember spinning some object on a string and being told that the *real* force was not the one I could most obviously feel—the force that wanted to tear the object from me and send it scattering to the floor; the real force was the one I was applying to keep the object near me, in my orbit. In Inscoe's work the forces acting in and on a community have this same counterintuitive physics. Men and women simultaneously love and hate the role they are bound to play, inside and outside at the same time, torn by the gravity of their own condition and yet having multiple chances to set each other free.

It is a little striking to consider that for those of us whose careers have benefited so much from John, who was always behind us, pushing at our backs, speeding us on our way, impelling us to succeed, the real force is the one we rarely acknowledge, the force that kept us in his company, in his orbit, just a little longer.

This volume is dedicated to him, to the gravity of his decency and kindness, and to the Inscoe connection.

NOTES

1. John C. Inscoe, *Writing the South through the Self: Explorations in Southern Autobiography* (Athens: University of Georgia Press, 2011), 24–25.
2. John C. Inscoe, *Mountain Masters: Slavery and the Sectional Crisis in Western North Carolina* (Knoxville: University of Tennessee Press, 1989).
3. Inscoe, *Writing the South through the Self*, 2.
4. On "placedness" see also Barbara J. Fields, "Dysplacement and Southern History," *Journal of Southern History* 82, no. 1 (2016): 7–26.
5. Collier Cobb, quoted in the *News and Observer* (Raleigh, NC), July 2, 1896.
6. Leonard Swett, "A Very Poor Hater," in *Lincoln as I Knew Him: Gossip, Tributes, and Revelations from His Best Friends and Worst Enemies*, ed. Harold Holzer (Chapel Hill, NC: Algonquin Books, 2009), 78; John C. Inscoe, *Mountain Masters: Slavery and the Sectional Crisis in Western North Carolina*, rev. ed. (Knoxville; University of Tennessee Press, 1996), xiv.
7. Inscoe, *Mountain Masters*, rev. ed., xvi.
8. Phillip Shaw Paludan, *Victims: A True Story of the Civil War* (Knoxville: University of Tennessee Press, 1981), vii.

CONTRIBUTORS

STEPHEN BERRY is the Amanda and Greg Gregory Professor of the Civil War Era at the University of Georgia. He is the author and editor of several books, including *House of Abraham: Lincoln and the Todds, A Family Divided by War* (2007) and *All That Makes a Man: Love and Ambition in the Civil War South* (2003). He is the secretary-treasurer of the Southern Historical Association and is a distinguished lecturer for the Organization of American Historians. Berry also oversees the web project CSI Dixie, devoted to the coroner's office in the nineteenth-century South.

RAS MICHAEL BROWN is an associate professor of history at Southern Illinois University at Carbondale. His book *African-Atlantic Cultures and the South Carolina Lowcountry* (2012) won the 2013 Albert J. Raboteau Book Prize for the best book in Africana religions. His latest article, "The Immersion of Catholic Christianity in Kalunga," was published in the *Journal of Africana Religions*. He is also a contributor to *Women of the Iberian Atlantic* (2012) and *Central Africans and Cultural Transformations in the American Diaspora* (2002). Brown's current manuscript, titled "Baptized in Kalunga: Christianity and African Religions in the Atlantic World, 1650–1850," examines the ways that African-descended people have directed the interactions between various forms of Christianity and multiple "traditional" African spiritual cultures.

JUDKIN BROWNING is a professor of history at Appalachian State University. He is the author and editor of several books, including *The Seven Days' Battles: The War Begins Anew* (2012) and *Shifting Loyalties: The Union Occupation of Eastern North Carolina* (2011). Browning's latest project, for which he was awarded an American Council of Learned Societies Collaborative Research Fellowship (with Timothy Silver), is an environmental history of the Civil War and is under contract with the University of North Carolina Press.

KATHARINE S. DAHLSTRAND is a PhD candidate in the Department of History at the University of Georgia. She served as the social media editor for *The Civil War Monitor* from January 2015 through December 2017. Her article "Temporary Triumphs: The Carpetbagger President of the Knoxville Industrial Association" appeared in the 2014 *Journal of East Tennessee History*.

Her MA thesis from Florida Atlantic University won the Traci Jill Edelman Memorial Award for the best MA thesis in 2014. She works with the Student Veterans Resource Center at the University of Georgia to collect oral histories of veterans attending the university.

MARY ELLA ENGEL is an associate professor and chair of the History Department at Western Carolina University. Engel's book *Praying with One Eye Open: Mormons and Murder in Nineteenth-Century Appalachian Georgia* is forthcoming from the University of Georgia Press. She has served as a research assistant for the Freedman's Teachers Project and has published articles in *Appalachian Journal* and *Atlanta History*. She also has contributed essays to *Reconstructing Appalachia: The Civil War's Aftermath* (2010) and *Blood in the Hills: A History of Violence in Appalachia* (2012).

MATTHEW C. HULBERT is a cultural and military historian of nineteenth-century America. Hulbert is the author of *The Ghosts of Guerrilla Memory* (2016), which won the 2017 Wiley-Silver Prize for the best first book in Civil War history from the Center for Civil War Research at the University of Mississippi. He is also the coeditor of *Writing History with Lightning: Cinematic Representations of Nineteenth-Century America* (2019), with John C. Inscoe, and of *The Civil War Guerrilla: Unfolding the Black Flag in History, Memory, and Myth* (2012), with Joseph M. Beilein Jr.

GEORGE W. JUSTICE is a lecturer of history at the University of North Georgia. He previously served as the University of Georgia research assistant to former Georgia governor Zell Miller and his archivist in the U.S. Senate. At the University of Georgia, he also worked as the assistant editor of the *Journal of Higher Education Outreach and Engagement*. He is the author of *Courthouses of Georgia* (2014) and was a finalist for the Georgia Writers Association's Author of the Year Award. In 2015, he was the University of North Georgia's Oconee campus faculty member of the year, and he received the Featherbone Communiversity master teacher award in 2016 and the University of North Georgia's Faculty Award for 2018. His current research involves Georgia's constitutional conventions and their role in southern sectionalism.

LUKE MANGET is an assistant professor of history at Dalton State College. His latest article, "Ginseng, China, and the Transformation of the Ohio Valley, 1783–1840," was published in *Ohio Valley History*. He has also published essays in *Environmental History* and *Appalachian Journal* and written reviews for *West Virginia History*, *Ohio Valley History*, and the *Civil War Monitor*. Manget is the recipient of the Winterthur Garden, Museum, and Library's short-term residential fellowship and the Hagley Museum's exploratory research grant, among other awards.

SAMUEL B. MCGUIRE is a lecturer in the History Department at Western Carolina University. He earned his PhD from the University of Georgia in 2015, and his research focuses on Civil War–era Appalachia. He has published essays on the Kirk-Holden War of 1870 in the *North Carolina Historical Review* (July 2014) and *Appalachian Journal* (Spring/Summer 2012). He has also written reviews for the *Journal of Southern History*, *Civil War History*, and other academic journals.

BARTON A. MYERS is an associate professor of history at Washington and Lee University. He is the author of the awarding-winning *Executing Daniel Bright: Race, Loyalty, and Guerrilla Violence in a Coastal Carolina Community, 1861–1865* (2009) and *Rebels against the Confederacy: North Carolina's Unionists* (2014) and coeditor with Brian D. McKnight of *The Guerrilla Hunters: Irregular Conflicts during the Civil War* (2017). Most recently, his critical essay "God of War: General Robert E. Lee on the Front Lines of Battle" was featured as the cover story in the *Civil War Monitor*. Myers's work has appeared in the national media, including the *Los Angeles Times*, the *Richmond Times-Dispatch*, Smerconish.com, Sirius XM's "The Michael Smerconish Program," CSPAN's "American History TV," and National Public Radio's *Virginia Insight*.

STEVEN E. NASH is an associate professor of history at East Tennessee State University. He is the author of *Reconstruction's Ragged Edge: The Politics of Postwar Life in the Southern Mountains* (2016), which won the 2016 Weatherford Award for best nonfiction book in Appalachian studies. He is also a contributor to *Weirding the War: Stories from the Civil War's Ragged Edges* (2011), *Reconstructing Appalachia: The Civil War's Aftermath* (2010), and *North Carolinians in the Era of the Civil War and Reconstruction* (2008).

KYLE N. OSBORN is an associate professor of history at King University. Osborn is the author of several articles, including "Reconstructing Race: Parson Brownlow and the Rhetoric of Race in Postwar East Tennessee," which was published in *Reconstructing Appalachia: The Civil War's Aftermath* (2010). His latest article, titled "Their Norths: Southern Travelers in Northern Society," appears in *Southern Cultures*. He has also published reviews in the *Journal of East Tennessee History*, the *Tennessee Historical Quarterly*, and other academic journals.

ROBERT C. POISTER is a PhD student in the Department of History at the University of Georgia and works full time for the university's Office of Development. His article "At Home on the Mountain: Appalachia in Lillian Smith's Life and Work" was published in *Appalachian Journal*. He has written book reviews for *Civil War History*, *Southwestern Historical Quarterly*, *Florida Historical Quarterly*, and other scholarly print and online publications.

KATHERINE E. ROHRER is a lecturer of history at the University of North Georgia. Her published articles include "Slaveholding Women and the Religious Instruction of Slaves in Post-Emancipation Memory" in the *Journal of Southern Religion* (2013) and "Lifting the Veil of Obscurity? Lucy Webb Hayes, American First 'First Lady'" in *A Companion to the Reconstruction Presidents, 1865–81* (2014). She has also published reviews for the *Journal of Southern History*, the *Journal of African American History*, *Civil War History*, and other academic journals.

BRUCE E. STEWART is an associate professor of history at Appalachian State University. He is the author *Moonshiners and Prohibitionists: The Battle over Alcohol in Southern Appalachia* (2011), the editor of *King of the Moonshiners: Lewis R. Redmond in Fact and Fiction* (2008) and *Blood in the Hills: A History of Violence in Appalachia* (2012), and the coeditor of *Modern Moonshine: The Revival of White Whiskey in the Twenty-First Century* (2019), with Cameron D. Lippard. He has also written articles for the *Journal of Southern History*, *Environmental History*, and other academic journals.

KEVIN W. YOUNG has academic interests spanning a wide spectrum of the humanities. A native of western North Carolina, he has written articles and reviews for *Appalachian Journal*, the *North Carolina Folklore Journal*, *Now and Then: The Appalachian Magazine*, and other journals and periodicals. His article "'The Largest Manhunt in Western North Carolina's History': The Story of Broadus Miller" appears in *Blood in the Hills: A History of Violence in Appalachia* (2012). He currently teaches at Appalachian State University and the University of North Carolina at Asheville.

INDEX

Abbot, Jacob, 79, 80
Adams, Cordelia, 51
Africa: Angola, 8, 30, 31, 32; Bambara, 25, 26, 28; Bight of Biafra, 8, 25, 27, 28, 29, 32, 33; Congo, 28, 30, 31, 32; Gambia, 24, 28; Gold Coast, 25, 27, 29; Sierra Leone, 25, 26, 27; Windward Coast, 25, 26
African American community, 5, 8–9, 12, 141. *See also* Ebo; Gullah; slave community; Wright, Richard
African American nationalism, 3, 15n8, 262n18
Allen, Richard Pinkney, 135, 136, 140, 141
American Colonization Society, 93, 95
Anderson, Benedict, 7, 61. *See also* imagined community
Anderson, Hannah Crawford Fain, 70
Anderson, John Fain, 9; ancestors of, 60; as amateur historian, 70; background of, 69–70; on Lincoln, Abraham, 72–73; as member of "post-heroic" generation, 61, 73; and Revolutionary generation, 70; unionism of, 71; on Washington, George, 61, 71, 72, 73, 74. *See also* Fain, Hiram; imagined community; Washington, George
Anderson, Samuel, 70
Angelou, Maya, 265
Angola, 8, 30, 31, 32
Asheville, NC, 114, 132, 135, 136, 141. *See also* stock law
Asheville Citizen, 179, 212; support for Buncombe County stock law, 180, 183, 184. *See also* stock law
Athens, GA, 13; education in, 230, 232, 236–37, 240. *See also* Lucy Cobb Institute
Atkinson, Nathaniel, 179
autobiography, 13–14; importance of, 248–49. *See also* Percy, William Alexander; Smith, Lillian; Wright, Richard

Avery's Creek township (NC), 178, 181, 183, 185
Avery, Isaac T., 40

Bacot, Ada, 79
Bailey, James, 177
Baker, Russell, 265–66
Bakersville, NC, 42; slaveholders in, 42–43
Bambara, 25, 26, 28
Baptists, 11, 162; oppose Mormons in North Carolina, 165–69. *See also* Brasstown, NC; Green, Henry; Methodists; Morgan, John; Mormons (Church of Jesus Christ of Latter-day Saints); Parry, Joseph Hyrum
Barber, D. P., 217–18
Barber, Davis, 118
Barber, Thomas, 118, 122
Barclay, James, 25, 26, 27, 33
Baton Rouge, LA, 12, 195, 197, 200, 202
Battle of Gettysburg, 11, 106, 116, 118–20, 128
Beers, Alfred B., 218–19, 220
Bell, John, 67, 102, 105, 114
Bell, John Stephen, 166
Bender, Thomas, 4, 6, 14, 15n10, 67
Bentley, Lizzie, 142
Berry, Wendell, 10
Bight of Biafra, 8, 25, 27, 28, 29, 32, 33
Black Mountain township (NC), 174, 181, 182, 183, 185, 186
Blalock, Malinda ("Sam"), 120, 126
Blalock, William McKesson "Keith," 120, 126, 127
Blankenship, Presley, 51
Blassingame, John W., 3, 266
Blight, David, 148
Brasstown, NC, 11; opposition to Mormons in, 165–69. *See also* Baptists; Methodists; Morgan, John; Mormons (Church of Jesus Christ of Latter-day Saints); Parry, Joseph Hyrum

275

Braswell, James, 122
Braswell, R. W., 122
Braswell, Robert, 122
Braswell, Thomas, 122
Breckinridge, John C., 67, 102, 114, 201
Brevard, Keziah, 80, 83–84
Brock, W. E., 216–17
Brockenbrough, John White, 100–101, 107
Brooks, James, 230
Brown, John, 82, 83
Brownlow, William G., 216
Broyles, Isaac, 44
Buck, Lucy, 86
Buncombe County, NC, 11, 12, 132, 136, 141; opposition to stock law in, 174–75, 178, 179–82, 184; support for stock law in, 178–79, 182–83, 184–85. *See also* commons culture; Hominy Valley; Jones, Johnstone; Pearson, Richmond; stock law
Burgwyn, Henry King, Jr., 118
Burke County, NC, 40, 41, 42, 49, 127
Burleson, Mary, 46, 48
Burleson, Simeon, 43, 48
Burleson, William, 49
Burleson, Wilson, 49
Burnett, Fred, 177
Burnside, Ambrose, 117
Burnsville, NC, 47; slaveholders in, 43–44
Burroughs, Samuel W., 219
bushwhackers, 157; in Missouri, 148, 150, 152, 153, 154, 155, 156, 157; in western North Carolina, 126, 127, 128. *See also* Blalock, Malinda; Blalock, William McKesson "Keith"; Caldwell County, NC; guerrilla violence; Noland, John; Quantrill, William
Byrd, Samuel, 45

Cades Cove, TN, 1–2, 7
Caldwell County, NC, 11, 113; bushwhackers in, 126–28; Confederate deserters from, 122–25; enlistment of Confederate soldiers from, 114, 115–16; food shortages and dissent in, 120, 121–22, 126, 128–29; opposition to conscription in, 120–21; during the secession crisis, 114–15; support for Confederate cause in, 116–17, 125; unionism in, 125–26. *See also* Lenoir, NC; Twenty-Sixth North Carolina Infantry
Calhoun, John C., 96, 97, 102
Candler, Thomas J., 179
Cane River, NC, 9, 40, 44, 45, 46, 47
Carpenter, Jacob, 41, 51
Carpenter, Margaret, 51
Carter, Hodding, 252
Carter, James, 48
Carter, James Earl, Jr., 266
Carter, W. R., 72
Chamberlain, Hiram S., 214
Charleston, SC, 25, 29, 33, 45, 62, 115, 136
Chattanooga, TN, 13, 177; and Forty-Seventh National GAR encampment, 211–13, 216–25; GAR Posts in, 214–15; as symbol of the New South, 213, 214, 215–16. *See also* Forty-Seventh National GAR encampment; Grand Army of the Republic (GAR)
Cherokee County, NC, 161, 162, 165, 168, 169, 186
Chesnut, Mary, 78
Chicago, IL, 255, 258
Children of the Confederacy, 234
Childs, Albertus, 41, 49–50
Childs, Eben, 50
Childsville, NC, 41, 49
Chinn, Richard, 197
Clawson, Rudger, 169
Clay County, NC, 161, 162, 165, 166, 168, 169
Clay, Henry, 95, 96, 102, 104, 205
Cobb, Collier, 267
Cobb, James, 252
Cobb, Lucy, 232. *See also* Lucy Cobb Institute
Cobb, Thomas R. R., 82, 232, 233
Coffey, Larkin, 119, 120
Cole, Frank O., 221–22
Common, Jim, 137
commons culture, 175, 177, 187; definition of, 176. *See also* open range; stock law
community, 1; county as, 4–5; definition of, 2–3, 4, 7–8, 14, 132, 134, 161, 248; house-

hold as, 5; neighborhood as, 5–6. *See also* African American community; Bender, Thomas; emotional community; imagined community; slave community
community coercion theory, 146, 158; definition of, 150–52. *See also* Noland, John
Congo, 28, 30, 31, 32
Connelley, William E., 154, 155, 156
Cook, Robert, 69
Courtney, Andrew H. "Dan," 118–19, 124, 126
Crawford, William, 186

Davidson, Mary, 101
Davis, Jefferson, 64, 85, 104–5, 200, 236; during the Civil War, 124, 125; as member of "post-heroic" generation, 62, 63, 67; on Washington, George, 66–67. *See also* Anderson, John Fain; Fain, Hiram; Washington, George
Deaver, Harrie, 140
Deaver, Reuben, 133, 134, 135
Dellinger, Logan Henry, 47
Democratic Party, 95, 114, 156, 200, 250; support for stock law in Buncombe County, 178–79, 184, 185, 186; in western North Carolina, 178. *See also* Buncombe County, NC; Jones, Johnstone; stock law
Desangaño plantation, Cuba, 202, 203, 205, 206, 207. *See also* McHatton, Eliza Chinn; McHatton, James
desertion, 116; in Buncombe County, NC, 139–40; in Twenty-Sixth North Carolina Infantry, 118, 122–28. *See also* Allen, Richard Pinkney; Buncombe County, NC; Night, Dick; Twenty-Sixth North Carolina Infantry
Dew, Thomas, 78–79, 80
Deyton, Nathan, 51
Deyton, William, 51
Douglas, Stephen, 102
Dunn, Durwood, 1

Ebo, 8–9; African origins of, 25–27; emergence in Lowcountry, 27–29; as social identity, 23–25, 30, 32–33. *See also* African American community; Gullah; slave community
Edlefsen, Edlef B., 165, 166
Edmonds, Amanda, 81, 83
Edmonson, Belle, 84
Edwards, John Newman, 153, 154, 155
election of 1860, 67, 102, 105, 114
Ellis, John, 115
Ellison, Frank, 135
Ellison, Ralph, 252
Elmore, Grace, 78
Emmerson, Ash, 197
emotional community, 9–10; in the antebellum South, 78–82; definition of, 78; and emotional revolution, 86; and female indignation, acceptance of, 84–85; transformation of during the Civil War, 82–84
Everett, Edward, 102

Fain, Eliza, 63
Fain, Hiram, 9; ancestors of, 60; background of, 63; during the Civil War, 64–65, 67; following the Civil War, 68; as member of "post-heroic" generation, 61, 73; racism of, 64; support for secession, 63–64; views on George Washington as symbol of defiance to tyranny, 62, 63, 64, 65, 67, 68, 69, 73–74. *See also* Anderson, John Fain; imagined community; Washington, George
Fain, John, 60
Fain, John Ruben, 70
Fain, Nicholas, 60, 70, 73
Fain, Richard, 63
Fairview township (NC), 182, 183, 185
Farragut, David, 216
Faulkner, William, 2
Fishburn, Julia Miller Junkin, 98
Fisher, Julia, 84
Fitzhugh, George, 97
Fleet, Mary, 82
Fleetwood, George W., 222
Fleming, Samuel, 43, 47
Flowers, Elkanah, 121
Forgie, George B., 61
Fort Defiance, NC, 114, 121

Fort Sumter, SC, 82, 83, 115, 136, 150, 230
Forty-Seventh National GAR encampment, 13, 211; former Confederates' participation in, 212, 216–17, 218, 219, 220, 222; parade during, 211–13; racial tensions during, 13, 217–18, 222, 224, 225; sectional tensions during, 13, 216–17, 218–22, 225. *See also* Chattanooga, TN; Grand Army of the Republic (GAR); imagined community
Freedmen's Bureau, 157, 177
Fullbright, A., 135

Gambia, 24, 28
Gardner, Thomas, 46–47, 48; sons and sons-in-law of, 48, 50
Garland, John Wesley, 44, 47–48
Gell, Monday, 24
Genovese, Eugene D., 4, 151–52
Glasscock, Eli, 152
Gods and Generals (2003 film by Ronald F. Maxwell), 107. *See also* Junkin, George
Gold Coast of Africa, 25, 27, 29
Graham, William, 98
Grand Army of the Republic (GAR), 13; African American members of, 211–12, 214, 215, 217, 223–24; description of, 214; Forty-Seventh National GAR Encampment at Chattanooga, 211–13, 216–25; national membership of, 214; race relations within, 13, 217–18, 222–23, 225; reunion with former Confederate soldiers at Gettysburg, 213, 216, 219, 220; Tennessee membership of, 214–15. *See also* Chattanooga, TN; Forty-Seventh National GAR Encampment; imagined community
Grant, Ulysses S., 107
Great Smoky Mountains National Park, 1, 7
Green, Henry, 165, 166, 167, 170
Green, Leander, 180
Greene County, TN, 139
Greenlee, George, 49
Greenlee, James, 43, 44
Greenville, MS, 256, 260
Gregg, William H., 154, 155, 156
Griffith, John, 42, 49

Griffith, John Orlando, 49
Grudger, H. A., 185
guerrilla violence, 11, 139; in Missouri, 148, 149, 153, 154, 155; in western North Carolina, 162, 170. *See also* bushwhackers; Caldwell County, NC; Noland, John; Quantrill, William
Gullah, 8–9; African origins of, 25–27; emergence in Lowcountry of, 27–28, 29–32; as social identity, 23–25, 30, 32–33. *See also* African American community; Ebo; slave community
Gwyn, James, 115

Hampton, Alfred, 51
Hampton, Rebecca, 51
Hansen, Henry, 218
Hardeman, Ann Lewis, 79, 82
Harmon, Hattie, 81
Harper, Ella Rankin, 116, 122, 125
Harper, George W. F., 113, 116, 120, 122, 127
Harper, Samuel, 113, 115
Harris, David, 79
Harris, Goodwyn, 123–24
Harrison, James "Pappy," 168
Havana, Cuba, 195, 196, 200, 204
Hawkins County, TN, 9, 62, 67
Hayesville, NC, 162, 166
Hendersonville, NC, 142
Hendrix, Tom, 140
Henry, Cornelia Catherine Smith, 11; after Civil War, 142–44; and Confederate cause, support for, 136; and enslaved people, 137–39, 141–42; family background of, 132, 133; and freedpeople, 142, 143; marriage to William Lewis Henry, 132; and white laborers, 140. *See also* Hominy Valley, NC
Henry, Dorcas Love, 133, 134, 135
Henry, James L., 134, 135, 136, 138, 143
Henry, Robert, 132–33, 134, 135
Henry, Robert M., 134, 136, 143
Henry, William Lewis, 11; after Civil War, 142–44; and Confederate cause, support for, 136; enslaved people of, 134–35, 136–37,

138, 139, 141; family background of, 132–33; marriage to Cornelia Smith, 132; military service of, 136, 137, 139; and Sulphur Springs Hotel, as owner of, 135–36; wealth of, 134; white laborers of, 135, 136, 140. *See also* Hominy Valley, NC; Sulphur Springs Hotel
Higham, Thomas S., 165, 166
Hobson, Fred, 250
Hodgson, Hugh, 234
Hominy Valley, NC, 132, 133, 134, 140. *See also* Henry, Cornelia Catherine Smith; Henry, William Lewis
Hood, Clementine, 124, 125
Hood, Sydney, 124, 125
Horton, Zephaniah, Jr., 45, 47
Horton, Zephaniah, Sr., 44, 45
Howell, Grady, 179

imagined community, 1–3, 6–7, 9, 12–13, 61–68, 213. *See also* Anderson, Benedict; community; Lost Cause mythology
Ingram, John, 181
Inscoe, John C., 8, 68, 246, 253; definition of community, 266–67; significance of, 265–69
Iverson, Alfred, 77, 78
Ivy township (NC), 182, 183, 185

Jackson, Elinor Junkin, 93, 98, 106
Jackson, Thomas "Stonewall," 10, 105, 106; and Junkin, George, 93, 94, 100, 107. *See also* Junkin, George
Jackson County, MO, 152, 153, 155, 157
Janney, Caroline, 148
Jim Crow South, 10, 13–14, 217, 225, 247, 248; defense of, 217–18, 222–24, 256, 258, 260; opposition to, 249–53, 255, 258–59, 260. *See also* Forty-Seventh National GAR encampment; Percy, William Alexander; Smith, Lillian; Wright, Richard
Johnson, Andrew, 107, 216
Johnston, Gideon, 27
Jones, Calvin, 115
Jones, George, 135

Jones, Jane, 142
Jones, Johnstone, 178; conflict with Richmond Pearson, 184–85; support for Buncombe County stock law, 178, 179, 182, 183. *See also* Buncombe County, NC; commons culture; Pearson, Richmond; stock law
Jones, Juanita, 187
Jordan, Ervin, 149
Junkin, David Xavier, 106
Junkin, Ebenezer Dickey, 98
Junkin, Eleanor Cochran, 98
Junkin, George, 10, 93; background of, 95; children of, 94, 98, 100, 106, 107; during the Civil War, 106–7; conflict with Brockenbrough, John White, 100–101; death of, 107–8; decline in status, 94, 103; moves to Philadelphia, 104; opposition to abolitionists, 96; opposition to secession, 104–5; political unionism of, 93, 95–96, 101–2, 103; proslavery views of, 95, 96–97; slaveholding of, 100; and "Stonewall" Jackson, 93, 94, 100, 107; support for American Colonization Society, 95–96; and Washington College, as president of, 98–103; —, resigns as president of, 103; and Washington College student body, 102–3; wife of, 98. *See also* Jackson, Thomas "Stonewall"; Lexington, VA; Rockbridge County, VA; Washington College
Junkin, George, Jr., 98
Junkin, George G., 106
Junkin, John Miller, 94, 98, 106
Junkin, Joseph, 98
Junkin, William Finney, 94, 98, 106, 107

Kaye, Anthony E., 6
Keeler, James, 72
Kilpatrick, J. C., 52
King, Anna, 81
King, Edward, 176
Kirk, George W., 127, 141
Kishee, 26
Knox, William Henry, 71
Knoxville, TN, 68, 70, 216

Krick, Robert K., 106
Ku Klux Klan, 177, 219, 236, 256

Lafevers, Harvey, 124–25
Laurens, Henry, 29
Lawrence Massacre (1863), 149, 153, 156, 157
Lawson, Ella, 142
Lee, Robert E., 105; applies for amnesty, 107; during the Civil War, 118, 119, 124, 127, 201; as president of Washington College, 93, 107
Lee, Susanna Michele, 68
Lenoir, NC, 11; during the Civil War, 115, 122, 125, 126, 127, 128; Confederate deserters from, 123, 124; description of, 114; enlistment of Confederate soldiers from, 116; support for Confederate cause in, 113, 125. *See also* Caldwell County, NC; Twenty-Sixth North Carolina Infantry
Lenoir, Rufus, 115, 116, 128
Lenoir, Samuel, 113, 115
Lenoir, Walter, 114, 115, 116, 125, 128
Lenoir, William, 114, 121
Letcher, John, 104, 105, 107
Leverett, Mary, 85–86
Leverett, Milton, 85–86
Lewis, Cecelia, 44, 51
Lewis, William, 44, 46
Lexington, VA, 10, 93, 94, 97, 106, 107; agriculture in, 100; during the Civil War, 105; during the secession crisis, 101, 102. *See also* Junkin, George; Rockbridge County, VA; Washington College
Lincoln, Abraham, 71, 200, 201, 268; and colonization movement, supports, 96; and election of 1860, 94, 102, 114, 136; and Emancipation Proclamation, 151, 153; opposition to, 78, 103, 115, 116, 117; on Washington, George, 72–73
Lincoln County, NC, 41, 47
Lost Cause mythology, 6–7, 10, 12, 72–73, 86, 225, 250, 258. *See also* imagined community; Rutherford, Mildred
Louis, Joe, 265, 266

Love, James, Sr., 135
Love, James R., 134, 135
Lower Hominy, 182
Lucy Cobb Institute, 13; ascendance of, 233–34; closure of, 13, 242; curriculum of, 232–33, 234–35, 237, 238–39; description of, 230–31; financial troubles of, 239–40, 241–42; founding of, 232; and similar southern academies and colleges, 232–33; and State Normal School in Athens, competition from, 237; student body of, 239. *See also* Mell, Mildred Rutherford; Rutherford, Mildred; Woofter, T. J.
Lumpkin, Katherine Du Pre, 252

Macon County, NC, 44
Madison County, NC, 55, 139, 143
Main, Council, 187
Mandingo, 25, 26, 28
Marquis, Patrick R., 153
Mason, Madison Charles Butler, 223–24
Matamoros, Mexico, 195, 204
Mathews, David, 2
McCarver, John, 119
McConnell, Thomas M., 219
McDowell, James, 41–42
McDowell County, NC, 43
McElroy, John, 43–44, 50
McGill, Ralph, 252
McHatton, Eliza Chinn, 12, 205–6; background of, 197; and Brooklyn, moves to, 205; in Cuba, 196, 200–201, 201–3, 203–4; expectations for son, 205–6; in Mexico, 198, 199–200
McHatton, Henry, 12, 205–6, 207
McHatton, James, 12, 206–7; background of, 197; business dealings of, 197–98, 199, 201, 203, 204–5; death of, 205; moves to Cuba, 200; moves to Mexico, 198. *See also* imagined community
McHatton, John, 197
McHatton, Robert, 197
McMahon, Nancy, 60
McNair, James, 181, 182

INDEX

McNeill, Sallie, 81–82
Mell, Mildred Rutherford, 240. *See also* Lucy Cobb Institute; Rutherford, Mildred
Methodists, 11, 162; opposition to Mormons in North Carolina, 165–69. *See also* Baptists; Brasstown, NC; Green, Henry; Methodists; Morgan, John; Mormons (Church of Jesus Christ of Latter-day Saints); Parry, Joseph Hyrum
Middle Passage, 23, 28
Miller, Nelson A., 124
Miller, Welthea, 224
Moore, James Daniel, 120, 125, 126
Morgan, John, 163; in north Georgia, 164–65; in western North Carolina, 165. *See also* Mormons (Church of Jesus Christ of Latter-day Saints); Parry, Joseph Hyrum
Morgan, Sarah, 83
Morganton, NC, 40
Mormons (Church of Jesus Christ of Latter-day Saints), 11; opposition in Georgia to, 165, 169; opposition in North Carolina to, 161, 165, 166–70. *See also* Baptists; Brasstown, NC; Methodists; Morgan, John; Parry, Joseph Hyrum
Morris, Christopher C., 5, 14
Morris, D. Butts, 195
Morris, Till, 141
Morrow, Gordon, 122
Myers, Sadie, 242

nationalism, African American, 3, 15n8, 262n18. *See also* imagined community
Neblett, Lizzie, 79
Neely, Jeremy, 148
New Orleans, LA, 197, 198, 201, 203, 205
Night, Dick, 140
Noland, Francis Asbury, 152, 157
Noland, John, 11, 149; in black Confederate debate, 149–50; before the Civil War, 152; and Quantrill Men reunions, reasons for attending, 155–56; and Quantrill's band, 153–55, 157–58; and *Ride with the Devil*, portrayal of in, 156–57. *See also* community

coercion theory; Lost Cause mythology; Quantrill, William; *Ride with the Devil*
Norris, Nineveh C., 140
North Toe River, NC, 9, 40, 41, 42, 49
Norwood, Joseph, 121
Norwood, Laura, 116
Notla, NC, 165, 169
Nugent, William, 78

Oakes, Loderick, 40–41
O'Brien, Gail, 5
Olmsted, Frederick Law, 53
open range, 175–76; closing in western North Carolina of, 186–87. *See also* commons culture; stock law
Oshnock, Kevin, 123

Paludan, Phillip Shaw, 268–69
Parker, Bill, 135
Parker, Jim, 137
Parry, Joseph Hyrum, 11; arrival to Georgia, 165; arrival to North Carolina, 166; background of, 163–64; opposition in North Carolina to, 166–69; whipping of, 169–70. *See also* Baptists; Brasstown, NC; Methodists; Morgan, John; Mormons (Church of Jesus Christ of Latter-day Saints)
Patten, George, 214
Patten, Zeboim, 214
Patterson, Robert, 179
Patterson, Samuel, 121
Pearson, Isaac, 42
Pearson, Richmond, 174, 186; background of, 177; conflict with Jones, Johnstone, 183–84; opposition to stock law, 178, 179, 182, 183–85. *See also* Buncombe County, NC; commons culture; Jones, Johnstone; stock law
Penland, Milton, 43, 49, 53
Penland, Robert, 49
Pendleton, William Nelson, 105
Percy, William Alexander, 13–14, 247, 248; and community, fulfillment within, 259–60; defends white southern traditions,

Percy, William Alexander (*continued*) 256–57; racial views of, 257–58; sexuality of, 260. *See also* autobiography; Smith, Lillian; Wright, Richard
Petersen, Paul, 149–50, 153
Petty, Elijah, 85
Philyaw, Gideon, 119, 127
Philyaw, Simeon, 119, 127
Piercy, Blake, 46
Piercy, Ephraim, 46
Polk, James K., 200
Populist Party (People's Party), 185, 186, 250
Preston, Margaret Junkin, 93, 94, 98, 100, 107
Pritchard, Gullah Jack, 24, 31, 33
Proffitt, James C., 51

Quantrill, William, 11, 148; as leader of Confederate guerrilla band, 150, 153, 154, 155, 156, 157. *See also* Noland, John

Raleigh, NC, 113, 114, 117, 163, 174, 178, 185
Rankin, Jesse, 125
Rankin, Nathaniel, 116–17
Rawick, George A., 3
Ray, Thomas Lee, 39, 45, 47; sons and descendants of, 44, 45, 46, 47, 49, 51
Ready, Cora, 80, 83
Republican Party, 64, 68, 82, 107, 143; opposes stock law in Buncombe County, 179–82, 184; in western North Carolina, 175, 177–78, 185, 186, 187. *See also* Buncombe County, NC; Pearson, Richmond; stock law
Ride with the Devil (1999 film by Ang Lee), 150, 156–57. *See also* Noland, John
Roach, Mahala, 80–81
Roberson, George, 49
Robinson, John, 97–98
Rockbridge County, VA, 94, 100, 102, 105, 106, 108. *See also* Junkin, George; Lexington, VA; Washington College
Rogersville, TN, 62
Rome, GA, 165, 222
Roosevelt, Theodore, 186

Rowland, Henry, 46
Rubin, Anne Sarah, 69
Rubin, Louis, Jr., 247–48, 255
Ruffner, Henry, 98
Rutherford, Laura Cobb, 232
Rutherford, Mildred, 13, 86, 231–32; death of, 242; on gender, 236–37, 237–38; and Lost Cause mythology, 235–36, 237; and Lucy Cobb Institute, as principal of, 233–35; —, as president of, 235–40; —, opposes merger with the University of Georgia, 241–42. *See also* Lost Cause mythology; Lucy Cobb Institute; Mell, Mildred Rutherford; Woofter, T. J.

Saint-Domingue, 24
Sandy Mush township, NC, 174, 182, 183, 185
Savannah, GA, 30
Schmeling, Max, 265, 266
Senegamia, 24, 25, 26, 27, 28
Seney, George I., 233
Setser, Thomas W., 117, 118, 119
Setser, W. E. "Eli," 117, 118, 119
Seward, William, 107
Shepherd, Dorothy, 46, 50
Shepherd, Joseph, 44, 46, 51
Shepherd, Thomas, 44
Sierra Leone, 25, 26, 27
Sinkler, Emily, 81
slave community, 8–9, 21–23, 33, 266; in the early Lowcountry, 27–28; scholarly interpretation of, 3–4, 6; in West and Central Africa, 25–27. *See also* African American community; community; Ebo; Gullah
Smith, Lillian, 13–14, 247, 248; opposition to racial inequality in the South, 249–50, 251–52, 258; paternalism of, 252; quest for fulfillment within community, 259; sexuality of, 250–51. *See also* autobiography; Percy, William Alexander; Wright, Richard
Smith, William, Sr., 133, 135
Snelson, J., 135
Sondley, Foster A., 181

Sons of Confederate Veterans (SCV), 150
Sons of Union Veterans (SUV), 211, 223
South Hominy township, NC, 183, 185
South Toe River, NC, 9, 40, 41–42, 43
Stamps, AR, 265
Standing, Joseph, 169
Steward, D. Minor, 222
Stewart, Jackson, 52
stock law, 12, 175, 186–87; opposition in Buncombe County to, 174–75, 178, 179–82, 184; support in Buncombe County for, 178–79, 182–83, 184–85. *See also* Buncombe County, NC; commons culture; Jones, Johnstone; Pearson, Richmond
Stoneman, George, 128
Sulphur Springs, NC, 11, 132, 133, 134, 140, 142, 144. *See also* Henry, Cornelia Catherine Smith; Henry, Robert; Henry, William Lewis; Sulphur Springs Hotel
Sulphur Springs Hotel, 132, 133, 134, 135, 136. *See also* Henry, William Lewis
Swannanoa township (NC), 182, 185

Taylor, Elizabeth, 60
Teems, Leander, 167, 168
Terry, C. C., 135, 138
Thompson, Ella, 78, 81, 84, 85, 86
Thompson, E. P. 150
Todd, George A., 219–20
Toe Valley, NC, 9; kinship ties among slaveholders in, 39, 40, 47–48, 52, 53–54; geography of, 40; settlement of, 39–40; slaveholders in 1850, 40–47; slaveholders in 1860, 48–52. *See also* Bakersville, NC; Burnsville, NC
Tönnies, Ferdinand, 15n10
Torrence, Ell, 221, 222
Tuttle, Columbus A., 127
Twenty-Sixth North Carolina Infantry, 115; deserters from, 118–19, 122–25; engagements during the Civil War, 117–20; enlistment of troops from Caldwell County, 115–16. *See also* Battle of Gettysburg; Caldwell County, NC; Lenoir, NC

Union, SC, 132
United Confederate Veterans (UCV), 217, 218, 219, 220, 222
United Daughters of the Confederacy, 234, 235, 236
University of Georgia, 232, 233, 234, 236, 238, 240–41. *See also* Lucy Cobb Institute; Rutherford, Mildred; Woofter, T. J.
Upper Hominy township (NC), 174, 179, 182, 183

Vance, Robert, 50
Vance, Zebulon B., 50, 115, 118, 123, 124, 127
Vardaman, James K., 257
Vesey, Denmark, 24, 33
Virginia Military Institute, 93, 99, 100, 105

Wade, John Donald, 247
Walker, Andrew, 154, 155
Walker, William, 162
Wallach, Jennifer Jensen, 251, 252
Washington, George, 9, 95, 98, 102, 103, 105; birthday as a national holiday, 65–66; later generations' perceptions of, 59, 61, 62–63, 64, 68, 69, 71, 72–73; views on slavery, 65. *See also* Anderson, John Fain; Davis, Jefferson; Fain, Hiram; imagined community
Washington College, 10, 93, 105, 106, 107; background of, 97–98; during George Junkin's tenure as president, 98–103. *See also* Junkin, George
Washington County, TN, 60, 70
Watauga County, NC, 180, 187
Watkins, James, 267
Watkins, Sarah, 79
Webb, Hulda, 52
Webster, William L., 169
Wells, Carse, 135
Welty, Eudora, 8
West, Stephen, 53
Whiskey Rebellion, 9, 71
White, Wilson A., 116, 117
Whitson, George, 181–82
Whittington, Benjamin, 51

Windward Coast of Africa, 25, 26
Wilder, John T., 177, 214
Wilkes County, NC, 115, 126
Williams, Joshua, 43
Wilson, Edward "Ned," 44, 45–46, 51
Wilson, James, 46
Wilson, William A., 48
Winebarger, John, 180
Whig Party, 95, 96, 102, 114
Woofter, T. J., 240–41. *See also* Lucy Cobb Institute; Mildred, Rutherford; University of Georgia
Wright, Richard, 13–14, 247, 248, 252; alienation from African American community, 253–55, 259; opposition to racial inequality in the South, 253; quest for fulfillment within community, 255–56, 259. *See also* autobiography; Percy, William Alexander; Smith, Lillian
Wyatt-Brown, Bertram, 268

Yancey County, NC, 43, 52, 177. *See also* Toe Valley, NC
Yancey, William Lowndes, 103
Young, Brigham, 164
Young, Rueben, 42–43; sons of, 50
Young, Strawbridge, 42; sons of, 42

www.ingramcontent.com/pod-product-compliance
Lightning Source LLC
Chambersburg PA
CBHW011755220426
43672CB00018B/2965